May '90

To Moe —

  Whose love of politics
and Boston makes us
"soul mates"

  With thanks for all
you have done for me
over the years —

          In friendship
              Kevin

de Gruyter Studies on North America 4

Schabert, Boston Politics:
The Creativity of Power

de Gruyter Studies on North America

Politics, Government, Society, Economy, and History

Tilo Schabert

Boston Politics:
The Creativity of Power

Walter de Gruyter · Berlin · New York 1989

Tilo Schabert
Professor of Politics at the
Friedrich-Alexander-Universität Erlangen-Nürnberg
Erlangen, Federal Republic of Germany

Library of Congress Cataloging-in-Publication Data

Schabert, Tilo.
  Boston politics.

  (De Gruyter studies on North America ; 4)
  Includes bibliographical references.
  1. Boston (Mass.) – Politics and government.
  2. Political leadership – Massachusetts – Boston.   I. Title.
  II. Series.
  JS608.S33   1989   320.9744'61   89-23357
  ISBN 0-89925-586-8   (U.S. : alk. paper)

Deutsche Bibliothek Cataloging in Publication Data

Schabert, Tilo:
Boston politics: the creativity of power / Tilo Schabert. – Berlin ;
New York : de Gruyter, 1989
  (De Gruyter studies on North America ; 4)
  ISBN 3-11-012102-6
NE: GT

∞ Printed on acid free paper

Dir, Ina

Every limit is a beginning as well as an ending. For the
fragment of a life, however typical, is not the sample of
an even web.

George Eliot

Le seul plaisir est de trouver des résultats inattendus au
bout d'une analyse rigoureuse.

Paul Valéry

Acknowledgments

The execution of this study would not have been possible without the assistance of a number of persons and institutions.

The award of a Heisenberg Senior Research Fellowship by the *Deutsche Forschungsgemeinschaft* enabled me for several years to devote myself entirely to research. Helmut Engelhard, administrator at the *Deutsche Forschungsgemeinschaft*, sustained my efforts with sympathy and challenge.

In 1980 and 1981 the Center for European Studies at Harvard University provided me with a temporary academic home whose special character proved to be quite supportive. I am grateful to Dr. Guido Goldman, Director of CES, for his generous invitation to be a Research Associate at the Center. During my stay at the Center, as well as afterwards, Ms. Abby Collins, Administrative Director of CES, contributed to the progress of my work in a good many ways. I thank her for having been an unfailing source of encouragement.

In 1980 and 1981 I could also enjoy the hospitality of the Joint Center for Urban Studies at Harvard University and the Massachusetts Institute of Technology. Arthur P. Solomon, David T. Kresge, H. James Brown, then successively the Directors of the Joint Center, kindly extended to me the privilege to use the facilities of the Center. Jan Lent, secretary in the Director's Office, responded always to my many questions swiftly and efficiently.

Since 1980 I have been able at various times to work at the *Institut d'Études Politiques* in Paris. François Goguel, Head of the *Fondation Nationale des Sciences Politiques,* and Serge Hurtig, Secretary General of the *Fondation,* were so kind as to offer me the splendid opportunity for consulting the extraordinarily rich research collections of the *Institut.* Mlle. Thérèse Tournier was helpful to me, in a most gracious way, whenever I visited the Institute.

I was granted for the fall term 1983 a German Kennedy Memorial Fellowship by the Center for European Studies at Harvard University. Through this award I could complete my research in Boston.

The Boston Redevelopment Authority provided me with the base upon which I could rest and from which I could proceed while I pursued my inquiries into Boston politics. Robert J. Ryan, Director of the BRA, let me roam about the "Fifth Floor" in full liberty (and he did not seem to mind my roaming about the rest of City Hall). It was his trust that made Boston such a rich field for my scholarship. Susan Allen acted as my *amica curiae* in the BRA, sparing no effort in my behalf. Through her guidance I reached the ultimate point of my quest. I entered the institution I studied.

Rita Smith assisted me in using the Research Library of the BRA; Ian Menzies and Jennifer Chao helped me to gain access to the files of the *Boston Globe.*

I take pleasure in expressing my gratitude to two friends, Hella Mandt and Helmut Hasche, and to my sister, Eva-Maria Schabert, for not deserting me at a time of distress.

Hans Fromm, Professor Emeritus of Germanic Studies at the University of Munich, lent his support to the project of this study at a crucial juncture.

The book is dedicated to Ina Schabert, my wife.

Baierbrunn, December 1988

Table of Contents

Chapter 1: The Autocracy, Condition of Creativity

Chapter 2: The Court, Locus of Creativity

Chapter 3: The Party, Carrier of Creativity

Chapter 4: The Government, Movements of Creativity

Chapter 5: The City, Space of Creativity

List of Abbreviations

BG	=	Boston Globe
BH	=	Boston Herald
BHA	=	Boston Herald American
BM	=	Boston Magazine
BMRB	=	Boston Municipal Research Bureau
BO	=	Boston Observer
BPH	=	Boston Phoenix
BRA	=	Boston Redevelopment Authority
CR	=	City Record, City of Boston
CSM	=	The Christian Science Monitor
IHT	=	International Herald Tribune
NJ	=	National Journal
NYT	=	The New York Times
OPS	=	Office of Public Service, City of Boston

List of Tables

Introduction
The Story of Politics

The Story to be Told

Human beings are creative beings, and politics is the principal mode of their creativity.

There are, of course, other endeavors which human beings as creative beings pursue. They draw pictures as painters, they make melodies as composers, they put on pieces of words as writers, they construct buildings as architects, they fabricate handicraft as artisans, they manufacture goods as workers. In the process of any of these pursuits they produce something tangible, something final: a portrait, for instance, or a still life, a song or a symphony, a poem or a scholar's book, a cottage or a church, a table or a vase, a machine or a garment.

It is in the pursuit of politics that human beings perpetually produce, and never produce anything tangible, anything final. Politics is pure creativity: it is a pursuit of creativity of which the "product" is the creativity that is pursued. Of all the modes of human creativeness, music is most comparable to politics. A musical composition, without being vocalized, is dead; it becomes actually a product of musical creativity only in the mode of its production: when it is performed and heard. Similarly, politics has no reality other than the process of politics being pursued; it occurs but through itself: in an act of politics. Once a musical composition is completed, however, the finished composition will remain, variations in the performance notwithstanding. Politics, in contrast, does not know finalized products; all that it yields is movement, a movement unto movements of creativity. The creation politics achieves is an unceasing creation. It is the human configuration of a *creatio continua*: the creative difference between form and confusion, duration and discontinuance, design and decomposition. Without politics, human beings would not exist. It is the "divine" creativity through which they exist.

This study proposes a portrayal of the process of creativity that politics is. It represents an inquiry into the *creatio continua* as which politics occurs. In view of its subject, the undertaking appears to be paradoxical. All things political are fluid things, the gist of the study goes. So what indeed is it that is suggested to be studied? What could the study have as a matter, if all that there is as its matter is perennially flowing away?

It is not possible to step into the same river twice. Yet, it is also possible each time to experience the flow of one and the same river. The paradox stands and it casts the entire study. The inquiry that is proposed truly is a paradoxical undertaking; it cannot take form in any other way and still be the intended study, for its paradoxical nature derives from the paradoxical nature of its subject.

All things political are fluid things. Within its fluidity, however, politics tends to transcend its fluidity. It produces things and forms, not the least of which are its own things and forms, the governments and regimes through which it takes place. A political creation is politics' final cause; it occurs to occur as the form of a polis, for instance, or a state, of a commonwealth, or a nation. In the mode of a political creation, politics, it appears, could come to an end; it would seem that it has produced the "things political" for which it had been the production. Yet, everything produced by politics has to be sustained by politics, else it is soon about to vanish. As the cause of its own reality, politics' reality depends upon the cause: upon politics. All politics tends to transcend itself, to come to an end. Yet, all politics transcends any end – any political form, and political creation – into which it may have come. The process of politics continues, else there is no "end" of this process.

A study of politics, then, does not have as its subject anything that "is." Its subject happens and it happens beyond the forms through which it appears, if it is approached as a subject of study. The alternative is clear: either politics is studied through its forms or it is studied as it happens. The former choice is the traditional one, political science in the scholastic mode. The latter choice has rarely been taken; it is infinitely difficult. The reality of politics is endless, the fluid reality that it is, transcending forever the forms that it fleetingly takes. Why fathom the flux of politics, indeed, when there are the finite forms, however changeful they might be, by which politics traditionally has been assumed as a subject that is understood?

An infinitely fluid reality is no justification for a finalizing mode of learning. On the contrary, it is a challenge for the inquiring mind, regardless of the existent forms of knowledge. To be sure, it would not be possible to apprehend politics, if finite forms of apprehension were not applied in the act of apprehension. Infiniteness is not to be grasped through infiniteness. Fluidity is not a supposition of fluidity. Understanding politics is indeed and cannot be anything else than a "finalizing" act. Yet, understanding politics is also a perennial act, as perennial as its subject. Politics eludes continually the forms of its reality, and, consequently, the forms of its being apprehended. It is pure reality or, to be entirely precise, it is all movement: the movement from which the forms emerge through which this movement – the movement of politics – can be discerned and, as the movement that has occurred, be apperceived.

The challenge, to which this study forms a response, is politics, the movement. The study, to say it again, does not propose a depiction of politics in the conventional modes. It proposes a story, the story of politics. It proposes a pursuit of politics, the pure reality that achieves all its reality only while it happens. The study of politics, as presented here, is the story of politics told by politics in the pursuit of this study.

The Places of the Story

In the course of the study the story of politics will be pursued at different places. The principal place will be a city: Boston. There were three reasons for this choice. A city was chosen because of the crucial advantage any city affords with regard to an inquiry into politics. In a city politics appears quintessentially. For one thing, the relevance of politics to every human concern is immediately evident, in view of the microcosm that each city forms. And then, the relevance of human relationships to the actual event of politics is equally manifest, in view of the proximity within which politics takes place in a city. Boston was chosen because of a classic and of a current feature in its existence. Politics in Boston has never been dull, uninspired, or unimaginative; all observers of Boston politics agree, beyond the considerable differences in their judgment, on the unique fascination which the Boston example of politics holds. And the fascination is compellingly enhanced by the recent *fortuna* of Boston. In the late 1950's the fate of Boston seemed to be sealed. It was a city in decay. Thirty years later, at the close of the 1980's, Boston shines in the realm of cities. It is a city in its full renaissance. And it is a city that documents, to an extent that could hardly be found elsewhere, the creativeness of politics. The new strength that Boston has gained has not been a result of pure luck. The wheel of the city's fortune turned primarily on account of the creative strength that politics lent to the life of the city. The improbable project of restoring the city to its former brilliance − it was politics that carried the project to success.

While Boston struggled with its fate, the position of Mayor of the city was assumed by a young politician who proved to be a most creative politician: Kevin H. White. Mayor White governed Boston for the unusually long period of 16 years, from 1968 to 1983. A close scrutiny of his administration provided the major amount of empirical material upon which this study is based. The search for politics, the quest for the reality of politics as creativity, did not stop there, however. Inquiries into the subject of Boston at large − its social, political, economic history, its people, its traditions, its architecture − expanded the foundation and the scope of the study. And then, a systematic exploration of politics as a field of study traced the texture of precedents and parallels within which the regime of Major White emerged as a paradigmatic example of creative politics, on the one hand, and through which the classic tradition of creative politics shone forth, on the other. The theme of the study was politics, politics as the principal mode of human creativity. And in the pursuit of this theme, the study became a comparative exposition of creative politics. Mayor White as a creative politician could be compared to other creative politicians, to Presidents Franklin D. Roosevelt and Dwight D. Eisenhower, to Chancellor Konrad Adenauer and President François Mitterrand, in particular. And the personal regime which Mayor White built could be compared to the personal regimes that creative politicians always have built: in antiquity, in the Renaissance, in our time; at the local level or at the national level; in Europe as well as in America.

The Themes of the Story

If it is true that politics is the creativity through which human beings exist, the creation of human society is the theme that an inquiry into politics pursues. Accordingly, this study has been given the subtitle *The Creativity of Power*. Still, the empirical foundation as well as the scope of the study entailed a thematic plurality within the general theme. While politics remained the field of inquiry, the exploration of the field moved along these thematic threads:

– Boston politics
– The administration of Boston Mayor Kevin H. White
– The historiography of Boston
– City politics
– American politics
– Urban "planning"
– The renaissance of cities
– Political science and its methodology
– Government
– Political power
– Political institutions
– The comparative history of political parties
– The theory of political finance
– The pathology of politics
– Temporal modes of politics
– Friendship and politics
– Election campaigns
– The political character of space
– The spatial character of politics
– Spatial creativity
– Political creativity.

Writing the Story, Reading the Story

A story wants to be told. It requires its form: a narrative by which it unfolds its drama and its truth. The form of the story must produce, on the part of the audience, the experience of a story and it must make the audience witness to the story's authenticity. Through the way it is told the story must become the story actually happening; it must become the narrative of the audience.

In the composition of the study, therefore, certain rules have been followed.

(a) To make the study as readable as possible, the material upon which it was built is only partly presented in the text. A presentation of all the material would have made the train of the text excessively cumbersome.

(b) The material not presented in the text is laid out in the footnotes. To their larger extent, the footnotes represent, therefore, more than mere footnotes. They form the apparatus of scholarship that is an integral part of this study.

(c) Throughout the study, very detailed analyses were combined with general thematic reflections. Each chapter and each paragraph within every chapter is introduced by a theoretical exposition of the next matter of inquiry. And at regular intervals a summary is given which formulates the generic relevance of the results drawn from the empirical analyses.

(d) The path of the inquiry and the inquiry itself are not disjointed. The usual section "On Method," splendidly isolated from the actual inquiry, will not be found. Rather, the methodological routing of the study is explicitly discussed whenever the material imposes the problem of choosing a "method": a way to approach the material along the mode(s) in which it presents itself. The pitfall of method was avoided by the method to reflect methodically the method of the study.

The story that will be told can be read in different ways. The audience will have options of reading to choose from. It is possible to take up from the study a guide of governing, a manual to be used by the apprentice as well as the professional. The apprentice might wish to employ it for rehearsals of his lore. The professional might wish to adopt it as a mirror of reflection. The study can also, of course, be seized as a text on Boston. Through this reading the study will offer a work of historiography, in which Bostonians will recognize the configurations of people and events that have shaped their recent past, and in which others will discern the tectonics of local affairs at that special site that is Boston. In the vein of a predominantly academic reading, an introduction to the science of politics will emerge from the study. The reader will be invited to a practice of understanding politics that is both "philosophical" and "empirical." The study might be read, finally, just for entertainment. This reading experience will occur when the reader primarily appreciates the detective train of research along which the study grew and took its form. A quest for knowledge, the reader will realize, has its own drift of drama.

These are some possibilities of reading this study. Each can be selected; or several can be chosen in a more complex act of reading. Other possibilities might be found. The study extends beyond its text. The text is given here. The extension is the product of an open process starting here. It is the product of the audience.

Chapter 1
The Autocracy, Condition of Creativity

τό τε γὰρ ἓν τὸ ὂν ἀεὶ ἴσχει καὶ τὸ ὂν τὸ ἕν·

For the One always holds What Is and What Is
holds the One.

Plato, *Parmenides* 143 a

1 Philosophical Argument: The Paradox of Liberty

Since a science of politics emerged, political liberty has been one of the principal problems, if not the primary problem of this science. All human beings aspire to a human existence fully achieved. They desire the freedom of being themselves. And all human beings exist but as social beings. Being themselves, for them, is being themselves in conjunction with each other. Society is the condition of freedom. Freedom, however, defies conditions. Human beings, then, face forever this paradox: to attain the freedom of being themselves, they must restrict the freedom of attaining it. To the degree that they seek the freedom wherein a truly human existence lies, they must keep the bonds within which alone they can have this freedom.

The whole political process arises from this paradox.[1] If it did not exist, politics would be unnecessary.[2] And a science of politics would be pointless. Yet, the paradox has remained and will remain, of course.[3] "Il n'est pas de

---

[1] Cf. G. E. G. Catlin, *The Science and Method of Politics,* London – New York 1927, p. 237: "The whole political process arises from the paradox that, in order to gain assurance of freedom in one direction, we must submit to certain restrictions which curtail our sense of general freedom." – Cf. also Catlin's further reflections, p. 238 f.: "In Politics, this sense of being irked by restraint, even though the restraints be means to one's own ends, is often termed the love of liberty, and is not infrequently coupled with a naive belief, characteristic of Whig England and of pioneer America, in the sufficiency of one's individual powers to deal with the emergencies of the social situation. One often observes that the lover of liberty declines the end for fear of having his liberty restricted by the means; [...]. That he who wills the end, e. g. of a purity in local politics, must also will the means, by being prepared to undergo the heat and dust of voting and electioneering himself, is one of the most difficult of lessons for free human nature to learn. [...] The believers in liberty do not love to recognize that, when it comes to a fight, discipline must be the means if their cause is to triumph."

[2] There have of course been attempts to overcome the paradox and hence to do away with politics, in order to achieve conditions of human community that would be "rational," "efficient," potentially "perfect." Cf. Chapter III, 13.

[3] The experience of politics as paradoxical is central to the political science of Plato, of course. "But this is the thing that has made me so long shrink from speaking out, because I saw that it would be a very paradoxical (*para doxan*) saying." (*The Republic* 473 e.) ... "Unless, said I, either philosophers become kings in our states or those whom we now call our kings and rulers take to the pursuit of philosophy seriously and adequately, and there is a conjunction of these two things, political power and philosophic intelligence, [...] there can be no cessation of troubles, for our states, nor, I fancy, for the human race either." (*The Republic* 473 d.) Cf. also p. 192 ff. and the Index of Subjects, "paradox."

liberté, sans organisation de cette liberté. − There is no liberty without an organization of this liberty."[4]

Quite appropriately, the science of politics has largely been, throughout its history, an inquiry into the "organization of liberty," that is, into possibilities of founding and preserving "political liberty" − the freedom of human beings under the rule of freedom.[5] The inquiry, as we know, did not bring forth flawless scenarios, nor did it produce infallible plans.[6] Political science proved to be a science "in-between," between notions of human perfection and the experiences of human frailty, between paradigms of order and the reality of disorder, between tenets of logical thought and the practical logic of prudence.[7] In one of its veins, however, the science of politics gained upon

---

[4] F. Mitterrand, Interview, in: *Libération*, nouv. sér., no. 923, May 10, 1984, p. 6.

[5] Cf. Plato, *Laws* 693 b,d − e: "[...] a State ought to be free (*eleuthéran*) and wise and in friendship with itself [...]. There are two mother-forms of constitution, so to call them, from which one may truly say all the rest are derived. Of these the one is properly called monarchy (*monarchia*), the other democracy (*demokratia*), [...] the rest are practically all, as I said, modifications of these two. Now it is essential for a polity to partake of both these two forms, if it is to have freedom (*eleuthería*) and friendliness (*philía*) combined with wisdom (*phrónesis*). And that is what our argument intends to enjoin, when it declares that a State which does not partake of these can never be rightly constituted. − It could not. − Since the one embraced monarchy and the other freedom, unmixed and in excess [...]." − Cf. further: O. von Gierke, *Natural Law and the Theory of Society 1500 – 1800*,Cambridge 1934; A. Passerin d'Entrèves, *The Medieval Contribution to Political Thought − Thomas Aquinas, Marsilius of Padua, Richard Hooker*, Oxford 1939; F. Watkins, *The Political Tradition of the West: A Study in the Development of Modern Liberalism*, Cambridge, Mass. 1948; M. Pohlenz, *Griechische Freiheit. Wesen und Werden eines Lebensideals*, Heidelberg 1955; W. Suerbaum, *Vom antiken zum frühmittelalterlichen Staatsbegriff − Über Verwendung und Bedeutung von respublica, regnum, imperium und status von Cicero bis Jordanis*, Münster 1961; E. Berti, *Il de re publica di Cicerone e il pensiero politico classico*, Padua 1963; E. Voegelin, ed., *Zwischen Revolution und Restauration. Politisches Denken in England im 17. Jahrhundert*, München 1968; I. Berlin, *Four Essays on Liberty*, Oxford 1969; R. D. Cumming, *Human Nature and History. A Study of the Development of Liberal Political Thought*, Chicago 1969; P. F. Moreau, *Les racines du libéralisme*, Paris 1978; A. Liebich, *Le libéralisme classique*, Sillery (Québec) 1985; P. Manent, *Les libéraux*, 2 vols., Paris 1986; idem, *Histoire intellectuelle du libéralisme*, Paris 1987.

[6] The classic statement on flawless scenarios (Rousseau's rule of the *volonté générale*, for example) and infallible plans (Montesquieu's trust in the *nature des choses*, for example) is Plato's: "[...] the probable outcome of too much freedom is only too much slavery in the individual and the state." (*The Republic* 564 a.)

[7] Plato and Aristotle, the founders, proceeded from this insight; in this century the insight has been restored by Eric Voegelin, Leo Strauss, and Hannah Arendt.

the paradox political liberty poses.[8] Political science came close to mastering the contradictious task of "organizing" our "liberty." It invented constitutional government.

Constitutional government is a "miraculous" mechanism. It produces political authority by denying it. It deliberately weakens the political executive and thereby compels him to seek the authority which he needs. Government is constitutionally shattered into pieces and he who wants to wield power in the welter of these pieces must, first of all, build up his own authority. In the mode of constitutional government power is but a fluid phenomenon to be seized in a continuous quest for power.

But how does the head of a constitutional government, from whom power has deliberately been withheld, gain the power to govern and still remain the head of a constitutional government?

In the practice of constitutional government the paradox of liberty poses itself as the paradox of power. A constitutional government, on the one hand, is a government "whose powers have been adapted to [...] the maintenance of individual liberty."[9] On the other hand, it is a government, and in a government "leadership and control must be lodged somewhere; the whole art of statesmanship is the art of bringing the several parts of government into effective cooperation for the accomplishment of particular common objects."[10] Constitutional government cannot do without power; political power is necessary. Yet, it should be the power of liberty — the power of that liberty that negates power.

What, then, should the head of a constitutional government do? Should he still seek power, the power that liberty appears to deny? Should he, in other words, be prepared to violate the law, the constitution?

The truth of constitutional government, however, is indivisible. There is no exception to the rule of law, for the commoner and for the prince alike. Constitutional government was founded not in defense of efficiency,

---

[8] "Science of politics" is meant here to denote political wisdom in general (hence the "science" every good politician knows) and not only the academic discipline called political science.

[9] W. Wilson, "Constitutional Government in the United States," in: *The Papers of Woodrow Wilson*, ed. A. S. Link, Vol. 18 (1908–1909), Princeton 1974, p. 69 f.

[10] Ibid., p. 105. — The idea that "leadership and control must be lodged somewhere" — the notion of a political executive — has been formulated, as to its real significance and importance, only in the course of modern, if not contemporary political thought. Cf. H. C. Mansfield Jr., "The Absent Executive in Aristotle's Politics," in P. Schramm, T. Silver, eds., *Natural Right and Political Right*, Durham 1984, pp. 169–196; idem, "Gouvernement représentatif et pouvoir exécutif," *Commentaire*, no. 36, 1986, pp. 664–672.

resolution, or competence but in defense of liberty. To violate laws, and be it just one, is to make the fatal switch from the rule of law to the capriciousness of man. However strong the head of a constitutional government must be in order to be able really to govern, he will never have a legitimate reason to forsake the sanctuary of liberty: the rule of law.

No, the power that liberty needs but appears to deny has to be found within the constitution of liberty. It cannot be obtained institutionally; the institutional frame, constitutional government, is an instrumentality for the maintenance of liberty, not for the acquisition of power.[11] The power to govern, institutionally dispersed, has to be sought through the institutional frame, in a para-institutional quest. "Leadership and control must be lodged somewhere." But somewhere is nowhere, until the head of the constitutional government has accumulated, there where he is, the power of the head of a constitutional government.

The paradox of power persists. It is the paradox of liberty, constitutionally transfigured. There is no solution to it, nor even a way to find a solution. But there is the art of gripping it: executive politics. In a continuous quest for power the political executive builds up a "system" of sources from which he can continuously draw *his* power. He masters the paradox of power by creating, within the framework of constitutional government, a para-institutional configuration of personal power. Against the shattered pieces of constitutional government he sets off monocratic powers — an autocracy.

2 Power and Architecture

The practitioners of the art of politics tend to take pleasure in the art of architecture; they view it as the perfect mode of symbolizing their might.[12]

---

[11] The definition of constitutional government as an "instrumentality for the maintenance of liberty" is Woodrow Wilsons's. Cf. "Constitutional Government in the United States," op. cit., p. 72.

[12] Cf. H. G. Evers, *Tod, Macht und Raum als Bereiche der Architektur*, München 1970 (Reprint); A. Reinle, *Zeichensprache der Architektur. Symbol, Darstellung und Brauch in der Baukunst des Mittelalters und der Neuzeit*, Zürich – München 1976; M. Ragon, *L'Architecte, le prince et la démocratie*, Paris 1977; H. A. Millon, L. Nochlin, eds., *Art and Architecture in the Service of Politics*, Cambridge, Mass. 1978; T. Schabert, "Moderne Architektur — und die Hütten der Epigonen. Menschliches Bauen als politische Kunst der Vergangenheit," *Der Monat*, Jg. 30, H. 2, Dec. 1978, pp. 127 – 133; J. Trilling, "Paris: Architecture as Politics," *The Atlantic*, October 1983, pp. 26 – 35; M. Warnke, *Politische Architektur in Europa. Vom Mittelalter bis heute — Repräsentation und Gemeinschaft*, Köln 1984.

The passion of politicians for the plastic potency of architecture transcends the variegations of governments and rulers. It enraptures kings and sheiks, tyrants and warlords, presidents and senators, mayors and aldermen, the dignitaries of the court in an empire as well as the representatives of the people in a republic. The symbolic potential of buildings, monuments, cityscapes attracts political power whatever its form, enticing rulers and regimes to reveal in the language of architecture the truth of their power.

A civic journey to Boston's new City Hall (completed in 1969) provides an excellent example, for the design of the surroundings and that of the building itself are obviously intended to inject into such a journey a symbolic significance. Let us imagine we were visiting Boston and, induced by architectural as well as civic curiosity, we were allured into approaching the seat of Boston's government. To what experience would our journey lead?

As we emerge from one of the streets which open into City Hall Plaza, we go through a series of transitions. Entering the plaza spread out in front of City Hall, we are reminded of the *piazza della repubblica* in an Italian city. Passing from our previous hurried pace to a leisurely tempo of walking, we conform our movement to the design of the plaza. We join other people in a public arena. The perimeter of our movement — like that of our fellow citizens — shrinks to the radius of the pedestrian, and our awareness of the social life in the plaza becomes more acute. We have stopped to be absorbed in private thoughts and instead feel a growing desire for the experience of civic community. An almost imperceptible influence steers us towards the entrances to City Hall. The slight slope of the plaza converging on the building infuses in all movements on the plaza a sense of direction; it seems to be natural that they gravitate towards the ground floors of City Hall. There, we can hardly fail to notice all the signs and communications telling us that the building serves the functions of public administration. Considering the design of the entrance hall and observing the activity which takes place in it, we discern, however, a larger purpose of the hall's architecture. By its design and the material used for its construction the hall forms a continuation of the plaza from where we came. The City Hall appears to be as much a public arena as City Hall Plaza; the symbolism of its architecture yields the perception of an open, transparent relationship between the people of Boston and their representatives in City Hall; architecture emphasizes the principle of democracy: there is but one sovereign "outside" and "inside" City Hall.

Indeed, considerable efforts are made to welcome everyone who visits this civic home. An information officer is seated behind a widely visible desk in the entrance hall and directs people to whatever counter or office they want to go. The spatial organization of offices is, in many parts of the building, by no means intimidating but permits visitors to see city employees working at their desks or to hear a group of them in a meeting room deliberate on some public agenda. At several key points in the building numerous pamphlets and brochures are displayed reporting upon the projects and archievements of this city's government. Browsing among them, we chance upon a booklet which arouses our particular interest, since it describes the place of our visit. As we read the short text, we understand that we are certainly welcome to cover the final stretch of our passage to the seat of Boston's government. For we are told that "[...] the Mayor's Office and the City Council Chamber [are] visible to all and directly accessible by a large stairway [from the entrance hall]."[13]

In accordance with the hierarchy of representative government, we turn first towards the Chamber of the City Council. Having climbed up the stairway, as directed, we easily find the doors to the Chamber. They are broad and well marked and — as we note by observing the people around us — they evidently represent the entrance to a place of civic congregation. The Council is in session and, by listening to its debate, we avail ourselves of this opportunity to obtain a lesson in civic instruction. At first, our perception is not sharp enough to pierce through the complex language of the debate and to grasp the real instruction which it conveys. For it is carried on by a body of people who obviously are seasoned politicians, steeped in the traditions of Boston, knowledgeable about the affairs and interests of her people, skilled in the procedures of the political process. And yet, as we gradually realize, they behave as if they were thrown into a kafkaesque dilemma being summoned to collaboration with a master who never appears but shrouds himself in elusion and secrecy. Can it be true? Is the transparent architecture of Boston's City Hall an illusion? Why does the Council despair of cooperating with the Mayor of Boston? Is the Mayor's Office perhaps not "visible to all and directly accessible"? Where actually is it?

Spurred by the sensational ring of this seemingly trivial question, we immediately decide to complete our civic journey by having a look at the Mayor's chambers. Back on the stairway which is supposed to lead not only to the City Council Chamber but to the Mayor's Office as well, we are at a loss as to where we should go. This time, architecture gives us no guidance. Making inquiries among passersby, we are directed towards the corner where

---

[13] BRA, *Government Center*, s. l., s. d. [p. 3]. Cf. also "Boston City Hall," CR, Vol. 75, No. 1, Jan. 3, 1983, pp. 4–5. This brief description includes the following statement: "The bricks of the plaza flow right into the South Entry Hall to tie the world inside the building to the world outside, and continue across the Hall and up the stairs, creating a 'path' to the floors above." — Boston's new City Hall was designed in 1961 and built between 1961–69. The design is not wholly original; it is inspired by Le Corbusier's design for the monastery of La Tourette (near Lyon) in France which was built between 1956–60.

the lifts are installed. Should the office of Boston's Mayor be there, tucked away in the elevator's corner? There are just walls of concrete and the lifts, and — indeed — deeper in the corner there is an opening protected by a desk behind which a policeman is sitting. He is eyeing us with a guarded look but lets us pass and venture further. Presently, another desk impedes our civic journey. A secretary, barely concealing her view of us as intruders, makes us explain the reason for our sudden appearance. Glancing around while thinking of an answer — what we say eventually about our civic curiosity proves to be totally inadequate, of course —, we discern a small room whose design suggests that it is meant to shield whatever lies beyond. There are a few chairs, but if anyone sat down, this person could not help being clearly a stranger. There are a few doors, but they carry neither a sign nor a mark and they are closed. Architecture is used to protect the office of Boston's Mayor against the public's view and to make it inaccessible. An architectural shield separates the people of Boston and their Mayor — who, on the other hand, can sneak in and out of his office by a private elevator linked directly to his car's garage. Our civic journey in Boston must remain incomplete, for the last part of the path to civic power is the Mayor's private way.[14] Now we apprehend the symbolic meaning of the antechamber in the elevator's corner. It is not a vestibule of democracy but the guardroom of an unaccounted might. Pondering over this power behind the architectural screen, we set off to turn away.

3 The Potential of Power

The City Charter of Boston vests the Mayor with a great amount of institutional authority. Associates of Kevin White did not mistake this authority when they spelled out the "great power [concentrated] in the Office of the Mayor" or observed that the holder of the office was "uninhibited to do whatever he likes to do as long as he moves within the law."[15]

The Mayor is the chief executive of the city government. He holds the prerogatives to appoint or to dismiss the heads of departments and to enlist the services of "secretaries" in his office to whom civil service laws do not apply — the latter prerogative was used by Kevin White several hundred

---

[14] Under Mayor White the "private way" was by no means a free and open way. It was divided into several separate sections; to reach the Mayor one had to proceed through a series of doors of which each was guarded by a vigilant secretary.

[15] Sources: Interviews.

times, the appointments of "secretaries" added up to a form of personal government, his "Court" (see Chapter 2).

The Charter also enables the Mayor to control the budgetary process. It is his privilege to initiate the annual budget of the City, to make all regular and supplementary appropriations, and to make transfers — "other than for personal service" — from any appropriation to any other. In contrast, the City Council can neither originate a budget nor "increase any item in, nor the total of, a budget, nor add any item thereto," but is just given the right to reduce or reject any item.[16]

The Charter gives the City Council only very limited possibilities of checking the power of the chief executive. The Mayor, on the other hand, enjoys a position of predominance over the Council. Every order, ordinance, resolution, or vote of the Council — with few exceptions — must be approved by the Mayor. If the Mayor exercises the veto, the Council can override it only by two thirds of all the Councillors' votes. Every order, ordinance, resolution, or vote concerning budgetary matters, however, will be void in consequence of a veto by the Mayor. The Council is empowered to change and to reorganize the structure of the city government, but by-laws or ordinances passed by the Council to that effect must again be approved by the Mayor. And not the Council but the Mayor will then have the prerogative to appoint — without confirmation by the Council — the head of every department or agency that is created as a result of such a reorganization.

The considerable power which the Mayor of Boston can wield by virtue of the legal authority vested in the office covers not only the city departments and agencies proper. It extends over the whole structure of local government in the Boston area. This extended power can be measured, for instance, by a simple numerical comparison on the basis of a table published in the *Municipal Register*. The table shows the procedures by which a number of positions are filled, by appointment or election, in the local government of the Boston area. Altogether, the positions of 153 public officials are specified. The Mayor of Boston clearly appears as the preeminent actor in the process of filling these positions — having the sole power to appoint no less than 113 of the 153 officials.[17]

In some cases the legal power vested in the office permits the Mayor to govern even in an absolutist way. The decision of Mayor White as regards

---

[16] Cf. "Excerpts from the City Charter," in: City of Boston, *Municipal Register for 1978 – 1979*, Boston 1979, p. 17 ff. and City of Boston Code [Statute, Ordinances, Regulations], [1975]. On city charters in general, cf. Ch. A. Adrian, *State and Local Government*, New York, 1976, 4th ed., pp. 89 – 97.

[17] *Municipal Register for 1978 – 1979*, pp. 45 – 48.

the franchise for the construction and operation of cable TV in Boston represents a classic example. For the law empowered the Mayor to grant this franchise as a result of just his own resolve. Legally he was not required to let any other institution or any other public official participate in the process of selecting one of the companies which were competing for the Boston franchise. While he entrusted to a fluid configuration of advisers[18] the task of preparing his selection, Mayor White fully maintained the absolute authority which he held in this particular case. The decision which he eventually reached was an *arcanum imperii* until he chose to make it known. And when he made it finally known, he phrased the announcement in the language of self-conscious power: "I am today announcing that I have chosen the Cablevision corporation to build and operate a citywide cable TV system for the City of Boston."[19]

4 The Construction of the Autocracy

The legal construction of the office enables the Mayor of Boston to enjoy and to exercise a formidable power. Any Mayor of Boston would attempt to avail himself of this power. So did Kevin White who was first elected Mayor of Boston in 1967 and held the office for 16 years from 1968 to 1983. And not only did he fully succeed. But he achieved much more: he amplified the mayoral authority to an extent that even a most liberal reading of the City Charter would not reveal.[20]

---

[18] "Fluid configurations of advisers" were principal instruments of governing in the administration of Mayor White. Cf. infra, p. 233 ff.

[19] Cf. *BG*, Aug. 13, 1981. On the background inform: M. Harmonay, D. First, "Mayor White, Media Mogul: The Politics of Cable TV," *Boston Magazine*, Sept. 1980; Al Larkin, "Cable TV Comes To Boston ... and It's Kevin White's Show," *BG Magazine*, Sept. 7, 1980; *BG*, June 22, 1981; July 17, 1981; Aug. 10, 1980, Aug. 16, 1981.

[20] Basic information about the political career of Kevin White can be found in: City of Boston, *Boston's Forty-Five Mayors*, Boston 1979, 2nd ed., pp. 46 – 54; Th. H. O'Connor, *Bibles, Brahmins and Bosses. A Short History of Boston*, Boston 1976, pp. 146 – 156; Ph. Heymann, M. Wagner Weinberg, "The Paradox of Power: Mayoral Leadership on Charter Reform in Boston," in: W. Dean Burnham, M. Wagner Weinberg, eds., *American Politics and Public Policy*, Cambridge, Mass. 1978, pp. 280 – 306; M. Wagner Weinberg, "Boston's Kevin White: A Mayor Who Survives," *Political Science Quarterly*, Vol. 96, No. 1, Spring 1981, pp. 87 – 106; B. Ferman, "Beating the Odds: Mayoral Leadership and the Acquisition of Power," *Policy Studies Review*, Vol. 3, No. 1, Aug. 1983, pp. 29 – 40; G. V. Higgins, *Style Versus Substance. Boston, Kevin White, and the Politics of Illusion*, New York 1984; J. A. Lukas, *Common Ground. A Turbulent Decade in the Lives of Three American Families*, New York 1986, pp. 585 – 623.

Probably Kevin White would not have attained to such an amplified power if he had exploited only the prerogatives of his office. There were, in addition, external factors which furnished the material basis for the heightening of his legal power:

(1) Considerable amounts of federal funds had to be allocated to neighborhoods, civic organizations, and public institutions in the city;
(2) a large number of urban renewal and redevelopment projects required political guidance and resolution;
(3) a growing clientele of developers and entrepreneurs wanting to invest in Boston's economic future looked on him as the principal in City Hall who negotiated and acted on behalf of the city.[21]

By seizing these opportunities, Mayor White considerably expanded the field of political activity in which his power could grow.

Finally, in addition to the legal power vested in his office and the heightened power derived from favorable external circumstances, he acquired a third source from which he could draw political power. Kevin White set up his own "political system,"[22] a configuration of associates, companions, and allies which served only *his* political purposes.[23]

From Kevin White's progress as Mayor of Boston emerged quite a remarkable phenomenon. It inserted an autocracy into the texture of the American republic.[24]

---

[21] Cf. B. Ferman, "Beating the Odds ... ," *op. cit.*; J. H. Mollenkopf, *The Contested City,* Princeton 1983, pp. 3 – 11, 188 – 212.

[22] The members of Mayor White's administration used the term "political system" to draw a distinction between themselves and the formal structure of Boston's government.

[23] Cf. infra, p. 127 ff.

[24] The term "autocracy" may sound severe as definition of a mayoral regime in an American city. The founding of the American republic, after all, made the word "autocrat" a foreign notion – spelled George III. Still, there is no logical or any other reason to refrain from using the term "autocracy" if it denotes most accurately the reality of political power that is studied. Moreover, the method of looking for precedents helps to avoid the pitfalls of subjective judgement. (The test of truth is a lack of originality.) In his classic, *The American Commonwealth,* James Bryce characterized the municipal government in the United States by, among other things, the "vesting of almost autocratic executive power in the mayor," the "mayor's absolute power over all the agents of the city government." The "entire character of the city government, for the four years which constitutes a Mayor's term," Bryce writes, "depends upon the man chosen for the office of the Mayor." (*The American Commonwealth,* abr. ed., New York – London 1920, pp. 433, 443, 442.) Mayor White did not escape this perception of mayoral power. Referring to the Mayor's predominance over Boston's redevelopment, Ian Menzies, a leading editorialist of the *Boston Globe,* described him as "architectural autocrat" (*BG,* Feb. 24, 1983). In the context of this brief linguistic reflection it appears interesting to note,

This autocracy established by Mayor White can not be grasped by the conceptual apparatus of a political science of institutions or public administration.[25] The formula "strong Mayor – weak Council" hardly defines a mayoral regime that grew into an autocracy. Nor would an "empirical" analysis suffice which would follow the methods of orthodox social science. Presumably "realistic," the analysis would presuppose a contrast between the "real" workings of Mayor White's regime and its institutional "form." Pursuing the logic implied by this presupposition, the analysis would become a probe into the "secrets" of the regime, its oligarchic structures, conspirational politics and, of course, corruption. Since its plausibility would apparently be augmented to the extent that "striking revelations" were made, the accomplishments of the analysis would be measured against sensationalist expectations rather than critial reflection. Progressively, the study of the regime would turn into a hunting for a limited set of "sensational" phenomena. Fascinating as it might be, however, this hunting would distort the view of the autocracy built by Mayor White. Yes, an autocracy is prone to corruption. But this is a piece of perennial wisdom which does not need to be proved once again – the pedantry of social science notwithstanding. And, besides, neither incidents of corruption nor one-sided allocations of public funds or other phenomena of this kind explain the existence of an autocracy in a democratic society. A study is needed which ascertains, first of all, the nature of its subject.

The autocracy built by Mayor White was the result of a progress in the aggregation of power.[26] The zero point of the progress was given by the

---

furthermore, that Mayor White actualized a regime quite congenial to the taste of other politicians in the Boston area. In a report of the *New York Times* (Dec. 10, 1983) the Massachusetts Legislature was called the "most autocratic in the country." Mayors are perceived as "autocrats" in other democratic societies as well. Cf. J. Becquart-Leclercq, *Paradoxes du pouvoir local,* Paris 1976, p. 199 ff. (J. B.-L. uses the term "monocrate"); Th. Ellwein, R. Zoll, *Wertheim. Politik und Machtstruktur in einer deutschen Stadt,* München 1982, pp. 228 ff., 235 ff.

[25] Political actors in Boston barely conceal their contempt for "academics" who do not see the inadequacy of this approach as clearly as they do.

[26] On the dynamics of power in the process of its aggregation, cf. Th. Hobbes, *Leviathan,* I, X: "For the nature of Power, is in this point [considered as "Instrumentall Power"], like to Fame, increasing as it proceeds; or like the motion of heavy bodies, which the further they go, make still the more hast." – The problem of "power" as a *continuing process of aggregating power* has not really been recognized in the literature on urban politics. In his study on New Haven Robert Dahl alludes to the problem but then deals with it by typically brief remarks: R. D. Dahl, *Who Governs? Democracy and Power in an American City,* New Haven 1961, pp. 308 – 309 ("The Art of Pyramiding"). In the literature on presidential leadership, however, the problem has become one of the central

formal position of being the Mayor of Boston. By using the possibilities of this position to the utmost extent, the Mayor amplified progressively the amount of his power. He "moved" in the actualization of his mayoral authority from the zero point − the legal authority vested in the office − to a position of aggregated power − an autocratic regime.[27] The progress he made in the course of this movement was the personal progress of Kevin White as Mayor of Boston. The power which he aggregated reflected *his* will, *his* aspirations, and *his* actions. It did not change the formal conditions of his authority but took place within the existent structures of governing in Boston.

A study of this autocracy has to be undertaken, therefore, as a simultaneous study of both its formal and its actual modality. Only then can the study be focused upon its true subject: the *movement* by which Kevin White acceded to the position of an autocrat within the constitutionally unchanged form of his mandate as the Mayor of an American city.

5 The Strategy of the Autocrat

A position of aggregated power can only be held if the aggregation of power is continuously sustained. Without incessant support the pile of power would quickly crumble and be reduced to the ground level of a purely formal authority. Any ruler who has built a regime emanating from an aggregation of power must, above all, be concerned with the continuing generation of power. For this ruler to govern means to struggle for power − and to struggle continuously. However constituted the regime may be, the search for sources of power and the need to preserve these to the extent that they are exploited are the paramount problems inherent in its composition.

Mayor White recognized the intrinsic problems of a powerful government, of course. And he knew the need to devise a strategy of governing by which he would be able to attain and − an objective of even greater importance − to reproduce continuously a position of aggregated power.

---

topics. This is largely due to Richard E. Neustadt's classic study: *Presidential Power. The Politics of Leadership with Reflections on Johnson and Nixon,* New York − Toronto 1960, 1976. A parallel classic dealing with the power problem of German Federal Chancellors is Wilhelm Hennis' study: *Richtlinienkompetenz und Regierungstechnik,* Tübingen 1964.

[27] Associates of Kevin White who have known him since his first term as Mayor of Boston refer vaguely to this "movement" in observing that during his later terms he displayed a governing behavior quite different from that of the earlier terms.

He contrived his strategy towards his ascendancy and he practiced it persistently while he was Mayor of Boston. However, the status of this strategy in relation to his rule has generally not been understood nor has it really been analyzed.

According to the common view, one can explain the strategy of Mayor White by an evocation of "similarities": a similarity between his government and the "administrative style" of President Franklin D. Roosevelt or a similarity between his rule and the "machine politics" of Richard Daley, Mayor of Chicago.[28] Implicitly, evocations of this kind attribute to Mayor White's strategy the status of an imitation. They suggest that all that is needed to understand it is a reference to the one or the other "model."[29]

And one could indeed point out that Mayor White and his associates themselves seemed to have corroborated this view. Kevin White let it be known that he was familiar with some of the "models";[30] close associates told people from outside his administration that he had studied "FDR's administrative style"; and, truly, the Mayor's staff convened for several seminars of instruction in politics Daley-style.[31]

The demonstrations of Kevin White and his associates notwithstanding, evocations of similarities do not really help to fathom the Mayor's strategy of governing and, in particular, to comprehend the correlation between the

---

[28] Cf., for instance, *BG*, April 6, 1976: "Kevin White is impressed with Daley's use of power. He has studied Daley's methods. If national avenues were shut to White, he would not be unhappy at the prospect of becoming an institutional mayor in Boston — as Daley is in Chicago." — *Newsweek*, May 11, 1981: Mayor White "[...] has long entertained national ambitions and he has been building a political machine to go with them. Last year he had a historian brief his top aides on how Mayor Richard Daley ran Chicago." — "White is fond of quoting Mayor Daley to the effect that filling potholes are what kept the Chicago Mayor in office" (Interview, Senior aide, White administration). Cf. further *BG*, May 15, 1981; *NYT*, Dec. 26 and Dec. 30, 1982.

[29] The list of "models" includes: FDR, Daley, John V. Lindsay (Mayor of New York), the governing of Boston as described in: N. Matthews, *The City Government of Boston*, Boston 1895; the Mayors of Boston as depicted in: E. O'Connor, *The Last Hurrah*, Boston 1956.

[30] They were represented by three books: F. R. Kent, *The Great Game of Politics: An Effort to Present the Elementary Human Facts About Politics, Politicians, and Political Machines, Candidates and Their Ways, for the Benefit of the Average Citizen*, Garden City 1923, Reprint New York 1974; M. L. Rakove, *Don't Make No Waves, Don't Back No Losers. An Insider's Analysis of the Daley Machine*, Bloomington 1975; idem, *We Don't Want Nobody Nobody Sent. An Oral History of the Daley Years*, Bloomington 1979. — Kevin White consulted with Milton Rakove about machine politics (*BPh*, Nov. 18, 1980).

[31] The instructor was Milton Rakove.

strategy and the nature of his rule. Their misleading tendency did not only discourage reasoned attempts to discern the political wisdom of the strategy. It fostered the easy excuse of cynical conclusions. Kevin White, it was held, had adopted the strategy on purely calculating grounds. He was portrayed as a schemer, plotting his ego trip to the excitement of power.[32]

Thus, covered by the judgment of cynicism, the strategy of the autocracy remained unintelligible. And the judges did not apparently realize the irony of their position. For they did help the autocrat and his aides to ward off any too close a curiosity about the reasons why, in fact, they were capable of making and operating an autocracy. Every autocracy tends naturally to be secretive about its inner workings. Its guardians must rejoice if critics even maintain that there is not more about it than a reflection of classicism, an imitation of models. There is nothing to be learned from imitations, reason the critic and with him the guardian; whatever there is to be learned about them can be learned by the study of the classic examples. There is nothing to be learned from White's autocracy; however the latter worked, it were the ways of Daley, of Roosevelt that were aped by Kevin White.

Yet, the art of politics knows but imitations, or, to put it positively, politics is an art whose practitioners tend to attest the classicism of politics; it is an art of classicists.[33] Time and again, the problems of governing are solved, or at least dealt with, in "similar" ways: by different people in different times under different circumstances. Every practitioner strives for mastering the technique of the art, for learning the politician's lore – and mostly does this without knowing, or caring, very much about precursors or forerunners, masters of the recent or sages of the remotest past.

An innocent ignorance makes many politicians (and most of their critics) believe that their political pursuits have an "original" importance. This error of judgment should not be surprising. For politicians do not usually happen to be scholars or amateur historians in the field of political studies. (In the course of longer careers, though, some few develop a strong interest in the field.) If they became more knowledgeable about the practice of their art at places and in times other than their own, however, they would soon "discover" what they would perceive to be "astonishing" parallels and precedents of their own pursuits. They would find "models" – extraneous as well as earlier "models" of their own present rule and of this rule's intrinsic strategy of governing.

---

[32] Conclusions of this kind present: F. Butterfield, "Troubles of Boston's Mayor Are Tied to Political Machine," *NYT,* Dec. 26, 1982; D. Clendinen, "Profile in Politics: Boston Mayor's Reformist Style Faded With His Fortunes," *NYT,* Dec. 30, 1982.

[33] Cf. infra, pp. 41, 168, 213–217.

Being the politicians that they are, they would very likely exploit their find. They would be drawing prestige and authority from those "models" *des autres lieux* and *des autres temps* which they appeared to "emulate." And they would of course not neglect to tend the fame and the aura of these "models." They were not afraid of imitations, certainly not. For they had then tasted the advantages of practicing the art of politics as classicists. The more their own rule resembled a "model," the less it would need its own *raison d'être;* the more they would appear to be emulating a "classical model," the more they were able to govern as they pleased — the mystique of the model would cushion the brute reality of their power. They would not reject but would embrace the knowledge of "famous" politicians and of "classic" ways to govern and to rule, "similar" to theirs. For their love of politics, they would want to actualize "imitations" — imitations that gave the originality of their political pursuits the resemblance of classicism.

Mayor White built an autocracy and he built the autocracy by a strategy of governing that resembled the strategies followed by other and indeed famous politicians. He emulated models and he emulated those models because this "emulating" gave the originality of his political achievements the resemblance of classic politics. The similarity between his strategy of governing and the classic strategies of politicians such as Roosevelt and Daley palliated the apparent *skandalon* of his autocracy: it traversed the texture of the American republic and yet it embraced a classic vein of American politics. It embodied the paradox of liberty: a politician's governing between power denied and power assumed.

Nevertheless, the Mayor could not help being original if he wanted really to govern. Pursuing the vision of being a politician of creative strength, he aimed at expanding as much as he could the authority vested in his office; he assumed autocratic powers — and he could not cease from seeking more power, and more power again and again, or else he would have betrayed his vision of political creativity. It was this inherent dynamics of his autocracy, balanced precariously between creative strength and flat authority, that made him apply a specific strategy of governing — that made him choose *his* approach to the problem of governing.

For the greatest danger to the autocracy was the autocracy itself. Being sustained by a continuing accumulation of power, it could not last unless it was organized in quite a certain way. To exist, the autocracy needed an organization through which it soaked up incessantly an uninterrupted flow of power that continuously reproduced all the power from which it emerged. Hence, Mayor White's autocracy was by necessity the principal concern of Mayor White's autocracy.[34] Its essence, an assumption of autocratic powers,

---

[34] Cf. W. Hennis, *Richtlinienkompetenz und Regierungstechnik,* op. cit., p. 39: "Not the least part of a political leader's attention must be paid not only to his politics but also to its conditions, to the preservation of his power above all." (My translation, T. S.)

depended upon its form — upon an organization of the Mayor's government
that was the catalyst of the Mayor's autocratic powers.

The Mayor had therefore to apply his political skills also to the *conditions*
for governing and not only to the *tasks* of governing. In a sense, organizing
a creative government — and that meant a powerful government — was of
greater importance than the process of governing itself. If the Mayor had
considered governing merely as a matter of "public administration" or "policy
management," he would have belittled the original moment of politics:
creativity. Yet he recognized the secret of power: he who knows that power
is an unsteady companion, the gift of circumstances, also knows how to hold
on to it. As the conditions from which power grows change continually, the
structures of political organization by which it is drawn from these conditions
have continuously to be changed accordingly. A politician who is forming a
government and who wants to use this government creatively, must build a
government that itself is a product of creativity — a government whose
"organization" is as fluid, as flexible, as variable as possible. In politics, a
chaotic government is the catalyst of creativity.

This is the logic of political creativity, the path of power pursued by
Mayor White when he built his autocracy. He "emulated" Roosevelt, of
course, and many other politicians, all those who had understood and seized
upon this logic.[35] But, again, it was an emulation through originality. Everybody can apprehend the logic, at any time, without any knowledge of
precedents or precursors. However, not all politicians have indeed found this
path of power, and most of those who did find it were either not capable or

---

[35] On Roosevelt, cf.: F. Perkins, *The Roosevelt I Knew,* New York 1946; R. Moley, "The
Issue Is Administration," *Newsweek,* Vol. 32, Aug. 30, 1948 and Sept. 6, 1948; H. A.
Simon, D. W. Smithburg, V. A. Thompson, *Public Administration,* New York 1950; S. J.
Rosenman, *Working With Roosevelt,* New York 1952; A. M. Schlesinger Jr., *The Age
of Roosevelt,* Vol. I, *The Coming of the New Deal,* Boston 1958 (in particular, pp.
519 – 552); A. J. Wann, *The President as Chief Administrator. A Study of Franklin
D. Roosevelt,* Washington, D. C. 1968; R. E. Neustadt, *Presidential Power,* op. cit., in
particular, pp. 225 – 231. – Contrary to earlier studies on Eisenhower as president, Fred
J. Greenstein has convincingly demonstrated the "creativity" of Eisenhower's presidency.
Cf. F. J. Greenstein, *The Hidden-Hand Presidency. Eisenhower as Leader,* New York
1982, esp. p. 244 ff. – A German counterpart of Roosevelt was Konrad Adenauer, the
first chancellor of the Federal Republic of Germany. On the extraordinary achievements
of his political leadership, cf. A. Baring, *Im Anfang war Adenauer. Die Entstehung
der Kanzlerdemokratie,* München 1982, 2nd ed., esp. pp. 19 – 30; A. Poppinga, *Meine
Erinnerungen an Adenauer,* München 1972, esp. pp. 26 – 33; idem, *Konrad Adenauer.
Geschichtsverständnis, Weltanschauung und politische Praxis,* Stuttgart 1975, esp. pp.
22 – 23. – As to my knowledge, a comparative study of "creative" political leadership
does not exist.

daring enough to travel the path for some distance. If a few have reached or are presently reaching the final destination, we may think that they are "similar." And indeed: they made the voyage to the fruition of power, every politician's fulfillment. But each made the voyage through himself alone. Kevin White emulated classic politicians. And thereby he became Kevin White, the classic politician.

6 The Principles of the Autocracy

Whatever relates to the process of governing and this process itself as well has to be regarded as a potential source of power.
This was the first and foremost principle of the autocracy.
Form the first one several other principles followed.

(1) The field of politics where the power of the autocrat can grow must be expanded to the largest possible extent; whoever joins the autocracy in whatever capacity has above all to be concerned with locating and exploiting new sources of power.

(2) All the power harvested in the field has to be absorbed by an "organization" which transports the new power to the sanctuary of the autocracy. Inversely, a system of exploitation must be established that spreads over the whole field extracting actually from it all the power which it yields.

(3) In the pursuit of power competitors can hardly be tolerated; and separate nuclei of power will be bypassed if the principals do not accept the offer of being coopted.

(4) As a government the autocracy cannot be "neutral"; its continual search for power consumes the process of politics, or conversely, politics is the aggregation of power. To govern means to appraise everything in terms of power: every event, every transaction, every fact and every idea, every person, every group.

These principles of the autocracy made politics the affair of all people whose life was in one way or the other affected by the government of the autocrat. They imposed a sharp alternative upon each of them. One could either participate actively in the intense politics stirred and stoked by the "government of Boston." Or one could resign to being a quiescent subject of the whips and whirls of Mayor White's politics.[36]

---

[36] That everything that happens under Boston's sun is "political" − this is a public truth in Boston, shared by everyone. And the truth stands up well in one's daily civic experience in Boston. Most Bostonians are therefore inclined implicitly to assume that it reflects a "natural" state of affairs. The autocracy was built on fecund ground.

7 The Invisible Government

In organizing his government the autocrat applied certain precepts of political conduct. The one that was paramount contradicted what is generally known as the science of "public administration" or "policy management": Thou shalt make your government invisible!

No one except Mayor White ever knew what his government really looked like.[37]

The autocrat deliberately kept his government in a state of confusion, throwing it again and again into the whirl of shuffles and commutations.[38] Still, there was a government of Boston — existing as a series of ephemeral configurations of persons and institutional organisms. The Mayor alone know the momentary configuration; for he had "organized" it temporarily to serve his immediate purposes; and he never disclosed this kind of *arcanum imperii*. Whoever else wanted to penetrate the government of Boston encountered but uncertainty, a city official as much as a stranger. And the uncertainty was never resolved. Information as to a momentary configuration — the "form" of the government at a given moment — became irrelevant before long as the government had taken shape in yet another configuration ... which restored the autocrat's *arcanum* and relegated everyone else to the perennial uncertainty.[39]

---

[37] Rexford G. Tugwell, assistant secretary of agriculture under Roosevelt, once explained: "Franklin allowed no one to discover the governing principle" (quoted in: A. M. Schlesinger Jr., *The Coming of the New Deal*, op. cit., p. 528). — On Eisenhower's five strategies of hidden-hand leadership, cf. F. J. Greenstein, *The Hidden-Hand Presidency*, op. cit., p. 57 ff.

[38] For comparative purposes, cf.: A. J. Wann, *The President as Chief Administrator*, op. cit., p. 30: "[...] Roosevelt's method of creating new agencies [...] did bring great vigor and enthusiasm into the conduct of administration. At the same time, however, it developed an exceedingly disorderly, if not chaotic, organizational structure which did considerable violence to the integrated 'unity of command' pattern generally admired by public administration authorities."

[39] Cf. for instance: "Interim Report on FY [fiscal year] 1983 Operating Budget of City of Boston, Coun. Tierney, on behalf of the Committee on Government Finance [Boston City Council], submitted the following: No adequate reports have been submitted on the following departments as requested by Committee Chairperson during the recently completed department budget hearing for Fiscal Year 1983 operating budget of the City of Boston and Suffolk County. — 1. No response relative to 17 F letters [...] as requested during hearing on Office of Property Equalization. 2. No response to Committee on Neighborhood Services relative to attached letters. 3. Contradictory reports on numerous city departments concerning quotas, numbers of employees; for example Administrative Services (all divisions), Public Works, Public Facilities, Park Department and Elderly

By "organizing" the government as a government in confusion, the Mayor grew in power. Through the general uncertainty as to the transitory configurations called "government," his legal responsibility for forming a government was transformed into the discretionary powers of an autocrat. In a technical respect the Mayor's exclusive knowledge as to the current configuration of organizational strings made him superior to anyone who discussed with him the business of government. Perceptually, his presence was felt everywhere, the governmental confusion of power notwithstanding. He was always there, even if he was rarely present. Whoever became involved in the process of governing and wanted to have a certain governmental policy pursued could hardly ignore his wishes, intentions, and plans. The reading of those was at least as important as any technical competence or practical knowledge. Finally, in a political respect, the Mayor could always remind everyone of his autocratic powers by making the suggestion – or, if necessary, the threat – that he might change the "rules of the game" by unhinging the governmental apparatus – or at least parts of it – and arranging everything anew in accordance with *his* wishes and *his* plans.

Nevertheless, the intention of "organizing" a government as a government in confusion really seems to be absurd. In a way, government is nothing else but the organization of politics. A government is generally viewed as a matter of "order," of "systematization," of "regularity." Any "government" lacking these qualities would accordingly seem not to be a government at all. What has Mayor White then done? Did he organize a government – that is essentially a system of stable institutions and regularized procedures? Or did he create a confusion – that is essentially a flux of chaotic institutional arrangements and unpredictable maneuvers?

Charting the course of great personal power, he could not really opt for a government of the former kind. Neither could he just say: let chaos be and this will be the government! He did something else. He forged a dyadic form of government which combined chaos with order, irregularity with continuity, flexibility with stability, confusion with consistency.

This dyadic form of government hinged upon a specific type of structures. To the extent that it was a *government,* it comprised necessarily certain administrative, managerial, and executive institutions. To the extent that it was an *unstructured government,* however, it was composed but of fluid and amorphous configurations. The autocrat produced – or more precisely:

[...]. 7. There appears to be many operlapping functions and duties in several departments [...]. 8. The Council has received little concrete written information involving six new departments totalling almost $ 2 million ($ 2,000,000) and seventy-four new positions [...]" *Proceedings of City Council,* Aug. 18, 1982, CR, April 18, 1983, p. 305.

animated — a para-institutional set of fluid configurations by which he could both govern a city and protect his grip on the city by a governmental confusion.[40]

8 Producing Institutions

Emerging from an institutionalization of habits and procedures, a government evidently consists of various "institutions": departments, agencies, commissions, boards, authorities, etc.[41] The term "institution" implies a notion of continuance and firmness. And a certain institutional continuity inhered the autocrat's dyadic government, too — but only a structural, not a material one. It was formed by a continuative structure of institutions. Yet this structure was fabricated as a flexible net of institutions and these institutions themselves were again fashioned as flexible figurations.

There existed a government, but the institutional form of its existence was fluid. The fluidity was swayed by two axes of change. They conjoined the two elements of the government's construction — form/structure on the one side and flexibility/fluidity on the other. They alone provided whatever "continuity" and "permanence" this construction had. They prevented its fluidity from becoming a surge towards dissolution.

The one axis of change involved the institutions by which the government was made up as well as the people who embodied these institutions. It defined their respective positions in relation to each other and marked thereby the locus of shifts in the institutional setup of the government. Typically, changes of the setup were initiated and carried out by the following method: from the institution(s) where they worked currently a number of people were

---

[40] Of both the presidency of Ronald Reagan and the presidency of François Mitterand in France could be said that they consisted in a "para-institutional set of fluid configurations." Cf. the preliminary accounts: D. Kirschten, "Decision Making in the White House: How Well Does It Serve the President?" *NJ*, Vol. 14, No. 14, April 3, 1982, pp. 584–589; idem, "Inner Circle Speaks With Many Voices, But Maybe That's How Reagan Wants It," *NJ*, Vol. 15, No. 22, May 28, 1983, pp. 1100–1103. — M. Schifres, M. Sarazin, *L'Elysée de Mitterrand. Secrets de la maison de France*, Paris 1985. p. 112f., 124f. — A concept of power that would take its "fluid nature" into account is sketched by Hans Buchheim in his article "Die Ethik der Macht," in: Institut der deutschen Wirtschaft, ed., *Wirtschaftliche Entwicklungslinien und gesellschaftlicher Wandel*, Festschrift Burghard Freudenfeld, Köln 1983, p. 42 ff.

[41] Concerning the problem of institutions as institutionalizations of habits and procedures, cf. E. Voegelin, "Der Mensch in Gesellschaft und Geschichte," *Österreichische Zeitschrift für Öffentliches Recht*, Vol. XIV, No. 1–2, 1964, pp. 1–13.

shifted to a place "outside" the existent institutions, yet "inside" the fabric of the government. The people who were brought together this way were then identified as an "advisory group," "policy committee," or as another such configuration. Thus they constituted a para-institutional body of deliberation and policy formulation. The further existence of the group and, in particular, its "form" depended upon the length, intensity, and, especially, outcome of the deliberations. The group was either disbanded or "put to sleep" or it was transmuted into a new agency or commission or authority or corporation or another such institution. In the latter case a new institution had been produced within the fabric of the government — quite naturally as it were.[42]

In some cases the unfoldment of the new institution did not affect the existing institutions. In other cases, however, parts from one or several existing institutions were transferred to the new institution or the latter even replaced one or more of the former. At all events, people — and not institutions — were the locus of shifts in the setup of the government. Or, to put it succinctly, there was a government in as far as there were fluid configurations of people.

9 Movement Among Institutions

The second axis of change structured the connections between the institutions as such. The institutions did not, of course, form a hierarchy or any similar fixed order. Rather they moved continuously, each in relation to every other. The impulses to their movements were given by the Mayor.

The autocrat caused among the institutions a movement in a vertical direction when he charged one of them with a special responsibility close to his interests; that institution received thereby a "higher" status within the momentary structure of the government. Usually all people whom concerned the new development were instructed — or knew by experience — that the rise of the institution was an "elevation" on probation. And the effectiveness

---

[42] In 1971, for example, the "Economic Development and Industrial *Commission*" (EDIC) emerged as a "liaison between business and the administration and a study group" (Interview source). Later in that year the EDIC was transformed by state legislation into a municipal corporation — the "Economic Development and Industrial *Corporation*" (EDIC) — having the power of eminent domain. In 1979 the EDIC employed about 100 people. — A forerunner of the EDIC had been established by the Mayor in 1969: the "Development and Industrial Commission" (DIC). However, the existence of the DIC was by no means terminated when the EDIC was founded.

of the test was often increased by a parallel "elevation" of a second or third institution. A competition ensued that resembled a trial since the two or three institutions were pitted against each other so long as the "jury" — the autocrat and whoever happened to be his counsellor(s) in this matter — had not handed down the verdict. When the "jury" had "passed the judgement," any support on the part of the autocrat was simply withdrawn from the institutions whose performance was negatively judged. Since they had principally an undefined status, they just dropped and were left wherever their movement "downwards" came to a standstill.

Whereas the rise of an institution of course excited its staff, the effects of a "fall" were often traumatic; they drained the sunk institution of its political viability. The morale, loyalty, and efficiency of the staff were seriously impaired, and drifts towards disintegration turned the institution more and more into a management problem.

However, from the Mayor's point of view, "natural" effects of this kind were not necessarily disadvantageous, for they offered him yet another opportunity to draw power from governmental confusion. He could step in and sort out the survivors, the political fighters from the victims, the bunglers; and he could reorganize the institution in disarray or transplant parts of it that were still viable — including the survivors — to a more suitable place in the momentary constellation of the governmental process.[43]

Among the institutions movements in a horizontal direction occurred, too. The autocrat caused such movements in as far as he identified policy areas, on the one hand, and assigned one or more of these areas to one or more institutions, on the other. If the policy areas were clearly defined and if the assignments were made at the ratio of one area to one institution, each institution moved away from every other. All institutions together tended thereby to represent the government in its *functional* dimension. If, however, the autocrat chose to convey only vague definitions and to make overlapping assignments, the institutions moved towards each other so close that conflicts ensued necessarily. Competing with each other for spheres of influence and policy relevance, the institutions represented the government in its *political* dimension.

Of course, the institutions never moved in one direction all at once. Different policy directives were given at different times and thus produced among the institutions an intricate geometry of movements and standstill: while some spread and moved apart, a group of other institutions drew close

---

[43] Franklin D. Roosevelt once said to Frances Perkins: "There is something to be said for having a little conflict between agencies. A little rivalry is stimulating, you know. It keeps everybody going to prove that he is a better fellow than the next man. It keeps them honest too [...]" (F. Perkins, *The Roosevelt I Knew,* op. cit., p. 360).

to each other and intersected; others again stayed momentarily at their place. The government as a whole was therefore never a purely "functional" or a purely "political" body. Through the geometry of its institutions this government oscillated continuously from "administration" to "politics" and from "politics" to "administration."

While the autocrat moved and produced institutions, his proxies in the government were not idle. Within the agencies which they directed they moved, shuffled, and commuted, too. They adopted the autocrat's strategy of governing. And they applied his precepts of political conduct: they kept their institutions in a fluid state, and this inner fluidity of their institutions was only swayed by two axes of change analogous to those that swayed the fluidity of the government as a whole. Thus they assisted the autocrat in making everything in the government as fluid as possible. Fluid institutions fitted the government's fluid form.

10 Politics Versus Government

By constructing his government as a flexible net of flexible figurations, the autocrat secured several political advantages.

First, he ensured the predominance of policy over institutions.[44] The form of institutions followed the evolution of policies. Initiating or changing a policy included always the possibility of reconsidering and, if necessary, restructuring the institutional apparatus by which this policy would have to be implemented. Institutional routine was thwarted. And the instrumental function of institutions, organizing politics, could not become a poor substitute for politics proper. The impulsiveness of politics prevailed; it kept the institutional form of politics in a state of fluid organization.

Secondly, the autocrat preserved possibilities of motivating the members of government. Its fluid form actualized in many institutional shifts, and each of these shifts could be used to excite a number of people in the government. Everyone, of course, was interested in a promotion, a raise, an assignment to a new and attractive task. Among those who felt they were concerned,

---

[44] "[...] Roosevelt kept some control over the development of policy [...] by purposely refusing to define jurisdictions in sharp, clear, and mutually exclusive terms [...] the lack of clarity in the assignment of responsibilities [...] gave his own personality a greater impact on the development of administrative policy than would have been the case had the Federal bureaucracy been organized in accordance with the dreams of a typical artist of organization charts" (H. A. Simon, D. W. Smithburg, V. A. Thompson, *Public Administration*, op. cit., p. 168).

every shift then kindled this interest. And since so many shifts occured, the autocrat could play upon the hopes of very many people in the government. All rightly viewed the continuing governmental confusion as the continuing chance of making an ever greater progress in one's personal career. Thus, through the way he "organized" his government, the autocrat created among its members a climate of high expectations, a climate of expectations which he cultivated carefully and exploited adroitly.

Thirdly, his shifting people continually from one place in the government to another gave the autocrat a considerable control over the heads of the government's agencies. A department head could not for a moment be certain that some members of the department had not again been recruited by the Mayor for tasks which he had determined — and that he would bother to inform their official boss. While the autocrat took the liberty of consulting about everything with whomever he pleased,[45] while he took the liberty of inviting whomever he wanted to join one of these configurations by which he constantly reshaped his government, the heads of the governmental agencies were not really in control: the people whom they would have wished to command had been shifted before they were ready to command. The autocrat's capricious rule confined them to a condition of administrative uneasiness and political uncertainty.

---

[45] This habit did not necessarily elevate the spirits of his associates: "Some of the policy specialists on [the] staff get frustrated when White has independent contact with people within their sphere of responsibility without telling them" (Interview). — As to parallels, cf. A. M. Schlesinger, *The Age of Roosevelt. The Coming of the New Deal,* op. cit., p. 523: "Roosevelt's persistent effort [...] was to check and balance information acquired through official channnels by information acquired through a myriad of private, informal, and unorthodox channels and espionage networks. At times, he seemed almost to pit his personal sources against his public sources." — F. J. Greenstein, *The Hidden-Hand Presidency,* op. cit., p. 147: "Eisenhower drew on plentiful rather than few sources of information and advice. Even within the White House the informal realities contradicted the impression of a formalistic hierarchy. [...] [p. 150:] He had an extraordinary broad network of acquaintances and friends with whom he corresponded and met. [...] In all, unofficial and official associates combined to provide Eisenhower with at least as diverse a flow of information and advice as any of the other modern presidents." — As to German parallels, cf.: W. Hennis, *Richtlinienkompetenz und Regierungstechnik,* op. cit., pp. 35 – 37 (about the information techniques of German Federal Chancellors, in general); A. Poppinga, *Meine Erinnerungen an Adenauer,* op. cit., pp. 27 f. (about the information techniques of Chancellor Adenauer). — As to the very similar information techniques of President Mitterrand, cf.: S. Cohen, "Les hommes de l'Elysée," *Pouvoirs,* No. 20, 1981, pp. 94 – 98; D. Molho, "Elysée an III: Les choses de la vie," *Le Point,* No. 607, 7 Mai 1984, pp. 40 – 41; idem, "Les stratèges du Président," *Le Point,* No. 644, 21 Janv. 1985, p. 36; M. Schifres, M. Sarazin, *L'Elysée de Mitterrand,* op. cit., pp. 110 ff.

11 The Exercise of Authority

The institutions by which a government is formed usually establish a pattern of authority lines. Their composition reflects a notion of "order" and therefore prescribes procedures of institutional interaction. Moreover, the internal organization of each institution follows certain concepts of professional work – like the division of responsibilities, for instance – and thereby produces additional lines of authority.

Such a concurrence of authority lines and institutional composition could not, of course, take place in the autocrat's government. The fluid structure of its institutions repelled formal authority. Every manifestation of authority was necessarily "fuzzy."[46] Authority was as fluid a phenomenon as the government itself.

The autocrat did not rely solely upon this "natural" confusion of authority. He reinforced the confusion on purpose by producing – and by animating continuously – a particular structure of authority. In doing so, however, he could not just choose any structure imaginable. Wanting to confuse the authority lines, he was nevertheless compelled to introduce some "order." Any governmental apparatus would be paralyzed if its activities were not regulated in a certain way. To make it work, areas of responsibility must specifically be assigned to singular people and singular institutions. Yet a structure of well-defined assignments would have been incongruous with the autocrat's government, in general, and with its intrinsic tendency towards "fuzzy" manifestations of authority, in particular. Again that peculiar kind of *fluid* structure was needed, a structure by which lines of authority were *drawn* and at the same time *confused*. Both conditions were met by the Mayor: authority was exercised within the government and by the government. But every exercise of authority also aggravated the confusion of competence within a field of competing forces. There existed many individual circles of

---

[46] A senior associate of the Mayor described the government's procedures as follows: "Everything is unstructured. Decisions are made totally without any decision-making structure. Everything changes all the time. It's very chaotic" (Interview). – Roosevelt, Arthur M. Schlesinger writes, "deliberately organized – or disorganized – his system of command to insure that important decisions were passed on the top. His favorite technique was to keep grants of authority incomplete, jurisdictions uncertain, charters overlapping" (*The Age of Roosevelt. The Coming of the New Deal,* op. cit., p. 527 f.). Cf. also R. Moley, "The Issue Is Administration," *Newsweek,* Vol. 32, Aug. 30, 1948, p. 84: "Subordinates often did not know for sure what they were to do, or what Roosevelt's answer was to a given problem [...]. His habit of giving vague assignments of authority brought about violent conflicts in his official family."

authority. Yet they overlapped and therefore did not mark lines of authority, they blurred them.[47]

To produce the overlapping circles of authority, the autocrat applied two particular methods.

First, he made duplicate assignments whereby two persons − or two institutions − were compelled to contest one area of responsibility which, however, neither could win exclusively. Usually, the contestants somehow managed to assert themselves and to maintain individual circles of authority within the same area of responsibility. But the extension of each individual circle was a matter of continual competition and dispute. The two circles of authority never formed a solid figuration. They always represented a contingent constellation in an unending contest. Each of the contestants was entitled to exercise full authority over the same area of responsibility. Yet whatever authority each of them held was but a partial and provisional authority. And they themselves were the instruments of their constraints.

The effectiveness of this method was considerably intensified by the request that employees − or agencies − perform tasks not just in one but in several areas of responsibility. Consequently, an employee or an institution was compelled to uphold the own circle of authority within a whole field of competing forces where every single area of responsibility was claimed by a number of contenders. In this field everyone's circle of authority was likely to overlap quite a few other circles of authority. Not only did one actor contest with another for the same area of responsibility, but everyone challenged the authority of everyone else in a general contest of competence. There were lines of authority, only these lines reflected but fluid movements.[48]

The second method consisted in assigning identical tasks to different persons − or institutions − and in not making anyone aware of them having counterparts. Circles of authority overlapped, but those who busied themselves in each other's fields did not notice at first that they were involved in a competition. The autocrat, standing aloof, could watch the course of the contest and discover the strengths and weaknesses of each competitor.

Persons or institutions were pursuing their tasks, but they had unwittingly been turned into competitors and were thus undermining each other's authority. All furnished the evidence for a critical judgment on everyone. Doing

---

[47] In their study of Mitterrand's presidency Michel Schifres and Michel Sarazin point out the advantage which a ruler enjoys in causing responsibilities to overlap: all initiatives have him as point of departure and point of arrival (*L'Elysée de Mitterrand*, op. cit., p. 111).

[48] "Le mouvement qui déplace les lignes (the movement which shifts the lines)" − this is the phrase which President Mitterrand used to interpret his political conduct. Cf. *Libération*, Nouv. série, No. 923, May 10, 1984, p. 7.

their work, they could not help being accomplices in the cold calculation of the autocrat. Assuming their responsibilities, they could not avoid crowding some of them off their field of responsibilities.[49]

Sooner or later the nescient competitors realized their situation, of course. Inevitably, this knowledge affected their personal sense of authority. They discerned not only their involvement in a contest with each other, but they understood also that they were players in a "game" over which they themselves had no control. As they grasped their situation, they perceived a confusion of authority – and the truth of this confusion. They were not allowed to exercise personal authority in any form other than the feeling that they lacked authority. They held authority and yet they were taught the lesson that they had no real authority. They were confused about the extent of their authority and yet they understood that they were not meant to experience authority in any other way. In the autocrat's government authority was a movement; it fled before those who wanted to possess it and it stayed with those who resigned themselves to its twists and turns.[50]

---

[49] Circumstances of this kind did not only exist within the government proper. There were similar circumstances in the broader area of civic affairs. Cf. M. D. Esch, J. E. Killory, *Boston Charter Reform, (A), (B), (C),* [case study] Kennedy School of Government, Cambridge, Mass. 1978, section (B), p. 7: "Over the summer [1976] the Mayor's staff had solicited the advice and support of various academic experts on the subjects of school and electoral reforms. [...] Working together, the academics and the Mayor's people formulated a detailed agenda of reforms. [...] The Creation of the Committee for Boston [a citizen's advisory committee [...] of eleven civic, religious, business and former government leaders] and the assembling of the panel of academic experts were two simultaneous, yet separate, operations, the latter group not knowing of the former's existence." – About the parallels in the Roosevelt administration cf. A. M. Schlesinger, *The Age of Roosevelt. The Coming of the New Deal,* op. cit., pp. 536 ff.; A. J. Wann, *The President as Chief Administrator,* op. cit., p. 69 f.

[50] The confusion of authority was not always upheld – exceptions were made. Cf. J. Bradley O'Connell, *The Boston Plan,* (A), [case study] Kennedy School of Government, Cambridge, Mass., 1979, p. 1: "The most recent effort to make Boston a national model for urban strategy was the Boston Plan, unveiled by the administration of Mayor Kevin White in August 1977. [...] it was an effort to coordinate the activities of a number of city agencies and authorities so that the city government could have a united position in dealing with the 'feds.'" – ibid., p. 14 f.: "Kevin White liked the idea of setting up a competition among the agencies, with each department formulating a comprehensive plan of its own and the 'winner' presumably becoming the lead agency in its implementation. [...] White subsequently [...] decided against a competition." – Still, the author of this study concludes: "All the officials agree that it is difficult to produce a coherent table of organization to depict the Boston city government. In January 1977 three city agencies had broadly defined functions such that each was somehow engaged in producing plans or formulating 'economic policy' for the whole city – the BRA, the Economic

12 The Autocrat and His Associates: The Distant Intimacy

In constructing his dyadic government, the Mayor produced not only fluid institutional structures but fluid personnel structures as well. Again, the notion of fluid personnel structures seems at first to contradict any sense of power. One cannot govern if one does not control the administrative and political behavior of the people who work for one's government. But how could this control be exerted if the "places" and the "identities" of the people forming the government are being interchanged continually in a flux of amorphous configurations? Will then the personnel not be encouraged to make up segments of independence?

The autocrat reconciled power with fluid personnel structures by entering into a special relationship with each of his associates. One of them explained what the nature of this relationship was: "You have an individual relationship with White even though you have to go through 20 people to reach him. White will not give you explicit directions. You run your programs with your own strengths, but in White's image [...]. After you are exposed to him, you either understand him or not."[51]

White brought a certain fascination of his personality to bear upon the people who worked for him. They were moved to believe in a special mode of communication between "The Mayor" and the associate: a communication whose intimacy was so intense that it largely transcended the need for formal conditions such as frequent meetings, direct contacts, or personal information. "The Mayor" and the associate could be separated from each other by considerable distances in time, space, and prestige — rare encounters only; or the supreme status, on the one side, and an inferior one, on the other; or a political life in the limelight, on the one hand, and a limited function in relative obscurity, on the other. Yet "The Mayor" could count on the associate's allegiance, and the associate did presume his or her ability to read "The Mayor's" mind and intentions.[52]

Development and Industrial Corporation and the Office of Program Development. Rivalry among these agencies and the overlapping of their responsibilities were thought to be obstacles to city coordination and efficiency. By January 1978 these agencies and their responsibilities remained intact; however, they had been joined in having city-wide economic policy functions by the Office of Federal Relations, the Employment and Economic Policy Administration, the Executive Office of the Boston Plan and the Boston Plan Executive Policy Committee" (ibid., p. 34).

[51] Source: Interview.

[52] Cf. the passage on 'the riddle of the two mayors,' THE MAYOR and the Mayor: infra, pp. 254–257.

The Mayor fostered the feeling of intimacy — from a distance. Naturally, every associate was anxious to have access to him. The Mayor treated with great skill this general wish. He had access to him tightly controlled, and thereby he transmuted it into a privilege that carried a rarified status or influence or opportunities for winning his ear and for becoming his confidant or all of this together. The Mayor bestowed the privilege at different times upon different people for different reasons, without regard to seniority or official standing.[53] Every associate could therefore hope that the autocrat would at some moment grant him, or her, the privilege of access, too. And the Mayor was likely to capture the associate's complete attention indeed — *if* the latter could for a while play a crucial role in one of his current undertakings. But, for the same reasons, none (with very few exceptions)[54] could be certain of the chance either of gaining access to the autocrat or, if the access had been granted, of enjoying this privilege for more than a moment. It had only been given for a specific purpose after all. Nevertheless, some time later the privilege could be restored again, for yet another moment, or even for a more extended span of time.

Thus the Mayor used access to him as a tool to envelop his associates in intimacy, on the one side, and to manage this intimacy quite pragmatically, on the other. The associates themselves grasped the Mayor's pragmatic calculations. As long as they hoped "to stay in the game," they did not object. They observed rather the "game," the "ups and downs," trying to "figure out" who — at the moment of observation — was "close" to the autocrat, who was "out" (having no longer easy access to him), and who was "rising" again or just for the first time. Numerous conversations were used to collect and to check pertinent information.

13 The Government and Its Personnel: Disjunctions and Discontinuities

As he produced fluid personnel structures, the autocrat followed a specific technique. A principal assistant alluded to this technique when he recounted

---

[53] Roosevelt's "habits of conversation out of channels," Schlesinger writes, "were sometimes disconcerting. He had little hesitation, if he heard of a bright man somewhere down the line in a department, about summoning him to the White House. Ickes [Harold L. Ickes, Roosevelt's secretary of the Interior] complained bitterly in his diary about 'what he does so frequently, namely, calling in members of my staff for consultation on Department matters, without consulting me or advising with me.' And often he bewildered visitors by asking their views on matters outside their jurisdiction" (A. M. Schlesinger, *The Age of Roosevelt. The Coming of the New Deal*, op. cit., p. 524).

[54] Edward T. Sullivan, Director of Administrative Services; Lawrence M. Quealy, Executive Assistant, Mayor's Office; the *alter egos*. Cf. also infra, pp. 68, 79.

how he began to work for the Mayor: "He knew political administration. He knew that signing me on didn't give me a real function."[55] The autocrat built his "political" administration (significantly, the assistant used this term rather than the term "*public* administration") by applying a technique of disjunctions. He separated persons – that is persons employed in the government – and functions, that is the *nominal* functions of those employees. By these disjunctions he established a dual personnel structure.

The official personnel records showed the *nominal* structure. It was maintained for several purposes: as a necessary formal manifestation of the government; to comply with legal, governmental, and administrative regulations; for the payment of salaries; and for screening from public view the real operations of the government. The *real* structure was invisible but existed all the same. It was constituted of employees who actually performed functions quite different from those for which they were listed in the personnel records or by employees who worked in agencies other than those to which they belonged officially.[56]

Persons and functions were separated and by this technique the Mayor had procured the enfranchisement of his autocracy. He could move people as well as jobs from one place to another in the government, and he could manage these movements without making them manifest in any formal way. Whereas the nominal personnel structure stood unchanged, persons and functions could be transferred at will. And the autocrat enjoyed a considerable discretion as regards the quantity, the extent, and the frequency of these transfers. If political or financial circumstances required an expansion of the real personnel structure, he could multiply the disjunctions. If a contraction seemed advisable, he could shift people and functions back into their official shells. Moreover, he could adapt the personnel structure to variable circumstances by only partially separating persons and functions. In such cases, employees devoted their working time to performing their official functions and one or more other ones as well. The actual allocation of the working time was usually made by the employees themselves. In general, they had a keen sense of their divided job.

By applying the technique of disjunctions, the Mayor obtained a fluid personnel structure. It emerged from the movements of expansion and contraction by which the difference between real and nominal personnel structures grew or diminished. The disjunctions ignited frequently public quarrelling

---

[55] *BG* (Sunday edition), March 9, 1969.
[56] Cf. also the pertinent reports in: *BHA,* March 17, 1981; *BG,* April 28, 1974; Jan. 23, 1976; Dec. 9, 1980; March 14, 1981; March 15, 1981; March 19, 1981; April 1, 1981; April 2, 1981; Febr. 4, 1982.

between the Mayor and the City Council.[57] But their issue, the fluid personnel structure, was very difficult to discern. Not only was it largely invisible, but it was also a manifestation of very elusive movements. Even close associates of the autocrat were as much and as often as everyone else at a loss as to the question who was actually doing what and where in the autocrat's "political" administration. It was virtually impossible exactly to know everyone's momentary place and momentary identity (or identities). And whatever it was that one knew, it was never more than a mixture of exact and outdated information. The autocrat's fluid personnel structure could only be known within a circle of irony. Outsiders struggled to penetrate the knowledge of insiders, and insiders availed themselves of outsiders to supplement their knowledge and to bring it up to date.

The autocrat, however, did not neglect the chance to further intensify the fluidity of the personnel structure, for he did not miss the possibilitiy of separating persons and functions in yet another way: by the technique of discontinuances. The Mayor applied this technique when he periodically launched shuffles and shake-ups of the personnel. Thereby persons and functions were separated not in the mode of functional disjunctions but in the mode of temporal discontinuities. Employees performed indeed the functions which they held officially. But they were recurrently cut off and were charged with different functions. These periodic shuffles and shake-ups kept the government and its personnel apart. There was a functional continuity of governmental services. But there was hardly any human continuity. Only a few officials in the government held one and the same position or pursued one and the same kind of activity over a larger number of years.[58] All the other people working in the government switched functions very frequently in a largely discontinuous series of jobs.

---

[57] Cf. *BHA,* March 3, 1981; *BG,* March 14, 1981; March 18, 1981; March 19, 1981; April 1, 1981; April 2, 1981; May 13, 1981; Febr. 1, 1982.

[58] Edward T. Sullivan, Director, Administrative Services, 1968 – 1983; Lawrence M. Quealy, Executive Assistant, Mayor's Office, 1968 – 1983; Joseph F. Casazza, Commissioner, Public Works, 1968 – 1983, Chairman, Public Improvement Commission, 1968 – 1983; Herbert P. Gleason, Corporation Counsel, 1968 – 1979; Joseph M. Jordan, Superintendent in Chief, Commissioner, Police Dept., 1975 – 1983; Francis W. Gens, Commissioner, Housing Inspection, 1968 – 1975, Building Commissioner, 1975 – 1979; Richard R. Thuma, Building Commissioner, 1968 – 1975; Theodore V. Anzalone, Commissioner of Assessing, 1968 – 1974; John F. Mulhern, Commissioner, Real Property Dept. 1968 – 1974; David L. Rosenbloom, Acting Commissioner, Health and Hospitals Dept., 1975 – 1976, Commissioner, Health and Hospitals Dept., 1976 – 1982; Robert J. Ryan, Director, Boston Redevelopment Authority, 1978 – 1984; Joanne Prevost, Commissioner, Real Property Dept., 1974 – 1980.

The technique of discontinuances increased the fluidity of the personnel structure. It furnished more of the power which the autocrat continually sought. However, this was not its only effect. It impaired also the collective memory of the people working in the government. The shuffles and shake-ups in which they were periodically involved prevented them from accumulating historical knowledge about the government's work. Being on the move in the discontinuous series of their jobs, they cold hardly develop a memory that related to one particular function and preserved this function's historical dimension. The fluid personnel structure caused a collective amnesia among the employees as regards the past of what they were doing.

Finally, the shuffles and shake-ups provoked the people working in the government to a variety of responses: (a) there were those who not only lived through the shuffles and shake-ups with ease but felt that these experiences stimulated their creativity; (b) there were those who found it difficult to approve of the autocrat's strategy of governing but were nevertheless prepared and skilled enough continually to adjust themselves to the quick succession of changes in the volatile field of fluid personnel structures; (c) and there were the victims — those who were not able to survive what they felt was a series of destructive experiences; they went through a number of shuffles and shake-ups and they were "burned out."[59]

14 The Chaos of Power

Kevin White governed Boston as Mayor by ruling the city as autocrat. There were the extensive legal powers vested in his office. Kevin White exhausted their absolutist dimension. There were circumstances quite favorable to the building of an autocracy. Kevin White exploited the vast potential of power they held. There were not a few possibilities of turning the conduct of government into a persistent acquisition of power. Kevin White used these possibilities relentlessly, he made the city preoccupied with the pursuit of his power.

---

[59] Cf. also BG, Aug. 4, 1974: "Undoubtedly, some who left the administration were 'affected' by White's system — a system which many of his current people describe as 'survival of the fittest.' Its White's contention that some people who have left have done so 'not out of any sense of bitterness, but because of an inability to compete in that kind of atmosphere. [...] When you have so much talent churning up so much activity, they begin to fight with each other for attention — my attention. This puts a strain on their relationships to each other, and it puts tremendous pressure on me — I think it's fair to say that unless you are a strong personality, you will get affected by it.' "

— He became an autocrat. In this first chapter I tried to explain the Mayor's extraordinary progress in the building of his autocracy. Organizing a disorganized government was the paradoxical but essential task. Governmental chaos brought creativity, the control of this creativity brought power. The Mayor mastered the chaos of power. He built an autocracy, and this autocracy emerged from a confusion of governmental power which he alone controlled. He proved to possess the skills that are necessary for forging fluid configurations of people and fluid structures of institutions.

— He became a classic politician. He adopted and pursued a strategy of governing which had before been used – in past and present times. The strategy of governing that builds upon the personal element of politics. The strategy of governing that attests to the classicism of politics. I have tried to explain the Mayor's perplexing status in the pursuit of this strategy: he did emulate it and he did invent it. He found the ways of classic politicians while he chose his own manner of governing.

— He became the original author of a perennial lesson. In the following I will try to render the lesson. The classic form of expressing political maxims of this kind is the *Mirror for Magistrates* as it was used during the Middle Ages and the Renaissance. I adopt the form to express the present lesson. This then is the *Boston Mirror for Magistrates*:

- First and foremost, emulate the wisdom of the rulers in Ancient Rome: *divide et impera* – divide and dominate.
- Prevent the existence of an umbrella group which covers the realm of your power. Divide and isolate people by a proliferation of commissions, advisory groups, task forces, etc. If the complexity of the governmental apparatus is criticized, propose the creation of a commission for the study of governmental reform.
- Do not establish precise lines of authority. Keep responsibilities blurred. Make overlapping assignments.
- Give your associates and aides some latitude for running their affairs. Foment competition. Reward the winner.
- Engage several agencies in projects on similar turf. Make them jockey for position.
- Distribute from time to time chips of influence among your aides and subordinates. They tantalize their yearning for power.
- Launch periodically into a shake-up of the governmental apparatus. Shuffle the personnel.
- Create two layers of government, a visible and an invisible one, by splitting governmental positions into nominal and real functions.
- Become an expert in substituting a web of personal relationships for the system of government.

If you steadily apply these methods, you will erect a chaotic but powerful rule of which you will be the sole master. You will delegate power and yet you will hold it all. You will incite countless power struggles. But you will pull the strings. Your associates and aides will be grateful to you for their bit of independence. And you will possess the advantage of having some others to blame, if anything goes wrong. They will frequently encroach upon each other's sphere of activity, and they will therefore be compelled to appeal to you as arbitrator and judge. Your policy of incessant shuffles and reorganizations will leave everyone in perplexity to the same degree as the meaning of your moves will be confined in your mind.

The manipulation of governmental chaos is the source of your personal power.

Chapter 2
The Court, Locus of Creativity

ᾗ μὲν ἄρα τὸ ἓν ὅλον, ἐν ἄλλῳ ἐστίν· ᾗ δὲ τὰ πάντα μέρη ὄντα τυγχάνει, αὐτὸ ἐν ἑαυτῷ καὶ οὕτω τὸ ἓν ἀνάγκη αὐτό τε ἐν ἑαυτῷ εἶναι καὶ ἐν ἑτέρῳ.

Inasmuch, then, as the One is a whole, it is in the other; inasmuch, however, as it is all parts that are, it is in itself; and thus is by necessity the One itself in itself and in the other.

Plato, *Parmenides* 145 e

1 Philosophical Argument: The Few and the Many

Politics is the process of creativity from which human societies emerge. Human beings form a society by participating in a sphere of common views, deliberations, and actions. They pursue a common life, and this pursuit of their community becomes manifest in a series of symbolic, spatial, social, and economic differentiations: from the process of their asserting expositively the existence of their community political symbolisms arise which express what is held to be the specific nature and the original purpose of the community; through the process of unfolding spatially the life of the community, lines are marked which define the particular place of the community in the physical as well as the human world; in the process of distinguishing themselves one from another and of relating to each other in specified ways the members of the community make up social and economic structures that reflect the different conditions of their individual lives in the community.[1]

This process of human differentiation is mediated by the process of politics. It is the mediating mode of politics through which the myriad threads of community are woven into a distinctive form of human society. Many members of the community are involved in the process of mediation. Only a few, however, are the agents of the mediation. The few represent the many. And by virtue of this representation all — the society — act in as far as the few — their representatives — perform acts of political mediation.[2]

When we think or talk about Boston, body politic of urban condition, we may visualize the city just in one of its various dimensions: Boston's geography, history, economy, architecture, Boston's culture, people, urban per-

---

[1] Cf. G. Vico, *Scienza Nuova* (1725), Book I, Sections 2 and 3; E. Voegelin, *Order and History*, Vol. I, *Israel and Revelation*, Baton Rouge 1956, Introduction, pp. 1 – 11, Vol. III, *Plato and Aristotle*, Baton Rouge 1957, Introduction, pp. 1 – 24, Vol. IV, *The Ecumenic Age*, Baton Rouge 1974, Introduction, pp. 1 – 58. – Vitruv, *De Architectura Libri Decem*, Book II, Chapter 1; St. M. Lyman, M. B. Scott, "Territoriality: A Neglected Sociological Dimension," in: ed. R. Gutman, *People and Buildings*, New York 1972, pp. 65 – 82; A. Rapoport, *Human Aspects of Urban Form. Towards a Man-Environment Approach to Urban Form and Design*, Oxford 1977, pp. 8 ff.; Ch. Norberg-Schulz, *Genius Loci. Towards a Phenomenology of Architecture*, New York 1980, pp. 6 ff., 50 ff.; K. Lynch, *A Theory of Good City Form*, Cambridge, Mass. 1981, pp. 131 ff.

[2] Cf. Plato, *Parmenides* and *Philebus* 14 c – 18 b. – E. C. Banfield, J. Q. Wilson, *City Politics*, Cambridge, Mass. 1963, pp. 21 ff., 58 f.; D. Sternberger, "Die Erfindung der 'Repräsentativen Demokratie,'" in: ed. K. v. Beyme, *Theory and Politics – Theorie und Politik*, Festschrift C. J. Friedrich, Den Haag 1971, pp. 96 – 126; H. Eulau, K. Prewitt, *Labyrinths of Democracy: Adaptation, Linkages, Representation and Policies in Urban Politics*, New York 1973, pp. 12 ff.; N. E. Long, "Federalism and Perverse Incentives," *Publius*, No. 2, 1978, p. 87.

sonality.[3] Regardless of the aspect one will happen to choose, Boston will appear as a distinctive site of urban civilization. And if we should view the city from more than one aspect, the image of Boston as an extremely differentiated and therefore unique city will undoubtedly capture our mind.

Nevertheless, the unique urban setting as which we appreciate Boston is by no means the same we know as the "City of Boston." However distinctive the urban form of Boston may be, it does not make Boston a body politic. Boston would not be the "City of Boston" if the purpose of creating a civic community and the aspirations of all the persons involved in this endeavor were not pursued by the representative acts which a few Bostonians perform on behalf of all the other Bostonians. There is Boston, the urban setting of a human community. But there is only a City of Boston in as far as this community appears in the form of political representation.

By the City Charter the Mayor of Boston can act as the city's preeminent representative. Mayor White performed the representation by reigning autocratically, and this might tempt us to conclude that under his rule "The Mayor" and the "City of Boston" were one and the same. However, a conclusion of this kind will not hold if it is judged against the very complex reality of Boston's political representation in the era of Mayor White. The autocrat dominated the politics of the city. But it was not he alone who represented the city.

Beyond the bronze doors shielding the Mayor's Office in Boston's City Hall a particular form of Boston could be found: the "City of the Fifth Floor," as it was fittingly called by one of its former inhabitants. For it was the "City of the Fifth Floor" where those dwelled who represented the "City of Boston." Or, to put it differently, the inhabitants of the "City of the Fifth Floor" were those few Bostonians who performed the representative acts by which all the other Bostonians, the many, acted as the "City of Boston."

2 Two Tales and Two Stages

The persons populating the "City of the Fifth Floor" liked to present themselves as the ruling elite of a great city. Indeed, the meeting with a senior official could be an aesthetic experience. One was ushered into a room whose interior

---

[3] As to the notion of "urban personality," cf. M. Keller, *Historical Sources of Urban Personality: Boston, New York, Philadelphia.* An Inaug. Lecture delivered before the University of Oxford on 3 March 1981, Oxford 1982; Cf. also J. Nolen, *City Making* (1909), in: L. M. Roth, ed., *America Builds. Source Documents in American Architecture and Planning,* New York 1983.

produced in the spectator's eye a symphony of colors. It was exquisitly furnished, the walls were adorned with original paintings of contemporary masters. The brilliant scenery of Boston's harbor and waterfront opened through the windows, it conduced to an aura of sublime elegance. A glass of an excellent Californian wine was offered, quite appropriately. And then the affairs of Boston were discussed. The senior official related a first-class experience in urban civilization. The story of Boston's present renaissance was told and it was the story of Boston and other great cities: London, Jerusalem, Paris, Zurich, Rome.

Indeed, the persons populating the "City of the Fifth Floor" liked to think of themselves as the selected few called to public service. The meetings with a special assistant to the Mayor could be a Waspish experience. Conversations about Boston politics were conducted by the assistant in the manner of a graduate seminar at Harvard University. At the first meeting barely a few words had been spoken and he had already established his credentials as Harvard *alumnus*. Clear enough, he had a superior mind and he was involved in a great cause serving the Mayor of Boston. With the candor of his youth he stated that he knew essentially what moral and political thought was all about. He expressed his willingness to come forward with some further expositions of his knowledge. He stipulated that a familiarity with the works of Robert Nozick and Willard V. Quine — who happened to have been his teachers at Harvard — would help to understand him.

Another associate of the Mayor excelled in speaking the smooth language of diplomatic parley. He charmed interlocutors with the imperturbable air of his words and thereby made them powerless to protest when he did not answer their questions or told them the bad news they did not want to hear. Judged from his urbane manner of communicating it would have been illogical to think that Boston, the city he represented, was not one of the great cities of the world.

The Mayor, finally, followed the classic taste of rulers when he spoke and acted as the representative of Boston. City Hall was the place where he carried on the business of governing. Acts of representation, however, needed their proper *décor*: a ruler's residence that symbolized the prestige of his domain. The stage of the Mayor was the Parkman House, an elegant town-house on Beacon Hill, Boston's most fashionable neighborhood.[4] At the Parkman House the Mayor received those visitors whom he wanted to treat with special care. The surroundings of the Mayor's residence evoked images

---

[4] The Parkman House (named after Francis Parkman) is located on 50 Chestnut Street. It is owned by the City of Boston and registered as a National Historical Landmark. A chapter on the Parkman family ("Dr. Parkman Takes A Walk") can be found in C. Amory, *The Proper Bostonians*, New York 1947.

of Boston in a state of glory. It was not difficult to grasp the symbolic signification of approaching the house and passing its threshold.

The *salon* as it is known in France represents the classic example of mixing culture with politics, entertainment with the practice of power. A dinner in the Parkman House was a similar event under similar circumstances — presided over by the Mayor who was likely to be at his best. There were not many opportunities at which the Mayor could sway the doyen of Boston's business community. Acting under the *mise-en-scène* of the Parkman House, however, he happened to have this opportunity.

No doubt, the Mayor and his people in the "City of the Fifth Floor" were quite successful in impersonating the urbane elite ruling a great city.

There are two tales to be told about them, however. For the image of a great city that they projected was dotted, curiously enough, with the details of a small town.

When the Mayor once received an invitation to address an international conference in Europe, he instructed an aide to gather intelligence about the nature of the speeches which the other participants in the conference intended to deliver. Phone calls were placed to contact individuals who could discreetly obtain and pass on the desired information. The Mayor, one was told, lacked the sufficient experience of representing Boston in the theater of Europe. The performances of the European speakers would probably be sophisticated events. How could the Mayor avoid an embarrassing disparity between these performances and his own? And could he expect a gathering of congenial people, considering the fact that no other Mayor of an American city had been invited?

Old friends of Kevin White's live where he lives, on Beacon Hill. They helped him to launch his political career and, in its further course, they were his associates in many roles: as neighbors, advisors, buddies, colleagues, political activists, emissaries, counsels, companions. The site of this density of relationship was the small space of their neighborhood where the behavior and the movements of people did not pass unobserved. In this respect, Beacon Hill is the marketplace of a small town. The townsfolk on the Hill could acquire their own knowledge about the Mayor's progress as politician. For this progress took place, to a certain extent, as a drama among neighbors. Knowing the cast, being familiar with the daily routines and human relationships, just being as curious as townspeople are, they could detect the signs, gestures, movements, and miens which symbolized the political drama performed by the Mayor and his people. They did not need to watch TV or to read the papers; they just had to lean out of their windows, for instance, to see the Mayor late in the evening sitting with his confidante on the doorsteps to her house, talking with her for hours, while the night passed. The nocturnal sessions on the doorsteps were repeated more often than not, enacting what was viewed as a scene in the civic spectacle of a small town.

A sense of mythology was preserved among the people of the "City of the Fifth Floor." The political drama which they performed was the stuff of which fables are made. They followed the script about a great city and they acted in the way of urban villagers. They thought that the world is their stage and they presumed that the village fabulist is the best critic of their play.

The special assistant to the Mayor, the former student of Nozick and Quine who knows essentially what moral and political thought is all about, displayed in his office one large portrait — not of Aristotle, or of John Locke, or of John Adams. No, it was a portrait of Kevin Hagen White. He did not betray any emotion as he talked about his jobs and his responsibilities, he was as cool as any technocrat. But the mien became vivid, the voice fell into modulations, and the words were stressed by gestures as he described what he thinks is the greatest ritual in Boston politics: the Mayor attending a wake. No, the Harvard *alumnus* in the Mayor's Office could not think of any good scholarly studies about Boston. But in his view such studies are unimportant anyway. All one could tell about Boston had been told in two fables. And while he wrote the titles carefully down he recited them as if he were casting a spell: *The Last Hurrah, The Last Hurrah, Liberty's Chosen Home, Liberty's Chosen Home.*[5]

3 The Field of Political Creativity

It happens very rarely, with Plato and Aristotle in Athens, with James Madison, John Adams, Thomas Jefferson in America, that the science of

---

[5] E. O'Connor, *The Last Hurrah*, Boston 1956. This novel recounts political life in Boston under the legendary James Michael Curley, Mayor of Boston between 1914–17, 1922–25, 1930–33, and 1946–49. Curley is portrayed in the novel as "Mayor Frank Skeffington." – A. Lupo, *Liberty's Chosen Home. The Politics of Violence in Boston*, Boston 1977. This quasi-fictional book offers an account of Kevin White's political career with a particular emphasis on the "busing crisis" of 1974–75. In June 1974 Federal District Judge W. Arthur Garrity had ordered the Boston School Committee to desegregate Boston's public schools by "busing." Throughout 1974–75 this attempt at desegregating school children (there were around 18,000 children involved) was accompanied with racial conflicts (steet demonstrations, racial assaults, strikes). An extensive report on the "busing crisis" was published by R. A. Dentler and M. B. Scott: *Schools on Trial. An Inside Account of the Boston Desegregatoin Case*, Cambridge, Mass. 1981. The authors wrote their report from the vantage point of "experts appointed by Judge Garrity to advise and represent him and to supervise his order to desegregate Boston's schools." A critical review of the book was published by J. L. Hanna in: *Policy Studies Review* I (4), May 1981, pp. 777–781, cf. also J. A. Lukas, *Common Ground*, op. cit.

politics and the process of politics concur, that the study of politics and the reality of politics are twins.[6] Under the relation which appears to be their "normal" one, the science of politics lags the process of politics. As a scholastic mode the science represents, by definition, reflections about politics *a posteriori*.[7] It is meant to capture politics in finite forms, such as words, concepts, symbols, a body of knowledge. Politics, however, is an open-ended process, moving invariably beyond all "scientific" charts that may have been made of its course. Its actual reality is always different from the one that is presently known.

There is no solution to the disparity between the finite forms of science and the fluid nature of politics. The science of politics, while being true to what it is, holds on to that "knowledge" about politics which it represents. The process of politics, while moving beyond the reality of its movement, becomes progressively a process of politics quite other than the one "known" by the science of politics. To some extent, knowledge about politics is always a knowledge bordering upon ignorance.

The experience of ignorance is of course the check upon the sluggishness of science. The disparity between science and politics cannot be caused to disappear. But its ultimate consequence, science turned into ignorance, is not a foregone conclusion. The process of politics can at any stage be reconsidered with the view of readjusting the present forms of political knowledge to the actual reality of politics. The readjustment will hardly be complete, because of the fluid nature of politics that continues of course to elude all finalizing explications.[8] Still, even a partial readjusting will prevent the science of politics from losing increasingly the reality of its subject.

---

[6] This is the reason I think why we continue to attribute a paradigmatic status to the Platonic-Aristotelian *episteme politike* and to the political science of the American Founding Fathers.

[7] Those who are primarily concerned with political science as a "science" (a natural science, as it were) would probably stress the point differently. They would argue the case of a future-oriented discipline: political science as the science of prospective political developments. They were right, of course (in a way they would probably not recognize). A science of prospective political developments operates with extrapolations of present trends into the future. These extrapolations are again based on data concerning politics having taken place *before* the time at which the extrapolations are made. In other words, the extrapolations are but reflections about politics *a posteriori*.

[8] Cf. Plato, *Statesman*, 269 D: "Absolute and perpetual immutability is a property of only the most divine things of all, things of a bodily nature do not belong to this class." — ibid., 294 A – B: "In a sense, however, it is clear that lawmaking belongs to the science of kingship; but the best thing is not that the laws be in power, but that the man who is wise and of kingly nature be ruler. Do you see why? — Why is it? — Because law could never, by determining exactly what is noblest and most just for one and all, enjoin

The current vocabulary of political science includes the notion of "executive power" and this notion is meant to denote the crucible of politics. It is intended to define that area of political reality where the representative acts are performed by which a multitude of people acts as one people, as the people of one body politic. The notion implies a movement of creativeness. It implies that somewhere in the process of politics something is "made" by the "execution" of power. It is through "executive power" that the Many emerge as the One, that there is *e pluribus unum*. Somewhere in politics acts of transformation occur: acts which make the multitude appear as a body politic. The notion of executive power implies a moment of transfiguration. There are the representative acts performed by a few on behalf of the many. And there is the body politic of all, the few and the many, that acts through these representative acts.

Moment of creativeness, moment of transfiguration — the current vocabulary of political science does not feature such expressions. We are offered instead the term "political leadership." It covers the crucible of politics by a

---

upon them that which is best; for the differences of men and of actions and the fact that nothing, I may say, in human life is ever at rest, forbid any science whatsoever to promulgate any simple rule for everything and for all time." — Aristotle, *Nicomachean Ethics,* 1094 b15 – 24: "The subjects studied by political science are moral nobility and justice; but these conceptions involve much difference of opinion and uncertainty, so that they are sometimes believed to be mere conventions and to have no real existence in the nature of things. And a similar uncertainty surrounds the conception of the Good, because it frequently occurs that good things have harmful consequences: people have before now been ruined by wealth, and in other cases courage has cost men their lives. We must therefore be content if, in dealing with subjects and starting from premises thus uncertain, we succeed in presenting a broad outline of the truth ... Accordingly we may ask the student also to accept the various views we put forward in the same spirit; for it is the mark of an educated mind to expect that amount of exactness in each kind which the nature of the particular subject admits." — Cf. also: E. Voegelin, *Order and History,* Vol. III, *Plato and Aristotle,* op. cit., pp. 293 – 303 ("The Range of Political Science"). And: W. Bagehot, *The English Constitution,* ed. R. H. S. Crossman, Glasgow 1963, 1978, 14th ed.: "Language is the tradition of nations; each generation describes what it sees, but it uses words transmitted from the past. When a great entity like the British Constitution has continued in connected outward sameness, but hidden inner change, for many ages, every generation inherits a series of inapt words — of maxims once true, but of which truth is ceasing or has ceased. As a man's family go on muttering in his maturity incorrect phrases derived from a just observation of his early youth, so, in the full activity of an historical constitution, its subjects repeat phrases true in the time of their fathers, and inculcated by those fathers, but now true no longer. Or, if I may say so, an ancient and ever-altering constitution is like an old man who still wears with attached fondness clothes in the fashion of his youth: what you see of him is the same; what you do not see is wholly altered" (p. 59).

compact symbol, the monolithic symbol of a prime political figure who "leads": "The President," "The Chancellor," "The Prime Minister," "The Governor," "The Mayor." And the symbol then suggests an answer before any questions have really been asked as to the person(s) and the place(s) by whom and where those essential acts of politics, the acts of transformation are performed through which the Many emerge as the One. The symbolic person, "The President" or "The Mayor," is thought to perform deeds of "leadership" and these deeds are imagined to occur at the symbolic person's symbolic place, "The White House" or "The Mayor's Office."[9]

The language of political science no longer grasps the reality of the representative acts through which a multitude of people becomes the one people acting as a body politic. It needs readjusting. Concepts such as "executive power" or "political leadership" and symbols such as "The President," "The Mayor" or "The White House," "The Mayor's Office," still suggest the simple reality of a "chief executive" residing in an official mansion, surrounded just by his family and one or two secretaries. Indeed, this is what the relevant constitutional provisions stipulate: an "executive branch" of quite idyllic proportions.[10]

---

[9] One could of course draw up a longer list, including such well-known symbolic places as: "L'Elysée," "Downing Street 10," "Das Bundeskanzleramt" (the German Federal Chancellery), "Der Ballhausplatz" (the symbolic place of Austria's federal government). ... As to the symbolism of the "Mayor's Office" in Boston a senior aide of Mayor White offered this de-mythologizing remark: "You have to be careful to define who you are talking about. There are lots of offices who answer 'Mayor's Office' when you call them on the phone" (Source: Interview). Still, the Mayor crafted the "myth" persistently. From the start of his administration he insisted that it "function cooperatively rather than separately and that the driving force come from the Mayor's Office" (*Report to Mayor Kevin H. White and the Boston Redevelopment Authority from Hale Champion, Development Administrator,* July 11, 1968, p. 4).

[10] According to Boston's City Charter, Mayor White should have enlisted only a few "secretaries." Cf. *City Charter,* Chapter 486 of the Acts [Commonwealth of Massachusetts] of 1909, Section 15, in: City of Boston, *Municipal Register for 1978 – 1979,* op. cit., p. 39. – Article II of the American Constitution states that the President of the United States "shall appoint Ambassadors, other public Ministers and Consuls, Judges of the Supreme Court, and all other Officers of the United States." It is doubtful whether by this was also meant the large presidential apparatus which we have come to know as the "White House" and the "Executive Office" (comprising 5000 or more persons). – Articles 5 – 19 of the French Constitution (Fifth Republic) define the responsibilities of the President of the Republic – and make no mention at all of any aide, colloborator, or staff, let alone such an elaborate governmental apparatus as the "Elysée" of today (comprising about 800 persons). – In the section of the *Grundgesetz* (Basic Law) of the Federal Republic of Germany pertaining to the Federal Chancellor (Art. 63 – 69) there is no reference to anything like the *Bundeskanzleramt* (Federal Chancellery) and

However, the executive branches of governments have grown, whereever we look, into giant plants. Their growth has been noticed, of course; it has been observed and attempts at describing it have been made. In particular, it has been noted either as a numerical phenomenon (the growth of the staff of American Presidents, for instance) or as an organizational phenomenon (the growth of the bureaucracy). It has *not* been studied as a phenomenon of political creativity and has therefore *not* been seized as what it is essentially: as the emergence of a "second government" which is tending to supersede the first, that is formally instituted government.[11]

While the science of politics continues to consider as governmental "reality" what its symbols and concepts evoke, governmental politics has been moving beyond the known institutions of government towards quite another reality of governing. To be sure, there is nothing "new" about this reality. As ever, the representative acts are performed by which a multitude of people acts as one people, as the people of one body politic. But the few who perform these representative acts are constituting a field of governmental configurations quite unlike any conventional "government." It precedes and it transcends all institutions of government. It is the fluid reality of politics that corresponds to the fluid nature of politics. It is the field of political creativity.

For the study of politics a phenomenon more fascinating than the field of political creativity could not occur. It is politics to be seen in the mode of its incipience. It is the process of political creativity made "visible." It is politics in the making.

What we see in studying the phenomenon are people: persons in government constituting governmental configurations. If we want to identify these persons and to apply an apt scientific definition for that purpose, we should continue to use the expression "the field of political creativity." However, if we want to name these persons and to speak about them as a group, we should choose a telling symbol. In fact, there is such a symbol already in use. It is borrowed from the language of monarchism, probably because this symbol conveys precisely the image of persons grouped around the formal emplacement of government, yet constituting by themselves governmental configurations: "The Court."[12]

---

the *Bundespresseamt* (Federal Press Office), the apparatus of the Chancellor as it exists today (comprising about 1300 persons).

[11] Cf. T. Schabert, "Das Paradox der Macht. Anmerkungen zur Regierungspraxis in Washington, Paris und Bonn," *Süddeutsche Zeitung*, No. 188, Aug. 17–18, 1985, p. 81.

[12] In a story about Herbert Gleason, an old friend of Mayor White's, we find Gleason called a "Yank in *King Kevin's Court*" (*BHA*, February 2, 1978). – In his study of *Presidential Power* Richard Neustadt writes: "Each [Johnson and Nixon] presided over

The field of political creativity is a phenomenon to be seen by the second government that is formed by the Court. Or, to put it differently, the Court is the locus of creativity in the process of politics. The Court defines the area of political reality where the representative acts are performed through which a multitude of people becomes the one people acting as a body politic. The Court is the crucible of politics.

As far as I can see, the Court has hardly been subject of scientific studies.[13] This might appear surprising. That there are second governments

a Royal Court, writ large" (op. cit., p. 27 f.). — We should further note that the expression "The Court" is part of a larger vocabulary of related symbols. In Michael J. Malbin's book *Unelected Representatives. Congressional Staff and the Future of Representative Government,* New York 1980, there appears not only the term "royal court" but also the adjective "feudal" (p. 21); and according to the *National Journal* (Dec. 15, 1984, Vol. 16, No. 50 – 51, p. 2386), American Presidents follow the rule "personnel is policy" in order to gain control over the "duchies and fiefdoms of the federal government." The Elysée, seat of the President of a *Republic,* is also called the "Château" or "La maison présidentielle" or even "La maison du Prince" (P. Viansson-Ponté, *Histoire de la république gaullienne,* Paris 1970, p. 140; M. Schifres, M. Sarazin, *L'Elysée de Mitterrand,* op. cit., subtitle; various newspapers). The French Press has applied to Mitterrand's "Court" also the term *gens Mitterrandia* that is a symbol which recalls the politics of the nobility in Ancient Rome. Stéphane Rials, in a straightforward scholarly survey of the French Presidency, introduces a section on the President and governmental committees by the title "Le prince en ses conseils" (*La présidence de la république,* Paris 1981, p. 112). — Students of "urban politics" do not appear to have been inspired greatly by reports on "Courts" (and similar phenomena) in "national politics." They have largely overlooked the phenomena of the Court. If they discussed them, the discussion was very brief — and it conveyed the impression that the significance of these phenomena as regards the study of politics was not really apperceived. Cf., as a typical example, the surprisingly short remarks on the "professionals" in: R. D. Dahl, *Who Governs?,* op. cit., pp. 305 – 306.

[13] First of all, there are hardly any publications dealing with the Court in some extensive manner. And the few publications which are available were not undertaken as strictly scientific studies. They represent works of journalism, quite carefully researched, it needs to be said. But their primary emphasis still lies upon information rather than analysis. Cf. especially: the various reports on the American Presidency in the *National Journal;* P. Viansson-Ponté, *Histoire de la république gaullienne,* 2 vols., Paris 1970 – 71; C. Dulong, *La vie quotidienne à l'Elysée au temps de Charles de Gaulle,* Paris 1974; M. Schifres, M. Sarazin, *L'Elysée de Mitterrand,* op. cit.,; the various reports on Mitterrand's Presidency in *Le Point;* "Kanzleramt," *Der Spiegel,* No. 24, June 6, 1966, pp. 32 – 40; R. Zundel, "Die Souffleure der Kanzler," *Die Zeit,* No. 28, July 8, 1983. — There exist — or have existed — quite a few sophisticated studies on the American Court (the "White House"), the French (the "Elysée") and the German Court (the "Bundeskanzleramt") produced by members of these Courts. Written solely *ad usum principis,* they remain unpublished — or were destroyed.

in contemporary politics is known, after all, or else neither the symbol *The Court* nor other similar symbols would have penetrated our current political language. But the symbol, telling as it is, has probably satisfied any further curiosity much too early: the area of political reality to which the symbol refers is still largely unexplored.

In the following I shall attempt an exploration. I shall try to analyze the emergence of a second government, that is the phenomena of the field of political creativity, by analyzing the Court of Boston under Kevin White.

The Court of Boston under Kevin White had no formal shape and could therefore not be discerned on the level of governmental organization. Empirically, it was a distinct field of political creativity. The different *manifestations* of this creativity could be observed and it was in the mode of such a study that the *field itself* could be perceived. The study then proceeded on two strata:

(a) on the stratum of manifestations which were the *units* of observation and study;
(b) and on the stratum of the field which was the *subject* of the study. Within this texture the stratum of manifestations represented the "surface" — where observations could be made — and the stratum of the field represented the "depth" — where those processes of political creativity occurred from which the manifestations emerged. While it proceeded, the study moved hither and thither between the two strata following the empirical pattern which they together formed. It would have deviated from this pattern, and thus ceased to be an empirical study, if each stratum — the manifestations of the field and the field from which those manifestations emerged — had been considered separately. The manifestations would then have been perceived just as figures of organization, their linkage would hardly have been recognized, and some would even have slipped off the range of attention. And the field would just have disappeared, since the figures of organization — to which its manifestations would have been reduced — would no longer have been transparent towards its reality.

The Court of Boston under Mayor White was a field of political creativity that manifested itself in a configuration of political organisms. While the organism known as "The Mayor's Office" was the most prominent one, others, like the one or the other "policy committee" or "task force," could be quite inconspicuous. Some organisms, the "colonies" of mayoral aides in other departments or agencies, for instance, did not have a stable existence; typically, a "colony" appeared at some point within an agency, grew or shrank, became insignificant or disappeared altogether. And in the one or the other case organisms of quite different names and of quite different shapes filled successively one and the same "place" within the Court; yet they were all organisms typical of this particular place; for example, the place of a "political organization" in the Court was never void, it was consecutively filled, but filled only in different ways.[14]

The study of the organisms revealed the Court a phenomenon of movement. Two different movements could be distinguished:

(a) a movement in a vertical direction between "depth" and "surface"; organisms emerged from the depth of the field, appeared at the surface as its manifestations, and disappeared again;

(b) a movement in a horizontal direction; organisms grew and shrank, their number increased and decreased, the field expanded and contracted; it was "pulsating."

The Court fulfilled three essential functions:

(a) It existed within the regular city government as a separate *personal* government of the Mayor who could use it at will. Its existence enabled him to a certain extent to govern irrespective of administrative procedures and bureaucratic interests. Regular city departments were duplicated by corresponding organisms in the Court and these organisms gave the Mayor a commanding "independence" in relation to the apparatus of the city government.

(b) Conversely, having the Court as a separate, personal government, the Mayor could control the regular city government. He may not have succeeded always in swaying the administrative performance and political behavior of department heads and the bureaucracy in each and every case, but the Court yielded the necessary means, a wealth of political intelligence, excellent expertise, a sizable manpower, which could be used to persuade, cajole, reward, or punish them.

(c) The Court formed the clearing-agency of Boston politics. Policy initiatives in Boston had hardly a chance to survive if they were not cleared by the Court. Those which pleased the Court were adopted and then further pursued in the Mayor's name. Those which did not fit in with the current preoccupation and objectives of the Court were usually not rejected outright; the Court dealt with these initiatives in a politically much more soothing way: it absorbed them. They were considered and discussed, but less intensively and less frequently the more time elapsed; when it became increasingly difficult to locate someone in the Court who still

---

[14] A senior and long-term aide of Mayor White stated, for instance, that he "was involved in White's political organization since the first days of the gubernatorial race, which began in 1968" (Source: Interview).

knew them, it was too late to back away from the Court and to save what had long ceased to be an "initiative."

On the other hand, the Court constantly generated policy initiatives. Its members would have thought that something was wrong if the Court did not vibrate with a hectic rhythm of policy production. A great deal of the production never reached the stage of serious consideration and only a fraction of the proposed policies were implemented eventually. But the constant generation of policy initiatives kept the Court functioning as Boston's predominant place of political vitality. As the source of an abundant amount of political impulses, it engulfed or exploited at least many other founts of political vitality.[15] The restless policy production of the Court seemed to be a waste of manpower, ressources, and time. Still, it provided the abundance of expert knowledge, policy anticipations, and political options, out of which the Court's power grew.

The Court, one should finally note, largely eluded public scrutiny. It was not discerned, really. There was no formal, legal, or institutional mode of grasping the manifestations of its existence. Besides, the Mayor and the other members of the Court artfully diffused any curiosity of outsiders. One knew that a group of persons existed who was performing the representative acts through which there was a "City of Boston" acting. The subject of this knowledge, however, was not explored any further. While "The Mayor has said" or "The Mayor's Office wanted this" was the conventional answer to everything one wanted to know about Boston's political life, the existence and the procedures of the Court were ignored. And yet, whatever it was that one would have wanted to know, the Court held the answer.

4 A Phenomenon of Politics That Defies Numbers

As a phenomenon of political creativity the Court could not be apperceived by quantitative methods of research. It defied numbers. There was hardly a question more simple than this: "How many members does the Court have?" Yet this question could at no moment be answered satisfactorily. Numerical

---

[15] Cf., for example, the following explanation given by a mayoral assistant: "The New Federalism [under President Nixon] has given us access to funds that had been frozen, but also has given us responsibility for coordinating their use, and accountability. We anticipated Community Development Revenue Sharing (probably one of the few cities that did), as well as HUD comprehensive planning grants, changes in Model Cities. We have had people planning, looking at federal program money as a whole [...]" (Source: Interview).

data could be collected but they did not render a precise quantitative profile of the Court.

They were not utterly useless, however. It is certainly helpful to know, after all, whether the Court had about 10 or as many as 1000 members. Even if it proved impossible to determine precisely how many members it had, the data which were available evoked a certain quantitative "image" of the Court. Such a quantitative image is of course but an approximation to reality, and this fact should be kept in mind. On the other hand, one could not conceive of the Court and not at least have an approximate notion of its numerical size.

There were several reasons why no precise data on the number of people in the Court could be collected:

(a) In a special report, *City of Boston Employees – How Many Are There?*,[16] the Boston Municipal Research Bureau[17] stated the fundamental problem as follows:

> How many people are employed by the City of Boston? The lack of reliable city personnel reports makes it difficult to answer that question accurately [...]. The number of people working for the city is a basic piece of management information which should be readily available in simple, straight-forward reports. In fact, nobody in City Hall today can provide that kind of document. [...] the number of employees in the Public Works Department on July 8, 1980 [for example], was 627 according to the Data Processing Unit's personnel report. It was 731 according to the Public Works' Personnel Unit and 652 based on the Budget Division's data.[18]

---

[16] BMRB, *City of Boston Employees – How Many Are There?*, Special Report No. 97, Boston 1980.

[17] The Boston Municipal Research Bureau, supported by contributions from businesses and individuals, is a research organization that monitors government spending and taxation in Boston. Compiling and publishing its independent reports on administrative, financial, and budgetary problems of the City, it is acting as a "watchdog agency."

[18] *City of Boston Employees – How Many Are There?*, op. cit., pp. 1, 3. – In a rare instance of public acknowledgment David Rosenbloom, Health and Hospitals Commissioner, agreed that "The Municipal Research Bureau's figures are generally consistent with published figures generated by the city's review of its activity" (*CR*, Feb. 2, 1981, Vol. 73, No. 6, p. 106). – In March 1983, though, the BMRB could register a certain improvement: "Documenting City employee numbers by department has been facilitated by the partial implementation of new employment information system. However, the Bureau staff must still manually audit payroll reports for various departments to achieve reasonably accurate data. The City has begun to implant its personnel/payroll system, and now all City departments except a few major line departments such as Police, Library, and Public Works are entered onto the system" (BMRB, *Changes in Boston's Personnel Levels*, Special Report No. 83 – 1, Boston 1983).

(b) The members of the Court who formed "colonies" in regular city departments nowhere appeared formally in their real function, as agents of the
autocrat. Instead they were listed officially as employees in their "host"
departments. Sooner or later, a certain number of them was recognized,
by colleagues, City Councillors, newspaper reporters,[19] and they were
then broadly characterized as the "Mayor's people." Nevertheless, anyone
wanting to procure a full quantitative knowledge about the "colonies"
was always one step behind in a process of hide-and-seek.

(c) The Court included people who received salaries which the City did not
draw from own but from other, mostly federal funds. In making an
attempt to determine the number of these employees, one would have
needed some sort of documentary evidence — even if it had been as
contradictory and deficient as the ordinary personnel records —, but
such evidence was virtually non-existent: "About 14% of those on the
total city payroll are paid for from federal and other special funds. Yet
there is no report to show the number of those employees by department
or funding source ..."[20]

(d) Finally, the existence of the Court was not susceptible to the standard
procedures of gathering information about governments. It was the
essential phenomenon of Boston's government under Mayor White. Yet
it was not identical with any institution, organizational arrangement, or
political organism of this government. Consequently, the Court as such
was not a unit of data collection.

Again, this does not mean that there were no data at all concerning the
Court. Numbers relating to the Court could be obtained from various sources.
But they really made sense only after the Court had been clearly apperceived.
It was necessary to "see" the Court, and only then it was possible to know
which data were relevant to a quantitative "image" of the Court.

On the basis of such relevant (and available!) data it can safely be said
that the numeric size of the Court grew continuously and that it grew
considerably as well. The growth can be deducted particularly from a series
of quantitative data on the "Mayor's Office" which was, however vaguely
defined, a significant part of the Court.

In 1968, that is in the first year of the Mayor's rule, about 133 people
were known to be employees in his "Office." Ten years later, the Office

---

[19] One City Councillor, Frederick C. Langone, in particular concerned himself with detect-
ing the hideouts of the "Mayor's people." — Agents of the autocrat in other departments
were often shunned by their colleagues after they had been recognized. — Unfortunately,
newspaper reporters tended to obscure the existence of colonies by their sensationalist
inclinations.

[20] *City of Boston Employees — How Many Are There?*, op. cit., p. 2.

comprised 825 employees and an unspecified number of "federally funded" people.[21] In 1980, while the City went through one of its fiscal crises,[22] the government was compelled to lay off a considerable number of workers and employees. In April 1980, for instance, the Mayor announced a personnel reduction program "of 400 to 500 employees, mostly from the so-called Mayoral agencies."[23] Thus the number of people working in the "Mayor's Office" decreased to 531 employees in 1981.[24] However, in March 1983, the Boston Municipal Research Bureau reported that the number of employees in the Office had risen again, by 15% between January 12, 1982 and January 11, 1983.[25]

---

[21] Cf. BG, June 16, 1981 and A. Ganz, G. Perkins (BRA), *Performance of Boston City Government 1967 – 81*, [Boston] April 1981, Table 4, pp. 13 – 16. In this table a few mayoral agencies – the Office of the Bicentennial, the Office of Development, the Office of Public Service, the Office of Federal Relations, the Office of Fiscal Affairs, the Office of Property Equalization – are listed separately. The number of their employees was included in calculating the total number of employees – 825 – in the "Mayor's Office." – Concerning "federally funded" employees, a mayoral aide explained that he had been "working on ways to finance the mayor's policy staff from federal funds." He "proposed using Model Cities funds." And he planned "to keep this secret from [the City] Council as long as possible. There will be an internal transfer that won't be too visible."

[22] The fiscal crisis was caused by "Proposition 2 1/2," an initiative petition sponsored by "Citizens for Limited Taxation" and approved in November 1980 by an overwhelming majority of Massachusetts voters. Proposition 2 1/2 became law on Dec. 4, 1980. It was designed "to limit a community's property taxes to 2 1/2 % of the full and fair cash value of its taxable property. For a city such as Boston, where FY [fiscal year] 1981 property taxes represent 10.2% of fair cash value, the law would require that the amount raised in property taxes be reduced 15% each year until the 2 1/2 % limit is reached. After that property taxes may only be increased by a minimum of 2 1/2% of the preceding year's total, regardless of the growth in assessments. [...] Full implementation of [Proposition 2 1/2] in Boston would take six years. In the end it would cut the current property tax levy between $ 318 to $ 391 million, a reduction of between 61 to 75%" (BMRB, *Proposition 2 1/2: Impact on Boston*, Special Report No. 98, Boston 1980). Concerning background information about the proposition, cf. BG, Oct. 31, 1980; Dec. 4, 1980; March 22, 1981.

[23] *City of Boston Employees – How Many Are There?*, op. cit., p. 4.

[24] Cf. BG, June 16, 1981.

[25] *Changes in Boston's Personnel Levels*, op. cit. – It is certainly worthwhile to note that the Mayor of Boston had a staff larger than that of the President of the United States. A few comparative numbers regarding the staff personnel in the White House Office: President Kennedy, 338 persons; President Johnson, 292 persons; President Nixon, 583 persons; President Ford, 525 persons. Cf. Subcommittee on Employee Ethics and Utilization, Committee on Post Office and Civil Service, U. S. House of Representatives,

5 A Phenomenon of Politics to Be Studied in Its Mode of History

Section 1: The Reality That Is History

As a phenomenon of movement the Court took shape in a sequence of changing manifestations. A comprehensive view of the Court can therefore be attained only by a longitudinal study which encompasses all the successive configurations of political organisms in which the Court consisted at different times. To apperceive the Court, one must apprehend its "history," that is the history of its manifestations, for this history is the Court. The Court has to be seen as a diachronic phenomenon: it was the Court which "historically" became the Court. In its history the Court disclosed its reality. Or, inversely put, the reality of the Court can be seized by grasping the Court in the mode of its history.

Viewed in their temporal sequence the changing manifestations of the Court form a distinctive structure. The structure is rendered by Table 1, the "historical profile" of the Court. The diagram depicts the manifestations of the Court within the matrix of two axes:

(a) a time axis which starts with 1967, the year in which Kevin White was for the first time elected Mayor of Boston; and
(b) a configuration axis which runs along the essential classes of manifestations.

Section 2: The Rhythm of Organizational Creativity

In the Mayor's first term the configuration of the Court's political organisms was quite simple. It became more complex only in the last year.[26]

The second term, however, was characterized by a considerable organizational creativity. A complex configuration of organisms emerged by this creative thrust. In retrospect, this term appears to have been the "golden age" of the Mayor's rule. Ascending the autocratic position which he came to cherish above all, the Mayor, and his enthusiast staff as well, took the City of Boston on a course of great reforms. The autocrat harbored the aspiration

---

Presidential Staffing – A Brief Overview; 95th Congress, 2nd Session, July 25, 1978, p. 57.

[26] The immediate cause of this development was probably the departure of Barney Frank, the Mayor's first chief of staff and first *alter ego*.

that the radiance of his achievements in Boston would project him into a national role.[27]

Many of the organisms which were produced in the second term carried over into the third, but the fervor of political creativity had dissipated.[28] Within the remaining configuration those organisms were most alive which served the purpose of accumulating power.

In the fourth term, finally, the Court took on yet another configuration. Most of the organisms which had been both carriers of policies and instruments of politics had almost completely disappeared. Only one of them remained, the "machine," unadorned as it were, alluring a degree of attention which the earlier manifold of organisms, much more intricate and more potent, had never attracted. This development was largely caused by financial constraints. Federal funds, in particular, dried up. As the scarcity of revenues became ever more acute, major organismus could no longer be supported.[29] Still, the Court's configuration in this term included a variety of "systems" destined to monitor the "policy output." The most notable was the "Office of Policy Management."[30] Its administrators aimed to make the apparatus of the city government more "efficient" and more "responsive" to the needs

----

[27] In July 1972 Kevin White's national aspirations were almost fulfilled when George McGovern, presidential candidate of the Democratic Party, briefly considered to appoint him his running mate as vice-presidential candidate. Edward Kennedy and his camp apparently opposed the nomination of White. McGovern chose eventually Senator Thomas F. Eagleton. Shortly after the Democratic Convention, however, McGovern was compelled to seek another running mate. Senator Eagleton had resigned from his place on the ticket. In the new round of candidates being considered Kevin White featured once again — but was not chosen McGovern's running-mate, once again. — The Mayor had invested considerable efforts in his vice-presidential campaign. The campaign was financed by Mortimer Zuckerman; Ira Jackson acted as "advance man." — From time to time there was an echo, albeit a feeble one, of the Mayor's national aspirations. Cf., for instance, the article "White reportedly charting national course" that appeared in the *BG* on October 31, 1980, and begins as follows: "Mayor Kevin H. White plans to visit China next May, as part of a strategy to give himself international exposure while exploring the possibility of running for the presidency in 1984, according to sources within his administration [...]"

[28] The earlier enthusiasm and creative thrust dissipated under the impact of two particular experiences: the "busing crisis" (cf. footnote 5) and the difficult circumstances of White's reelection in the fall of 1975.

[29] As for example: the web of BRA district directors and, in particular, the elaborate network of Little City Halls (cf. infra, p. 132 ff.).

[30] The Office of Policy Management was the brainchild and pet object of Micho Spring, the Mayor's political twin during his last years in City Hall (cf. infra, p. 81 f.).

| | | | election |
| 1980 | 1981 | 1982 | 1983 |

icho Spring   Bob Ryan   leave: Rosenbloom
                Deputy Mayor   Mundel

                managers/politicoes

                   policy management   Finis Principatus Kevini Albi

nagers/ politicoes

   policy management   Vice Mayor

                 Deputy Mayors

          cabinet

             working groups

    Deputy Mayors

Mayor

et

   working groups

     James Kelly   James Kelly

                machine

   machine

The zealots   The zealots

of the citizens (and potential voters). While the language symbol, policy management, was new, the idea, an efficient city government, was of course quite old.[31]

6 Institutional Change

Major changes in the Court's configurations occurred in each term during the last year, that is the year preceding a mayoral election. The changes took place first in the depth of the field and became then visible partially within the year that preceded the election. They fully reached the surface of the field, that is the level of distinct manifestations, only after the election.

During 1968 and 1969 the chief of staff, Barney Frank, was the preeminent figure among the mayoral aides. Frank left in January 1970, and the Mayor afterwards did not want to appoint a new chief of staff, he was "loathe to create that role [Barney Frank as chief of staff and *alter ego*] again."[32]

Instead, the autocrat talked about a staff reorganization. Throughout 1970 a competitive diversity of sub-groups and individuals characterized the internal life of the staff although the general trend pointed to a type of staff organization whereby a group of specialists would collectively advise and assist the Mayor. A staff organization of this type emerged after the mayoral election during the first year of the Mayor's second term. It became fully operative in 1972.

In 1974 the configuration of the Court altered in two respects:

(a) A political organization of the autocrat had existed before, but its various manifestations[33] were now being amplified by specific forms of a purely "political" organization. A first step towards this amplification was the appointment of a mayoral assistant who spent his time organizing the Mayor's followers.[34]

---

[31] The rhythm of organizational creativity in the White House, very similar to that in Boston's City Hall, is described in: R. M. Pious, *The American Presidency,* New York 1979, pp. 248 – 250.

[32] Source: Interview. – A former colleague of Frank explained: "Barney had the Mayor's complete confidence. Never had to talk to the mayor before making a decision. The mayor has been a bit concerned since Barney left about letting another situation like that develop" (Source: Interview).

[33] As for example: the web of BRA district directors which served the professional purpose of urban planning and was used, besides, as a vehicle to gather political intelligence.

[34] Kirk O'Donnell.

(b) The Mayor introduced the "system" of Deputy Mayors. Among the constantly changing manifestations of the Court this "system" represented a singular case. It persisted in the Court as a major and continually active organism.

In 1978 the position of a chief mayoral assistant appeared again in the Court. As in the other instances of institutional change, it became fully visible only in the first year of the subsequent term. In the same year the organization of the Mayor's followers was rehearsed on the occasion of the so-called "classification campaign."[35]

The last major institutional change took place in late 1981 when the Mayor appointed the director of the BRA, Robert J. Ryan, Deputy Mayor for Development. Ryan, who remained head of the BRA, had not only become a close aide of the Mayor, but, more importantly, represented the one field of governmental activity, urban planning and development, upon which the Mayor increasingly depended in maintaining his power, his autocracy.

In the course of the same development − which again became fully manifest only in 1982 − a number of people both from the Mayor's staff and the BRA gained a more influential status in the Court and, as a result of their expertise and responsibilities in the area of urban development, gravitated towards each other, forming the Court's central organism of power in its final years.[36]

7 Configurations and Institutions

The reality of politics emerges from a continual process of movements between "informal" configurations and "formal" institutions. Political institutions exist and people pursue politics by being active within the realm of these institutions. But in pursuing their political activities − meetings, deliberations −, they do not completely conform to the formal pattern of institutions. They constantly enact this pattern of institutions, of course. But

---

[35] In 1978 the Massachusetts voters passed a "classification" amendment which was designed to restructure the system of classifying (= assessing) property for tax purposes. By the amendment communities are allowed to tax commercial property at a higher rate than residential property. The White administration anticipated a fiscal relief for Boston and its property owners and therefore, by the classification campaign, urged the Boston voters to approve the amendment. Cf. also BMRB, *Down the Homestretch on Revaluation and Classification,* Special Report No. 82−8, Boston 1982. − Campaign manager for Boston's tax classification efforts was John F. Weis.

[36] Cf. infra, p. 312.

they also fill the institutional framework with a host of informal configurations. Both processes occur simultaneously, the enactment of institutions and the practice of forming configurations. The formal dimension of politics reaches into the informal one and the informal dimension reaches into the formal one. An inquiry into the reality of politics therefore cannot be undertaken on the assumption that this reality is defined just by its visible manifestations at the moment of study, for these manifestations have emerged from an interplay of informal-formal and formal-informal processes. They reflect not a reality which is what it is but a reality which is what it becomes. The manifestations of this reality are manifestations of movements and the study of these movements must consequently be the central part of any inquiry into that reality, the reality of politics.[37]

A simple exercise suffices to discern in the reality of Boston politics the movements between "informal" configurations and "formal" institutions. I shall compare the Court with the institution that was its formal equivalent: the "Mayor's Office." The comparison will be made on the basis of

(a) the historical profile of the Court, as it is being drawn here;
(b) and the organizational profile of the "Mayor's Office," as presented by the *Official Directory* of Boston's city government (see Table 2).

One would probably assume the directory to have the great advantage of being a document of precision; whereas the value of the Court's profile, one might think, would lie in its heuristic status. The quantity of information provided by the directory would be rather extensive, one might believe, while the profile would offer mostly information of a structural kind. Perhaps one might even be prepared for drawing the conclusion that the directory is in every respect an essential piece of evidence and that, in contrast, the Court's profile represents nothing more than some additional illustration.

Table 2: Organizational Profile of the "Mayor's Office", as presented in the City Directory, City of Boston

1968	(1)	Administrative Assistant
		Special Assistant
		Executive Assistant
		Press Secretary
1968	(2)	Special Assistant
		Special Assistant
		Executive Assistant

---

[37] A similar statement is Victor Turner's: "The social world is a world in becoming, not a world in being [...] and for this reason studies of social structure *as such* are irrelevant" (*Drama, Fields and Metaphors. Symbolic Action in Human Society,* Ithaca 1974, p. 24).

1969	(1)	Executive Assistant
		Special Counsel
		Special Counsel
		Press Secretary
1969	(2)	Executive Assistant
		Special Counsel
		Special Counsel
		Director of Communications

1970 = 1969 (2)

1971		Special Assistant
		Special Counsel
		Director of Communications

1972 (1) = 1971

1972	(2)	Chief Administrative Assistant
		Special Assistant
		Director of Communications

1973 = 1972 (2)
1974 = 1973 = 1972 (2)
1975 = 1974 = 1973 = 1972 (2)
1976 (1) = 1975 = 1974 = 1973 = 1972 (2)

1976	(2)	Vice Mayor
		Chief Administrative Assistant
		Special Assistant
		Director of Communications
1977		Vice Mayor
		Special Assistant
		Director of Communications
1978		Vice Mayor
		Deputy Mayors
		Special Assistant
		Director of Communications
1979		Vice Mayor
		Deputy Mayors
		Special Assistant
		Press Secretary

1980 (1) = 1979

1980 (2)		Vice Mayor
		Deputy Mayors
		Executive Assistant
		Administrative Assistant
		Press Secretary

Excerpts from the *Official Directory*, published intermittently in the *City Record*, 1968 – 80.

Yet the precision of the profile is greater than that of the directory; and the larger amount of relevant information can be obtained from the Court's profile rather than from the directory. It took the directory four years to report — "officially" as it were — the existence of Deputy Mayors in Boston's city government. The directory starts with featuring the "Mayor's Office," but the sketchy information it presents about this institution is hardly enlightening — in fact, the directory's "information" conceals the real configurations of the Court and the historical sequence of these configurations. For example, from 1968 onward the post of a "special," "executive," "chief administrative" assistant is listed in the directory continuously (it is not said whose assistant), but there is no trace of the very different governmental and political roles which associates of the Mayor played when they filled successively this position.

In a sense the Court's profile is more "official" than the directory. It is not the profile but the directory which is intelligible only for someone who has the benefit of an insider's knowledge. The informal dimension reaches into the formal one and the formal dimension reaches into the informal one. In studying the informal configuration of the Court, one follows a movement towards the true, "official" forms of Boston's government. And in reading the formal, but arcane presentation of this government, one follows a movement towards the host of "informal" configurations with which it is filled. And within the interplay of these two movements the reality of politics comes into view.[38]

8 Persons Define Places of Politics

The Court produced its "princes," very few individuals who enjoyed at one time among its many members a very special status. The ascendancy of the "princes" symbolizes especially the process of political creativeness of which the Court was the figuration. None of the individuals who became "princes" originally possessed a special place in the Court. To be still more precise: there were no places, special or otherwise, carved out in the Court.

Yet when one of those individuals acquired gradually a particular status in the Court, it appeared as if this person filled a place in the Court which evidently belonged to its configuration. The Court, it seemed, included the

---

[38] In his study on the Eisenhower Presidency Fred J. Greenstein makes a similar comparison between the *United States Organization Manual* entry for the Eisenhower White House office, on the one hand, and the "informal realities" of Eisenhower's staff organization, on the other. Cf. *The Hidden-Hand Presidency,* op. cit., pp. 144 – 147.

place from its very beginning. And yet this particular place had become known only by the person who was defining the place by his or her presence in the Court.[39]

The Alter Ego

In the history of the Court's configuration the place of the Mayor's alter ego was taken twice, by two different individuals of whom each combined the personal role of principal adviser with the official role of chief assistant.[40] Once it had been defined, the place remained known and members of the Court who aspired to shoulder the autocrat's burden attempted to move in the place presuming apparently that it was "there." But they did not succeed in defining by themselves the place of the Mayor's alter ego and hence there was no such place *actually*. Instead, the aspirants just managed to assume the position of faction leaders in the internal wrangles of the Mayor's staff,[41] or to play the Mayor's principal, the latter keeping his distance,[42] or to share with someone else the autocrat's ear.[43] Nevertheless, the place of the alter ego, once defined and known now as a place which could again be defined by a person in the Court's configuration, continued to be a focus of attention, for the members of the Court and for the public alike. Everyone was prepared to see the alter ego, and there were indeed "alter egos" who did not so much define the place where they were seen as occupy it in the eyes of Court observers.[44] Thus, when it became apparent that a member of the Court had

---

[39] As to the "Court" of President Reagan a connection between "personal inclinations" and "positions" in that "Court" has been observed: "What has happened during the first three years of Reagan's term is that his aggressive and ambitious aides have simply sorted themselves out, gravitating toward the positions that best suit their own personal inclinations and their notions of how they might best assert power and influence" (D. Kirschten, "Under Reagan, Power Resides With Those Who Station Themselves at His Door," *NJ*, Vol. 16, No. 8, Feb. 25, 1984, p. 361).

[40] During 1968 and 1969 the place was filled by Barney Frank, and from 1979 through 1983 it was filled by Micho F. Spring.

[41] Colin Diver and Bob Weinberg.

[42] Robert Kiley.

[43] Robert Kiley/Ira Jackson.

[44] When Robert Kiley left City Hall the *Boston Globe* reported: "Deputy Mayor Robert R. Kiley is possibly the most important person ever to leave Mayor Kevin H. White during his eight years of office [...]. He was, according to one aide, a 'super chief' within the administration [...]. 'Kiley has been the closest thing to an indispensable person,' said a top aide [...], there is concern [...] among some aides that Kiley's departure will leave a gap in the administration that may never be filled" (*BG*, March

again entered upon the role of principal adviser and chief assistant to the Mayor, the person in the place of the alter ego met with universal recognition, as if a place in the Court had been taken by the person to whom this place really belonged.[45]

The Court Theologian

Many intellectuals (or professors, for that matter) gave advice to the autocrat. Neither acquired a particular status in the Court, by virtue of learned reports or reasoned opinions alone. In the Court advice from these quarters ranged among lower fares, to be had often at the price of someone's vanity. Still, the Court knew an intellectual "prince": The Court theologian. The person who defined the place of the Court theologian emerged from within the Court.[46] This ascent from "inside" the Court was by no means an accident. Through the Court theologian the Court grasped the Court's existence, essence, and fate. To the members of the Court it appeared that their theologian formulated a calling which only one of them could know. When the Court theologian emerged, he made a figure of the Court happen: he took his place.

The Court theologian combined the intellectual gifts of strategic and conceptual thinking with literary skills, administrative adroitness, and political imagination. He represented, strategically as well as organizationally, the greater, that is, national aspirations which the autocrat pursued from his first reelection in 1971 until the fall of 1974. In 1975 he left his official post in City Hall but he did not leave his place in the Court. He continued to produce policy ideas and strategies and, in particular, to formulate the Mayor's plans and goals; inaugural speeches came from his pen. The Court theologian concerned himself also with the future of the Court. He recruited new members for the Court, young people whom he initiated into the life of the Court and whose professional career he helped to advance once they had gained their own position in the Court's configuration.

26, 1975). – In a rare instance Herbert Gleason was described as White's alter ego: "It may be unfair, but some at City Hall not only regard Gleason as White's man, but profess hardly to see him at all apart from the mayor. One veteran councillor said, 'He's the mayor's alter ego.' The relationship is such that it all but makes the man disappear" (BHA, Febr. 26, 1978).

[45] The person: Micho F. Spring, who began to work for the Mayor in 1976, started on her ascent in 1978 and became the alter ego in 1979.

[46] Ira Jackson.

The Politics Pro

Surprisingly, several years, six years precisely, passed before someone appeared and defined in the Court the place of the politics pro. The Court's soul was of course politics and hence every member of the Court was a "pro" — or did not partake in the Court for very long.[47] Governing amounted to politics and politics amounted to governing, a "good government" expressed indeed the soul of the Court.[48] During the first six years, then, the senior aides to the Mayor who ran the city's government also pursued politics in the interest of the Court, did "political work," as it was later called.

When the politics pro appeared[49] this relation was reversed. He held an official position in the Mayor's Office. But the position was largely a shell for purely political pursuits, distant activities that did not fall exactly into the range of the government's business proper. They were aimed at building the autocrat's party.[50]

The appearance of the politics pro as a figure of the Court brought on ambivalent views among the members of the Court and, even more so, on the part of the public. Politics was the soul of the Court; yes, this was true, almost everyone would have concurred. But using the government as an instrument for the pursuit of politics in the interest of the Court, was this not a different matter? To equate in an ostensible manner the process of politics with the interests of the Court, was this still legitimate? An answer was not easily found, if indeed there was any.[51]

Doubts notwithstanding, the figure of the politics pro was a much-favored object of public curiosity[52] and, by contraries, a phenomenon of uneasy feelings among members of the Court which they tried to cope with by hush attitudes. In the Mayor's fourth term the figure fell into disrepute. The person who had defined the place of the politics pro in the Court's configuration was no longer there and the successors[53] went about their duties, political work, under a very thin pretence of governmental service. They still filled a place in the Court, but it was now the place of the Court's acolytes.

---

[47] To be precise, there were members of the Court who proved to be apolitical; they could survive, though usually for a brief period, by finding in the Court an ecological niche.

[48] Senior members of the Court liked to express their "ideology" through the slogan: "Good government is good politics and good politics is good government." This was the slogan of Chicago's Mayor Daley as well. (Cf. E. C. Banfield, *Political Influence. A New Theory of Urban Politics*, New York 1961, Paperback edition 1965, p. 247.)

[49] Kirk O'Donnell.

[50] Cf. infra, p. 137 ff.

[51] Cf. infra, p. 196 ff.

[52] Cf. *BG*, Sept. 2, 1981; March 8, 1983.

[53] James Kelly and Dennis Morgan.

The Entrepreneur

The process of politics is to a large extent a sequence of crises. And in Boston crises abound. To be their stage was the business of the Court. Not all that happened during the autocrat's era was handled by the Court. Politics decided about politics, about the kind of crisis to be faced and the kind of crisis to be disregarded.[54] From the crises which the Court met emerged a few individuals who proved themselves able to reconcile exigencies facing the City, on the one hand, with the political concerns of the Court, on the other. Through their political skills applied to "selling" the City in the business community, to stemming off the City's financial collapse, to managing the building boom in Downtown Boston, they defined the place of the entrepreneur in the Court's configuration.[55] While they filled their place,[56] the entrepreneurs filled it quite distinctively. In the moment when events came to a head, the City of Boston appeared to act through the acts of the Court's entrepreneurs.[57] However, the entrepreneurs quickly disappeared from the ascendent, once the whirl of events had subsided. The configuration of the Court culminated in the place of the entrepreneur. But the persons defining that place defined a place *within* the Court's configuration.

9 Persons Settle the Stages of History

The people in the Court bore a mentality of their own. The bonds of association, evidence of this mentality, were strong. There was never a meeting which all members of the Court attended.[58] There existed, however, the

---

[54] Cf. B. Ferman, "Beating the Odds: Mayoral Leadership and the Acquisition of Power," op. cit.

[55] Concerning the figure of the entrepreneur in urban politics, cf. J. H. Mollenkopf, *The Contested City,* op. cit., esp. pp. 3 ff., 210 f.

[56] James V. Young was the Court's entrepreneur in matters of finance; David Rosenbloom filled the place during the fiscal crisis caused by "Proposition 2 1/2" (cf. footnote 22); and Robert J. Ryan assumed entrepreneurial responsibilities in the area of urban development.

[57] Cf. infra, pp. 79, 305 f.

[58] Still, from time to time, the Mayor convened larger groups of Court members. These meetings served many purposes of course – governing the spirits of the people in the Court was not the least of them. At one such meeting held in 1973, for example, the Mayor severely criticized everyone in presence of all others. Some suffered a "nervous breakdown," as a witness recalled. All went out of this "group-therapy session down on their knees" (Source: Interview).

invisible community of all those who shared the special experience of having acted in the field of political creativity that was the Court.

Nevertheless, within this community very important distinctions were made. The members of the Court did not view each other indiscriminately. They divided themselves into "era groups." For their acting in the Court, in so far as it engaged in founding and preserving a political body, marked the "time" of their life in the Court and it marked the fellowship they experienced in the Court during this time. Their acting in the Court created the condition for remembrance. It created the condition for history.[59]

Members of the Court identified themselves vis-à-vis all other members as a "group" by pointing to a particular "era" in the Court's past or present. It was the era during which "they" had formed, or were forming, the Court as a fellowship in politics. Thus the Court became a series of era groups and, viewed as a sequence in time, this series described the "history" of the Court.

The people of the Court shared the special experience of having acted in the Court. They did not share this experience as an actual experience, however. As such the experience differed: there were different pieces of recollection, different modes of remembrance, different spans of memory.

There were persons *in* the Court who marked the history *of* the Court. They shared one experience through many different experiences, and through the recollection of these experiences they recorded distinct stages of the one experience they shared. They recorded one history. And they settled different stages of this history. The successive stages of their history as the Court.

The sequence of era groups coincides approximately with the sequence of the Mayor's terms. The groups were not given individual names and hence I suggest the following terms to denote each group: "the founders" (1967 – 71), "the movers and shakers" (1971 – 75), "the professionals" (1976 – 79), and "the zealots" (1979 – 83).

The Founders

The first era group was largely composed of the Mayor's old-time family friends. Typically, many of them dwelled where he dwelled, on Beacon Hill. While acting in the Court, the members of this group generally concentrated their work upon the "substantive side of politics," as they liked to say. An idealistic view of public service spurred on their efforts of government. Still, in governing actually they displayed a tendency just to react to events and

---

[59] I am paraphrasing a passage in: H. Arendt, *The Human Condition*, Chicago 1958, p. 8 f.:
"Action, in so far as it engages in founding and preserving political bodies, creates the condition for remembrance, that is, for history."

developments. They did not cling to a perfectionist paradigm of government. They "loved" politics, but they did not translate their passion into the ambition to anticipate and to control everything that could possibly "crop up" in the process of politics of which they partook.

The Movers and Shakers

An aggressiveness in tackling the problems of governance, a view of politics as a subject to be mastered by "plans," a technocratic persuasion – these were the attitudes of the era group that followed. The group did not shun two great ambitions: the ambition to set up Boston under their rule as a paradigm for any future urban policy in America; and the ambition to carry Kevin White into the Oval Office on the wings of Boston's prominence. The members of the group defined themselves by such epithets as "idealists," "liberals," "professionals," thereby suggesting a disposition commensurate with the great ambitions. They had primarily been recruited because of their professional skills, and therefore they believed at first that they should draw a line between "government," or "professionalism," on the one hand, and "politics," or "partisan politics," on the other. It was their group, in particular, that was using the slogan "good government is good politics"[60] to advertise the Court. And they stuck to it, although they reached the conclusion that a government to be "good," it must be very political.

Quantitatively, the second era group was much larger than the first one. Its socio-geographic composition had become more diverse, too. Not just the circle of the Mayor's family friends, but also other social pools, inside and – even – outside Boston, had been tapped to recruit the "movers and shakers." Many talents were needed, weren't they, to steer Boston and the Mayor towards a position of splendor in America politics.

The Professionals

Most of the movers and shakers had already left the Court when the Mayor's third term began. Now the Court chiefly concerned itself with consolidating its power in the city and with pursuing a few key projects there. The Renaissance of Boston was still pursued, but more realistically. The great ambitions had shrunk to the natural interests of elected officials. The Court

---

[60] Or, as a mayoral aide put it: "We wanted to run the city and – by doing this – help to re-elect White" (Source: Interview).

wanted to continue its existence, and tying its fate to the Renaissance of Boston held the greatest promise of success.

Congruously, the third era group was largely composed of professionals, a set of "political" professionals and a set of "expert" professionals. Both sets tended to undertake their work separately rather than jointly; the type of administrator who combined political thinking with technical expertise no longer prevailed. The professionals shared neither the reformist enthusiasm of the founders nor the great plans of the movers and shakers. They consolidated and continued what had been started before the era of their own acting in the Court.

The Zealots

The fourth and last era group displayed again quite distinctive characteristics. When this group emerged, the Mayor had ruled for twelve years — which was a considerable span of time in a democratic society. Several waves of "young people" had followed the first generation of "young Turks" who had helped Kevin White to become Mayor of Boston. This group now was not only "young" in terms of the average age of its members (around 28). It was also very "young" in view of the temporal distance to the founders, the "young Turks." While the members of the group just dimly perceived the origins of the Mayor's rule in a remote past, they viewed the rule itself as a matter of course: there existed the Mayor's autocracy and the only question was how this autocracy could be made even more autocratic.

With this era group the nexus between the "origins" of the Mayor's rule — when its enthusing novelty was still its sole quality — and the late moment of its existence broke. The group was by no means indifferent to the vitality of the rule, quite to the contrary. It took great pains to "renew" the autocracy. But these efforts were not meant to be a "return to the origins" and thus to be a true renewal.[61] Instead, they were fights to fortify the group's singular experience: the complacency of an ingrown autocracy.

---

[61] The classical statement on the renovation (*rinnovazione*) of a political rule by a return to the origins (*riduzione verso il principio*) is to be found in Machiavelli's Discourses (*Discorsi*), at the beginning of Chapter 1 of the Third Book (Cf. N. Machiavelli, *Il Principe e Discorsi sopra la prima deca di Tito Livio*, ed. S. Bertelli, Milano 1960, p. 379 f.). For an English translation, cf. *The Prince and the Discourses*, with an Intr. by M. Lerner, New York 1940, 1950, p. 397 f.: "There is nothing more true than that all the things of this world have a limit to their existence; but those only run the entire course ordained for them by Heaven that do not allow their body to become disorganized, but keep it unchanged in the manner ordained, or if they change it, so do it that it shall

A large majority of the group's members, then, adopted the attitude of zealots in the cause of Kevin White. The experience of the autocracy determined their perception of politics, and their zeal consumed their political consciousness. The zealots went about governing as if they had to protect a beleaguered camp.

Among those who watched or dealt with the autocracy the defensive aggressiveness of the zealots did not go unnoticed. It particularly irritated the members of earlier era groups. The "alumni" would have liked to think of their successors as people who embodied their own — somewhat idolized — past: those exhilarating, and irretrievable, days of "public service." Instead, they encountered an insolence which they felt was certainly not justified by imperious statements of the sort: "I work for the Mayor's Office." Claiming that *they* had been inspired by an ethos of public service, the alumni looked at the zealots with contempt, and concluded: "They just want to keep the Mayor's power."[62]

10 Political Archaeology

The contempt which the alumni felt towards the zealots was not a purely historical matter. Some members of the Court from earlier eras had stayed on and thus were still acting in the Court during the era of the zealots. These "elders" did not fully conceal their critical attitude towards the "young" and their way of running the Court. The zealots, however, peddled their views and pushed their prestige. Between elders and zealots the Court had cloven.

This cleavage was only one of the various scissions in the Court that arose from the historical sequence of era groups. Or, "historically" put, through the sequence of era groups the Court had acquired a historical structure. When they divided themselves into era groups, the members of the Court situated themselves historically, and in the moment of this historical awareness they saw among themselves a scale of layers of which each represented

---

be for their advantage, and not to their injury. And as I speak of mixed bodies, such as republics or religious sects, I say that those changes are beneficial that bring them back to their original principles. And those are the best-constituted bodies, and have the longest existence, which possess the intrinsic means of frequently renewing themselves, or such as obtain this renovation in consequence of some extrinsic accidents. And it is a truth clearer than light that, without such renovation, these bodies cannot continue to exist [...]. This return of a republic to its original principles is either the result of extrinsic accident or of intrinsic prudence."

[62] Source: Interview.

another era. A sequence of the past was discerned as a structure in the present. A crucial transfiguration occurred: the notion of era groups had been a matter of recollection; the notion of layers, however, was a matter of status, prestige, importance. "History" became "hierarchy."

The composition of the Court contained its history, and this history had formed the social fabric of the Court. Or, in methodological terms, the study of the Court's composition is the study of the Court's history, and the study of the Court's history is the study of the Court's organization. Thus, it was not purely an archaeological interest which induced us to pursue the movements of these persons who defined in the Court places of politics and the movements of those who settled the stages of its history. To know these movements helped us to see how a field of political creativity emerges through its manifestations. We grasped a fragment of analytical knowledge which we would not have wanted to miss. Still, our archaeological pursuits were intended also to produce a fragment of practical knowledge: insights into the workings of the Court. We practiced archaeology and we shall presently continue to do so, but it is *political* archaeology. The movements of persons which we pursue are the elementary movements of politics. They will not be known if we study only the composition, the structure of political bodies. We must dig deeper, through the layers of composition, the layers of history, towards the field of movements, the field of creativity where politics defines what politics is.[63]

11 The Many Emerge As the One

The movements of persons making the Court were movements in the mode of organization. They suggested a transfiguration. What was the Court? The answer is: persons. The persons in the Court. And this answer tells all. The Court had no reality beyond the reality of the persons in the Court.

Yet, these persons made the Court "appear" — *the* Court. There was a body of politics. There were political organisms, distinct configurations of people. There was the Court. A phenomenon of organization. What was the Court? The answer could be: A system. An entity of power to be used for the purpose of governing. And this answer would mark a transpersonal

---

[63] The necessity of an "archaeological acquisition of knowledge" (*archäologische Forschung*) in the study of politics is briefly alluded to in: M. P. C. M. van Schendelen, "Das Geheimnis des Europäischen Parlaments: Einfluß auch ohne Kompetenzen," *Zeitschrift für Parlamentsfragen*, Jg. 15, H. 3, Sept. 1984, pp. 415–426.

objectivity. The Court had an existence of its own, quite apart from the persons who just happened to be members of the Court.

Two answers, and only one can be right. No doubt, persons formed an organization or, equally true, an organization existed to which a number of persons belonged. But whose primacy was it? The primacy of persons over the organization? Or the primacy of organization over the persons? Did a preeminence of persons preclude the organizational manifestations *of* the Court from being more than fluid configurations of individuals *in* the Court? Or did the emergence of these manifestations entail a process of organization that subjected the persons in the Court to a system of schematized behavior?

Through the progress of our analysis the moment of transfiguration in the movements of the persons making the Court appears to have split. It seems to us that we see two different matters: the tangible but infinite presence of persons, on the one side, and the transpersonal, hence objective existence of an organization, on the other. And reviewing our progress towards this discovery, we might well be induced to conclude that it has been a progress of analysis towards the actual shaping of things: "from" the persons making the Court "to" the Court made of persons.

If we held on to this conclusion, however, we would "forget" the empirical datum from which our analysis proceeds. We would commit the classical error of substantiating inference, reifying what "exists" only in the mode of analytical abstraction and has no independent existence whatsoever apart from the datum in whose analysis it "appears."[64]

---

[64] Cf. Plato, *Cratylus,* 388 c: "A name is, then, an instrument of teaching and of separating reality (*ousia*), as a shuttle is an instrument of separating the web." – Aristotle, *Posterior Analytics,* 100 a 3 ff.: "Thus sense-perception gives rise to memory, as we hold; and repeated memories of the same thing give rise to experience; because the memories, though numerically many, constitute a single experience. And experience, that is the universal when established as a whole in the soul [...]. Let us re-state what we said just now with unsufficient precision. As soon as one individual precept has 'come to a halt' in the soul, this is the first beginning of the presence there of a universal (because although it is the particular that we perceive, the act of perception involves the universal, e. g. 'man,' not a 'man, Callias')." – *Metaphysics* 1087 a 15: "Knowledge, like the verb 'to know,' has two senses of which one is potential and the other actual. The potentiality being, as matter, universal and indefinite, has a universal and indefinite object; but the actuality is definite and has a definite object, because it is particular and deals with the particular." – Cf. further *Metaphysics* 1003 a 10, 1053 b 17, 1060 b 20, 1087 a 2. – For contemporary versions of this classical "methodological" wisdom, cf. M. J. Adler, *The Difference of Man and the Difference It Makes,* New York 1967, esp. pp. 156 ff., 346 ff.; H. Eulau, *Micro-Macro Political Analysis. Accents of Inquiry,* Chicago 1969, Introducton: "On Units and Levels of Analysis," pp. 1 – 19.

The data from which our analysis proceeds are the movements of persons making the Court. When we consider these movements structurally, that is, as movements in the mode of organization, they continue of course to be the movements of persons. The persons whose movements they are do not "disappear" simply because of our analytical progress "from" looking at them, the persons, "to" looking at the phenomenon of organization, the Court, which these persons are producing. Or, inversely, our analysis would be increasingly devoid of reality if its "progress" impelled us to see an "organization" rather than the persons making it.[65]

Methodically remembering the path of one's method is the method of avoiding the pitfalls of methods. We proceeded "from" looking at the persons making the Court "to" looking at a phenomenon of organization, the Court. In taking this path, we followed those movements in the mode of organization that occurred as the movements of persons making the Court. Strictly, then, not a "method," a method satisfactory to the postulates of methodology, but these movements themselves were our path of inquiry. We did not study an "organization," but searchingly traced and retraced the movements of which a phenomenon was made that appeared as an organization. Really, we never ceased looking at the persons making the Court. But, looking at them more carefully, we discerned in the ongoing movements of these persons moments of transfiguration: persons forming through the pattern of their movements forms of organization.

For the purpose of further analysis in the following I shall speak of "organisms of the Court" or "configurations of Court members." However, we should keep the methodical status of these concepts in mind. They describe only what we "see" in the course of our analysis; they do not define any reality of an "organization."

We observe the movements of persons. We shall see these persons "appear" in certain forms of organization. We shall probe our vision of "organisms" and "configurations." And we shall discover movements of persons.

Configurations of Court members arose on account of pragmatic politics. In order to set about its work, the Court needed to become an "actor."

---

[65] Concerning the conventional understanding of "organization," cf.: L. v. Wiese, "Organisation," in: *Handwörterbuch der Sozialwissenschaften,* Vol. 8, ed. E. v. Beckerath et al., Stuttgart 1964, pp. 108–111; A. L. Stinchcombe, "Formal Organization," in: ed. N. J. Smelser, *Sociology. An Introduction,* New York 1967, 1973, 2nd ed., pp. 23–65; P. M. Blau, "Theories of Organization," in: D. L. Sills, ed. *International Encyclopedia of the Social Sciences,* Vol. 11, s. l., 1968, pp. 297–305. – As to the historical and analytical narrowness of contemporary "theories of organization," cf.: E.-W. Böckenförde, "Organ, Organismus, Organisation, politischer Körper," in: O. Brunner, W. Conze, R. Kosseleck, eds., *Geschichtliche Grundbegriffe. Historisches Lexikon zur politisch-sozialen Sprache in Deutschland,* Vol. 4, Stuttgart 1978, pp. 519–622.

Pragmatic politics requires that there is "someone" who promotes a policy and operates within the governmental apparatus, who negotiates and enforces purposes and resolves, who appears in the arena of politics. To do politics, the Court had to act politics: visibly, distinctly, authoritatively.

The Court entered acting as an agent in politics by coalescing into organisms such as the "Mayor's cabinet," "policy committees," "mayoral offices," or "campaign organizations." Under paradigmatic conditions the process of coalescence was attuned to the exigencies of politics. Then the Court was ready to respond to any new political development by producing a political organism which matched the new situation that had arisen. While a perfect attunement was rarely the case, of course, the "life" of the organisms – that is, their appearance, their existence, their disappearance – closely reflected the political "pulsations" of the Court coping with the vicissitudes of politics. In acting as an agent in politics, the Court "pulsated" – organisms appeared and disappeared, grew and shrank, interlocked, split, and mutated. These "pulsations" could be perceived as one observed the "life" of the organisms. They provided the material for the study of the Court as an actor. Through empirical observation one could apprehend the coalescence of Court members into organisms, and the alterations and the disappearance of existent organisms. And thereby one could detect the political "actor" in the manifestations of the Court.

The Mandarins

In the course of the Court's existence three government officials emerged who conducted independent operations. These operations, however, were neither separate nor marginal operations. On the contrary, they were quite essential to the political pursuits of the Court.

Their peculiar nature sprung from the special status of the officials who ran them. Each of these officials incorporated within the scope of his or her operation the Court's highest authority: the MAYOR.[66] Each was a sectional Mayor, as it were. Or, to use a more telling term, these three government officials were the Mandarins of the Court.

There was a Mandarin in the domain of human services,[67] a Mandarin in the domain of administrative services,[68] and a third Mandarin whose domain was the politics of the government's policies.[69]

---

[66] On the difference between "Mayor" and "MAYOR," cf. infra, p. 254 ff.
[67] Lawrence M. Quealy.
[68] Edward T. Sullivan.
[69] Micho F. Spring.

Mandarin Quealy officially held the position of a "special assistant to the Mayor." He had already worked for Mayor John Collins, the predecessor of Mayor White, and he served in the latter's administration from its beginning in 1968. His extensive experience in the government of Boston — almost a singular distinction — was one of the two assets that made him a Mandarin. The second asset was his wealth of personal contacts. "Larry," as he was generally called, knew everyone in the city, in Boston's neighborhoods as well as in City Hall.

Mandarin Quealy's operation was composed of himself, a small staff, and the network of his contacts. Its purpose was undoubtedly important: it personalized the government. "Larry" gave the government a human face. He helped people to shed the awe, anger, and frustration with which they had become filled running into the intricacies of the government's bureaucracy or the arrogance of government officials. "Larry" provided guidance, he opened up direct channels, he showed how to take shortcuts. If a citizen wanted to talk to the Mayor, he could call upon Quealy and Quealy did not only respond but did so in a manner that made one feel that one was indeed talking with the Mayor.[70]

Individuals as well as community groups addressed to Mandarin Quealy all kinds of requests and complaints. Typically, a citizens group would have been waiting for a long time to obtain from the City a commitment to build a playground in their neighborhood — or the commitment would have been made but no action had been taken. Quealy would be asked to intervene on behalf of the neighborhood. When he lent his support, the project of the playground would "suddenly" move quite rapidly towards its completion. Or, to quote two other typical examples, Quealy would assist someone in getting a zoning variance or he would support a neighborhood association with its request that the impact of a projected high-rise on the surrounding residential area be mitigated by imposing a limit upon its height.

Certain requests could better be handled by a city councillor or a member of the Massachusetts Legislature. Mandarin Quealy would still render his assistance in referring such a request to the councillor, state representative, or senator whom he could trust with it — and would, on that occasion, widen his operation by winning a new contact or reviving an old one.

The Mayor appreciated the role of Mandarin Quealy. He had him acting as his personal representative to neighborhood associations, community leaders, or citizens groups. The neighborhoods were not Quealy's exclusive domain, of course, but every other government agency which became active

---

[70] The Mayor, on the other hand, called upon Quealy's services when he was "gearing up" his election campaigns. Cf., for example, *BG,* Nov. 2, 1982.

in this area had to come to terms with this Mandarin's operation. While the Mayor's most elaborate "system" of neighborhood services, the "Office of Public Service" and the network of "Little City Halls," spread over Boston,[71] Quealy's operation continued on a parallel course — and it did so quite independently. In some cases, even, the "City" would not act in the domain of neighborhood services without having before consulted with Mandarin Quealy.

Mandarin Sullivan outwardly occupied a position more elevated than Quealy's. He was the head of the Administrative Services Department since 1968 and he held the title of "Vice-Mayor" since 1976. Sullivan grew into a Mandarin on account of his vast administrative responsibilities and his long, loyal service to the interests of Mayor White. The most important aspect of his role as a Mandarin was his privilege to make his own choices regarding the scope and the subjects of his participation in the governmental process. The Mayor would ask Sullivan from time to time to take up a certain task. On the whole, however, Sullivan defined his own role. He showed an interest in a pending issue or in the implementation of a policy and he was accorded, almost automatically, the rank of the leading official.

Mandarin Sullivan's operation habitually included three particular tasks: bargaining with labor unions on behalf of the city, representing the Mayor and the city to municipal associations, and cultivating the relations with administrators, labor representatives, urban officials in the world of public administration outside Boston. Dealing with these tasks, Sullivan acted more or less independently.

Micho F. Spring joined the White administration in the fall of 1976, emerged as the Mayor's chief assistant and *alter ego* in 1979 – 80, and was appointed "Deputy Mayor for Policy Management" in September 1980. She was a Mandarin because she was the Mayor's alter ego. Her singular status in the Court was attested every day by the other persons in the Court. Many held the view that they had checked with the "Mayor" politically sensitive questions when they had checked them with Micho Spring. Some people even retained a few "chips" of information, data, strategy, and so forth, when they had a meeting with the Mayor. There was still that other presence of the "Mayor," Mandarin Spring, and holding one's own in her presence could prove to be even more important.

Besides, Mandarin Spring had succeeded in amplifying her personal role of being the Mayor's alter ego by establishing herself in the formal role of "managing" the apparatus of the government as well as its policies. In this capacity Spring conducted an ambitious and elaborate operation that

---

[71] Cf. infra, p. 132 ff.

encompassed all of the government. She had her own staff which included experts for every major governmental activity, and she had been given the authority to "evaluate" the performance of all personnel, including department heads, regarding their "efficiency" in implementing policies and delivering public services. She – or one of her staffers – enjoyed the prerogative of being free to meddle in any new policy of any city agency.[72] The prestige of her operation in the Court was such that many members of the Court anticipated Mandarin Spring's control and therefore chose to invite her – or one of her staffers – to participate in their policy planning at a stage when any of her suggestions, wishes, or objections could still fully be considered and, if advisable, adopted.

The Mayor's Office

The best known and yet the least understood organism of the Court was the "Mayor's Office." It was indeed a phenomenon of organization that easily defied a precise definition. The expression "Mayor's Office" by which this phenomenon was generally known was only a nominal shell; it diffused rather than facilitated an understanding of the phenomenon. "There are lots of offices who answer 'Mayor's Office,'" a former Court member observed,[73] indicating the nominal confusion regarding this organism of the Court. It would have been possible to establish a list of all those offices and to present a host of impressive designations such as the "Mayor's Office of Policy Management," the "Mayor's Office of Federal Relations," the "Mayor's

---

[72] Cf. CR, Sept. 22, 1980, p. 1: "Mayor Kevin H. White, on September 8, outlined a new set of criteria designed to improve the management of city government by quantifying and evaluating the performance of city departments [...]. Some of the new objectives will be aimed at making city government run more smoothly administratively [...]. Department reports will be compiled quarterly and will be verified and evaluated by the policy management staff through independent data collection and assessment methods. [...] The departments will be monitored by the Policy Management staff specialists in fiscal affairs, transportation and energy, development, neighborhood services, and education and human services." – In an interview a member of the "policy management staff" offered some further explanations. The staff would "verify" and "evaluate" the "performance of city departments" by "polling" residents of Boston. In doing so, the staff would not be interested in getting at the "real" performance of the departments; they would rather be interested in finding out how this performance were "perceived" by Boston residents. In other words, performance was "measured" not so much in terms of good services, but in terms of good public relations. A short biography of Micho Spring can be found in: CR, Sept. 29, 1980, p. 916 f.

[73] Source: Interview.

Office of Elderly Affairs," the "Mayor's Office of Public Safety," the "Mayor's Office of Housing and Development," and so forth and so on. However, such a list would not only have needed to be revised constantly, it would also have suggested a false notion of the phenomenon under inquiry. The numerical and the nominal manifestations of the "Mayor's Office" changed continuously. It happened more often than not that some "Mayor's Office of ..." already had long been defunct when the news about its existence reached the level of public awareness. And the mayoral offices differed widely in their textures, functions, and jurisdictions. In one case the name "Mayor's Office of ..." could represent a large core group of mayoral advisors, in another case it could just stand for the one-man operation of a marginal Court member.

The "Mayor's Office" was known as an organizational phenomenon. Yet a search for its "organization" would have unearthed not any organization — save the deceptive array of "mayoral offices." In what then did its existence consist and how had it been formed?

There were persons, members of the Court, who constituted the "Mayor's Office." They each held a position somewhere in the governmental apparatus. And they all together were identified with a political organism that generally was called the "Mayor's Office." The existence of this organism was very real, yet it never existed in an established way. It was not a consequence of organization, yet it emerged from an aggregation of persons.

The organism "Mayor's Office" appeared wherever a number of persons congregated acting the "Mayor's Office." And this organism was shaped whenever such a congregation occurred. Its constitution did not date from one formative event but was a continuing process. It was constituted as often and in as many cases as persons in the Court formed themselves into the "Mayor's Office."

It emerged from an aggregation of persons. Principally, any number of persons in the Court could coalesce into any kind of aggregation and act the "Mayor's Office." And the persons in the Court used this competence quite liberally indeed.[74] Nevertheless, they generally tended to coalesce into a few major types of aggregation which persisted, more or less, in the continuing constitution of the "Mayor's Office." Thus, the aggregation of persons from which the "Mayor's Office" emerged happened, to a considerable extent, within a specific structure of aggregation.

It was through this structure of aggregation that the "Mayor's Office" appeared.

The structure was composed of four types of aggregation.

---

[74] Cf. infra, p. 233 ff.

(a) A relatively small group of persons constituted the *bureau* of Mayor White: the Mayor himself, his secretaries, an appointments secretary, a receptionist, a few assistants, and one or two close advisers.[75]

(b) The *staff* of the Mayor — all his assistants, aides, advisers, policy planners — was a much larger group functioning as an aggregation of persons essential to the appearing of the "Mayor's Office"; it will presently be considered more closely.

(c) The aggregation formed by the *Vice Mayor* and the *Deputy Mayors* was a "system" of administration rather than an instrument of planning and action, though individual axes of deliberation and decision making ran from the Mayor to the Deputy Mayors and the Vice Mayor.[76] This aggregation interlaced with the "cabinet," as will shortly be explained.

(d) Finally, there were the *proconsuls,* former members of the mayoral staff, who had been advanced to heads of government agencies. Each proconsul directed a division of Boston's government and directed it as a constitutive member of the "Mayor's Office."[77] Within the "Mayor's Office" the proconsuls appeared in various roles: as Deputy Mayor, member of the "cabinet," the head or member of a "policy committee," a "task force," or simply as the principal executive of a mayoral policy.[78]

---

[75] In the spring of 1981 the bureau comprised the following persons/positions: Christopher Bator, Special Assistant; Stephen Dunleavy, Assistant; Donna Floyd, Receptionist; Buford Kaigler, Special Assistant; James Kelly, Special Assistant; Leslie Macissac, Administrative Secretary; Dorothy Novak, Assistant; George Regan, Director of Communications; Elizabeth A. Roy, Administrative Assistant; Kathy Ryan, Administrative Secretary; Micho Spring, Deputy Mayor; Carolyn Toronto, Secretary; Kevin H. White, Mayor.

[76] Examples: the axis "White — Deputy Mayor Kane" in the field of arts, festivities, cultural events; the axis "White — Deputy Mayor Ryan" in the field of urban development; the axis "White — Vice Mayor Sullivan" in the field of municipal administration. — Each axis existed and functioned on account of a *personal* rapport between the Mayor and Deputy Mayor X or Y, and therefore tended to be an exclusive structure.

[77] Two examples: (a) David Rosenbloom, 1973 Director, Parkman Center for Urban Affairs (this institution was usually described, somewhat hyperbolically, as "Mayor White's urban think tank"), 1975 Executive Assistant to the Mayor, 1976 – 83 Commissioner of Health and Hospitals. — (b) Robert J. Ryan, 1974 Assoc. Commissioner, Assessing Department, 1977 Director, Office of Property Tax Equalization, 1978 Director, BRA. Constitutionally, the BRA is not a city agency within the jurisdiction of Boston's Mayor. In 1981 a senior associate of Mayor White described Ryan nevertheless as "almost a staff person" (staff meaning the Mayor's staff; Source: Interview).

[78] In 1980 – 81 David Rosenbloom, for instance, chaired the "Mayor's Committee on Proposition 2 1/2." He ran the city's health and hospitals system *and* at the same time orchestrated the cuts in the city's budget necessitated by proposition 2 1/2 (see footnote 22 as to this proposition).

The Staff

Between 1968 and 1971 the Mayor drew advice, assistance, and expert knowledge from a very small staff. In fact, the few persons in his administration with whom he met to discuss the conduct of his government were not really staffers but leading officials in the government.[79] A supporting staff provided some technical assistance, but the work of these aides was poorly organized. They were all "generalists," "people," as a Court member explained, "who could become instant experts on anything."[80]

In 1972 the staff expanded considerably and became a core aggregation of "policy specialists" in the Court. It continued to exist as such until 1975.[81]

After 1976 the aggregation of mayoral aides took on still another form. First, the previous specialization lessened; staffers emerged who possessed both technical expertise and the administrative-political skills which the autocrat's government particularly required. Secondly, a certain number of aides moved into line departments where they joined the "colonies," another type of organisms of the Court.[82] Thirdly, the staff became layered through the operation of Mandarin Spring. Her "policy management" introduced an uneasy differentiation of a higher tier from a lower tier.

All these developments resulted in a greater complexity of the staff which it kept, as well as its numerical size, until the end of the Mayor's rule.

In its expanded and increasingly complex form the staff was fulfilling the following functions:

(a) It made up a large pool of information and political intelligence. Staff meetings, if they went well, could produce a fairly complete map of the current scene of politics in Boston, Massachusetts, Washington, and other relevant places.

---

[79] Typically, a meeting would include: (a) Kevin White, Barney Frank, and, later, Robert Weinberg (chief assistants), Francis Tivnan (Director of Communications) or (b) Kevin White, Barney Frank, Theodore Anzalone (Assessing Commissioner).

[80] Source: Interview.

[81] The following list details the principal areas of specialization and the names of aides who were responsible for policies in these areas. One can appraise the size of the aggregation by considering that a number of subordinate staffers was attached to each of these experts, in some cases a few, in other cases two dozens. The list: Ira Jackson, Robert Kiley (generalists); Robert Schwartz (education); Andrew Olins (housing); Fred Salvucci (transportation); Frank Tivnan (communication); David Niklaus (government reorganization); Kirk O'Donnell (neighborhood issues); Ann Lewis (women in politics); Mary Davidson (social services); David Strohm (community development planning); Peter Richardson (urban development); Nancy Huntington, Teri Weidner (special projects).

[82] Cf. infra, p. 91 f.

(b) The collective expertise of the staff enabled the Court to deal with the government agencies and with the line departments, in particular, on an equal level. Each specialist and his sub-staff "monitored" the agencies and departments which fell under his "jurisdiction." The collective expertise also helped the Court to hold its own in the process of bargaining with governmental agencies in the State (Massachusetts) or in Washington, and to hold its own as well when it responded to the pressure of interest groups.

(c) The staff could be used as an instrument for long-range planning and as a laboratory for the analysis and the resolve of policy issues.

(d) As an aggregation of experts whose personal backgrounds, professional experiences, and political views widely differed, the staff reproduced the social and political environment within which the Court operated. This representative quality of the staff, forming a microcosm of American society, was particularly crucial at the time when the Mayor pursued his national ambitions. In moments of creative interplay among staff members the diversity of views could develop its own momentum and spark the staffers to a confluene of ideas and purposes; their group then acquired, however temporarily, the additional quality of a symbiotic thrust.

(e) Finally, the staff functioned as a pressure group whom each of its members or a group of them could enlist to "push something through" in the political world "outside" the Court. Since every staffer knew people in this world, the staff as a whole provided a wealth of contacts which no staff member alone could have accumulated. By giving each other access to these contacts, the staffers greatly intensified, individually as well as collectively, their political influence.[83]

The preceding account describes the staff as it existed from 1972 to 1983. However, one qualification must be made.

Between 1972 and 1975 the staff members interacted with each other in the mode of peers. Though of course there were differences in rank and pay, they performed as a team.[84] In 1975–76 and the succeeding years the staffers lost this latitude in sharing their responsibilities;[85] their relations became

---

[83] Cf., for comparative purposes, M. J. Malbin's study on the influence of congressional staff: *Unelected Representatives. Congressional Staff and the Future of Representative Government,* op. cit.

[84] As individuals *within* their group they knew competition and conflicts, of course. Acting as members *of* their group, however, they performed as a team.

[85] This is one of the reasons why, in later years, the period 1972–75 was regarded increasingly as the "golden age" of the staff.

increasingly stratified and this stratification put constraints on their interaction. They went about their work as a group that had become divided into different segments.

12 Creativeness and Efficiency

Emerging continually from a chaos of power, the government of Boston's autocrat was always in need of more efficiency. It needed the discipline whose very negation it was. Being founded against order, it could not be made really efficient.

Nevertheless, the need to preserve whatever efficiency it had could not be neglected either. It was meant to be a government that would work, after all. What then was done? Was the efficacy of this government periodically reviewed? It seemed so, for public announcements regarding an increase of this government's efficiency were made quite abundantly throughout the time it existed. And were then its works reorganized indeed? They were and they were not, for every "reorganization" was severely restrained by an inherent inhibition: persons came first in the "organization" − or "reorganization" − of this government. Theirs was a primacy over institutions.

All attempts to make the autocrat's government work efficiently were therefore undertaken in a particular way. When certain members of the Court had proved, over a period of time, that they possessed particular talents for particular tasks, they were gradually recognized as persons who by their very presence and their activity were defining distinct roles of government. Ever so often these roles were ratified and given an institutional name. Or, in other words, the "government" was kept in a state of "efficiency" by adjusting its "form" to the functions which Court members in the government had already carved out for themselves.

Each of these recognitions was customarily announced as another "reorganization" of the autocrat's government ("to provide better services for the citizens of Boston"). But the mode of recognition did not vary very much. There were actually three principal modes:

(a) to nominate someone "Vice Mayor" or "Deputy Mayor";
(b) to include someone in the "Mayor's cabinet"; or
(c) to appoint someone member or head of a "policy committee."

None of these titles, positions, and institutions represented any constitutional provision of Boston's government. But each became a prominent part of the Mayor's rule. Each acquired the status of governmental authority. But none represented more than some persons clustered together under some institutional name.

The Vice Mayor and the Deputy Mayors

The cluster of Deputy Mayors was introduced in February 1974. By his appointment each Deputy Mayor was formally recognized as "supervisor" and "coordinator" of all government agencies within his area of responsibility.[86] In 1976 one of the Deputy Mayors[87] was promoted "Vice Mayor" and thus was recognized in a role which he had inofficially fulfilled since the early years of the Court. The cluster of Vice Mayor and Deputy Mayors continued to exist in the Court until the end of the Mayor's rule.[88]

The Cabinet

From the beginning of the Mayor's rule a number of persons in the Court clustered around him and formed an organism of aides and advisors that was called the "cabinet." There were periods when the Mayor met with the cabinet once or twice a week; in other periods cabinet meetings were chaired by Vice Mayor Sullivan, and the Mayor did rarely attend. The cabinet did not have the formal structure nor the formal status of a decision-making body. Still, policies, and politics of course, were discussed, approved, or disapproved. Members of the cabinet could agree on anything, but nothing was a binding "decision." On the other hand, though, the cabinet was composed of persons who carried responsibility in setting the policies of the government. This individual status of each cabinet member was affirmed when, towards the end of the Mayor's first term, each was given the responsi-

---

[86] Edward T. Sullivan, Director of Administrative Services, became "Deputy Mayor for Administrative Services"; Robert Kiley, assistant to the Mayor, became "Deputy Mayor for Policy Planning and Human Services" (or: "D. M. for Policy Planning and Neighborhood Services." Typically, the areas of responsibility were only vaguely defined); Robert J. Vey, Director of the Public Facilities Department, became "Deputy Mayor for Capital Improvement and Construction" (or "D. M. for Capital Improvement and Physical Operations").

[87] Edward T. Sullivan.

[88] Among the Deputy Mayors several changes took place between 1974 and 1983. 1975: Kiley (who had left the government) was replaced as Deputy Mayor by Katharine D. Kane who at that time directed the "Mayor's Office of Boston Bicentennial." In 1976 the Deputy Mayors were: Kane, Vey, and Clarence Jones, Director of the "Mayor's Office of Human Rights." In 1980: Kane, Jones, and James V. Young, the city's Treasurer-Collector. In 1981: Kane, Micho Spring, Robert J. Ryan, Director of the BRA. In 1983: Kane, Spring, Ryan, and Lowell R. Richards, Treasurer-Collector.

bility for overseeing a number of government agencies (the Deputy Mayors and their similar tasks notwithstanding!).[89]

Policy Committees

The Court produced innumerable "policy committees," "task forces," "working groups." Its members congregated incessantly into clusters of this type. They went about governing —
— by forming committees;
— by keeping them alive temporarily as tools for interacting, for debating and formulating policies;
— by disbanding these committees or, rather, by letting them just disintegrate;
— by forming new committees, new task forces,
repeating the same course of action.

In view of the mode of procedure which they decidedly preferred, the members of the Court constituted a government of committees.[90]

---

[89] In 1968 – 69 the cabinet included: Barney Frank, William I. Cowin, Samuel V. Merrick (all Mayor's Office); Edward T. Sullivan, David W. Davis (Deputy Director, Administrative Services); Hale Champion (Administrator, BRA); Paul Parks (Director, Model Cities Program); Herbert P. Gleason (Corporation Counsel); Theodore v. Anzalone (Assessing Commissioner); Daniel J. Finn (Director, Office of Public Service); Herman Hemingway (Assoc. Commissioner, Housing Inspection). In 1974: Robert R. Kiley, Ira Jackson, David Niklaus (all Mayor's Office); Robert J. Vey (Deputy Mayor); Frank M. Tivnan (Director of Communications); Herbert P. Gleason; Robert T. Kenney (Director, BRA); Theodore V. Anzalone; James V. Young (Collector-Treasurer); Gerald W. Bush (Director, Commerce and Manpower Department); Paul Parks; Kirk O'Donnell (Director, Office of Public Service). In 1976: Edward T. Sullivan, Katharine D. Kane, Robert J. Vey, Clarence Jones, James V. Young, Kirk O'Donnell, Frank M. Tivnan, Larry Quealy, David Niklaus. In 1981: Edward T. Sullivan, Katharine D. Kane, Micho Spring, David Rosenbloom (Commissioner, Health and Hospitals); Robert J. Ryan (Director, BRA).

[90] At the national level, the reality of executive power too is characterized by a proliferation of committees, task forces, working groups etc. It would be a major research task, for instance, simply to survey the "offices," "concils," and similar entities that flourished in the Reagan White House: National Security Planning Group, Office of Policy Development, Cabinet Councils (six), Office of Policy Information, White House Planning and Evaluation Office, group of legislative strategists, Office of Public Liaison, Office of Legislative Affairs, Office of Administration, Political Affairs Office, congressional relations staff, Intergovernmental Affairs Office, Management and Administration Council, Legal Policy Council, etc., etc. — Since the establishment of the Fifth Republic the government of France has increasingly become a government of committees. Cf. P. Verrier, *Les services de la présidence de la république*, Paris 1971, p. 13 f.: "C'est un nouvel aspect des moyens d'action du Président de la République que l'on aborde avec l'étude

As tools of governing the committees were very pliable and therefore ideal instruments of political manipulation. When they were handled with skill, the effects using them could be very strong. Of course, the selection of committee members was the decisive element in forging an effective committee. In making a selection, skillful operators observed the following rules:

(a) The policy issue to be dealt with by the committee is the principal criterion of choosing the committee members.

(b) Each is chosen on account of his or her personal assets: the expertise, experience, and political savvy that bears upon the specific task of the committee.

(c) The members of the committee are not recruited as representatives of the government agencies where they hold their official positions (and their superiors ought to know as little as possible about their assignments in advance). The understanding is that they serve the interests of the Court.

(d) The members of the committee are chosen primarily in view of the committee's specific task. Any change in the nature of this task is followed by a change of the committee's composition.[91]

---

des conseils et comités qui se tiennent à l'Elysée [...]. Le gouvernement par conseil, toujours prisé en France, fait aussi partie de la 'panoplie' de la Ve République et il est bien connu que la participation du chef de l'Etat à ceux-ci est loin de consister en une simple formalité." In his study on *Les conseillers du Président* (Paris 1980) Samy Cohen again stresses the importance of the "conseils élyséens, structures de délibération les plus élevées de l'Etat." He explains: "Depuis 1959, se tiennent à l'Elysée deux types de conseils: le *Conseil des Ministres* [...] et les *conseils restreints* ou *conseils interministériels* [...] les conseils restreints tiennent une place extrêmement importante dans le contrôle que le Président de la République peut exercer sur les affaires du pays et ce n'est guère par hasard si depuis 1959 ces conseils n'ont cessé de se multiplier. [...] Puis il y a les autres conseils − en fait les plus nombreux − qui n'ont ni composition, ni compétence particulières et qui se réunissent selon les circonstances sur les sujets les plus divers: orientations budgétaires, éducation, énergie, espaces verts, préparation des sommets franco-allemands" (p. 66−67). Cf. further: C. Dulong, *La vie quotidienne à l'Elysée au temps de Charles de Gaulle*, Paris 1974, 1975, Ch. VI, pp. 171 ff.

[91] The project of the "Boston Plan" (see Chapter 1, footnote 50) provides a good example of this rule. The plan was put together by a policy committee whose members were all mayoral aides: Andy Olins (housing adviser), John Drew (Office of Federal Relations), Bob Schwartz (education adviser), Jack Murphy (personnel adviser), Micho Spring (mayoral assistant). The stage of preparing the plan was followed by the stage of "selling it in Washington." In view of the latter task the Mayor decided to have a new policy committee. It had quite a different composition: John Drew, Charles Atkins (Employment and Economic Policy Administration), Andy Olins, Robert Walsh (BRA), George Seybolt (EDIC), Bradley Biggs (Boston Housing Authority), Emily Lloyd (Mayor's Office), John Weis (Office of Planning and Program Development).

Colonies

The members of the Court were not identified regularly by their titles, nominations, or official functions. To make the Court transparent would have meant to reveal a great deal of political intelligence. Occasionally, the names and the functions of members of the Court were made known, but then this was done upon political considerations and not for the benefit of public knowledge.

There were then organisms of the Court of which it would seem that they never existed if only official records were used to discern all the extension and the complete structure of the Court. Not a few members of the Court were dispersed throughout the apparatus of the government and nevertheless performed functions in the Court, functions which were often quite important. They constituted the outer Court, its "colonies" in government agencies whose dominant actors were not mostly members of the Court.[92] In appearance they were employed by these agencies, and they supposedly worked under the direction of the respective agencies heads, but, in fact, they worked at tasks which were set by the interests and the agendas of the Court.

The colonies in the outer Court came into existence because of three reasons:

(a) The colonies were the Court's tools for exerting its control over the apparatus of the government. Through implanting its colonies the Court spread over the government like a spider's web.

(b) While the number of employees in the mayoral offices and the number of these offices as well were burgeoning, the Mayor's budget did not grow to the same extent. By creating the colonies, the budgetary restrictions on the employment of Court members could largely be overridden. The web of colonies provided the Court with a system of financial support.

(c) The Court preferred to shroud its operations in elusiveness and enigmas. The colonies constituted a system of concealment perfectly attuned to this prepossession.

Numerically, the size of the colonies varied considerably. In some cases the colony consisted of just a few persons. In other cases it consisted of two

---

[92] For comparative purposes, cf. N. W. Polsby's statement concerning the system of colonies in the administration of President Nixon: "Centralization of policy making was only half of the latter day Nixon administrative program. The other half consisted in systematic attempts to place functionaries who can best be described as political agents in the bureaus and departments, administrators whose job it was to report to the White House on the political fidelity of the executive branch" (*Consequences of Party Reform*, Oxford 1983, p. 92; the sources of evidence are listed by Polsby on page 220, footnote 10).

or three dozen persons. Some mayoral offices were set up almost wholly as a colony. The total number of colonists at a given time varied between 40 and 150 persons.

As colonists, members of the Court held various kinds of posts. An assistant to the Mayor was listed as "assistant corporation counsel," for instance,[93] or the editor of the *City Record* as an employee in the Traffic and Parking Department,[94] or the Mayor's press aide as "planner" in the Economic Development and Industrial Commission.[95][96] Or they were colonists of double standing: their employment was financed by funds from the Federal Government, and these funds were administered by an agency that hosted colonists.[97]

The Political Organization

All major organisms of the Court have been surveyed — except one. The organism that remains to be considered did not represent the one or the other movement of creativity in the Court but reflected the very essence of the Court as a field of political creativity. It was called the "political organization" by the members of the Court, and outsiders called it the "political machine." Both terms evoke some truth about this organism but also suggest conclusions which fall short of an adequate understanding. The "political organization" was a very complex phenomenon. It has been categorized much too easily. It requires a separate, detailed analysis. Such an analysis will be undertaken in the next chapter.

---

[93] Michael Kelly in 1972.

[94] Joseph Fahey in 1976.

[95] George Regan in 1976. As "planners" in the BRA were listed, for instance: Andrew Olins, the Mayor's housing adviser, Emily Lloyd, the Mayor's transportation adviser, in 1976; Jim Leitner and Lisa Savereid, both participants in Mandarin Spring's operation, in 1982. As a "planner" in the Neighborhood Development Agency figured Maureen Schaffner, senior mayoral aide.

[96] On the EDIC, cf. Chapter 1, footnote 42; G. T. Nedder, ed., A Business Community Guide to City Hall, s. d., p. 14 f.; H. Roth, B. Dacey, R. Ryan, Boston Guide to Development, Boston 1981, p. 13 f.

[97] Ira Jackson, the Court theologian, was paid as an employee in the BRA with money from the federal 701 program, in 1974; a group of pollsters from Mandarin Spring's operation and a dozen staffers from the Mayor's Office of Public Safety, were paid as employees in the Neighborhood Development Agency (NDA) with money from Community Development Block Grants, in 1982. On the NDA, cf. H. Roth et al., Boston Guide to Development, Update, [1981].

13 On Studying a Phenomenon of Creativity: The Process of Alternating Perceptions

The Court and the government of Boston were interwoven with each other in manifold and intricate ways. The Court emerged from within the government and the government was shaped by the Court.

Yet, as interwoven as they were, the Court and the government were two distinct phenomena. As subjects of our analysis they appeared necessarily in alternate modes: in the mode of being two different entities and in the mode of being a single governmental conformation. The Court members alias government officials, or the government officials alias Court members, themselves displayed a subtle understanding of their two-way existence. They appeared to have acquired an acute sense of judgment enabling them to recognize the oppurtune moments either for marking the distinction between Court member and government official or for enacting the blend of both pursuits.

The alternate modes in which Court and government appeared constituted the empirical structure of our analysis. Court and government could be viewed separately as well as conjunctionally. Their complex reality of being two distinct yet closely interwoven phenomena required a specific method of inquiry. There are two modes of perceiving this reality but neither fully reveals it. The one mode of perception had to alternate with the other and it was only within this process of alternating perceptions that the reality of Court and government appeared.

In the present chapter the Court was studied as a distinct phenomenon. Still, in the course of the analysis references to the government were continuously made. The Court relates to the government, of course, any separate consideration notwithstanding. Presently the relation between Court and government will be discussed as a final point of this chapter. In this concluding reflection the two phenomena will necessarily appear as two different entities. Yet one should bear in mind that they are also something else: a single governmental conformation.

(a) The Court kept the government under political control. Court members issued directions to governmental employees.

(b) The Mayor related to agency heads in various ways, either directly or indirectly, frequently switching from one mode of relationship to another, making exceptions all the time. To a large extent these contacts were screened by members of the Court. On the other hand, Court members acted as intermediaries between executives in the government and the Mayor. Agency heads were usually not particularly eager to meet face to face with the Mayor.[98] They expected to be more "efficient" (a euphemism for being more independent) when they avoided such meetings.

(c) The Court provided the place and the means of arbitration in the case of inter-agency or intradepartmental conflicts.

(d) The persons in the Court (many of them were graduates from Harvard or M. I. T, Wasps, or would-be Wasps) and the persons in the government (mostly career civil servants, bureaucrats) tended to regard each other with uncertainty, suspicion, contempt. They formulated the experience of their relationship by such expressions as: "dangerous,"[99] a "trading of favors,"[100] or "cultural warfare."[101]

14 The Movements of Inquiry Into the Movements of Governing

The preceding analysis of the Court pursued a series of movements. It proceeded from reflections upon a phenomenon of organization, the Court, and thus, as a movement of inquiry, it pursued the constitutive process from which the Court emerged. It followed movements that could be discerned as the constitutive movements of the Court. The subject of the inquiry was not a completed "organization" of governmental creativity. The subject were movements of organizing the creativeness of government.

In probing the Court the inquiry followed a movement from the Court as a field of political creativity to the Court as a configuration of political organisms. The movement led into the Court's dimensional structure, its "depth" and its "surface," its "invisible" reality, and its "visible" manifestations. By the pursuit of the movement within this structure the Court could be seized in the mode of its ongoing constitution: incessant movements of organizing *within* the Court, the field of political creativity, towards an organization *of* the Court, towards a configuration of political organisms. The extension and the fabric of the field could be discerned by apprehending the configuration of political organisms to which the movements of organizing verged, and the significance of the configuration as the organizational representation of the field could be understood in the pursuit of the movements

---

[98] On a similar "avoidance of face-to-face relationships" among French administrators, cf. M. Crozier, *The Bureaucratic Phenomenon,* Chicago 1964, pp. 220 ff.

[99] Source: Interview.

[100] Source: Interview.

[101] Transcript of a lecture presented by Barney Frank on March 3, 1977 to a class (Government 246, Prof. E. C. Banfield) at Harvard University, p. 19.

of organizing from which it emerged. The field remained necessarily an evanescent phenomenon; the configuration, on the other hand, resembled a distinct form of government.

The inquiry has followed the movement of governmental creation.

In scrutinizing the human fabric of the Court, the inquiry followed a movement from the beginning of the Court to its *dénouement*. It pursued the Court's history. The history of the Court could be read by a study of the persons who constituted the Court. Their movements in relating to each other, hierarchical, temporal, socio-spatial movements, described an historical texture discernible as the unfolding, the golden age, and the crepuscule of the Court.

The inquiry has recorded the history *of* the Court in following the movements of the persons *in* the Court.

In assessing the organizational manifestations of the Court, the inquiry followed a movement from a relatively simple to an increasingly complex structure. It pursued a movement of differentiation. The Court could be observed in the process of acquiring continually a greater diversity of manifestations. Incessant movements of organizing *within* the Court, changing aggregations of persons, varying lines of authority, shifts of influence, produced an hypertrophic growth *of* the Court's manifestations.

The inquiry has discovered the organizational openness of the Court; a differentiating movement continuously carried it beyond its actual form of organization.

In comparing the organisms of the Court, the inquiry followed a movement between a state of equilibrium and a state of agitation. It pursued the Court's pulsation. The Court lived on the growth, expansion, and contraction of its organisms. The comparative study of the organisms disclosed the meaning of the Court's organizational hypertrophy. Organizations have an inherent tendency towards a state of equilibrium, a state of uniformity, routine, sluggishness. The prevalence of this tendency is signaled by a lack of organizational confusion, a lack of recurring reorganizations, a lack of incentives to exceed one's competence, in short, a lack of creativity. The Court's organizational hypertrophy signaled a prevalence of just the opposite tendency, the tendency towards a state of organizational agitation. The Court offered a confusing complexity of overlapping organisms. It was reorganized very often. Its members were quite evidently inspired with an expansive view of their competencies.

The inquiry has seized the essence of the Court, locus of creativity.

Chapter 3
The Party, Carrier of Creativity

ἄγει μὲν δὴ ψιχὴ πάντα τὰ κατ᾽ οὐρανὸν καὶ γῆν καὶ θάλατταν ταῖς αὐτῆς κινήσεσιν, αἷς ὀνόματά ἐστι βούλεσθαι, σκοπεῖσθαι, ἐπιμελεῖσθαι, βουλεύεσθαι, δοξάζειν ὀρθῶς, ἐψευσμένως, χαίρουσαν, λυπουμένην, θαρροῦσαν, Φοβουμένην, μισοῦσαν, στέργουσαν

Soul then guides all ... by its own movements, of which the names are: volition, reflection, forethought, deliberation, opinion, true or false, in joy or distress, confidence or fear, hate or love ...

Plato, *Laws* 897 a

1 Philosophical Argument: Time, History, and Society

The continuum in which human societies move is generally called "time," and the record of the continuum is generally called "history." Under the presently prevailing mode of historical perception[1] the configuration of time, history, and society is understood as a phenomenon of equivalence: the "time" of "history" is measured by calendar years, and the sequence of those calendar years is thought to be the continuum in which societies exist – moving from the stage of a "beginning" to stages of "higher" development, emerging from a "past" and entering a "present," setting out from the "present" and heading towards a "future." The history of a society appears to extend along a single axis of time; hence it is conceived of as an advance on this one axis from points "downwards" to points further "up," and it is understood that this advance defines exclusively what could be viewed as "history" of the particular society.

The study of the continuum in which human societies – or human beings as "historical" figures – move must probably lean, to a certain extent, upon a compact and uniaxial view of the continuum. There has to be a "beginning" of a "history" and there has to be an "end" or else the history to be told would simply evanesce by its own infinity. There has to be the continuous "life" of a particular "person" portrayed in a biography or else the biographical text would have no subject but the disparate pieces of "biographical" documents.

Neither the "truth" or "reality" of the historical continuum nor the "character" or individual "existence" of a historical figure can fully be grasped in this way, however. The general image of history as an advance along a single axis of time mirrors the *mode* of understanding the historical continuum but does by no means reflect the *reality* of this continuum. A careful scrutiny of a particular society in a particular "historical" situation will always reveal a society full of contradictions, perplexing features, insoluble tangles of events. Within its "historical" situation one will certainly find a thread of time along which the society appears to have "advanced" or to be "advancing." But – this *one* thread of time alone does not define the existence of the society in a continuum of "history." It is *a* thread of time within a continuum where "time" occurs in manifold ways: as a "time of advance" or as a "time of renaissance," as a "time of ruptures and discontinuities" or as a "time of parallel and corresponding events," as a "time of anticipation" or as a "time of retroflexion." Each human society appears to be full of contradictions, perplexing features, and insoluble tangles of events because every human

---

[1] Cf. T. Schabert, "Modernity and History," *Diogenes,* No. 123, Fall 1983, pp. 110–124.

society moves within a continuum of different "times" of which each has its own rhythm, tempo, and direction. A society's "history" then is a continuum of existence within a manifold of different "times." To record the history of a society means to record the movements of this society within a plurality of historical axes.[2]

As an urban society Boston exists and moves in different historical ages. The city lives in the age of high technology and it lives in the age of tribal customs. The city adapts its architectural form to the age of skyscrapers and it sustains its classical architectural tissue of the Nineteenth century. The city dwells in the age of television when it elects its governors and it appears to be a medieval city-state considering the fabric of its government.

The autocracy of Mayor White drew its force from a political organism that represents the paradigmatic example of Boston being situated "historically" in an age other than our present time. Conventionally, the organism was decribed as a "political machine" and, in accordance with this description, considered as a genuine manifestation of American city politics. If it was viewed in a comparative perspective at all, the range of comparison was confined to the uniform tradition of "machine politics."

Typically, the academic literature on the subject (political machines and related matters) has kept a parochial perspective although it has become quite sophisticated as regards its methodology and quite extensive as regards its quantity. It still reflects but the world of Plunkitt's *Tammany Hall* − without having preserved, however, the originality of Plunkitt's provocation.[3]

---

[2] Cf. the passages on the "pluralité des dimensions historiques," in: R. Aron, *L'opium des intellectuels,* Paris 1955, pp. 59, 146 − 152; J. Barzun, *Clio and the Doctors,* Chicago 1974; J. M. Freeman, D. L. Krantz, "The Unfulfilled Promises of Life Histories," *Biography,* No. 3, 1980, pp. 1 − 13; the passages on the "tradition of medieval constitutionalism in American political thought" and the "disharmony of American politics: history versus progress," in: S. P. Huntington, *American Politics. The Promise of Disharmony,* Cambridge, Mass. 1981, pp. 34 ff. and 222 − 229 respectively.

[3] Cf. W. L. Riordon's classic: *Plunkitt of Tammany Hall* (1905). − The subsequent series of studies on machine politics and its tradition includes: G. Myers, *The History of Tammany Hall,* New York 1917; F. R. Kent, *The Great Game of Politics,* Garden City 1923; H. F. Gosnell, Ch. E. Merriam, *Chicago. A More Intimate View of Urban Politics,* New York 1929; H. Zorbough, *The Gold Coast and the Slum,* Chicago 1929; H. Zink, *City Bosses in the United States: A Study of Twenty Municipal Bosses,* Durham 1930; Ch. P. Taft, *City Management: The Cincinnati Experiment,* New York 1933; J. T. Salter, Boss Rule. Portraits in City Politics, New York 1935; G. M. Reynolds, *Machine Politics in New Orleans,* New York 1936; H. F. Gosnell, *Machine Politics: Chicago Model,* Chicago 1937; D. D. McKean, *The Boss: The Hague Machine in Action,* Boston 1940; M. Meyerson, E. C. Banfield, *Politics, Planning and the Public Interest. The Case of Public Housing in Chicago,* Glencoe 1955; R. A. Straetz, P. R. Politics in Cincinnati,

To be sure, Boston continues to be a city in the world that was illuminated by the "Tammany philosopher"; in the *Boston Mirror for Magistrates* Plunkitt's "plain talks"[4] reverberate. Yet, the political organism which was conventionally described as the Mayor's "machine" made Boston also a part of a historical world which is much larger and more diverse than the world of *Tammany Hall*.

This historical world is constituted by an axis of comparable political organisms in different societies — personal "interests" appearing as political "parties." Kevin White ascended to the position of Mayor of Boston, kept this position, and ruled over Boston for 16 years largely by virtue of such a "personal party" — the Kevin White Party. The political organization of personal interests represents — in very general terms — an early, pre-modern form of party organization.[5] It is in "historical" societies, therefore, that we

---

New York 1958; W. S. Sayre, H. Kaufman, *Governing New York City,* New York 1960; E. C. Banfield, *Political Influence. A New Theory of Urban Politics,* New York 1961; T. J. Lowi, *At the Pleasure of the Mayor. Patronage and Power in New York City 1898 – 1958,* New York 1964; S. Mandelbaum, *Boss Tweed's New York,* New York 1965; W. Moscow, *The Last of the Big-Time Bosses: The Life and Times of Carmine De Sapio and the Rise and Fall of Tammany Hall,* New York 1971; W. Bean, *Boss Rueff's San Francisco: The Story of Union Labor Party, Big Business and the Craft Prosecution,* Berkeley 1972; R. E. Wolfinger, *The Politics of Progress,* Englewood Cliffs 1974; M. L. Rakove, *Don't Make No Waves, Don't Back No Losers,* op. cit.; M. L. Rakove, *We Don't Want Nobody Nobody Sent;* op. cit.; A. Bridges, *A City in the Republic. Antebellum New York and the Origins of Machine Politics,* New York 1984.

[4] Riordon's Plunkitt of *Tammany Hall* carriers the subtitle: "A series of very plain talks on very practical politics, delivered by Ex-Senator George Washington Plunkitt, the Tammany Philosopher, from his rostrum — the New York Country court house bootblack stand."

[5] F. R. Kent and R. E. Park, two observers of "political machines," alluded to this point: "That the men and women who, through inherited or natural desire, or through selfish interest or ambition, go into politics should form an organization is wholly human and natural. The habit of men to organize dates back to those distant days when human beings first began, for purposes of protection, to congregate in bands. It was then the first politicians appeared, the first primitive political machines were formed, the first boss, in the person of the chief of the tribe, developed" (F. R. Kent, *The Great Game of Politics,* op. cit., p. 346). — "The political machine is, in fact, an attempt to maintain, inside the formal administrative organization of the city, the control of a primary group. The organizations thus built up, of which Tammany Hall is the classic illustration, appear to be thoroughly *feudal* [my emphasis, T. S.] in their character" (R. E. Park, "The City: Suggestions for the investigation of human behavior in the urban environment," in: R. E. Park, E. W. Burgess, R. D. McKenzie, *The City,* Chicago 1925, 1967, 4th ed., p. 35). Both statements, as allusions to the "feudal" or "primitive" origins of "political machines," are strikingly speculative — in comparison with the actual, pre-modern

find the classic antecedents of the Kevin White Party — in Ancient Rome, Italian city-states during the Middle Ages and the Renaissance, in England during the first half of the eighteenth century.[6] In these societies "interests," organized as "parties," were used to structure the process of seeking and sustaining the power to govern — and this was the function of the Kevin White Party, too. To the extent that the Kevin White Party formed the government of Boston — and it did so to a considerable extent —, it made Boston an American city "contemporaneous" with, for example, Rome's late Republic, medieval Lucca, England "at the Accession of George III."

Boston became the City of Boston ruled by the Court, a city where the lesson of politics could best be read in the version of a *Mirror for Magistrates*. Boston was moving along an historical axis which cuts our conventional image of "history" — "history" proceeding with the course of calendar years. The city entered into another "history" — the "history" of societies where the art of organizing a personal party, that is a party of "friends,"[7] has been

---

history of parties, personal interests, personal organizations. Cf. L. Namier, *Monarchy and Party System*, Oxford 1952; Th. Schieder, "Die Theorie der Partei im älteren deutschen Liberalismus," in: idem, *Staat und Gesellschaft im Wandel unserer Zeit*, München 1958, pp. 110 – 132; S. Cotta, "La nascità dell'idea di partito nel secolo XVIII," *Atti Facoltà di Giurisprudenza Università Perugia*, LXI, 1960; R. v. Albertini, "Parteiorganisation und Parteibegriff in Frankreich 1789 – 1940," *Historische Zeitschrift*, 1961, pp. 529 – 600; L. Namier, *Crossroads of Power. Essays on Eighteenth-Century England*, London 1962; E. Faul, "Verfemung, Duldung und Anerkennung des Partei-wesens in der Geschichte des politischen Denkens," *Politische Vierteljahresschrift*, 5. Jg., H. 1, März 1964, pp. 60 – 80; M. A. Cattaneo, *Il partito politico nel pensiero dell'illuminismo e della rivoluzione francese*, Milano 1964; H. C. Mansfield Jr., *Statesmanship and Party Government: A Study of Burke and Bolingbroke*, Chicago 1965.

6 Cf. M. Gelzer, *Vom römischen Staat. Zur Politik und Gesellschaftsgeschichte der römischen Republik*, Leipzig 1943, vol. II; L. R. Taylor, *Party Politics in the Age of Caesar*, Berkeley 1949; L. Simeoni, *Le signorie*, 2 vols., Milano 1950; R. Walcott Jr., *English Politics in the Early Eighteenth Century*, Cambridge, Mass. 1956; L. Namier, *The Structure of British Politics at the Accession of George III*, London 1957, 2nd ed.; Ch. Meier, *Res Publica Amissa. Eine Studie zu Verfassung und Geschichte der späten römischen Republik*, Wiesbaden 1966; D. Waley, *The Italian City-Republics*, New York 1969; J. Heers, *Le clan familial au moyen-âge. Etude sur les structures politiques et sociales des milieux urbains*, Paris 1974; L. R. Taylor, "Nobles, Clients, and Personal Armies," in: L. Guasti et al., *Friends, Followers and Factions. A Reader in Political Clientelism*, London 1977, pp. 179 – 192; L. Martines, *Power and Imagination. City-States in Renaissance Italy*, New York 1979; R. C. Trexler, *Public Life in Renaissance Florence*, New York 1980, esp. pp. 131 – 158.

7 The *locus classicus* on the political dimension of friendship is Aristotle's discussion of friendship (*philia*) in his *Nicomachean Ethics* (Books VIII and IX). "[...] friendship appears to be the bond of the state; and lawgivers seem to set more store by it than

shown to be the essential art of politics. Considering the story which these societies tell, we do not view a process in the ongoing time of the physical world, but view a process in the rhythmic time of continuing creation — we view the creativity of the politician. Once a full view of this process has been gained, one can easily recognize all the societies which are "contemporaneous" with each other beyond the "ages" suggested by the conventional image of history. Naturally, the quality of being contemporaneous with each other pertains to the respective societies only with respect to the process under review — being governed by a party of friends. Not as Boston has Boston become a "contemporary" of medieval Lucca, but as Boston whose government was formed by the Kevin White Party.

A party of friends is a deceptive phenomenon. One would usually think that it draws its existence from the associative sentiments and interests of the individuals who take part in it. Indeed, if there were no understanding among those individuals, it would not exist. Yet, what exactly is the understanding, what exactly are the associative sentiments and interests by which it comes to be? Everyone has friends but not everyone joins a party of friends. Most people pursue interests which are alike but they do not pursue these interests as political allies. What then is the difference between friends as friends and friends as political allies? And why is there such a difference at all? Why, in other words, do people being friends form a party?

---

they do by justice, for to promote concord, which seems akin to friendship, is their chief aim, while faction, which is enmity, is what they are most anxious to banish. And if men are friends, there is no need of justice between them; whereas merely to be just is not enough — a feeling of friendship also is necessary" (NE VIII 1155 a 25 – 30). — It should be noted, however, that Aristotle draws a distinction between three different kinds of friendship: (a) The friendship based on utility (*hē dia to chrēsimon philia*). "Thus friends whose affection is based on utility do not love each other in themselves but in so far as some benefit accrues to them from each other." — (b) The friendship based on pleasure (*hē dia tēn hēdonēn philia*). "[...] we enjoy the society of witty people not because of what they are in themselves, but because they are agreeable to us." — (c) The perfect kind of friendship — formed by "those who resemble each other in virtue [...]" and "[...] wish each alike the other's good in respect of their goodness" (*hē dia to agathon philia*). Their friendship "lasts as long as they continue to be good; and virtue is a permanent quality. And each is good relatively to his friends as well as absolutely, since the good are both good absolutely and profitable to each other. And each is pleasant in both ways also, since good men are pleasant both absolutely and to each other [...]" (NE VIII 1156 a 10 – 1156 b 15). Cf. also: H. H. Joachim, *The Nicomachean Ethics. A Commentary,* Oxford 1966, 4th ed., pp. 244 ff.; A. Moulakis, *Homonoia. Eintracht und die Entwicklung eines politischen Bewußtseins,* München 1973, pp. 70 ff.; Plato, *Lysis* 219 b – 223 a.

Evidently, friendly bonds alone do not explain the emergence and existence of a party of friends. Thinking about this form of a party, one is easily prompted to draw a misleading conclusion about its origins — they seem to be so obvious as it is a party of *friends*. Contrary to what one would believe, however, friends do not form a party because they are friends. The origins of their party must be sought outside their friendly relations — they form a party of friends because they find that this is the way to be a party in politics.

The Kevin White Party did not spring from a private prepossession of Kevin White. It arose out of necessity. Kevin White, the person, pursued the intention of becoming Mayor of Boston. The pursuit of this *personal* goal meant, by its very nature, a *political* quest, a quest for public support — from seeking the human and financial resources for building a campaign to seeking the majority vote in a mayoral election. The candidate alone would never have had a chance of reaching his goal. To win, he needed the support of a large configuration of people — of very many individuals who all shared the belief that Kevin White should be Mayor of Boston, that one should vote for him, join his campaign organization, become his adviser, contribute to his campaign funds. The personal aspiration of the candidate indeed made sense only inasmuch as it became the collective aspiration of the people who supported him.

This coalescence of aspirations occurred in a somewhat "miraculous" process: many people directed their resolution, energy, time, knowledge, and expertise towards a goal which none of them had had in common with any other of them before.[8]

However, they had a common goal to the extent that the candidate was a catalyst in the "miraculous" process — by aggregating a social field, by translating his personal quest into the quest of a "party."

How then can a candidate aggregate a field of supporters? Should he descend into the street, put up a stand, and speak to the crowds? Or should he sit in his study, write political manifestoes, and have them published in newspapers? Should he found a debating society, invite people of education, and discuss with them cosmic issues? Or should he canvass in the neighborhoods, visiting people in their homes, chatting with them in the pub at the corner?

The candidate will most likely consider to choose one or more of these approaches — specifically as approaches to campaigning. And he will do something else. He will look at existent aggregations, at social structures

---

[8] Cf. Cicero, *De Amicitia* XXV, 92: "Nam cum amicitiae vis sit in eo ut unus quasi animus fiat ex pluribus [...]" — "The effect of friendship is to make, as it were, one soul out of many [...]."

within which he — an individual though a candidate — could move to reach for an audience and to build a following.

Every human society is structured, and the candidate will find aggregations of people. There are great differences among human societies, however, as regards the degree to which they are structured. On the one side, a society predestines by its structures every manifestation of social life. On the other, a society reflects in its fluid structures the continuing variations of social life.

If we imagined a scale from the type of wholly structured societies to the type of fluidly structured societies and marked the place of Boston on this scale, it would lie near the extreme of the latter type of societies. The urban society of Boston is a structured society, of course — and in view of its ethnic composition very much so. But, to a far greater degree, it is a society in which certain "classical" social structures hardly exist, and the few structures which do exist are extremely fluid.[9]

The "Brahmins," once forming a Bostonian aristocracy, have abdicated a long time ago; the few who are still active in civic affairs content themselves with caring for the *Boston Athenaeum* and the *Museum of Fine Arts;* if, occasionally, one of them reenters the public arena, he is promptly stigmatized as a Brahmin turned maverick. The business community — potentially the kernel of a bourgeois class — features in the city in a visiting capacity; its members mostly reside in communities outside Boston where they lead the detached life of wealthy suburbanites; they are not Bostonians really but commuters to the city's economy, and their interest in Boston is largely defined by the business interests they pursue on weekdays during their office hours.

As regards their political allegiance, the voters in Boston are overwhelmingly "democratic." However, their allegiance to the "Democratic Party" is more a matter of persuasion than a subject of organization. As "Democrats" they would not vote for a "Republican," of course; but they would also not vote for a "Democratic" candidate simply because he is a "Democrat": the contenders in elections are mostly "Democrats" anyway — as the field of candidates reflects the predominantly "democratic" mood of the Boston electorate.[10] Elections therefore are largely contests of persons — within the

---

[9] The urban society of Boston is not a-typical. The American polity in general has more and more approached a state of "atomization." Cf. the section on "Building Coalitions in the Sand," by A. King in: idem, ed., *The New American Political System,* Washington, D.C. 1978, pp. 388–395.

[10] Municipal elections in Boston — for the Office of Mayor, the City Council, the School Committee — are nonpartisan elections. The formal discounting of party labels notwithstanding, voters and candidates think and act in terms of party affiliations. In 1979, for instance, John W. Sears, a notable Republican in Massachusetts politics, won

"Democratic family."[11] If they want to prepare for winning, candidates must build their *personal* organization of "Democrats" — there is no such thing as a "party organization," a continuing structure of active Democrats, that would carry, during the time of an election, a chosen member to the victory as candidate.

As a city in America Boston has followed the general trend towards a mass society where the mobility of the individual has widely diluted the binding sway of social structures. All the individuals who dwell in the city do not, of course, "disappear" in a sea of monads; there exist associative groups among them. But the number of these groups is endless, they often do not last very long, and their institutional form usually is but a fragile fixture. They convey very much the image of a society in continuous fluctuation.[12]

Everywhere in America local government is fragmentized and Boston does not represent an exception. A constitutional device for the preservation of political freedom,[13] the fragmentation of institutional authority does not

---

a seat on Boston's City Council. Not only did everyone duly note that no other Republican had managed to be elected Councillor in thirty years, but his colleagues and the public alike continued to consider Sears primarily as a "Republican" — regardless of his partaking in the politics of an informal, fluid coalition of Councillors (of which all the other members were Democrats) that in general opposed the politics of another such coalition (of which all members again were Democrats).

[11] In American politics those who call themselves "Democrats" or "Republicans" constitute a "family," a fluid political association composed of a variety of distinct parts, rather than a "party," a stable political formation composed of equal parts, respectively. The French, in particular, grasp the reality of political "parties" with a greater linguistic precision: as regards their functions all *partis* are "parties," to be sure, but then some "parties" more resemble a *famille* while others resemble a *club* or a *mouvement* or a *fédération* or a *rassemblement*. Cf. T. Schabert, "Ansätze zu einer Phänomenologie der politischen Parteien in Frankreich," *Zeitschrift für Politik*, Jg. 25, H. 4, Dec. 1978, pp. 357–376.

[12] Such an image of Boston emerges, for instance, if one studies *The Boston People's Yellow Pages,* published by "Vocations for Social Change" (a "nonprofit resource center for work and social change"). The first edition of the *People's Yellow Pages* appeared in 1971; the 1980–81 edition listed on 172 pages about 1400 human service groups and community organizations in the Greater Boston area.

[13] Cf. Publius [A. Hamilton, J. Jay, J. Madison], *The Federalist Papers,* [1788], No. 51 [Madison], ed. C. Rossiter, New York 1961, pp. 321–324: "In order to lay a due foundation for that separate and distinct exercise of the different powers of government, which to a certain extent is admitted on all hands to be essential to the preservation of liberty, it is evident that each department should have a will of its own; and consequently should be so constituted that the members of each should have as little agency as possible in the appointment of the members of the others. [...] But the great security

prevent the emergence of strong agencies, nor does it necessarily obstruct the rise of "power brokers" to a position of virtually unlimited influence within the fragmentized system of government.[14] Yet, within this system a concentration of power is always a consequence and not a precondition of politics; "structures" of might are likely to disintegrate at the moment the art of the politician(s) who created them is withdrawn. The American system of local government does not assist politicians in making their career; they themselves must possess the resources to master this maze of institutions.

How then — to repeat our question — could Kevin White, the candidate, aggregate a field of supporters? How could he build a following in a society as fluidly structured as Boston? How can a candidate bridge the gap between himself alone and all those people whom he needs to win, if in his quest for support he cannot rely on mediating structures? Is the quest then quixotic?

The candidate is alone as a candidate; he is not alone as a person. He has a family and he has friends; he has relatives and he has neighbors; he has schoolmates and he has colleagues in the profession. The members of his family have friends and his relatives have friends; his neighbors and his colleagues have friends; his schoolmates and his friends have friends. As a person the candidate can "discover" himself in a wide social field — and within this field he can first be "recognized" as the person who is *the* "candidate." The field opens the first social space where the candidate can perceive his "appeal" — and where his person can become the focus of interest for people whose drifting political interests and energies seek their figure of guidance, a candidate.

---

against a gradual concentration of the several powers in the same department consists in giving to those who administer each department the necessary constitutional means and personal motives to resist encroachments of the others. The provision for defense must in this, as in all other cases, be made commensurate to the danger of attack. Ambition must be made to counteract ambition. [...] Whilst all authority in it [the federal republic of the United States] will be derived from and dependent on the society, the society itself will be broken into so many parts, interests and classes of citizens, that the rights of individuals, or of the minority, will be in little danger from interested combinations of the majority." — Cf. also: E. C. Banfield, J. Q. Wilson, *City Politics*, Cambridge, Mass. 1963, pp. 63 ff.; E. C. Banfield, *Political Influence*, New York 1961, (= Paperback Edition 1965), pp. 263 ff., 324 ff.; Th. E. Cronin, *State and Local Politics: Government by the People*, Englewood Cliffs 1976, 2nd ed.; S. H. Beer, "In Search of a New Public Philosophy," in: A. King, ed., *The New American Political System*, Washington D. C. 1978, pp. 5–44; P. Woll, *Constitutional Democracy. Policies and Politics*, Boston 1982, pp. 19 ff.

[14] Cf. R. A. Caro, *The Power Broker. Robert Moses and the Fall of New York*, New York 1974 (= Vintage Books Edition 1975).

"Field" and "candidate" constitute each other; they emerge from two movements towards a distinctive appearance that are mutually contingent; the candidate appears more strongly, as the field moves towards him, and the field acquires clearer contours, as the candidate moves ahead in his quest for support.[15]

The person Kevin White became the candidate Kevin White by pursuing the quest of the person Kevin White being recognized as the candidate Kevin White. The place of this recognition was the social field within which Kevin White was situated as a person: his family, his relatives, his schoolmates, his colleagues, his neighbors, his friends. While his quest advanced, the field became ever wider: friends of colleagues, of neighbors, of friends, of relatives gravitated towards the candidate. The personal quest increasingly appeared as a political quest, and the field of people clustering around the candidate took on the shape of a "party" – all the early supporters of Kevin White excelled in "politics"[16] and they perfectly knew what they were: "Kevin White democrats."[17] The personal that is political "interest" of Kevin White and the political that is personal "interest" of his supporters coalesced and from this coalescence emerged the "Kevin White Party."

The emergence of the Kevin White Party in Boston occurred as a "historical" event in a manifold of "times." Each of these times can be chosen to tell the story of its origins and evolution. None, however, could be seized as the single thread that would lead to a full view of the event in "history." They must all be explored, if one wants to know the "history" – or rather the structure of "histories" – which define the event. The event is an event in different "historical" times. Its history is its story told in each of its times.

---

[15] Cf. Ch. H. Cooley, *Human Nature and the Social Order* [1902] in: *The Two Major Works of Charles H. Cooley,* Intr. by R. Cooley Angell, Glencoe 1956, p. 319 f.: "The prime condition of ascendancy is the presence of undirected energy in the person over whom it is to be exercised; it is not so much forced upon us from without as demanded from within. The mind, having energy, must work, and requires a guide, a form of thought, to facilitate its working. All views of life are fallacious which do not recognize the fact that the primary need is the need to do. Every healthy organism evolves energy, and this must have an outlet. In the human mind, during its expanding period, the excess of life takes the form of a reaching out beyond all present and familiar things after an unknown good; no matter what the present and familiar may be, that fact that it is such is enough to make it inadequate. So we have a vague onward impulse which is the unorganized material, the undifferentiated protoplasm, so to speak, of all progress; [...]." And p. 324: "Thus the idea of power and the types of personality which, as standing for that idea, have ascendancy over us, are a function of our own changing character."

[16] *BG,* March 9, 1969.

[17] *BG,*Dec. 29, 1967.

The pursuit of the story throughout the manifold of times delves into the depth of history — towards the knowledge of meaning in view of the event.
In pursuit of the story this manifold of times will be explored:

(1) The life of the Kevin White Party from 1960 to 1983; its existence as a configuration of people in the *time of calendar years*.
(2) The continuity of the social field from which organizational manifestations of the party successively emerged; its sustenance as a party of friends in the *time of social creation* — where other, "contemporary" parties of its kind can be found, apart from the "ages" of conventional history.
(3) The continuous presence of the persons who constituted the party; the existence of the party in the *time of personal relationships* — where the bonds of loyalty and common experiences transcend the vicissitudes of politics.
(4) The genesis, evolution, and disintegration of a distinctive aggregation of people clustered around a common quest — the personal quest of their candidate; the emergence of the party in the *time of a "miraculous" process* — the process of social creativity.

The Kevin White Interest

2 The Interest and the Party

A personal party is formed as a tool to be used in the process of obtaining and exercising political power. Ultimately, it is an instrument of governing. The more it fulfills this function, the more it acquires a certain quality: it becomes a carrier of public responsibility. Sooner or later, in a farther advanced stage of evolution, it will shed its private bearing, its original constitution as a personal party, and fully grow into a public body, into the institutionalized form of a political party.

Personal parties tend to become political parties, as any comparative study of "parties" in politics will show.[18] The Kevin White Party took on this tendency, too, but never really became a political party. It remained basically an "interest,"[19] that is a party of persons who were interested in promoting

---

[18] The "second American party system" emerged in the 1820's from *personal parties*. Cf. M. J. Heale, *The Presidential Quest. Candidates and Images in American Political Culture 1787–1852*, London–New York 1982, p. 81: "Following the disintegration of the old two party system, presidential candidates in the 1820's had inescapedly been forced to seek the prize in their personal capacities; they were not the agents of party. Yet parties were necessary, and it was in a sense personal parties which took shape around Adams and Jackson." – p. 75: "Despite the self-effacement of the principals, these were highly personal parties. They were not associated very clearly with programmes or measures, but rather were defined by their candidates. This was reflected in the nomenclature of the campaign organizations. On the one hand there were the 'Administrative Conventions,' the 'Friends of the Re-election of John Quincy Adams' and the 'anti-Jackson committees,' and on the other there were the 'Jackson Convention,' the 'Friends of Andrew Jackson' and the 'Hickory Clubs.'" – p. 83: "The election of 1828 marked the origins of a new two-party system. In time the personal parties which had taken shape around Adams and Jackson became impersonal parties, that is, lasting political organizations which survived changes in leadership and which possessed programmes and characters of their own. [...] Presidential candidates came and went, but the parties themselves survived, at least until the 1850's, and offered the nation a choice between contrasting political philosophies." – Cf. also the studies quoted in footnote 5 and: V. O. Key, *Politics, Parties, and Pressure Groups*, New York 1942, 1964, 5th ed., pp. 218–249.

[19] "Interest" is understood here as defined in the *Oxford English Dictionary*: "A business, cause, or principle in which a number of persons are interested; the party interested in such a business or principle; a party having a common interest, a religious or political party, business connexions etc. [...] 1714 Pope 'He said that I was enter'd into a cabal with Dean Swift and others to write against the Whig Interest.'"

Kevin White as politician – and in making their own career in government through the career of Kevin White. The political views prevalent among its members were not forged into a "party ideology" nor were its organizational manifestations shaped into a "party apparatus." Nor was its internal life laid down in statutes or was a steering committee of "party leaders" elected by its members. The Kevin White Party did in no way shed its private bearing, it served but the cause of Kevin White – and yet it formed the government of Boston, it carried public responsibility as every political party does. It continued to be a personal party – and yet it worked as if it had indeed become a political party.

A party of friends arrested in its movement from being an "interest" to being a "political party" represents a peculiar phenomenon. It is involved in the course of its evolution and does not follow this course to its end. It continuously appears to become what it never does become. It is the peculiar phenomenon to which the functional description of a political party fully applies while its essence is defined by a private interest. What has made the Kevin White Party to be this peculiar phenomenon?

America or, more precisely, the political fabric of the American republic confined the Kevin White Party to its peculiar condition. Being arrested in its movement beyond its private bearing, the Party testified the vigor of the existing forms of public life in America. While the Kevin White Party formed the government of Boston, the city hardly knew a "Democratic Party." The "Democrats" governed but they governed as "Kevin White Democrats." If a party of Democrats existed in the public life of the city, it existed mainly in the mode of the Kevin White Party.

Still, the Kevin White Party did not assume a political identity and – in the ensuing act of formalization – a political position outside the Democratic family. Among its members the attachment to the common cause – an attachment which sometimes was displayed quite fanatically – did evidently not supersede one's personal affinity to the Democratic belief. The primary forms of American public life proved to be stronger than the actually ascendant form of politics in Boston. The Kevin White Party could become the party of government in an American city, but it could not become an American party. The elementary realm of public life where political parties must find their roots was structured so firmly that it bent the Kevin White Party in its movement towards its "natural" end: the party formed the government of Boston, but American politics defined the texture of the government formed by the party.

Confined to its peculiar condition as a private interest forming a government, the Kevin White Party presented – unavoidably, one is inclined to say – a subject for continual misunderstandings and, frequently, gross misinterpretations. Crude concepts prevailed and were echoed by the media like a set of public truths. What existed necessarily as an instrument of governing, was depicted as a product of machine politics in its pure, that is, "dirty" form. What was animated by the art of friendship, was described as a cancer of corruption. What was a quest for a chassis of politics in a city of fluid shapes, was construed as a flagrant example of bossism. The distortion of views threatened to make any different approach appear heretical, if not pointless. There were so many "knowledgeable" observers and most of them, perceiving what they believed to be the crooked political scene in Boston, flatly refused to entertain the thought that "politics in Boston" could be worth a scholar's attention.[20] The present study might show heresy to be indeed a mode of scientific discovery.

One cannot apprehend such a phenomenon as the Kevin White Party if one does not view it within its proper context – the comparative history of personal parties. In the following an attempt is made to sketch this context in two ways. First, a series of relevant historical studies will be discussed with the view of conceptualizing the natural composition and the scientific representation of personal parties. Secondly, the concepts derived from this procedure will be arranged systematically; the result will be a conceptual matrix for the study of a personal party, a party of friends (cf. p. 116).

Under the republic in Ancient Rome patrician families were the preeminent actors in politics.[21] They established, maintained, and exerted their political influence by pursuing the politics of a "party." The members of a family, their friends, and the friends of their friends would form an alliance of interest (*necessitudo*) and use this alliance for the advancement of their interests in the public sphere. An alliance of friendship was passed from generation to generation and each saw that new friends were added to one's party.[22] Considerable efforts were made to organize the communication and interaction with and between all the friends with whom one was allied. The personal nature of this organization was tenaciously maintained; the *necessitudo* was "organized," but it continued to be defined by the personal relationships among the friends who were forming it. Concerning their socio-spatial origins,

---

[20] Yet, even if the Kevin White Party were perceived purely from within the tradition of machine politics, it would still appear as a phenomenon quite different from the classic example of bossism in Boston, "Czar" Martin Lomasney. Cf. H. Zink, *City Bosses in the United States,* op. cit., pp. 69 – 84; L. Ainley, *Boston Mahatma: Martin Lomasney,* Boston 1949.

[21] Cf. M. Gelzer, *Vom römischen Staat,* op. cit.; L. R. Taylor, "Nobles, Clients, and Personal Armies," op. cit.; M. Gelzer, *The Roman Nobility,* Oxford 1969; G. Boissier, *Cicero and His Friends. A Study of Roman Society in the Time of Caesar,* New York 1970.

[22] Cf. Ch. Meier, *Res Publica Amissa,* op. cit., p. 40 f.

alliances were frequently rooted in neighborhoods (*tribus*) or professional guilds (*collegia*); besides their original purpose the guilds served as political clubs. A drove of followers and a string of assistants enlarged the immediate circle of friends and family members. Followers were drawn into the orbit of the party by patronage, which was deliberately used also to increase their number. Finally, the head of the "party" — that is the head of the patrician family — established himself as a patron (*patronus*), protecting a throng of clients by using the political weight of his party, to which the more clients very likely turned, the more influence — that is followers and friends — it accumulated.

The personal parties of the patrician families dominated the public life in republican Rome to a rather great extent. Candidates for political office who wanted to succeed without the support of such a party very often failed; they could not find enough votes where voting was largely an act of friendship.[23]

---

[23] ibid., pp. 10 f., 39 f. — To become Mayor of Boston in 1983 was equally a matter of friendship, family ties, and local roots. The mayoral election of 1983 (the primary election held on October 11, 1983 and the final election held on November 15, 1983) proved that Boston voters still very much prefer candidates who were born in Boston and have lived among their friends in the city ever since, over candidates who may have lived and worked in the city for many years — but were not born in Boston and therefore could not help being "outsiders." Robert R. Kiley, a former aide to Mayor White and Deputy Mayor of Boston, manager of the Massachusetts Bay Transportation Authority for many years, and resident of Boston since 1972, was branded an "outsider" from the very beginning of his campaign for the office of Mayor — he was a native of Minneapolis and not of Boston! (Cf. R. L. Turner, "An Outsider, But Kiley Has Strong Assets," *BG*, Jan. 1, 1983.) Kiley could not overcome this great liability by his sense of humor (at campaign rallies he quipped: "I had to be born in Minneapolis to be near my mother"). In a field of nine contenders he remained a long-distance runner, faring very poorly in the public opinion polls. Kiley abandoned the race several weeks before the primary election. Again, it was observed that "Part of his trouble in attracting votes was that, in a city where voters still ask which parish a candidate was raised in, Mr. Kiley was not a native. Although he is of Irish-American ancestry, like many Bostonians, and went to Roman Catholic schools, he was born in Minneapolis" (*NYT*, Oct. 6, 1983). — By contrast, Raymond L. Flynn, the contender who eventually won a majority of voters in the final election and thus became the successor of Kevin White as Mayor of Boston, is tied up with Boston in the ideal way — by birth, family roots, friendship, a locally centered life and career. Cf. this panegyric portrait of Flynn, the "friend": "Flynn has put together a campaign that is fueled by ideology and by blood ties [...]. These elements of the Flynn campaign rubbed elbows recently at a house party in the heart of St. Margaret's Parish in Dorchester. The neighborhood is socially conservative, Irish, and working-class. So it was no surprise to encounter a formidable collection of stout retirees here, with tattooed forearms and a trace of brogue. They are men who worked all their lives as laborers or, like Flynn's late father, as longshoremen, before

In the city-states of Renaissance Italy the sphere of public life was again textured by family ties and friendships. The spatial structure of the cities — a small size, on the one hand, and a large proportion of public space, on the other — conduced people continually to intermingle; everyone's private life was to a large extent a life in public. As they pursued their daily affairs in the dense space of their community, friends, neighbors, relatives met each other many times, observed everyone's actions easily, exchanged news and plans very quickly — and became immersed in jealousies, quarrels, and feuds with equal ease. They were friends and enemies, neighbors and adversaries, relatives and rivals, citizens and partisans. Acting as citizens, they formed therefore "parties" quite naturally, as it were. They followed the lines of division along which they were already pitted against each other in their private lives.[24]

Parties of friends were the carriers of politics as well in England during the first half of the eighteenth century.[25] Considered as a political society, England had become an arena of modern individuals; an atomistic society of self-centered, egotistical people. Nevertheless, the same people were prepared to serve the country (they could then be of service to their friends, besides). To engage in this service, they needed vehicles for collective action. Public vehicles, the vehicles of a truly political society, could not be found in the atomized society which they themselves had brought about. There were but

---

the age of container shipping replaced men with machines on the docks. They are the living history of their neighborhoods, and Flynn is the pride of their generation. At the close of one of the candidate's monologues on getting special-interest groups out of City Hall, Mike Griffin, a former longshoreman, rose to address the crowd of 50 or so. As he spoke, *it was clear that for him, what the candidate had said wasn't nearly as important as who he is* [my emphasis, T. S.]. 'I said to your father 15 years ago that you'd be the first boy from Southie to be mayor of Boston,' Griffin proclaimed" (M. Rezendes, "Left, Right, and Flynn. Profile of a Blue-Collar Crusade," *BPh*, Oct. 4, 1983. Cf. further: J. V. Murphy, "Southie Cheers Victory of Their 'Hometown Boy,'" *BG*, Oct. 13, 1983).

[24] Cf. L. Simeoni, *Le signorie*, op. cit.; D. Waley, *The Italian City-Republics*, op. cit.; L. Martines, *Power and Imagination*, op. cit.; G. B. Picotti, "Qualche osservazioni sui caratteri delle signorie italiane," *Rivista Storica Italiana*, Nuova Serie IV, Vol. XLIII, Gennaio 1926, Fasc. I, pp. 7–30; J. Heers, "Partis politiques et clans familiaux dans l'Italie de la Renaissance," *Revue de la Méditerrané*, Vol. XX, 1960, pp. 259–279; N. Rubinstein, *The Government of Florence under the Medici: 1434 to 1494*, Oxford 1966, esp. pp. 131 ff.; Ch. Meek, *Lucca 1369–1400. Politics and Society in an Early Renaissance City-State*, Oxford 1978, esp. pp. 344–362.

[25] Cf. R. Walcott Jr., *English Politics in the Early Eighteenth Century*, op. cit.; L. Namier, *The Structure of British Politics at the Accession of George III*, op. cit.; C. Jones, ed., *Party and Management in Parliament 1660–1784*, Leicester 1984.

private bases for cohesive carriers of collective action: family connections, neighbors, friends, professional associates, political associates.[26]

Below the surface of England's atomistic society private connections became the carrier of politics. Or, in other words, the story of politics in England at that time is, to a considerable extent, the story of these connections. Given the nature of the connections, the telling of the story is a very difficult task: all that can be told eventually has first to be secured in a cumbersome process of assembling, comparing, and correlating a great many scattered data.[27]

A primacy of persons characterized also the political process in France under the Third Republic.[28] In elections voters freely shifted their allegiance, producing an electoral landscape of extremely fluid shapes. Votes were cast primarily in consideratoin of a candidate's personality, one's own personal interests which he would represent, and the loyalty which one owed to him. Again, personal relationships and private connections were the sole continuing carriers of politics. Similar to other societies ruled by personal parties, the Third Republic required its analyst to work like a detective, sifting an endless amount of details, slight bits of information – in order to be able finally to discern the *tableau politique* that he wanted to find behind the fluid appearances of this Republic's political reality.[29]

---

[26] It is interesting to note that Christian Meier draws a parallel between Namier's studies and his own study of personal parties in Republican Rome. Cf. *Res Publica Amissa,* op. cit., pp. 187 ff.

[27] Cf. R. Walcott Jr., *English Politics in the Early Eighteenth Century,* op. cit., p. 35: "Membership in the same class or profession and more particularly the relationship between neighbours, between the members of a family connexion, between the dependants of a magnate, and between politicians who having been associated in office elected afterwards to hold together – these furnished effective bases for cohesive groups. By correlating scattered data on the antecedents, economic interests, family and personal relationships, and political affiliations of individual Members of Parliament, we should be able to identify many personal and family groups."

[28] Cf. A. Siegfried, *Tableau politique de la France de l'Ouest sous la Troisième République,* Paris 1964, 2nd ed.

[29] Cf. ibid., p. 410: "On voit alors les questions de personnes primer toutes les autres. Tel canton vient à la République par sympathie pour un candidat républicain populaire, ou bien parce qu'une personnalité influante et riche a su grouper autour d'elle un certain nombre de dévouements d'intérêts. Mais tel autre canton revient avec une égale facilité vers la Droite, parce qu'un châtelain riche et remuant ou bien un prêtre combatif ont su y constituer un noyau d'opposition. De part et d'autre, les mouvements ne survivent guère aux hommes qui les ont suscités, et dans ces conditions l'évolution électorale – si même on peut se servir de ce mot – devient incompréhensible à quiconque n'a pas eu la patience de descendre jusqu'à ces infimes détails anecdotiques." – A more recent

The preceding historical sketch has yielded a set of notions pertinent to the phenomenon of a personal party, a party of friends. As they are arranged in a systematic fashion, the notions constitute a conceptual matrix for the study of personal parties (see Table 3).

Table 3: Matrix: A Party of Friends

	interest	organization	machine	party
(a) *connections* family neighbors friends professional associates political associates followers clients			*formal differentiation*	
(b) *primacy of persons* atomized society fluctuations density in space The candidate				
(c) *representation* scattered data correlations tableau politique				
natural composition				

and quite typical example of a personal party is described in: P. A. Allum, *Politics and Society in Post-War Naples,* Cambridge 1973, p. 325 ff. Cf. further: A. Zuckerman, "Clientelist Politics in Italy," in: E. Gellner, J. Waterbury, eds., *Patrons and Clients in Mediterranean Societies,* London 1977, esp. pp. 68 – 73.

The matrix features two axes; the one describes the natural composition, the other delineates the formal differentiation of a party of friends. The two sequences of concepts follow a personal party in its "natural" evolution: from being an interest to being a political party and from being a family connection to being a web of widely extended connections. Under the heading "primacy of persons" those conceptual tools are listed which help to perceive the socio-spatial origins of a party of friends. And the problems of analyzing personal parties are conceptualized under the heading "representation."

The matrix can be used as a checklist. A party of friends is "found" wherever characteristic features correspond to the concepts itemized in the matrix.

In the following the matrix will be applied to elucidate further the phenomenon of the Kevin White Party. As we shall see, the systematic arrangement of relevant concepts will make "intelligible" a collection of minute data which otherwise might seem to be just a product of pure positivism. The matrix is the medium where the logic of research, gathering "scattered" data, and the logic of study, seizing a *tableau politique,* meet.

The Kevin White Party emerged from Beacon Hill, the classic neighborhood of Boston's social and political elite.[30] Throughout its existence a considerable number of its most important members resided in this neighborhood. The history of the party began in 1960 when a group of residents formed an "interest" around Kevin White and took control of the Democratic Committee in their ward, Ward 5. The members of the interest coalesced around Kevin White because they felt that he held the greatest promise as their candidate for political office. Moving among his neighbors and friends, Kevin White became the candidate in a field of supporters gravitating towards him, the friend as candidate. The group of "young Turks" in Ward 5 included Herbert Gleason, resident and neighbor of Kevin White on Beacon Hill, lawyer and, later, corporation counsel in Boston; Katherine D. Kane, resident and neighbor of Kevin White on Beacon Hill and, later, Deputy Mayor of Boston; Lawrence Cameron, Kevin White's partner in a law firm; Barbara Cameron, his wife who would become Commissioner of Assessing in Boston's government under Mayor White.

The candidate was elected Secretary of State in Massachusetts, and the Kevin White Interest grew by a number of political associates, notably Richard

---

[30] On Beacon Hill, cf. A. Chamberlain, *Beacon Hill,* Boston 1925; C. Amory, *The Proper Bostonians,* New York 1947; G. F. Weston Jr., *Boston Ways. High, By and Folk,* Boston 1957, 1974, 3nd ed.; W. Muir Whitehill, *Boston. A Topographical History,* Cambridge, Mass. 1959, 1968, 2nd ed.; S. E. Morison, *One Boy's Boston 1887–1901,* Boston 1962; The Boston Society of Architects, *Architecture Boston,* Barre, Mass. 1976; L. H. Tharp, *The Appletons of Beacon Hill,* Boston 1973.

M. Dray, attorney in the Secretary's Office; Edward T. Sullivan, Deputy Secretary of State and, later, Vice Mayor of Boston; Robert Q. Crane, State Treasurer and long-time friend of Kevin White's.

When the Secretary of State became a candidate again, pursuing a quest for being the Mayor of Boston, further connections enlarged the Kevin White Interest:

(a) Friends and political associates, including in particular Harold Katz, the personal lawyer of Kevin White; Theodore V. Anzalone, State Director of Corporations under Secretary of State White and, later, the Mayor's aide in many capacities: Commissioner of Assessing (succeeded in this capacity by Barbara Cameron), fund raiser, Italian family man, the friend who knew friends everywhere; James Hosker, the campaign pollster and very close friend who would continue to calculate the Mayor's electoral chances, Frank Dooley, Kevin White's classmate at the Law School of Boston College.

(b) Friends and neighbors on Beacon Hill, notably Samuel P. Huntington, professor of government at Harvard and author of position papers for the candidate (and, later, for the Mayor); Nancy Huntington, the wife of Dr. Huntington who would serve as Director of Public Celebrations in the first White administration and, more important, would become the personal friend in whom the Mayor most confided.

(c) The Harvard connection, an enduring connection throughout the Mayor's tenure. Its first fellows were Barney Frank, tutor in government and, later, the Mayor's principal assistant; Hale Champion whom Kevin White, after his election, would appoint head of the Boston Redevelopment Authority; Samuel V. Merrick, who was hired as special counsel to the Mayor; David Davis whom Hale Champion recommended to the Mayor as expert on fiscal affairs (and who later became Harvard's budget director, rejoining Champion who had returned to the university).

(d) The Kennedy connection, notably Senator Edward T. Kennedy who helped to raise funds for Kevin White; and Richard N. Goodwin who assisted in writing the candidate's speeches (the Kennedy connection broke in 1972, cf. p. 62).[31]

---

[31] Quite similar to the quest of Kevin White, the campaign of presidential candidate John F. Kennedy originated in a personal "interest": "The nine men who met at his father's Palm Beach home to plan the strategy for John F. Kennedy's nomination were not party leaders: they were relatives, friends, and employees (only one was a professional politician) – persons attached to him as a person, not as a party figure." (E. C. Banfield, *Here the People Rule. Selected Essays,* New York – London 1985, p. 50.)

In the comparative history of personal parties the Kevin White Party deserves a prominent place.[32] It arose from private connections and although it formed the government of Boston over nearly two decades it remained an alliance of family connections (including the members of the White family, of course),[33] neighbors, friends, professional and political associates, and − increasingly, while it dispensed power − followers and clients. It emerged from a small, but distinct urban area − from the classic space of a *neighborhood,* the *contrada* in an Italian city-state, the *tribus* in Ancient Rome. And the confines within which its operations took place were the confines of a small town; close spatial relations intensified the personal relations by which the party worked.

This party of friends was a principal carrier of politics and public responsibility in an atomized society of fluid shapes − Boston, America. Its existence prevented the quest of Kevin White, a political candidate, from being quixotic. Attracting friends and followers, this candidate could transform his personal quest into a political quest, into the collective quest of all the people who were connected with his "party" − the political "interest" coalescing around Kevin White.

A *tableau politique* of the Kevin White Party is drawn in the present chapter of our study. The nature of its subject requires a very detailed representation; the technique of representation is comparable to the method of the pointilliste: technically, the *tableau* is composed of dots and strokes in abundant detail; pictorially, all the details blend together only in a certain distance, and it is this distance − the comprehensive view of the observer − that actually makes the *tableau.*

The "distance" from where the Kevin White Party can best be seen is the "history" of personal parties. Or, to put it inversely, the "history" of personal parties is the "place" of Boston in the era of the Kevin White Party.

---

[32] To appraise the *classic* achievement of the Kevin White Party, cf. the section on "Die Organisation der Macht," in: Ch. Meier, *Res Publica Amissa,* op. cit., pp. 174 ff.

[33] As regards the White family, cf. A. Lupo, *Liberty's Chosen Home,* op. cit., Chapter 6: "The Old Boston: Political Genes of a Man and The City." − On the "family factor" in Boston and Massachusetts politics, cf. E. Killory, *Boston Charter Reform (B),* Kennedy School of Government, 1978, p. 5.

3 The Interest and Its Legitimacy

"To have friends, is Power," notes Hobbes in *Leviathan*. A person alone may have but the "naturall Power" of an individual: an "eminence of the Faculties of Body, or Mind: as extraordinary Strength, Forme, Prudence, Arts, Eloquence, Liberality, Nobility." A person who has friends, however, has augmented his "natural" power by the power of his friends: "they are strengths united."[34]

---

[34] Th. Hobbes, *Leviathan,* (Part I, Chapter X), ed. C. B. MacPherson, Harmondsworth 1972, p. 150 (= Penguin Books). – Cf. also Aristotle, *Nicomachean Ethics* 1099b1: "For it is impossible, or at least not easy, to play a noble part unless furnished with the necessary equipment. For many noble actions require instruments for their performance, in the shape of friends or wealth or political power." – In discussing power as a phenomenon emerging from a field of friends I am drawing on the Kevin White Party for empirical evidence. However, the general relevance of the phenomenon ought to be stressed, and therefore I refer to a few exemplary observations made in the realm of presidential politics.

(a) When Hubert Humphrey pursued the presidential nomination of the Democratic Party, he counted upon his friendships to carry him to his goal: "Enjoying people as I do, I naturally seek new friends and keep old friendships going. As a matter of course, some of these friendships do have political value, and every politician is human enough to develop some friendships primarily for their potential political value. So I suppose it is honest to say that, within the limitations of my position and the strictures placed on me, I did instinctively try to develop a political base while I was Vice President, building primarily on the base I already had from my senatorial career – my long, happy relationships with the labor movement, the Jewish and black communities, liberal farm organizations. I had also been expanding my contacts in the business world." (H. H. Humphrey, *The Education of a Public Man,* Garden City 1976, p. 368.)

(b) On the other hand, President Carter's lack of success in dealing with Congress originated in his lack of friends on Capitol Hill: "He has no friends on Capitol Hill. 'He just doesn't have that wellspring to call on,' said one Southern Senator. 'When you get in trouble, that's when you need your friends to come to your defense, and he just doesn't have that.'" (St. V. Roberts, "Carter Discord With Congress: President Is Apparently Seeking to Ease Stains," *NYT,* June 5, 1979.) – "On Capitol Hill Carter failed to forge strong alliances. He had made no close friendships among Congressmen even after he had chaired a national committee to recruit Democratic candidates for Congress and state offices, an arrangement that enabled him to politick all over the country for 20 months. He still had no close congressional relationships after he had won the Democratic nomination and then the election. This was curious enough, but more revealing, he still had none four years later. A former Democratic Senator summed it up: 'There was no one up on the Hill who would go the last mile for him.'" (H. Donovan, "The Enigmatic President," *Time,* May 6, 1985, p. 22.)

(c) President Eisenhower, Fred J. Greenstein reports, acquired political influence through cultivating "personal relationships": "In congressional relations, because the committee

The power emanating from the combined forces of one's friends can be used to acquire still more power; Hobbes therefore includes it among a class of powers which he calls "instrumentall Powers" such as "Riches, Reputation, Friends and the secret working of God, which men call Good Luck." Power amplifies power and the amplified power accelerates the amplification of power: "For the nature of Power, is in this point, like to Fame, increasing as it proceeds; or like the motion of heavy bodies, which the further they go, make still the more hast."

Friends amplify their power by a concentration of their "united strengths" upon *one* friend within an expanding field of ever more friends. The power of each is amplified by the power of all, and from the power of all emanates the power of one that is the "greatest" power:

---

and leadership way stations are controlled by semiautonomous individuals, each with his own idiosyncrasies, personality analysis played a particularly key role. Personal relations based as much on art as spontaneity, for example, were crucial in Eisenhower's establishment of unexpectedly amiable relations with Taft [the Majority Leader]. [...] Eisenhower's sensitivity to personalities enabled him to identify and therefore bypass blocks in his channels for influencing Congress." (F. J. Greenstein, *The Hidden-Hand Presidency*, op. cit., p. 78 f.)

(d) According to his testimony, Alexander Haig, President Reagan's first Secretary of State, lacked sufficient status and influence within the Reagan administration; he was not, as he explains, a friend among friends in an "Administration of chums": "Clark [William Clark, Deputy Secretary of State under Haig and, later, Reagan's national security adviser] had a single, overwhelming qualification: he was an old and trusted friend of the President's. I was not, and in an Administration of chums, bonded together by years of faith and hope and hard work on the campaign trail, this was a handicap." (A. Haig, "CAVEAT. Realism, Reagan and Foreign Policy," *Time*, April 2, 1984, p. 33.)

(e) The following "generalizations that apply in any [presidential] administration" are offered by Ken Hechler in his memoir on the Truman administration: "A president surrounds himself with people whom he trusts. They share his goals, or are flexible enough to embrace and enthusiastically support them. They are on the staff to help the president in his job, rather than grind personal axes for themselves. They should have a point of view broader than the executive departments and agencies or special interests. [...] Every president – and Truman was no exception – appoints people from his home state whom he has known a long time. Thus he tries to insure there is mutual trust and loyalty between the president and staff members. Doing so does not always insure competence and ethical behaviour. There is a tendency to keep friends beyond the point of usefulness if they should get into difficulties." (K. Hechler, *Working With Truman. A Personal Memoir of the White House Years*, New York 1982, 2nd ed., p. 35.)

Cf. also Th. H. White, *The Making of the President 1960*, London 1961, pp. 1–5, 27–31, 49–55; Th. H. White, *The Making of the President 1964*, New York 1965, pp. 89–97, 131–139.

> The Greatest of Humane Powers, is that which is compounded of the Powers of
> most men, united by consent, in one person, Naturall, or Civill, that has the use
> of all their Powers depending on his will; such as is the Power of a Common-
> wealth.[35]

The "greatest" power is a precarious gift. It is the power to govern, the
sway of one will over the will of everyone else in a "Commonwealth." It can
be and, indeed, is very often an awesome power; seemingly boundless, as it
imposes its laws and rules upon myriads of individuals.

It is also the power, however, that itself is its greatest enemy, if its holder
asserts himself as the one whose will is the law. He who does everything and
controls everything becomes the weakest of all. Power stretched to boundless
might, explains Fénelon in *Télémaque,* saps the foundation upon which it is
built:

> When Kings become accustomed to recognizing no more any law other than
> their own absolute will, and when they no longer restrain their passions, they
> can do everything: however, being able to do what they want, they are sapping
> the foundations of their might; they lack principle and rules for the conduct of
> government. Everyone eagerly wants to flatter them: they no longer have a
> people; all what they have are slaves, and their number dwindles every day. Who
> will tell them the truth? Who will tame this torrent? Everything erodes [...].[36]

To have friends is power. And without friends power erodes. The greatest
of human powers, the power to govern, is a precarious gift because of its
provisional nature. Since it flows from the friendship, the consent of the
people in a "Commonwealth," the power of a government always needs
friends, or else it will cease to flow. It does not exist by itself but must
continually be renewed by the approval, trust, and loyalty of those who
originally agreed to it as their "strengths united." It is a precarious gift, a
provisional power to the extent that it requires a continuing legitimation of
its existence.[37]

---

[35] Th. Hobbes, *Leviathan,* op. cit., p. 150. – Cf. also Cicero, *De Amicitia,* VII, 23: "Quod
si exemeris ex rerum natura benevolentiae coniunctionem, nec domus ulla nec urbs stare
poterit – But if you should take the bond of goodwill out of the universe no house or
city could stand." – *De Amicitia,* XXIII, 86: "Una est enim amicitia in rebus humanis,
de cuius utilitate omnes uno ore consentiunt – For the one thing in human experience
about whose advantage all men with one voice agree, is friendship."

[36] Fénelon, *Télémaque,* (XVII), idem, *Oeuvres,* ed. A. Martin, Paris 1837, Reprint 1882,
Vol. III, p. 132 (My translation, T.S.).

[37] The relationship between power and the "principle of mutualism" is discussed by Hans
Buchheim in: *Die Ethik der Macht,* op. cit., pp. 53 ff. – On the legitimacy of power
derived from personal parties, in the context of the Roman *res publica,* cf. Ch. Meier,
Res Publica Amissa, pp. 13 f., 34 ff. – On the problems of legitimacy and legitimation

The flux and reflux of power – between people and government – cannot occur without mediating structures. They translate the abstract process of power into the reality of relationships between persons. Among those structures, "parties" represent the most important medium for translating power into politics among people. Frank R. Kent, the author of *The great game of politics*, a classic study of "political machines," expressed this "truth" succinctly:

> The truth is that political organizations are absolutely essential to the conduct of the government – city, state, or national. This is a government by parties. [...] Without organization there would be no parties. Without parties there would be no government [...]. If the party organizations were suddenly swept out of existence, we would have a period of chaos and disorder.[38]

Kent and a couple of other heretics apart,[39] the "truth" about parties has not many friends among contemporary students of politics. They mostly hold "enlightened" and therefore prejudiced views about this subject. They are fully prepared to accept parties as political structures that dispense power, constitute governments, share the burden of public responsibilities. They are much less inclined to approve of parties as personal relationships that concentrate power among friends, form a fabric of governing within the system of government, build a *clientèle* with the benefits of power.

The modern theory of politics implies a prejudice against the human factor in the shaping of a society's political life. Instead of being a science of people

---

in general, cf. A. Passerin d'Entrèves, "Legality and Legitimacy," *The Review of Metaphysics*, Vol. XVI, No. 4, June 1963, pp. 687 – 702; P. Bastid et al., *L'idée de légitimité*, No. 7, *Annales de philosophie politique*, Paris 1967; Th. Würtenberger Jr., *Die Legitimität staatlicher Herrschaft: Eine staatsrechtlich-politische Begriffsgeschichte*, Berlin 1973; N. Achterberg, W. Krawietz, eds., *Legitimation des modernen Staates*, Beiheft No. 15, *Archiv für Rechts- und Sozialphilosophie*, Wiesbaden 1981; T. Schabert, "Power, Legitimacy, and Truth: Reflections on the Impossibility to Legitimize Legitimations of Political Order," in: A. Moulakis, ed., *Legitimacy*, Berlin 1985, pp. 96 – 104. – The problem of power and its legitimacy within the context of *French* local politics has been discussed by Pierre Grémion (*Le pouvoir périphérique. Bureaucrates et notables dans le système politique français*, Paris 1976, pp. 416 – 439) and Jeanne Becquart-Leclercq ("Légitimité et pouvoir local," *Revue Française de Science Politique*, Vol. 27, No. 2, 1977, pp. 228 – 258). Grémion observes, for instance: "Ce n'est pas, suivant le schéma constitutionnel, le Conseil municipal qui est à la source de la légitimité du maire, mais à l'inverse, c'est souvent la légitimité du maire qui est première et c'est de lui que dépend la légitimité du Conseil. Le maire tire sa légitimité d'un *contact direct* avec l'ensemble de la population au-delà de toute structuration de cette population en groupes d'intérêts" (p. 418).

[38] F. R. Kent, *The Great Game of Politics*, op. cit., p. 344 f.

[39] E. C. Banfield, M. L. Rakove.

as persons in politics, it is rather a science of artefacts: the "State," the "political system," the "laws" of politics (understood in a mechanistic sense), "institutions" and their "functions," or such hybrid constructions as the "one-party State" or the *Staatspartei*." This science – planned to be a "natural" science of politics – presupposes a political reality whose *loci* are its own artefacts rather than the persons who pursue the activity called "politics." Naturally, nobody can overlook the importance of personal relationships in the pursuit of this activity nor the fact that it involves patronage, for instance. But then the science of artefacts cannot really recognize these human conditions of politics; they contradict what it teaches: the seizure of politics by rationalization. Since they cannot be ignored, the modern, rationalist theory of politics responded by a tacit prejudice: relegating the human conditions of politics to a grey zone of "informal" dealings or repelling them outright as "aberrations."

Therefore, the "truth" about parties – that is the legitimacy of parties as personal relationships, as party of friends – has usually been formulated in an apologetic way, if it was articulated at all.[40] From an empirical, not from a "scientific" point of view, this is somewhat surprising. The flux and reflux of power – that is the legitimation of a government – can be observed in the most direct way, if it is mediated by a party of friends. The artefacts of governments appear as what they are: knots of physical, spatial, and administrative organization that people use (and have therefore invented) in the process of being engaged in politics. And the *loci* of politics will be found not in a "system" of institutions (called "government") but in the relationships of the people who move within the web of institutional knots which, by their

---

[40] Cf. for instance: G. M. Reynolds, *Machine Politics in New Orleans,* op. cit., p. 236 f.: "In bringing together the scattered powers of government and focusing them for effective political action, the organization [= the Choctaw Club] did a real service. Since effective centralization was not provided by law, it was necessary for it to be achieved through party control." – R. K. Merton, "The Latent Functions of the Machine," in: E. C. Banfield, ed., *Urban Government. A Reader in Administration and Politics,* New York 1961, p. 181: "Proceeding from the functional view, therefore, that we should *ordinarily* (not invariably) expect persistent social patterns and social structures to perform positive functions *which are at the same time not adequately fulfilled by other existing patterns and structures,* THE THOUGHT OCCURS THAT PERHAPS [my capitalization, T. S.] this publicly maligned organization [the political machine] is, *under present conditions,* satisfying basic latent functions." – J.-F. Médard, "Le rapport de clientèle, du phéno-mène social à l'analyse politique," *Revue Française de Science Politique,* Vol. XXVI, No. 1, Febr. 1976, p. 123: "En effet, les systèmes politiques modernes, malgré le dévelop-pement du droit, de la bureaucratie, l'importance des idéologies politiques, n'ont pas éliminé les relations personelles: les rapports collectifs restent médiatisés par les rapports individuels, il faut en tenir compte pour une vue réaliste de nos sociétés."

movements, they are constantly reweaving. After a certain period of careful observation, the personal relationships that are the *loci* of politics will be clearly discerned: as distinctive aggregations of people, as a party of friends, for instance, such as the Kevin White Party.

This party of friends that formed the government of Boston labored continuously for its own and thereby the legitimacy of the government it formed. Various institutional mechanisms were set in motion to further the flux and reflux of power between the government and the people of Boston (they will be described in the following two paragraphs). The members of the party were not only taught to "please the people," but certain incentives were used to spur their enthusiasm for helping the party with its many tasks: "To inform and help people, relate them to and through the civil service bureaucracy and regulations, to attend community meetings and lead neighborhood causes, provide services, provide jobs, provide a social life, provide contacts."[41]

Naturally, winning a mayoral election every four years was the principal objective of the Kevin White Party. In these election years it served as the instrument for legitimizing the rule of Mayor White by attracting a majority of votes to Kevin White's candidacy. However, between the elections, the burden of the party as regards the legitimation of the Mayor's rule, became even greater: the flux and reflux of power had to go on, the power in City Hall needed friends in order to remain effective as a power to govern. In its varied manifestations the party mediated the flow of power between City Hall and the city, between the few and the many, between the Court and the people of Boston. It produced "legitimacy"; not the legitimacy lent by elections, but the legitimacy furnished by friendships, alliances, clienteles, patronage.

In an urban society of such fluid shapes as Boston the "greatest" power — the will of all united in one will — could hardly emerge and exist as an effective power to govern without the original *and* continuing legitimation by a personal party, a party of friends.[42] We should question current beliefs and consider that a government formed by friends is not necessarily a government of a twisted sort. Friends are friends, of course, and the party they make is induced by a personal "interest." In Boston, however, a personal interest of friends emerged as the indispensable bond by which the "discordant particles" of this urban society united to a body of political power.[43] Certainly,

---

[41] Source: Interview.

[42] On the parallel in Ancient Rome, cf.: R. Heinze, *Vom Geist des Römertums*, Leipzig – Berlin 1938, pp. 25 – 58 (the chapter entitled "Fides").

[43] On the necessity of bonds of friendship in the politics of the Roman Republic, cf. Ch. Meier, *Res Publica Amissa*, op. cit., pp. 22 ff., 36 ff.

in judging the Kevin White Party, one should not ignore the presence of all the "friends" who had an interest in its well-being. But, above all, one should constantly keep in mind what it was that made its existence "legitimate."

In his study on *The Structure of British Politics at the Accession of George III* Lewis Namier explains the legitimacy of personal parties, parties of friends, in the English Parliament. The explanation given by him and Soame Jenyns, the authority he quotes, is evidently meant to apply not only to the English Parliament but to other political bodies as well. As regards the emergence and existence of the Kevin White Party in Boston, it is quite instructive:

> In 1784, after a Parliamentary experience of almost forty years, Soame Jenyns, when writing on Parliamentary reform, declared that an independent Parliament consisting of Members 'unawed and uninfluenced, and guided only by the dictates of their own judgment and conscience,' never existed and never could exist.
>
> 'Take away self-interest, and all these will have no star to steer by [...]; a Minister [...] must be possessed of some attractive influence, to enable him to draw together these discordant particles, and unite them in a firm and solid majority, without which he can pursue no measures of public utility with steadiness or success. An independent House of Commons is no part of the English constitution [...].
>
> A numerous assembly uninfluenced is as much a creature of imagination, as a griffin or a dragon [...]. Parliaments have ever been influenced, and by that means our constitution is perpetually misrepresented and misunderstood. They are seldom, very seldom, bribed to injure their country, because it is seldom the interest of Ministers to injure it; but the great source of corruption is, that they will not serve it for nothing. Men get into Parliament in pursuit of power, honors, and preferments, and until they obtain them, determine to obstruct all business, and to distress Government; but happily for their country, they are no sooner gratified, than they are equally zealous to promote the one, and support the other.[44]

---

[44] L. Namier, *The Structure of British Politics at the Accession of George III*, op. cit., p. 213 f. – Cf. also: Xenophon, *Memorabilia*, II, vi, 27: "kai men hoi symmachein ethelontes eu poieteoi, hina thelosi prothymeisthai – Moreover, those who are willing to become allies must be well treated that they may be willing to exert themselves."

The Structure of the Party:
Members, Metamorphoses, and Metastases

4 Members: The Unreflective Creation
of a Political Body

They affirmed that they would not form a political body, never muster all of them that there were, and, anyway, would just have some sort of personal relationship to a number of colleagues in the government. Yet, they invited each other to celebrate, held or planned large gatherings, assembled the names and addresses of all those who belonged to them, producing lists that counted easily six hundred or a thousand people.[45]

They did not regulate the life of their party by statutes, nor did they ascribe the cohesive politics which they pursued to any rules. Yet they conformed to a distinctive attitude towards power and politics and displayed it in public with an astounding consistency.

They did not shape the body of their party by a formal hierarchy, and no one's standing in the party was determined by elections, formal agreements, or any other similar procedure. Yet they always had a positive sense of importance, knowing very well who the leaders and who the troopers of the party were, who had risen to a position of higher standing and who was jostling in the sidelines.

They did not stay in touch with each other in a regular way, neither observing a calendar of party meetings nor using other means of internal communication, like a bulletin, for instance. Yet they kept up a flow of information among them by which important news traveled in a flurry. Applying themselves to the media of personal contacts, luncheon appointments, telephone conversations, dinner parties, casual encounters, they formed quite a sophisticated "system" of communication.

They did not care about articulating the political beliefs which they might have had in common; nor did they establish any criteria or rituals to decide who belonged to their party and who did not; they themselves had not taken

---

[45] In the summer of 1983, for instance, plans were made to gather all friends of Kevin White's for a "farewell party" — KHW had decided not to seek once again the position of Mayor in the upcoming election. Harron Ellenson, a member of the Kevin White Party, started to prepare a list of all the friends to be invited, but did not complete her task since the plans for the party were called off. Ellenson's provisional list, dated from August 1, 1983, includes the names and addresses of 525 "friends."

an oath of allegiance nor professed an ideology. Yet they discriminated with great care among those who came from the "outside" and appeared to have bent their views upon the "inside." Whoever was eventually admitted to the world of the party had several times been the subject of a judgment passed by a trusted member of the party: "He [or: she] is okay."

A party of friends such as the Kevin White Party is a political body whose formal presence emerges from a process of unreflective creation. It was not planned, designed in the way a parliament, for instance, would be designed by the framers of a Constitution; it was not laid out, constructed by its founders first in the mode of a blueprint; it was not invented, built by deliberate acts of organization; its formal presence was not the accomplishment of conscious efforts: the efforts that brought it forth belied any manifestations of organized creativity. If the purpose to create a political body is thought necessarily to have been part of its existence, then it did not exist.

Yet it did exist. And it existed in the mode of a political body, having a presence of structure and form, producing an appearance of organization. It functioned in the way of a political party, transposing the political aspirations of a few friends into an effective political organization, forming a government.

The Kevin White Party represented a primary manifestation of social creativity. It emerged from a process that took place as persons who were connected with each other by personal relationships proceeded to actualize their connection; they concentrated in an aggregation; from the concentration of their connection grew a highly differentiated form of their presence – the Kevin White Party.[46]

I call this process of differentiation the process of unreflective creation. Again, the people who were involved in the process did not plan to unfold a differentiated social field, to give their relationships a continuing presence of structure and form. The emergence of a differentiated aggregation of people from a concentration of the connection between them eludes the ordinary logic of social designing. If it occurs, as it occurred with the Kevin White Party, it represents undoubtedly an act of social creation – but an act of an *unreflective* social creation.

Naturally, the participants in this act of creation could partake in an act of social creation because they already knew each other in the mode of primary relationships: family ties, friendships, spatial proximity, personal alliances. By maintaining these relationships, they were already using a

---

[46] It might be of interest to consider here that cities, the most *differentiated* forms of human congregation, emerged in ancient history from a *concentration* of human populations. Cf. Ch. L. Redman, *The Rise of Civilization. From Early Farmers to Urban Societies in the Ancient Near East*, San Francisco 1978, pp. 215 ff.; M. Hammond, *The City in the Ancient World*, Cambridge, Mass. 1972, pp. 7 ff., 13 ff., 45 ff., 54 ff., 148 ff.

potential of social creativity; and by actualizing their connection, they actualized this potential – producing, to an increasing extent, primary manifestations of social creativity.

They differentiated themselves as the Kevin White Party, forming the distinctive structure of a political body.

The core of this structure was the "political family." It consisted of not more than three dozen persons;[47] its character as a "family" sprang from the prevalent mode of relationship between these persons. They were connected with each other by kinship (the White family), by marriage (the Camerons, the Huntingtons, Robert J. Ryan married to the daughter of Robert Q. Crane), or by a close, familial association. And they formed a family that was thoroughly "political"; almost all of them held a position (or several positions) in the governmental structure established by the head of their family, Kevin White; the few others served the party in "unofficial" but nevertheless political functions.[48]

The political family reproduced the cosmos of the interests of Kevin White – and these were the interests of the party. Besides the connection of Kevin White's family and old friends, the political family included: members of the Court (Kane, Sullivan, Ryan, Jackson, Spring); pollsters and political consultants (Marttila, Hosker, Walsh); developers and other persons active in the business of urban development (Druker, Farrell, Zuckerman, Colbert,

---

[47] Kevin H. White, Kathryn G. White (the wife of KHW), Caitlan, Mark, Beth White (three of their five children), William J. Galvin, William Galvin Jr., Robert Y. Murray, Carolyn Connors (in-laws of KHW); Barbara and Lawrence Cameron, Theodore V. Anzalone, Richard M. Dray, Herbert Gleason, Samuel and Nancy Huntington, Harold Katz, James Hosker, Robert Q. Crane, John Marttila, Jack Walsh, David Sawyer, Jack Connors, Joanne Prevost, Robert J. Ryan, Edward T. Sullivan, Katherine D. Kane, Robert L. Farrell, James G. Colbert, Micho Spring, Mortimer Zuckerman, Ira Jackson, Tully Plesser, Bertram A. Druker. – This list does not reflect temporal variations; it describes the membership of the political family comprehensively.

[48] Quite a few of the positions held by members of the political family have already been mentioned (cf. pp. 39, 85, 89 f.). A few more examples: B. A. Druker, Chairman, Auditorium Commission; R. L. Farrell, Chairman, BRA; J. G. Colbert, Treasurer, BRA; R. J. Ryan, Director, BRA; Micho Spring, Trustee, Library Department; B. G. Cameron, Member, Public Facilities Board. The members of the White family were involved in the politics of the party as follows: W. J. Galvin, Chairman, Kevin White [campaign] committee; W. Galvin Jr., Head, Committee for a Better Boston [fundraising]; Kathryn, Caitlan, Mark White, consultants to the Kevin White committee; Beth White, paid expert in photo services, Kevin White committee; R. Y. Murray, Member of the Board, Massachusetts Parking Authority; Carolyn Connors, consultant, Kevin White committee and, very briefly, employed by the City. – T. V. Anzalone served as Treasurer of the Committee for a Better Boston.

the Court member Ryan); journalists (Alan Lupo, Colbert); a fundraiser and a versatile politician (Anzalone and Prevost).[49]

The small number of the members of the political family contrasts with the large number of all other members of the party. However, this multitude evidently adhered to a remarkable tendency towards forming a cohesive structure in space: most pursued their individual lives and careers, moved hither and thither between positions in the private sector and the government, or the academia, switched professions – and they remained parishioners of Greater Boston. And if the one or the other moved to New York or Washington, or, more rarely, to such places as Santa Fe or Seattle, he or she did not cut the ties to the party. Invitations were extended, axes of professional and political cooperation were built, possibilities for a job back in Boston were discussed.

In the pursuit of their professional careers, members of the party introduced another element into the structure of the party. Leaving their positions in the city government and moving to positions in other institutional settings (public or private), a number of them congregated sometimes as a "cluster" in one or more of those settings. They established "metastases" of the party beyond the city government proper.[50]

Over the years, the party took an also the characteristics of an employment agency operating as a discreet unit of job referrals. In case of need or interest, members of the party circulated their resumes among fellow members; this mutual assistance was mostly thought to be a matter of direct, personal relationships rather than a form of loyal service to the party. Apart from patronage (which was always supervised by a certain member of the Court and dealt largely with the distribution of low-level city jobs), no one in the party undertook "organized" efforts as regards the professional advancement of its members. Yet the people in the party knew each other, and they continued to know each other long after they had left their occupations in the city government. Cooperating in the way of an "invisible" employment agency, they "just" actualized personal relationships. But, they perfectly knew, of course, that by actualizing their personal relationships they were actualizing their relationships within a distinctive social field.

Thus the structural differentiation of the party included the awareness of all those who came to understand themselves as the "alumni" – as the

---

[49] On R. J. Ryan, cf. CR, Vol. 73, No. 35, Aug. 31, 1981, p. 709; on J. Marttila and J. Walsh, cf. S. Blumenthal, *The Permanent Campaign. Inside the World of Elite Political Operatives*, Boston 1980, pp. 202–216 and pp. 59–71, respectively; on B. A. Druker, cf. CR, Vol. 74, No. 23, June 7, 1982, p. 438; on J. G. Colbert, cf. CR, Vol. 73, No. 12, March 23, 1981, p. 703; on J. A. Prevost, cf. CR, Vol. 74, No. 13, March 29, 1982, p. 204.
[50] cf. infra, p. 141 ff..

persons who shared the experience of having participated and of continuing
to participate in the connection of a personal party, a party of friends. Many
displayed this awareness in the more compact form of a distinctive mentality.
They partook of tacitly approved opinions and unwittingly adopted habits,
of a store of purified memories and well-tailored legends, and, not without
adverse effects, of a xenophobia towards "outsiders." Socially, the mentality
inspired enthusiasm, but also instigated dissent. It became the major factor
in the process of social selection from which the party was built. If one could
not chime in with the mentality, one either did not join the party or quickly
left it again.

Through this process of selection and rejection, the party proved that it
existed.

5 Metamorphoses: The Junctures of Creativity

The party represented a process of social creativity not only in the mode of
its own differentiation. It also catalyzed a social and political creativity in
the mode of public administration and government. Itself forming a chassis
of politics, the party formed a government — the government of Boston.

In further considering this process — the party forming a government —,
we should, first of all, keep in mind what exactly the phenomena were to
which the word "party" and "government" refer. The terms denote two
aggregative fields of persons that did not exist in the way of two firm
"institutions." They were rather two different manifestations of the *same*
configuration of people within the *same* process of social creativity. Or, still
more precisely, members of the party became active as members of the
government and thereby formed the aggregative field called "government" —
all the while continuing to form the aggregative field of the party.

The process of the party forming the government unfolded by various
stages:

(a) From the party issued the Court, and from the Court arose the government.

(b) The party brought on campaign organizations, and in successful campaigns the government was founded. (The election campaigns will be
discussed in the next paragraph.)

(c) The party constituted a reservoir for the recruitment of government
officials. There was never a lack of candidates, since a member of the
party who resigned from a position in the government usually "returned"
to a holding position in the party from where he or she emerged again —
as was frequently the case — to assume another governmental office. In

addition, a rejuvenation of the government was accomplished by the self-perpetuation of the party. Novices — mostly proteges of senior members — were drawn into the spell of the party and eventually became dedicated servants of the government formed by the party.[51]

(d) Finally, the party mediated the flux and reflux of power between the government and the people; it produced legitimacy; it buttressed the creative potential of the government by securing the support of friends and clients among the people in the city.

In the process of affording power, legitimacy, and creativeness the party took shape in different approaches to institutionalization. Or, to put it inversely, certain institutional forms embodied the changing manifestation of the party. It appeared in a state of metamorphoses, in the continuing presence of different institutional forms.

A metamorphosis of the party occurred whenever the process of social creativity represented by the party approached another form of organization; whenever the creative potential diffused throughout the party — that itself was but a field of persons — was actualized by a fabric of directives given to members of the party; whenever the movements of these persons within the new fabric of directives converged to an institutional carrier of creativity.

Purpose and organization, the quest for achievement and the labor of persistence, political imagination and administrative discipline met in the metamorphoses of the party. Whenever they occurred, the metamorphoses drew the power of creativeness from the discordant particles of political life. They represented what I suggest to call "junctures of creativity."

The most ambitious approach of the party to embody in an institution the process of affording power, legitimacy, and creativeness was named "Office of Public Service" (OPS).[52] In the heyday of its achievement — which coincided with the third term of Mayor White (1976–79) — the OPS was regarded as the "most prestigious" agency in the City. It had succeeded for quite a while to attract many young men and women who were inspired by the idea that they worked for the cause of "good government" by working for the OPS. Most had taken up their first job in a governmental agency when they joined the OPS and, dedicated as they were, thought of themselves as being "the best and the brightest" in the administration of Mayor White.

---

[51] In 1981, for example, two participants in the operation of Mandarin Spring held their positions in the government as proteges of two Court members — who themselves did not hold a position in the government at that time: Lisa Savereid as protege of Ira Jackson, Alex Taft as protege of Emily Lloyd.

[52] The OPS is subject of a detailed study: D. Lorrain, *La gestion municipale à Boston*, unpublished research report, Fondation des villes, [Paris] 1976.

Not a few proved, by the course of their later careers, that the OPS had indeed provided excellent opportunities for a successful education in the trade of politics and government.[53]

An official brochure, published by the City in May 1978, described the OPS as follows:

> The Office of Public Service (OPS) operates the city's Little City Hall program. Eighteen Little City Halls, located in each neighborhood of the city, provide a broad spectrum of direct services and information to Boston residents. The program has been instrumental in bringing about greater citizen participation in the local governmental process, and has increased the sensitivity and responsiveness of the city's line departments to the special needs and concerns of neighborhood residents. Little City Hall managers and staffers are thoroughly versed in all aspects of city government.[54]

In the view of their founders and, later, administrators, the OPS and the Little City Halls fulfilled an essential need in the social and political life of Boston. They professed that the representation of the neighborhoods in the politics of the city had "broken down."[55] To be regarded as a legitimate

---

[53] The names of all former employees in the OPS cannot be mentioned. A few names, however, need to be listed. The respective persons either worked for the OPS in particular capacities or continued to be actors in Boston's political world: Fred Salvucci, Kirk O'Donnell, Peter Meade, Stuart Robbins, Isaac Graves, Robert Fichter, Gail Rotegaard, David Davis, John Vitagliano, Claudia Delmonaco, Ed Dwyer, William Holland, Robert J. Ryan, Larry Quealy, Andy Olins, Roberta Delaney, Dennis Kearney, William Edgerton, John Spears, Doby Flowers, Gerry Marcinowski, Bruce C. Bolling, Robert R. Kiley.

[54] City of Boston, *Neighborhood Boston. A Guide to Human Services,* [Boston] 1978.

[55] It was the City Council, according to this view, which did not fulfill its "natural" function as a body of neighborhood representation. Cf. M. D. Esch, J. E. Killory, *Boston Charter Reform (A),* Kennedy School of Government, 1978, p. 14: "The structure of the City Council has gone through three major changes in this century. In 1909 [...] the former partisan, bicameral assembly, with one branch elected at-large and the other by districts, was consolidated into a nine-member, non-partisan, at-large body, similar to the present Council [...]. In 1924 Boston moved back to a twenty-one member Council elected by wards, desiring to create a greater emphasis on neighborhood representation. Twenty-five years later, in 1949, the city returned to the nine-member at-large form prompted by a feeling that local issues were dominating the Council. [...] the era of Mayor Collins in the 1950's promoted the growth of the city and particularly the expansion of large urban developments and highways. Where no Council member had a stake in the affected neighborhood, the objections of residents were more easily ignored. [...] The last decade has seen a return, especially under Mayor White, of involvement of the neighborhoods with development plans and local concerns." – Since 1983 the Council is again largely based on "district representation": it is a body of thirteen members of which nine are elected by single-member districts and four at large. Kevin White did not appear to be overly enthusiastic about this change: "The new plan

authority, to win the support and approval of the people, to enlist the citizens as its constituents, a government of Boston needed a medium of direct interaction with the residents in the city. The OPS and the Little City Halls were intended to be this medium. At his first campaign for the office of Mayor, Kevin White, the candidate, pledged that he would establish a Little City Hall in each neighborhood, if he were elected. He kept his promise when he had become Mayor. The first of the eighteen Little City Halls opened in East Boston on July 25, 1968. Another nine were established in the same year; three in 1969, three in 1970, and two in 1972. In early 1981 the number of Little City Halls was reduced from 18 offices to 14; the remaining offices were all closed on June 16, 1981.[56]

The Little City Halls served their purpose in two ways, in an "official" one and in a more "unofficial" one.

The official part of the OPS-operation consisted in a variety of services. At a Little City Hall citizens would receive a marriage license, tax abatement applications, birth and death certificates, rent control information, public housing information, resident parking stickers, income tax assistance, dog licenses; at a Little City Hall they would register for voting, lodge a complaint about unsatisfactory municipal services, ask for help in an emergency or for assistance in dealing with the city bureaucracy.

The unofficial part subsisted on the official one and, for this reason alone, was supposed to reinforce the effectiveness of the services delivered by the Little City Halls. It reflected − unofficially and therefore more directly − the politics and the interests of the party.

On this side, then, the OPS-operation introduced an unmediated democratic process bypassing the institutions of representative government, in particular the line departments of the city government and the City Council.

Constituting a separate system of providing the people in the city with the services of the city government, it acted as a check upon the city bureaucracy. To the degree that it was controlled by the OPS, the bureaucracy could become neither too negligent nor too overbearing. And, of course, both the OPS and the bureaucracy could not help testing each other, forming a frame of competition for the delivery of municipal services − to the benefit of the

---

gives the neighborhoods at this time 'better representation,' he [White] said. But he added that he would not be surprised, 'if 30 years from now, they scrapped this and went back to a citywide council. And that change would be healthy." (*BG*, March 9, 1982.)

[56] The Little City Hall program was terminated under the impact of "Proposition 2 1/2" (see Chapter 2, footnote 22). Being close to bankruptcy, the City of Boston, it was said, could no longer afford to finance the program.

party in need of constituents and friends, supporters and voters, power and legitimacy.[57]

Employing a large number of people who developed their individual talents and skills, the OPS became a body of experts in urban management that duplicated the ordinary municipal administration. (And there was, we should not forget, the operation of Mandarin Quealy — which paralleled both the municipal administration and the OPS.) Quite a few of those experts moved into line departments where they continued to practice the political trade that they had learned in the Office of Public Service. They helped to permeate the interests of their party through the government of the city.

Until 1975 a research and planning division existed in the OPS enabling the agency to draw on relevant data when it championed its causes and projects. Among the staffers of the OPS it became a matter of competitive discipline (and pride) to prove one's point with "facts and figures." Within a system of local government which was not particularly apt to establish reliable and useful statistical records, this discipline again amplified the effectiveness of the OPS. And the greater effectiveness did not only include a higher technical expertise but also a greater political influence: read in the context of pertaining political knowledge (and political imagination), the "facts and figures" yielded very often quite a bit of "political intelligence." Not surprisingly, the research capacities of the OPS were eventually absorbed by the political machinery of the Court.

At the time of elections, when the party was "geared up" for campaigning, the "OPS-system" was deliberately used for procuring political intelligence. Information on the views and attitudes of the people as regards the government — and, of course, the party — was gathered from the network of Little City Hall managers and their staff — the "ears" of the party in the neighborhoods. Often the gathering of information useful for the campaign was undertaken in quite a systematic way. A group of activists in the OPS would, for example, compile a document listing everything that the government of Mayor White had done for each neighborhood.[58] This set of information would then be used to identify, with the help of a computer, small areas in the city for a specialized and — as this procedure helped to economize the resources — frequent mailing of campaign literature. In the mode of such activities the OPS took on very much the contours of the party and, specifically, the contours of the party as a political organization.

---

[57] According to measurements taken by the OPS, a typical line department handled 14 to 20 complaints and the OPS 500 complaints (!) a day.

[58] In view of the mayoral election in 1971 such a document was produced by Gail Rotegaard, Robert Fichter, and Missy McAlea.

Finally, the politics of the party and the financial policies of the government converged in the OPS. In the annual process of elaborating the budget of the city the OPS fulfilled the function of the critical institution. The managers of the Little City Halls – or members of their staff – reported on the needs *and* the political behavior (as regards the administration of Mayor White) of each neighborhood. These reports were then used as a basis to decide on the allocation of funds to the neighborhoods.[59] The party that formed the government made decisions which were prepared by a governmental agency that was formed by the party.[60]

The OPS and the Little City Halls represented one of the various approaches of the party institutionally to embody the process of affording power, legitimacy, and creativeness. These approaches to institutionalization did not pile upon each other in an arbitrary or accidental way. They reflected a significant sequence, a movement of the party from being a party of friends to becoming a political party. However, as has already been stated, the party was arrested in this movement and tied up in the peculiar state of fulfilling the functions of a political party while remaining a party of friends. In its metamorphoses the party moved towards the form of a political party, but instead of becoming a political party it consistently relapsed into the form of a personal party: it continued its movement by successively repeating a metamorphosis into a "political organization."

The manifestation of the party in the form of a political organization was accompanied by misunderstandings. For the public, these largely prevented an objective view of the political organization and the nature of its existence. Their impact was such that members of the organization – that is, of the party – set themselves the trap, for instance, where they were caught by one of their "natural" adversaries, a City Councillor:

> In December 1979 I walked out of City Hall. The place was swarming with these young employees, nice suits, good faces, slightly longer hair, good manners, just out of Kennedy School. I met one of them, asked him what he was doing here [in City Hall]. 'I am precinct captain.' *After* the election [election held in the fall of 1979 for the Mayoralty and the City Council]

---

[59] Cf. D. Lorrain, *La gestion municipale à Boston,* op. cit., pp. 104–115. – To a certain extent the BRA too was involved in the "politics" of the budgetary process.

[60] After 1976 the OPS ceased to be the critical institution in the process of allocating funds. Under the typical condition of instutional confusion the OPS "shared" its responsibilities in the process with the newly created "Resource Allocation Committee," the "Office of Program Development (OPD)," and the neighborhood planning staff of the BRA.

was over! The man is employed by the City and, if asked, immediately thinks of himself as the *political* 'precinct captain.'

The City is heavily politicized. These people have met every fortnight. Now they are meeting every week. White always thought in terms of a man who wants to have a crowd of people around him who support him. They spend 2 – 3 hours at least a day doing politics for White.[61]

And another member of the party, a journalist, chose not quite a felicitous formula when he described a leading figure in the organization as the "capo di tutti capi" of all the Little City Halls.[62]

Against such misconstructions it is emphasized here that the political organization was another metamorphosis of the party in the process which it represented in various institutional forms: the process of mediating the flux and reflux of power between the government and the people; of producing legitimacy; of buttressing the creative potential of the government; of securing the support of friends, followers, and clients among the people in the city.

The repeated metamorphoses of the party into a political organization began in 1971 when members of the party, former campaign workers and activists in the OPS and the Little City Halls, debated about the need of creating a "separate political organization." They thought that the OPS could not pursue the politics of the party to a full extent. And they knew (having made hundreds of phone calls) that many campaign workers wished somehow to continue their affiliation with one another and to socialize as members of a "White organization."

From two metamorphoses of the party, namely the OPS and the campaign organization, arose another metamorphosis, the political organization, and the political organization again spread out into the OPS, the Court, and new campaign organizations.

In creating the political organization, its founders aspired to extending the social field of the party into the electorate. They conceived of it as

---

[61] Source: Interview. – In criticizing the continuing presence of the party *after* the election the Councillor seemed to imply a temporal rule (or "principle of legitimacy") as regards the existence of political organizations: they are "tolerable" (if not necessary) only *during* the time of elections. Every candidate for a seat on Boston's City Council builds or revives of course his (her) own personal organization, however small it may be, as the time of election approaches (cf., for instance, R. L. Turner, "Connolly Builds an Organization," *BG*, Nov. 23, 1982). The question then is not the existence of political organizations but the legitimacy of their existence in different "times" of political perception – evidently this Councillor and the members of the Kevin White Party whom he met approached each other in different "times," and "clashed."

[62] Alan Lupo, *BG*, June 8, 1976.

a structural tool by which voters — the ultimate resort of the Kevin White Interest — would be brought into the alliances, connections, personal relationships from which the party drew its existence as a political body.[63]

As regards this aspiration quite an important observation should be recorded. Historically, the ethnic cleavages in the population of Boston had been reflected by similar divisions in the political representation of the citizenry.[64] The political organization of the Kevin White Party broke away from this tradition of ethnic politics. In a city haunted by ethnic and racial prejudices it spread across the ethnic divides and made Irish Catholics, Blacks, Jews, Italian Catholics, Yankees, Midwest Protestants, people of Scandinavian, Spanish, Armenian, Greek extraction participants in a party of friends.

The political organization was designed to be set up like a social pyramid. Kevin White stood at the top alone, while a throng of "volunteers" — in 1981 organization officials numbered 3000 in all — did "political work" for the party at the bottom. In between there was a hierarchy of organization officials which consisted of (from the top to the bottom): a "Committee of Five" (including a kind of executive secretary who was directly responsible to Kevin White), the "ward coordinators" (including the Committee of Five whose members served concurrently as ward coordinators), and the "precinct captains."[65]

---

[63] Cf. V. O. Key Jr., *Politics, Parties, and Pressure Groups,* New York 1942, 1964, 5th ed., p. 339: "The organization is often pictured as a dictatorship; a description that fits in some localities at some times. More often the organization assumes the form of clusters of personal loyalties about nuclear individuals."

[64] Cf. C. K. Burns, "The Irony of Progressive Reform: Boston 1898–1910," in: R. P. Formisano, C. K. Burns, eds., *Boston 1700–1980. The Evolution of Urban Politics,* Westport-London 1984, pp. 133–164; Ch. H. Trout, "Curley of Boston: The Search for Irish Legitimacy," ibid., pp. 165–195.

[65] In 1976 the two echelons of ward coordinators and the Committee of Five were represented by the following persons: Kirk O'Donnell, Robert Vey, Buford Kaigler (Com 5), James Kelly, Claudia Delmonaco (Com 5), George Nedder (Com 5), Elaine Guiney (Com 5), Everette Sheppard (Com 5), Jane Deutsch, Richard Hall, Katherine Ryan, Ray Willingham. — In 1980 the same echelons were represented by: John Coviello, Sonny Buttiglieri, Roberta Delaney (Com 5), William Howard, James Stack, Karen Devereux, Katherine Kane, Bob Toomey (Com 5), Tom Driscoll, Paul Carey, Reggie Johnson (Com 5), Kevin Killarney, Hank Previte, Jack Williams, Richard Rouse, Mark Weddleton, Jim Jones, Wyola Garrett, Vin Kent, Brian Leahy (Com 5), James English, Gerard McHale, Tom Gannon, Gerard Horgan, Lora Baldwin, Evelyn Campbell, Dick Cecca, Edward Kelly, Dennis Morgan (Com 5), Ed O'Donnell, Michael Hanlon, Bernie Callahan, Barry Fadden.

All ward coordinators and a large number of the precinct captains were employed in the government.[66] The executive secretary occupied an office adjacent to that of the Mayor and he had his own small staff. The other officials of the organization held jobs in various agencies and departments; certain institutions appeared to be more preferable than others, though.[67] Consequent upon the nature of its activities, the organization tended to interfuse those institutions which had the greatest potential of winning — or cultivating — clients and supporters; it pervaded the OPS and the Boston Redevelopment Authority (and its offshoot, the Neighborhood Development Agency) in particular.

The ward coordinators — according to the *design* of the organization — met every Monday at noon in City Hall. Later, in the evening, ward coordinators and precinct captains gathered for a meeting. The following day, every Tuesday, each precinct captain and his volunteers came together in the evening. Each volunteer was responsible for about 150 households — being the addressee for complaints, on the one side, and the benefactor who brought redress — through the party as intermediary, of course — on the other. With the help of a computer, organization officials and participants in the operation of Mandarin Spring measured the rate of successful interventions on the part of each volunteer and the number of votes which Kevin White — or another member of the party — received in the area of the volunteer's responsibility at the time of elections. Thus, the "performance" of each volunteer could be appraised — statistically and hence objectively, as it were — and be used for evaluating the relative status of the volunteer in the party and, more importantly, in the pecking order of the employees in the government. Precinct captains and ward coordinators were subject to the same kind of appraisal. If the performance was judged to be unsatisfactory and if he or she was employed in the government (as most of them were), he or she was likely to be "punished" in various ways: a deferred promotion, a referral to an undesired job, no increase or even a reduction of the salary. In the ultimate situation, when an agency or a department was about to "fire" a certain number of employees, the "rating" of a party member was often a crucial

---

[66] Cf. BMRB, Special Report, No. 82 – 3, *Boston's Personnel Reduction Program*, Febr. 26, 1982.

[67] In 1981 the ward coordinators (numbering 33 in all) were employed in the city government as follows: OPS (9), Housing Inspection (1), Mayor's Office (6), Health/Hospitals (3), Fire (1), Housing Impr. Progr. (1), Personnel Office (1), Elderly Comm. (1), Police (1), Office, Property Equaliz. (2), Budget (1), BRA (1), Park/Recreation (1), Retirement Board (1), Public Facilities (2), Real Property (1).

factor in the process of deciding who should and who should not be dismissed.[68]

Through this scheme newly hired employees in the government were induced in a short time to realize the basic imperative of their job. They had to take the precaution of presenting themselves as "volunteers" and of attending "political meetings" (for the frequency of their attendance would be measured). And a number of employees who were not residents of Boston — contrary to the requirement that every employee of the city reside in Boston — thought that they were well-advised in "adopting" a precinct in Boston to do "political work" there as volunteer or precinct captain.

The social reality of the organization was of course largely determined by its design. Yet it did not approximate the type of institution which its founders had had in mind. Among all other manifestations of the party the organization most clearly exposed its peculiar state: being a personal party that fulfilled — by necessity — the functions of a political party and yet was arrested in its movement towards becoming such a party. Although the party formed a carrier of political legitimation, the legitimacy of its most political manifestation — the organization — was not fully recognized, neither by the public nor by the volunteers, precinct captains, and ward coordinators themselves. There was a smack of "illegitimacy" in the general perception of the organization.

Most "political workers" in the organization therefore displayed feelings of shame and guilt — among themselves and, even more so, in the presence of "outsiders." They knew that they could not really avoid to do what they were doing (the organization could command their loyalty, after all) and they were partially convinced that the party — and that meant also the organization — represented an essential part of the process by which Boston

---

[68] In Spring 1981 Local 285 of the Service Employees International Union, representing 3 500 City of Boston employees, lodged a complaint against the White administration with the Massachusetts Labor Relations Committee. It contended that the status of city employees — promotions, pay raises, dismissals — had been affected by their political activity. Specifically, the Union alleged that in September 1978 and in April 1979 salaries of city employees were raised very unequally: while employees who had been active as ward coordinators and precinct captains had received wage increases averaging about $ 70 a week, other employees drew increases averaging only $ 5.75 a week. On May 29, 1981 Mayor White testified before the Commission. In the course of the hearing he had to admit that the political effectiveness of city employees as ward coordinators, precinct captains, and volunteers had been appraised and rated. He was further compelled to concede that the information and the ratings as regards the performance of employees in the mayoral election of 1979 had been put down in a so-called "black book" and that this book had been consulted by him frequently.

was governed. But the unsettled nature of the party, the private bearings of its public mission, confused their judgment. In their experience of the party (forming the government) the lines between "private" and "public," "personal" and "official," "politics" and "government" were blurred. If they told this experience, they told their bewilderment: what was it that made a government dependent upon a party of friends?

To cope with their bewilderment, the political workers in the organization developed strategies of evasion. They laughed at the party and its politics; or they gratuitously assumed the righteousness of the party's cause and methods; or they did their political work as perfunctorily as possible; or they allowed themselves to become filled with resentment against the party and all the aftermath of its existence.

Through its political organization the party brought a large field of supporters under a certain discipline; but it did not tap from this field all the creativity which it potentially held. In the mode of this metamorphosis − the organization − the party approximated a political party as much as the conditions of its existence allowed; but then it became itself the cause for the limitation of its achievements. As it reached its greatest extension in its most organized form, it began to hamper the very process of creativity it represented.

6 Metastases: The Configuration of Creativity

In forming a government the party did not act in a social space that was "empty." Politics as the quest of people for social creativeness never proceeds from an absolute beginning. A *tabula rasa* for the creative act of the politician does not exist.[69] The matter of politics are human beings who, by nature, have always been involved in a constitution of their common life.[70] As a creator the politician cannot but concreate, since the matter of his creativeness

---

[69] Cf. the passages on "le sens de l'histoire," in: R. Aron, *L'opium des intellectuels,* op. cit., pp. 145 ff.; the passages on "action" in: H. Arendt, *The Human Condition,* Chicago 1958, pp. 175 − 199; the passages on "practical knowledge" and the "science of politics" in: M. Oakeshott, *Rationalism in Politics,* London 1962, pp. 7 − 36; the passages on "conduct *inter homines*" in: M. Oakeshott, *On Human Conduct,* Oxford 1975, pp. 31 − 60.

[70] Cf. the passages on "man's *bios politikos*" in: H. Arendt, *The Human Condition,* op. cit., pp. 22 − 58; the passages on the "Poleogony" in: E. Voegelin, *Order and History,* Vol. III, *Plato and Aristotle,* Baton Rouge 1957, 1964, 2nd ed., pp. 96 − 104; the passages on "*Noese*" (noetic exegesis) and "*Primärerfahrung*" (primary experience), and on the "*konkrete Bewußtsein*" (concrete consciousness) in: E. Voegelin, *Anamnesis. Zur Theorie*

exists but in the mode of social creation. The quest for social creativeness is a quest for participation; politics begins at the products of politics.

In forming a government the party began to take part in a field of configurative action that was constituted by many other governments, governmental agencies, public authorities, and similar institutions. The social space into which the government formed by the party would extend imposed its own structure and forces of movement. The party could not just form a government; there was the principal condition of social creativity: in order to govern, it had to enter the structure of governments and to apply the forces of political movements that defined the place where the government would have to occur. Nowhere is *utopia* where a government might be formed at an absolute beginning in an absolute space. There is no government if a place of governing does not already exist.

The field of configurative action in which local governments partake has been described as a "maze" or a "labyrinth."[71] The metaphors convey the notion of a governmental structure that is the antipode of creativity. They suggest a confusingly intricate arrangement for governing where governments are forced to spend their energies in just finding a way to govern, long before they are able to govern creatively.

Thus the party confronted a considerable challenge – inasmuch as it continued to be a carrier of creativity while it formed a government among other governments. Not only did these governments impose a structure upon the field in which the government formed by the party would partake, but they also seemed – by the nature of this structure – to dispel the creativeness which the party was carrying into their field.

Not surprisingly, the labyrinth within which local governments operate is still largely unexplored.[72] Concepts or conceptual phrases such as "intergovernmental relations" or "links between local and national systems of government" betray an art of classification which seems to be the more precise the

---

der Geschichte und Politik, München 1966, pp. 290 ff., 340 ff., (for the English version cf. E. Voegelin, Anamnesis, tr. and ed. by G. Niemeyer, Notre Dame 1978, pp. 150 ff., 200 ff.); the passages on "Classical Political Philosophy," in: L. Strauss, What Is Political Philosophy?, New York 1968, pp. 84 ff.

[71] H. Eulau, K. Prewitt, Labyrinths of Democracy, op. cit., pp. V, 611–613.

[72] Cf. M. Kesselman, "Research Perspectives in Comparative Local Politics: Pitfalls, Prospects, and Notes on the French Case," in: T. N. Clark, ed., Comparative Community Politics, New York 1974, pp. 353–381 (esp. the passages on "American Local Politics" pp. 353 ff. and the passages on p. 363 f.); R. C. Fried, "Comparative Urban Policy and Performance," in: F. J. Greenstein, N. W. Polsby, eds., Handbook of Political Science, Vol. VI, Politics and Policymaking, Reading 1975, pp. 310 ff.; S. H. Beer, "Federalism, Nationalism, and Democracy in America," The American Political Science Review, Vol. 72, No. 1, March 1978, p. 19 f.

less it has seized of its subject. Other notions like *député-maire* and *cumul des mandats* (the formulae for the French version of the labyrinth)[73] or "topocrats" and "intergovernmental lobby"[74] denote the field of configurative action that appears as a labyrinth but do not make the intricacy of its constitution and its structure of movements fully transparent. Quite a felicitous expression is the term *Politikverflechtung*, introduced by German social scientists,[75] but again it does not express a probe into the field as deep and exhaustive as it ought to be. Any effort to grasp the labyrinth of political administration by one concept is probably futile if not inadequate in principle. Interestingly, the most sophisticated attempt at seizing its reality applies an elaborate net of formulae and concepts.[76]

As in other instances of this study, the inquiry must follow the constitution of its subject.[77] In forming a government among governments the party entered an institutional maze, found ways to govern under this labyrinthine arrangement, and − most importantly − succeeded in extracting from the forces of political movement in the maze a considerable strengthening of its own creativity. The party made its passage through the maze and to follow it on this passage is the method to explore its condition in the field of configurative action in which it took part when it formed a government among other governments.

The party made its passage by carving for itself, to a considerable extent, the condition of its participation in the field. It created a complex of metastases within the configuration of governments which constituted the field. It did not attempt to change the structure which other governments imposed upon the field. Any such attempt would have necessitated a "reformist" attack on

---

[73] Cf. M. Laurent, *A l'écoute des villes de France,* Paris 1976, p. 11 ff.; J. Lagroye, "A la recherche du pouvoir local," *Sociologia Internationalis,* Vol. 15, 1977, pp. 77 − 90; P. Birnbaum, *Les sommets de l'etat. Essai sur l'élite du pouvoir en France,* Paris 1977, pp. 78 ff., 115 ff.; M. Reydellet, "Le cumul des mandats," *Revue du Droit Public et de la Science Politique en France et à l'Etranger,* No. 3, Mai − Juin 1979, pp. 693 − 768.

[74] Cf. S. H. Beer, "Federalism, Nationalism, and Democracy in America," op. cit.

[75] Cf. F. W. Scharpf, B. Reissert, F. Schnabel, *Politikverflechtung,* Kronberg 1976; J.-J. Hesse, ed., *Politikverflechtung im föderativen Staat,* Baden-Baden 1978.

[76] H. Heclo, *A Government of Strangers,* Washington, D.C. 1977; and idem, "Issue Networks and the Executive Establishment," in: A. King, ed., *The New American Political System,* Washington, D.C. 1978, pp. 87 − 124. − Heclo's conceptual net consists of formulaes and terms such as: "configurations," "open networks of people that impinge upon government," "the loose-jointed play of influence in political administration," "webs of influence [that] provoke and guide the exercise of power," "issue networks," "the kaleidoscopic interaction of changing issue networks," "the clouds of issue networks," "a play of influence that is many-stranded and loose."

[77] Cf. supra, pp. 50 f., 77 f.

the labyrinth of local governments or, in other words, another American Revolution. It chose – wisely, one is tempted to say – to do something else. The party penetrated the structure by metastases, extending itself – like a web – over the configuration of institutions within which the government it formed was operating. Confronting an institutional maze by which its creativeness might have been dispelled, the party prevailed. Its metastases carried its creativeness into the maze and by this way the party forged within the labyrinthine arrangement of governments its own configuration of creativity.

Ingression

The metastases came into being in various ways. Some were produced by political planning, others developed contingently and were recognized as metastases only after they had evolved.

A very "productive" metastasis – "productive" from the party's point of view[78] – existed in the *Massachusetts Port Authority* ("Massport"), the "body politic and corporate" which is in charge of the state-owned airports in Massachusetts, the Port of Boston facilities, and the Mystic River Bridge.[79] It arose in one of the more contingent ways, namely by ingression. Members of the party moved from other places of employment to Massport where they formed a metastatic cluster. Its numerical composition varied, of course, as some people moved on again to other jobs, and a set of other people then constituted the metastasis.[80]

Also in the mode of ingression evolved a metastasis at Harvard's Kennedy School of Government. By comparison, the role of this metastasis in the party's configuration of creativity was more restricted and – more delicate. The government formed by the party would not have succeeded in the pursuit of certain projects if it had not received the support from the metastasis at Massport. No crucial importance of that kind inhered the metastasis at the Kennedy School. And those who belonged to it understated their involvement in the party's affairs: since knowledge was a matter of convenience, the

---

[78] Cf. infra, p. 244 f.

[79] The Massachusetts Port Authority was established by Chapter 465 of the Mass. Acts of 1956 (the "Enabling Act"). Cf. *A Reprint of the Massachusetts Port Authority ENABLING ACT, Chapter 465 of the Acts of 1956 as Amended Through December 1981* (With Appendices), s. l., s. d.

[80] At one time or the other the following members of the party belonged to the metastasis at Massport: David W. Davis, Robert Weinberg, Isaac Graves, Elliott Friedman, Charity Brown, Jane Deutsch, Denis Blackett, John Vitagliano, Richard Meyer, Teri Weidner, Lisa Zankman.

structural presence of the party was explained by a coincidence of personal relationships. In matters of recruitment, professional advancement, rhetorical skills, useful connections, however, the traces of the party led through the metastasis at Harvard.[81]

Transplantation

Ordinarily, the state government of Massachusetts and the government of Boston do not cooperate very well; they tend to approach each other with apprehension if not animosity. The antagonism between Boston − the sophisticated city − and Massachusetts − the rural hinterland − reproduces what appears to be a pattern in American state politics.[82]

This antagonism was alleviated for a while, when Michael Dukakis was elected Governor of Massachusetts in 1974. Dukakis did not belong to the Kevin White Party but had cultivated a close political relationship with its principals. He had been running mate of Kevin White when the latter himself had sought (unsuccessfully) the Governorship in 1970, and he had hired a member of Kevin White's political family, Jack Walsh, as the manager of his gubernatorial campaign.

As Governor-elect Dukakis looked for people with whom he could build his administration − and it was the party where he particularly found such people. Quite a few members of the party moved from their positions in the government of Boston formed by the party to the government of Massachusetts under Governor Dukakis − in the mode of a transplantation. Their movement across the traditional chasm between the two governments was accompanied by the encouragement of their friends in the party who believed that they would now have, as one observer put it, "the proverbial friend on

---

[81] Participants in this metastasis were: Hale Champion, Ira Jackson, Nancy Huntington, David W. Davis, Gail Rotegaard, David Mundel.

[82] J. W. Bookwalter, *Rural Versus Urban. Their Conflict and Its Causes: A Study of the Conditions Affecting Their Natural and Artificial Relation*, New York 1911; S. Desmond, "America's City Civilization: The Natural Divisions of the United States," *Century*, Vol. LVIII, Aug. 1924, pp. 548 − 555; J. R. Smith, *North America: Its People and Resources, Development, and the Prospects of the Continent as an Agricultural, Industrial, and Commercial Area*, New York 1925; A. J. Vidich, J. Bensman, *Small Town in Mass Society. Class, Power and Religion in a Rural Community*, Princeton 1958, 1968, 2nd ed., esp. pp. 317 − 347; W. C. Havard, L. P. Beth, *The Politics of Mis-representation. Rural-Urban Conflict in the Florida Legislature*, Baton Rouge 1962; D. J. Elazar, ed., *American Federalism. A View from the States*, New York 1966; A. K. Cambell, ed., *The States and the Urban Crisis*, Englewood Cliffs 1970.

practically all our major headaches" – that is a metastasis – in the State House.[83]

Implantation

A series of metastases were established in the mode of implantation. Using his political influence and, in particular, his power of appointment by which he could fill seats on the boards of public agencies and commissions, Mayor White implanted metastases of the party in the Boston Redevelopment Authority, the Massachusetts Convention Center Authority, the Beacon Hill Architectural Commission, the John B. Hynes Vets. Auditorium Commission, the Boston Fair Housing Commission (among others).[84]

Configuration

In their quest for resources – seeking federal funds in Washington, for instance – members of the party continually looked out for allies in the federal government and bureaucracy. Naturally, they were especially interested in forging relationships with those participants in federal politics who had previously been activists in the party. They found a number of such participants and could, in one case or another, establish what I suggest to call an axis of configurative action – a form of alliance which was based on a personal rapport but was implicitly restricted to such issues – as they came along – in which both sides, on their respective grounds, had taken a common political interest.[85]

In addition, the government formed by the party organized lobbies for the promotion of its interests in the federal capital. Members of the party were

---

[83] The metastasis in the (first) Dukakis administration (1975 – 78) was formed by: Robert Kiley, John Snedeker, David W. Davis, Paul Parks, Fred Salvucci, Charles Barry, Denis Blackett, Rick Borten, Charles J. Beard, David Standley, Conchita Rodriguez, James M. Stone, David Liederman.

[84] These metastases were constituted by: Robert L. Farrell, James G. Colbert, Clarence Jones, James K. Flaherty, Joseph J. Walsh (BRA); Micho Spring, Robert J. Ryan (Convention Center A.), Robert Q. Crane (State Treasurer, by statute chairman of the Conv. Center A.); Emily Lloyd (Beacon Hill Architect. Comm.); Bertram Druker, Theodore V. Anzalone (Auditorium Comm.); Jerome L. Rappaport (Fair Housing Comm.).

[85] Cf. D. H. Haider, *When Governments Come to Washington. Governors, Mayors and Intergovernmental Lobbying,* New York 1974; M. J. Malbin, *Unelected Representatives,* op. cit.; H. Mollenkopf, *The Contested City,* op. cit., pp. 258 ff.

sent to Washington for the purpose of lobbying, and professional lobbyists were recruited as well. As part of these efforts the government maintained offices in Washington where the lobbyists sent from Boston were assisted by a small staff.[86]

The organization of lobbies and the forging of axes of configurative action were mutually supportive enterprises, of course.[87] They yielded metastases in the mode of configuration – fabrics of influence that had to be revived from issue to issue but, in successful instances, greatly enhanced the creativeness of the party.[88]

Foundation

Metastases, finally, were set up in the mode of foundation. Most of them were formally established as "agencies," "commissions," or "councils" and inserted as such into the institutional imbroglio of the city government. As metastases, however, they remained under the control of the party. On the other hand, there were metastases which were incorporated as associations of "private citizens," that is members of the party acting as private citizens. They extended the institutional presence of the party – its configuration of creativity – beyond the realm of governments. Thus the party existed, apart from the government it formed, as a Party, Incorporated.[89]

---

[86] The general lobby office of the city (= The Court) appeared under the term "Office for Intergovernmental Relations" or similar expressions. Parallel efforts of lobbying were undertaken by the BRA and the City's Health and Hospitals Department, for instance. – The party's efforts of lobbying date from February 1968 (that is the very beginning of the White administration) when Samuel V. Merrick was appointed the Mayor's "special counsel on federal affairs." Merrick had been a former aide to W. Willard Wirtz and Arthur Goldberg, Secretaries of Labor in Washington, and he had also worked for the U.S. Senate Labor Committee and the National Labor Relations Board in Washington.

[87] The former activists in the party who had become participants in national politics included: Kirk O'Donnell (Office of Tip O'Neill, Speaker of the House of Representatives); David McDonough (National League of Cities); Isaac Graves (Office of U.S. Senator Paul E. Tsongas); Ann Lewis (National Committee, Democratic Party).

[88] For federal fiscal years 1978–80, for instance, Boston achieved the highest per capita level of federal funding of any Northeast-Midwest city. Cf. CR, Vol. 72, No. 39, Sept. 29, 1980, p. 1.

[89] The metastases set up in the mode of foundation included: the Economic Development and Industrial Corporation (cf. p. 29); the Employment and Economic Policy Administration, and the Boston Consumers Council. – The party was "incorporated" in particular by the "Boston Foundation" whose "directors" included prominent members

A survey of the party's metastases leads to a startling yet conclusive discovery. It succeeded in establishing its own configuration of creativity within the labyrinth of governments and institutions in which it took part while it formed a government. In the midst of this maze the party controlled its own system of annexed agencies, affiliated organizations, satellite groups, extensions, and legal formations. It was this system by which members of the party operated as members of Boston's government. They embodied an alliance of friends, clients, and supporters that had effectively become the real government of Boston.

In consequence of its nature the party's configuration of creativity did not have a permanent but rather a constantly changing structure. Its range and composition varied perpetually in a process of expansion and contraction; new metastases emerged while existent satellite groups were disbanded, or agencies which had been annexed grew again more independent.

The affairs of Boston were largely transacted through this configuration. Its reality was seized very well by seasoned members of the party. They knew how to act by the configuration and to use the channels of creativeness which is provided; they knew how to direct a project via the metastases through the labyrinth of governments. Not a few achieved a virtuosity that enabled them to act with a considerable degree of discretion, independence, and imagination — that is to actualize social creativity. Yet the nature of the configuration also ensured that fundamental uncertainties remained for *anyone* acting through the configuration — or else it would not have existed as resource of an autocracy.[90]

---

of the party: Kevin White, Herbert Gleason, Katherine Kane, and Elizabeth Cook. Another participant in the activities of the Boston Foundation was Newell Cook, City auditor and party member. It was the Boston Foundation, for instance, that supported the physical center of the Court, the Parkman House. It also served as a legal and constitutional tool for creating out of private and public funds one single pool of financial resources — over which the party could again exert a complete control, as a result of this hybrid construction.

[90] Cf. infra, p. 251 ff.

The Life of the Party: A Morphology

Every phenomenon *of* politics is a phenomenon *in* politics. No observer of politics is free to choose an absolute standpoint for his scrutiny; any knowledge of politics requires the experience of politics, and experiences are made by human beings but in the mode of participation.[91] The phenomena of politics are not equally discerned by everyone at all times. Or, inversely put, different people experience politics in different ways; all perceive the phenomena of politics individually according to personal circumstances and modes of participation in politics.[91]

As knowledge about politics results from individual perceptions, the general relevance of such knowledge is often denied. People, it is argued, do have very different experiences and views of politics. Any attempt to generalize these experiences and views would necessarily be an exercise in arbitrariness. The scepticism of the argument appears to be well-founded as long as one does not see the structural law that inheres the experience *of* politics by the participation *in* politics. Insights into the process of politics are drawn from within this process, and they reflect not an absolute but a relative point of view. Yet it is precisely this relative point of view upon which all knowledge about politics hinges: as a knowledge rooted in and as a knowledge abstracted from the participation in politics.

The individual perspectives from which people view politics do not prevent a general knowledge of politics. To the contrary, their variety inspires and directs the pursuit of such knowledge. Each perspective has been gained by extracting a *knowledge of politics* from a *participation in politics,* by observing politics from a relative point of view determined by insight and experience. Each perspective reflects an ongoing movement from the particular to the general, from impressions to insights, from experience to knowledge. Or, inversely put, this movement by which the phenomena of politics are discerned goes on as long as politics is viewed from individual perspectives. The notion of attaining an Archimedean standpoint beyond the movement, knowing everything about politics by knowing politics in one's town, is certainly a tempting idea. However, any aspiration for the Archimedean position would deaden the movement from which it derives. What would be viewed as

---

[91] Cf. E. Voegelin, *Plato and Aristotle,* op. cit., pp. 82 ff.; idem, *Order and History,* Vol. IV, *The Ecumenic Age,* Baton Rouge 1974, pp. 11 – 20, 176 ff., 183 – 192; idem, *Anamnesis,* op. cit., pp. 288 – 300 (for the English translation cf. *Anamnesis,* ed. G. Niemeyer, op. cit., pp. 147 – 160).

[92] Cf. Leo Strauss' reflections on the "character of political knowledge" in: *What Is Political Philosophy?,* op. cit., pp. 15 ff.

phenomena of politics would cease to be nourished by experience and would necessarily degenerate into subjects of arbitrary thinking. To know would mean to repeat what had once been known but had since become dead knowledge – "knowledge" removed from the participation in politics that alone provides a perspective for discerning the phenomena of politics. It is not the individual perspective which constitutes an arbitrary approach to a general knowledge of politics but rather the claim to possess this knowledge apart from the movement of individual experiences and views towards knowledge.[93]

As has been shown, there were many who in one way or the other participated in the politics of the party. They were friends or clients, relatives or business associates, young recruits to the party or contributors to the funds for the party's campaigns, developers, architects, or contractors. They viewed the party from different perspectives and in these perspectives the party appeared in different forms. In the view of the client the party was an organization of patronage and in the view of the businessman it was a supply of valuable contacts with decision makers in the government. The developer regarded the party as an alliance of interests with whom he had to reach an agreement and the contractor was attentive to the party as the form of his entree to the government as employer.

The party was different things for different people. It was perceived in different forms. Each of these forms represented an attempt to grasp the party as a phenomenon of politics. Each seized but an aspect of the phenomenon which was a "true" aspect, however – since it reflected the experience of participating in the politics of the party.

As a phenomenon of politics perceived by the participants in the politics from which it emerged, the party existed in the mode of a movement towards the knowledge of the phenomenon. This movement was represented always in different forms. The party "lived."

7 Friends and Clients

There were thousands of people in whose eyes the personal relationships by which the party was formed were also – and especially – economic

---

[93] The rule applies also to the explication of the rule: In the present study the phenomenon of the party is analyzed in the mode of a scientific inquiry. It is viewed from the perspective of a scholar and it appears therefore in the form of a subject of inquiry that is dissected with the tools of scientific analysis. In a scholar's perspective the party could not appear in any other form – to be a "subject of inquiry" is its "true" form under which it is discerned as a phenomenon of politics in the course of the scholar's inquiry into the politics from which it arose.

relationships. They flocked in the party as "friends" and "clients." They participated in the politics of the party with the view of receiving economic benefits. In their mode of perception the party appeared as an alliance of friends that organized the sharing out of public patronage. In Boston, as in other American cities, the use of patronage had been the principal mechanism by which generations of poor and powerless immigrants — often the subject of discrimination ("No Irish need apply") — had secured themselves a staple of livelihood and, increasingly, a basis of political power.[94] At the time when the party formed the government of Boston public patronage had become a venerable tradition in the politics of the city — quite apart from its original, compelling cause, the predicament of hapless immigrants.

And the party did everything but break the venerable tradition. It continued the practice of public patronage — in its "purest" form. As regards its social function, patronage had been superseded by the welfare state which mitigated poverty and other economic hardships (like unemployment, for instance) in ways more generous than public patronage could ever afford. As regards its civic function, patronage had been followed by electoral victories which made the immigrants and their descendants the leading political class in the city.

Therefore the boons of patronage could be shared out by the party on purely political grounds — as "rewards" for persons who in one way or the other had helped to further the interests of the party. Naturally, the rewards consisted in economic benefits — jobs, contracts, commissions — but their recipients were mostly selected upon political rather than economic considerations.[95]

The friends in the party who were clients of the party as well rendered the party various services, and they expected various benefits from the party. Three groups of clients could be distinguished.

---

[94] Cf. Th. H. O'Connor, *Bibles, Brahmins and Bosses,* op. cit.; O. Handlin, *Boston's Immigrants 1790—1880. A Study in Acculturation,* Cambridge, Mass. 1941, rev. ed. 1959; B. M. Solomon, *Ancestors and Immigrants. A Changing New England Tradition,* Cambridge, Mass. 1956; W. V. Shannon, *The American Irish,* New York 1966; B. Stave, *The New Deal and the Last Hurrah,* Pittsburgh 1970; St. Thernstrom, *The Other Bostonians. Poverty and Progress in an American Metropolis 1880—1970,* Cambridge, Mass. 1973; R. P. Formisano, C. K. Burns, *Boston 1700—1980,* op. cit.

[95] A penetrating analysis of patronage is to be found in: Th. Eschenburg, *Ämterpatronage,* Stuttgart 1961. — Among other things, Eschenburg draws a distinction between *Herrschaftspatronage* ("patronage as an instrument of governing") and *Versorgungspatronage* ("patronage as the practice of recompense"). It is useful to bear in mind this analytical distinction between the two forms of patronage — just because of their being intertwined so often in the process of politics. — Cf. also the passages on patronage in: V. O. Key Jr., *Politics, Parties, and Pressure Groups,* op. cit., pp. 338—341, 366—369.

(a) The government formed by the party provided jobs for a throng of several thousand "patronage workers" − 3000 persons on the average. The term used to designate this group of clients was well chosen; patronage workers were people who had first "worked" for the party − usually at the time of elections − and were then "rewarded" for their "political work" by being appointed to a post (ordinarily a low-level job) in the government. There was always a particular member of the Court who was responsible for keeping and updating a list of candidates for patronage jobs − the "patronage secretary."[96] When a job opened up in an agency, the personnel officer of this agency was required to notify the patronage secretary who in turn suggested whom among the candidates should be given the job. Agencies avoided to accept a suggestion of the patronage secretary only if a mismatch between the skills of the candidate and the job requirements was too evident. Having been given a job in the government, the patronage worker was expected to remain loyal to the party and to continue his or her political work. By the nature of his or her employment it was stipulated that a promotion or a transfer to a more desirable job would again depend upon political considerations − favorable judgements on his or her political work.

(b) Architects and developers constituted a second group of clients and friends of the party. Boston experienced a building boom and there were much more architects and developers wanting to have a share in the boom than could be accomodated. The party found that it could arbitrate a competition in which a great deal of professional prestige and very large sums of money were involved. Architects and developers, on the other hand, cultivated the party and, as will shortly be explained, demonstrated their allegiance to the party's cause in making generous campaign contributions. Again a list was put together on which the names of those architects and developers (or development companies) appeared who stood high in the party's favor. Whenever a developer and an architect had to be chosen for a particular development project, the party − that is the person(s) acting as the party − could "know" the choice or at least the finalists before any decision had actually been made. The process of selection usually tended to focus on those bidders or candidates who could show an outstanding record of professional achievement − whoever would be "chosen" eventually would be a first-class professional − and *then* turned into the process to identify (not to choose) the candidate who had been or could be expected to be a participant in the politics of the party. "All other things being equal" (as the quasi-official formula went), politics decided what decision had to be made.

---

[96] As patronage secretaries served: Joanne Prevost, Allen Austin, Jack Murphy.

(c) The third group of clients, finally, was formed by contractors who wanted
to do business with the city. Contractors were compelled – by the law,
as it were – to participate in the politics of the party. Every contract
which involved expenditures above a certain amount specified by the law
(in 1972: $ 2.000) had to be signed by the Mayor. Acting on behalf of
the Mayor, a particular member of the Court dealt with all the contracts
which fell under this rule.[97] His or her function did of course not only
consist in the task of preparing the letters of intent and the contract
documents to be signed by the Mayor. There was another, more important
obligation. Contracts were, in principle, competitively bid and could
therefore again be used to turn contractors into clients. Wanting to do
business with the city, a contractor was well-advised if he knew about
and participated in the politics of the party. From his perspective doing
well in business meant having friends and patrons in the party.

8 Connections

In all modern societies laws and governmental regulations permeate the social
and economic life. Everyone has become dependent upon a governmental
approval for almost everything. Modern societies, like addicts, would be
deprived of their sustenance if governments withdrew their regulatory infusions. Besides, governments usually do not act against their own interests;
they too have become addicted to their power of tutelage.

If understood as a political tool, the power of tutelage can be used – and
exploited – with great effect in the process of politics. To the government
it provides possibilities of leverage vis-à-vis the citizens; and to the citizens
it presents opportunities for negotiating with the government. Compelled to
cooperate by a plethora of laws and regulations, government and citizens are
continuously drawn into the politics of winning approvals, reaching an
agreement, finding a compromise.

The government formed by the party did not represent an exception to
this importance of politics regarding the relationship between citizens and
government in modern societies. Consequent upon its nature, however, it did
enhance the politics of public-private relations in Boston. Being a government
that amounted to a very elusive political rule, it obliged everyone to seek
approvals, variances, permissions from the government with an extraordinary

---

[97] The flow of contracts was supervised for quite a while by Barbara Cameron, the
prominent member of White's political family who served the party also in other
capacities: as fundraiser and Commissioner of Assessing.

amount of efforts. Like everywhere else almost everyone was subject to the government's tutelage for almost everything. Yet, in this case, the tutelage was exercised by a government that eluded any straightforward contacts. One needed access to the government, and the government withdrew from one's approach. There was but one way to get in touch with the government — by approaching it from within the medium of its existence, that is by participating in the politics of the party.

In the view of citizens who needed access to the government the party appeared again in a particular form. They perceived it as a body of intermediaries whose assistance one could obtain to pursue one's private interests even in the elusive sphere of the government. And the party included a number of persons, of course, who specialized in the delicate task of reconciling private interests with governmental imperatives and policies. By the services of these particular persons the party provided a medium of connections between citizens and government. It represented the necessary link in the politics of public-private relations: a party of liaison politicians.

Both government and citizens were interested in the services of the liaison politicians. Each side needed the technique of the *quid pro quo* in the process of negotiating an agreement, and yet each side wanted also to maintain its public, its private stance, respectively. The discretionary undertakings of the liaison politicians therefore appeared to be quite indispensable: they protected both government and citizens against adverse events and developments. The citizen could participate in the politics of the party by using the services of a liaison politician and could yet remain publicly "aloof." The government could convey certain requests to the private sector (for campaign contributions, for instance, in return for favors it had granted) and could yet appear uninfluenced by special interests.

The liaison politicians of the party engaged in three different types of mediation.

(a) They established and maintained connections between citizens and government in a open, quasi-public process. This type of mediation was usually adopted when citizens represented their interests by collective efforts and, correspondingly, in a public mode — as a community group or as a neighborhood association, for instance. Agreements on issues such as design guidelines or zoning variances for a development project were then negotiated within a triangular configuration of government, liaison politician(s), and civic group(s).[98]

---

[98] The controversy concerning the "Cabot Estate" is a case in point. Located in the middle of Boston's famed Emerald Necklace, a series of parks created by Frederick Law Olmsted, the estate was bought on July 1, 1969 by Pasquale Franchi, a developer. In

(b) There were private interests, of course, of which those who pursued them thought they should be taken on by liaison politicians with as little public attention as possible. It was this kind of mediation for which the services of liaison politicians were used most extensively. Any direct contacts between private interest(s) and the government were avoided. And it was understood that the liaison politician(s) lent "professional" services: as lawyer(s) or consultant(s). Still, everyone knew what the liaison politician was really doing, a mediation, and that this mediation was a matter of politics. A great number of mediations of this kind were continuously going on, and most of them were ignored by the public. The less the public knew, the more could the number of mediations grow.

---

the fall of 1970 Franchi submitted to the BRA a plan to build on the estate three 40-story high rises containing 2 000 units. Among other things, the proposal implied a change of zoning regulations (from single family use to a designation for high rise luxury apartments). The developer met with strong opposition from citizens in the neighborhood, Jamaica Plain, and conservation groups. In Dec. 1970 the Jamaica Plain Little City Hall created a "Citizens Advisory Committee" to review, in conjunction with the BRA, the development plans. Later a "Cabot Estate Task Force" was formed which included representatives from the Town of Brookline, the BRA, the Office of Public Service, the Boston Parks & Recreation Department, the Boston Conservation Commission, the Advisory Committee — and one area resident. After four years of negotiations and controversy the developer and the Task Force agreed upon a set of development guidelines which had won the approval of the Citizens Advisory Committee and of Mayor White. As a result, Mr. Franchi submitted in August 1973 a new proposal for a cluster development of 178 units at the average height of 2 1/2 stories. A month later, this new plan was officially approved by the BRA and the Boston Zoning Commission.

During this long process of negotiations the crucial link between developer, community interests, and the City government was provided by a party member — William Edgerton, first Jamaica Plain Little City Hall manager and, later, Deputy Director of the OPS. In a letter to Pasquale Franchi, the Director of the BRA, Robert T. Kenney, clearly spelled out Edgerton's role as liaison politician: "The best route for reaching the required zoning variances would be the PDA [...] [A PDA designation allows the developer to get a passage of exceptions to zoning codes rather than applying for individual variances]. [...] In order to minimize any possible reason for opposition or delay during this process, a close community-city-developer coordination will be appropriate. [...] To insure that the process proceeds with deliberate speed, Bill Edgerton, Deputy Director of the Office of Public Service will serve as the City's liaison with community groups. Bill is available to you to discuss your dealing with the community" (R. T. Kenney, *Letter of March 9, 1973 to Mr. Pasquale Franchi*).

The process by which a Cable TV franchise was awarded for Boston provides another illustrative example. In this case, a number of party members were involved in the activity of being liaison politicians: Peter Meade, Herbert Gleason, Alan Austin, William Ezekiel, Jack Walsh.

The party forming the government, however, did *not* forget the services it had rendered to private interests. If, as a result of the spatial density under which the process of politics took place, a leading member of the party met by chance in the street someone whom the party had recently helped and he was not properly recognized by the respective person, this individual was surely reprimanded, on the spot, unequivocally. Once you had become a friend among friends, you had better observe the tacit conditions of their friendship.

(c) The third type of mediation, finally, was defined again by the particular nature of certain interests and pursuits. Boston had its redlight district — called the "Combat Zone." There were people pushing drugs, prostitutes, and enterprises run by the Mafia (not only was the Combat Zone controlled by two families from outside Boston, but the Mafia attempted also, at various occasions, to take its share in Boston's building boom). Again, both sides, neither the government nor the interests operating outside the law, could afford to ignore each other. Yet, any direct contacts or negotiations were out of question. They had to meet without really meeting, they had to reach agreements without really negotiating.

They met and they agreed upon matters of mutual interest, "connected" by the figure of the liaison politician. As regards the "connection," the liaison politician did not really "mediate" but moved — as an individual person — in both "worlds," and back and forth from one world to the other. This movement was the connection. As a figure, the liaison politican was appreciated in both worlds. As a person, however, the liaison politician was shunned in either of the two worlds. Many requests but not many invitations were issued to the party's figure in the "shadow."

9 The Ethology of Nepotism

The behavior of people is the process of their learning the modes of their social existence. Politics is one of these modes, and by having experiences of politics they learn being participants in politics. Their experiences of politics inform the standard of conduct which they observe as participants in politics. They follow the political *ethos* which they have learned in sifting the process of politics in which they partake. Their political behavior is the process of mastering their political situation.

People are involved in political situations that vary greatly. Besides, any political situation tends to change. Hence, the process of mastering a political situation is a process whose subject itself is a process. Political behavior, that is, the process of learning the political mode of one's social existence, cannot abide with stances of stability, patterns of permanence. It implies, quite contrarily, floating dispositions towards the shifts and flow of political situations. It requires the habits of mental and social movements: forethought, sagacity, prudence and deliberation, persuasion, adjustment. It cannot be taught but has to be learned, and it cannot be learned other than by experience and practice. Nor can it be learned once and for all, since learning it *is* what has to be learned. Political behavior is the process of learning the process of political behavior.[99]

The habits which the process requires are not actualized by all people to the same degree. Many people do not pursue politics as a practice of prudence; at various stages in the process of learning the process of political behavior they shrink from further movements towards movement as a mode of their social existence; actualizing habits other than prudence – ambition, possessiveness, vanity, or idleness, for instance – they differentiate the process of learning the process of political behavior into a series of different and, in particular, persistent types of political behavior. They enter into the enactment of fixed dispositions towards politics.[100]

The people who participated in the politics of the party in general knew very well how to circumvent the snares of typical modes of behavior in view

---

[99] Cf. Aristotle, *Nicomachean Ethics* (NE) 1103b1 – 5: "We become just by doing just acts, temperate by doing temperate acts, brave by doing brave acts. This truth is attested by the experience of states: lawgivers make the citizens good by training them in habits of right action – this is the aim of all legislation." – NE 1103b22: "Our moral dispositions are formed as a result of the corresponding activities." – NE 1103b31: "Our actions determine the quality of our dispositions." – NE 1104a3 – 10: "Matters of conduct [...] have nothing fixed or invariable about them [...] but the agents themselves have to consider what is suited to the circumstances on each occasion." Cf. further NE, 1105a29 – 33, 1109a20 – 24, 1139a30 – b5, 1142a14 – 15, 1098a15 – 16.

[100] Cf. Plato, *Republic* 544B – 545A, 581C, 582A – E; Aristotle, NE 1179b10 – 19: "For it is the nature of the many to be amenable to fear but not to a sense of honour, and to abstain from evil not because of its baseness but because of the penalties it entails; since, living as they do by passion, they pursue the pleasures akin to their nature, and the things that will procure those, pleasures, and avoid the opposite pains, but have not even a notion of what is noble and truly pleasant, having never tasted true pleasure. What theory (*logos*) then can reform the natures of men like these? To dislodge by argument habits long firmly rooted in their characters is difficult if not impossible." – NE 1140b4 – 5: "It follows that prudence (*phronesis*) is not the same as science. Nor can it be the same as art. It is not science, because matters of conduct admit of variation; and not art, because doing and making are generally different, since making aims at an end is distinct from the act of making, whereas in doing the end cannot be other than the act itself: doing well is in itself the end."

of the vicissitudes of political life. Theirs was a party of creativity, not of orthodoxy. As regards the situation of belonging to a party of friends, however, a number of its members enacted, in a certain respect, the kind of behavior typical of a party that is sustained by family ties and the bonds of friendship. They practiced nepotism – learning so well what they learned in the process of participating in a personal party that it became the steadfast disposition to share out the fortunes of the party among sisters and brothers, husbands and wives, sons and daughters, nephews and in-laws.[101]

The party members practicing nepotism learned what they learned in considering their lives as participants in the politics of the party. They realized the anthropological form of the party, its rise from connections among relatives and friends. And they knew, of course, that the connections which made the party also made the government of Boston. In their eyes kinship appeared as the genetic principle of both government and party. If a member of the party wanted his nephew to be appointed to a post in the government, the wish could be granted therefore without any hesitation: to go ahead with the appointment simply meant to give the nephew in the party the "official" status of a nephew in the government.[102]

Those who practiced nepotism perceived also the emotional claims of the party. One could not participate in the politics of the party for any extended period of time and not be devoted very much to the life and the interests of the party. The demands upon one's time, energy, and loyalty were high, bearing heavily on the character of one's private life. It was much easier to render the services which the party required if one's family shared one's devotion to the party and offered practical help as well as emotional support.

---

101 This is a select list of kins to party members who at one time or the other were appointed to government posts: David J. Shea, son-in-law of BRA board treasurer James G. Colbert; Ann Lewis, sister of Barney Frank, aide to the Mayor; Carolyn G. Connors, sister-in-law of Kevin White; Robert Y. Murray, husband of Mrs. White's sister Nancy; Vincent Long, son of Ralph Long, deputy head of the Mayor's Office of Communication; Thomas Hosker, nephew of James Hosker, old friend of the Mayor's; Elizabeth Holland, wife of William Holland, director of the OPS; Owen Donnelly, son-in-law of Vice Mayor Ed Sullivan; Theodore Anzalone Jr., son of Theodore V. Anzalone, fundraiser and old associate of the Mayor's; Robert Toomey's son Robert and wife Joanne; Dennis Morgan's sisters Helen and Susan (both Toomey and Morgan were leading figures in the political organization).

102 An exemplary and recent parallel at the national level can be found in France in the government of President Mitterrand which evidently espoused kinship as a guiding principle of its appointments policy. Cf. J.-M. Gourevitch, M.-Th. Guichard, "La marée des 'têtes d'œuf,'" Le Point, No. 622, Aug. 20, 1984, p. 36; D. Molho, "Les stratèges du Président," Le Point, No. 644, Jan. 21, 1985, p. 36; J. Bouzerand, "La constellation Mitterrand," Le Point, No. 660, May 13, 1985, pp. 46–47.

Really, the participation in the politics of the party was a concern that touched the whole family. The party, on the other hand, of course could not take all this devotion for granted — it had to offer something in return: appointments in the government.

Furthermore, every devotee of the party naturally was a prey to fears about the fortune of the party as well as the personal luck in the struggles for influence and status within the party. Only fools would have expected the life in the party to be an experience of security and continuity; the turmoil of power from which it arose produced by necessity a succession of failures, upheavals, and strokes of adversity. One turn of events — a falling from the grace of the Mayor, a lack of success in completing a project, or, worst of all, electoral defeat — and the party's devotee could find himself or herself left out in the cold. And, as everyone knew, the party itself would not hold its governmental power forever. All could come to a sudden end. In one way or the other, however, the economic well-being of many party members was tied up with the affairs of the party. Therefore they took risks, those individuals and, in particular, those families who centered their lives upon the interests of the party. The risk that all could come to a sudden end could not be averted. Yet, its possibility became a lesser threat, if the financial consequences were alleviated beforehand: if not only one but two or three members of a family were given a job in the government.

This ethology of nepotism, finally, served as a code of communication among the habitués of the governmental offices controlled by the party. Practices of recruitment and employment intertwined with connections among relatives and friends. Professional and private communication interlaced. Jobs and kinship were interchanged. A tacit knowledge encompassed certain rules of political and administrative behavior. [103]

And the party approached a distinctive, classical form of political continuity. It moved towards establishing lineage as a principle of selecting candidates for offices in the government of Boston. It bent its own interests on the future of Boston, making Boston politics the destiny of families.

Connecting the continuity of a commonwealth with lineage is an ancient tradition, of course. And it was, during the era of the Brahmins, a very Bostonian tradition, too. [104] Yet, the party did not and could not really succeed

---

[103] For a phenomenological description of different types of nepotism, cf. Th. Eschenburg, *Ämterpatronage*, op. cit., pp. 18 ff. — On the "function of spoils," cf. V. O. Key Jr., *Politics, Parties, and Pressure Groups*, op. cit., pp. 366 – 369.

[104] Cf. E. D. Baltzell, *Puritan Boston and Quaker Philadelphia. Two Protestant Ethics and the Spirit of Class Authority and Leadership*, New York 1979; R. Story, *The Forging of an Aristocracy. Harvard and the Boston Upper Class*, Middletown 1980; F. C. Joher, *The Urban Establishments. Upper Strata in Boston, New York, Charleston, Chicago,*

in reviving this tradition in contemporary Boston. Any revival would have clashed with the prevailing historical, social, and political conditions of governing Boston. They made it inconceivable that the party moved beyond nepotism towards the foundation of a political regime of select families. The general knowledge – and acceptance – of these conditions arrested its natural movement, once again. Making the connections among family members and friends the connections among officials in the government, the party could but remain in the twilight of nepotism.

10 The Political Epoch

Polities follow the rhythm of politics. Their existence varies with the variations in the process of politics. A polity is not, as many suppose, just a setting, a framework, an institutional order, a system, or a "black box" within which a process of politics could be thought to occur – as something quite separate, as it were.[105] The opposite, of course, is true: a polity is what politics makes. It exists by virtue of its being a community in a state of politics and inasfar as always different situations of politics in the community follow one after another, the polity always exists sequentially in a different way. The variations in its existence – its "forms" – reflect the rhythm of the moments of politics in a community.[106]

---

and Los Angeles, Urbana, Ill. 1982; idem, "The Politics of the Boston Brahmins: 1800 – 1860," in: R. P. Formisano, C. K. Burns, eds., Boston 1700 – 1980, op. cit., pp. 59 – 86.

[105] A representative statement of this view, according to which political science ought to detour politics, was given by David Easton: "Our primary concern is, to be sure, with the functioning of the political system. For understanding political phenomena, we would have no need to be concerned with the consequences in and of themselves that political actions have for the environmental systems. [...] But the activities of the members of the [political] system may well have some importance for their own subsequent actions or conditions. [...] A useful way of simplifying and organizing our perceptions of the behavior of the members of the system [...] is to do so in terms of the effects [...] inputs have on what we may call the *political outputs*. These are the decisions and actions of the authorities. Not that the complex political processes internal to a system that have been the subject of inquiry for so many decades in political science will be considered in any way irrelevant. [...] the outcomes of these internal political processes [...] can [...] be usefully conceptualized as the outputs of the authorities. Through them, we are able to trace out the consequences of behavior within a political system for its environment." (D. Easton, "Categories for the Systems Analysis of Politics," in: idem, ed., *Varieties of Political Theory*, Englewood Cliffs 1966, p. 151 f.).

[106] Cf. Plato, Laws, Book III; Aristotle, Politics 1278b6 ff.; E. Voegelin, *Plato and Aristotle*, op. cit., pp. 240 – 253, 336 – 350.

A community proceeds from one moment of politics to another, for instance, when elections are drawing close, and politics takes on the form of campaigning or when a new government thrills the community with the sense of a new beginning, when a crisis in the community aggravates the climate of politics, or when the tasks of governing can largely be dealt with by administrative routine, when new social or political movements emerge from the community and seek to uproot the established procedures of governing, or when a charismatic politician gains ascendancy over the community and interweaves its life with his own career.[107]

Among these variations in the life of a political body there is one which is the most political of all moments of politics. I suggest to call it the "political epoch." It is the moment of truth: the moment when politics as the essence of a political body and politics as the workings of a political body appear as the *one* process of politics of which "making policies" and "being political" are but two aspects that coincide. The political epoch reveals what it is that makes policies, political bodies, political communities. Neither institutions, nor laws, or systems of decision making. Politics.

11 Priming the Party

To the extent that it was a political body that formed a government, the party could not consistently equate the business of governing with the pursuit of politics. It had to make the government appear as a government and was thus compelled somewhat to distance itself — being the party of politics that it was — from the daily conduct of governmental affairs. In the ordinary course of things the party was not particularly interested in evincing its presence as the carrier of politics that moved the government. While the government worked, the party seemed to be "dormant."

---

[107] The temporal variations of political forms — the variations of every political body in a continuity of time through the appearances of this body in continuously different forms at successively different times — have largely been neglected as a field of study by contemporary political science. A very few of its practitioners have touched upon the field: in a short paragraph of his work *Politics, Parties, and Pressure Groups* (op. cit., pp. 163 – 165) V. O. Key Jr. suggested "differentiations of the usages of the word 'party,'" observing that at one time the term referred to a "party-in-the-electorate," to a "party-in-the-government" at another time, or to a "party-in-the-legislature" at again a different time. Cf. further the passage on the "Symbolism of Time" in A. L. Strauss' essay on "Strategies for Discovering Urban Theory," in: L. F. Schnore, H. Fagen, eds., *Urban Research and Policy Planning*, Beverly Hills 1967, pp. 87 – 88.

It "awoke" and began to vibrate with vitality, however, whenever a mayoral election or a similar moment of politics approached.[108] Every mayoral election was a political epoch in the life of the party. Its essence — drawing the power of creativeness from the discordant particles of political life — and its workings — capturing this creativeness in the form of a government — appeared at once in the open process of electoral politics. While it was "geared up" for an approaching mayoral election, the party became visible as what it was: as the carrier of politics that moved the government.

The party became primed with friendships and loyalties. First of all, the webs of personal relationships were activated of which the current configuration of the party existed. Then, the more formalized textures of friends, followers, and clients, like the Office of Public Service and the Little City Halls, were employed as channels of communication linking the party and the electorate. Above all, however, every effort was made to transmute the entire party into the most political — and therefore most conspicuous — of all its manifestations: into a political organization.

At the time when a mayoral election approached, the political organization absorbed the party. The organization became the party, summoning the services of all the party's members, friends, and sympathizers and mustering everybody into the setup of the election campaign. As a "campaign organization" the political organization did not differ very much from the structure which has already been described.[109] The "ward coordinators" instructed and supervised the "precinct captains," and the precinct captains energized and directed the "volunteers," the "street people." The usual techniques were employed to motivate and to discipline this army of political workers.

Nevertheless, the campaign organization represented the party in its political epoch. In striving for the success of its candidate, the party fought for its life. Organizing the campaign therefore meant organizing the quest of the party for a new life. The bonds of friendship were the soul of the party. In making friends it became alive. An election campaign of the party was by necessity a campaign to renew old and to build new friendships.

Mayoral campaigns therefore were focused geographically upon the neighborhoods. There, in the neighborhoods, tissues of friendship existed with which the party — in the course of years — had become interwoven. The campaign organization drew its energy, drive, and manpower from these issues. Distributing campaign literature, putting up posters, hosting a kaffeeklatsch — these and the other labors of electoral politics were organized in

---

[108] Similar moments of politics were: the classification campaign (see Chapter 2, footnote 35), elections for the City Council, White's effort of presidential campaigning.
[109] Cf. supra, p. 138 ff.

the way of a friendly assistance among neighbors. Not the party invited to campaign activities but neighbors, and they extended the invitations as friends to friends in their neighborhood, and they acted as friends on behalf of their friends in the party. From the perspective of the campaign organizers the friends of the party who enjoyed the standing of "opinion leaders" in their neighborhoods were particularly good friends; their loyalty and support deserved the care which only special friendship can provide; each was introduced attentively to the needs and expectations of the campaigning party by the friend in the party who knew him or her best, preferably a friend who happened also to be a high-ranking government official and senior party member. Among friends it was not really necessary to remind anyone that the party had cared for its friends − and particularly its good friends − during the time between the mayoral elections. While they assisted the party now, in the political epoch of the mayoral campaign, the friends of the party knew that they worked for their own welfare in the future.

Besides the neighborhoods ethnic communities afforded tissues of friendship, tissues of a greater quality and strength than the ties that formed the party. Therefore, mayoral campaigns were also organized along ethnic lines. The principle of organization was again the identity of a friend in the party as a friend among friends in an ethnic community. For example, under the direction of a Chinese member of the party who was also a respected figure in the Chinese community, special campaign meetings were held for the members of this community. Similar events were staged for the members − often dispersed throughout the city − of other ethnic communities.

In its quest for a new life, in its campaign to renew old and to build new friendships, the party applied the most modern techniques of electioneering. As a campaign organization it combined the "old" with the "new," the "ancient" with the "modern." It drew its existence from the timeless culture of friendship, and it renewed its existence by the most recent artistry of American election campaigns.

A campaign staff was assembled, financed to a large extent by funds from business. Rather than making "official" campaign contributions, many firms preferred to put campaign staffers on their payrolls.[110]

The staff researched earlier elections in Boston and the present composition of the city's electorate, gathered data from voter surveys and polls, processed

---

[110] In 1975, for example, the campaign staff included: Patricia Aaron, Victoria Bartol, Jeffrey Bernstein, Pamela Call, Newell Cook, Steven Decosta, Robert Fichter, Mary Lou Gens, Mary Ellen Grealy, Nancy Jerome, Stacey Lesser, Ann Muenster, John Murphy, Nancy Murphy, Kirk O'Donnell, Jill Peltin, Maureen Schaffner, Elizabeth Sommer, Thomas Vallely, Paul White, Ralph Whitehead.

all relevant information, and stored it in a computer at the campaign head-quarters. As a result of these efforts in the vein of a "science" of campaigns, the staff could identify, for instance, the segments of those voters who registered at a characteristically low rate — like the tenants in Boston. The theoretical analysis of the electorate was of course untertaken because of its practical implications. The campaign organization saved money, time, and energy, as it knew the segments of voters with a low registration rate: these voters would not be courted as much as the groups of those voters whom the campaign planners could expect to turn out in great numbers at election day.

With the assistance of political consultants who were paid substantial fees,[111] the campaign organization "polled" and "canvassed" all registered voters in Boston. Polling was used to detect the "issues" that mostly concerned the voters, and canvassing was used to find out the voters who were likely to endorse the party's candidate, the Mayor.

The "White voters" — as they were called — were particularly encouraged to come forward and to concern themselves with the campaign and its organization. They were all potential friends and not a few of them would, if properly cultivated, shift gradually from the status of anonymous voters to that of trusted friends within the party's fabric of friendships. The technical sophistication of the campaign enabled the party precisely to know the source upon which it could draw to renew its existence. There were friends of the party "out there" in the electorate. But how could the party know and recruit them if they did not do what they could hardly be expected to do, namely present themselves on their own initiative? The computer bridged the gap, not unlike a matchmaker, tracing in the form of print-outs the hitherto invisible bonds between the party and all its potential friends. To canvass actually meant to blend the art of friendship and the artistry of election campaigns. Canvassing was courtship, performed in the mode of computer analyses and played out in the mode of an election campaign.

Significantly, the party sought the public endorsement of other political organizations like the trade unions, for instance; but it had no interest in drawing upon the manpower of these organizations. It did not need manpower but friends, and friends cannot be borrowed.

Friends cannot be borrowed nor can they be employed at will. The culture of friendship which carried the campaigning party to a renewed life existed but within definite boundaries. These boundaries were marked by the percep-tion of different people that they were "friends." They helped each other and

---

[111] S. Blumenthal, *The Permanent Campaign*, op. cit., informs about the services of political consultants employed by White campaigns. Cf. further: L. J. Sabato, *The Rise of Political Consultants. New Ways of Winning Elections*, New York 1981.

because they helped each other the party did exist. In concerning themselves with the campaign of the party they did not assist the "party" — an entity they would have refused really to know. They assisted each other.

On the one hand, then, the party was enlivened by all the loyalty which friends actualize in the pursuit of mutual interests. On the other hand, however, it was drained of all life the moment its friends were asked or expected to engage themselves in activities that had nothing to do with their culture of friendship. Beyond this culture the party did not and could not exist. It could always find new friends — and therefore exist. It could never use friendship for any purpose other than friendship. If it tried, it ceased to exist.

12 The Currency of Power

Political campaigns cost money, and they cost ever more money.[112] Whence does the money come? Who nurtures the quest for political power? What is it that smoothes the vicissitudes of political life?

The matter of political finance is wrapped in much obscurity yet, though in some polities more than in others.[113] If it is discussed in public at all, the debate tends to settle — all too readily yet inevitably, as it were — on the theme of "corruption."[114] Politicians will either be accused of enriching themselves by applying their power to extract "tributes" from their constituencies; or they will be charged with the practice of selling chips of their influence to whomever bids enough. It will even be held, in a more acute agitation about the mores in politics, that the politicians' greed infests the

---

[112] Cf. H. E. Alexander, *Financing Politics. Money, Elections, and Political Reform*, Washington, D. C. 1976, 1984, 3rd ed.; idem, ed., *Campaign Money. Reform and Reality in the United States*, New York 1976; idem, ed., *Political Finance*, Beverly Hills 1979; D. Bonafede, "Costly Campaigns: Consultants Cash in as Candidates Spend What They Must," *NJ*, June 16, 1983, pp. 789–792; R. E. Cohen, "Costly Campaigns: Candidates Learn That Reaching the votes Is Expensive," in: ibid., pp. 782–788.

[113] If public knowledge about political finance were measured in various countries on a scale ranging from "mystery" to "transparence," the U. S. would appear somewhere along the intervals towards transparence while France, for instance, would figure in deepest mystery. The Federal Republic of Germany, partly due to pertinent laws, partly as a result of recent trials concerning political bribery (the "Flick case"), would seem to be dangling between transparence and mystery.

[114] Cf. E. Drew, *Politics and Money. The New Road to Corruption*, New York 1983; J. T. Noonan Jr., *Bribes*, New York 1984, pp. 621–651 ("The Donations of Democracy").

process of policy making proper. What politicians do will be thought of as "deals" between buyers and sellers.

However, the public also expects the politician to make himself known, to advertise his policy maps, to reach for the support of constituencies, to win votes. It expects him to wage political campaigns, to compete with many others for the same office, and to struggle for the approval which it might or might not bestow upon him, and to seek the single voice of power from the discordant sounds of the multitude. How can the public expect the politician to do all this and not to spend a great deal of money?

The question belongs to a class of inquiries whose satisfactory pursuit is still a wanting enterprise in scholarship. An adequate answer could be formulated only within a theory of political finance. A certain nescience as to the nature of this theory might be one reason why it has not yet been achieved. Anyone envisaging it must first pierce through a curtain of erroneous perceptions. Contrary to common belief, any attempt at a theory of political finance would fail its subject, if it aimed primarily at clarifying the connections between "power" and "money." It would cling to a dichotomy that reflects a puritan uneasiness as regards the necessities of power. This uneasiness is widely spread as a political mood, in Boston, in America, and elsewhere. It is an attitude not free from hypocrisy.[115] Power should preferably have no relation to money whatsoever; however, if it cannot be had without any investment and expenditure of money, this brutal condition should at least be firmly restricted to a separate realm, back from the conspicuity of power. This puritan mood makes the politician the victim of a dichotomy from which he cannot escape: he cannot seek nor maintain political power and forsake the use of money altogether; he cannot help committing the blend of "respectable" and "pecuniary" politics; he cannot disprove a suspicion of wrongdoing which he constantly proves simply by being a politician.

There would be no politicians, if most of them did not succeed somehow in ostensibly keeping apart what really cannot be kept apart. Each must try to stride in the brightness of respectable politics and to shun the shadows of pecuniary politics. Some will slip and stumble, struggling betwixt and between, marking inadvertently the spot of suspicion. They will be victimized.[116]

---

[115] Cf. S. P. Huntington's analysis of the "American cognitive dissonance [...], the gap between moralism and hypocrisy," in: *American Politics,* op. cit., p. 74 ff.

[116] On September 28, 1984 Theodore V. Anzalone (see pp. 118, 130), "the subject of much adverse publicity," as a writer of the *Boston Globe* had it (*BG,* March 26, 1984, p. 19), was acquitted of extortion and conspiracy charges by a federal jury. For three years Anzalone had been a subject of U. S. Attorney William F. Weld's investigation of alleged corruption within the White administration. Anzalone's name, due to the nature of his involvement with Kevin White and the Kevin White Party, could be seen as standing

And some will be found to have deliberately dwelled in the darkness of corruption.

The puritan mood also prevents its many adherents from perceiving correctly the ingenuity of the skilled politician in handling the problem of political finance. They do not seem to understand the strategy which politicians have adopted to neutralize the pitfalls of the problem. Mayor White, by virtue of his own skills and those of his fund-raisers, accumulated considerable amounts of financial contributions to his election campaigns. The magnitude of his "war chest" — as media writers called it — appeared to manifest an inflated claim to power. However, it reflected the successful attempt to turn the necessity of raising funds into a freedom of choice. The more the amount of campaign contributions grew and the more the number of contributors increased, the less was the party in Boston obliged to bend its own interests and policies to the interests and expectations of each and every contributor. It partially "lost" its freedom of action by seeking pecuniary support, and it "regained" a greater liberty by striving to raise lots of funds from as many sources as possible.

Beyond the erroneous perceptions that still prevail, the primary task of a theory of political finance would be to discern properly the phenomena that constitute its subject. The most important of these phenomena is what I suggest to call the "currency of power."[117] In the world of politics this currency fulfills a function similar to that of "money" in the common world. It is the medium of exchange by which politics is transacted. To its users the currency of power offers a variety of units: favors, contracts, grants, jobs, desirable policy decisions, campaign contributions, votes, manpower, patronage, connections, access. They form the elementary units of political accounting by which it is possible to "manage" the transactions of politics. The users of the currency incur and settle "debts," accumulate "credits" to their standing (broadening their political clout), or run to taking "loans" (eroding their status in politics). No actual bookkeeping is done, of course, and the accounts are stored in memories only, but in each case of transaction hard calculations

---

for the Mayor and his administration. Cf. *BG*, Oct. 29, 1982; Dec. 17, 1982; June 27, 1983; March 6, 1984; Sept. 29, 1984 and the related reports in: *NYT*, Jan. 9, 1983; *BG*, Jan. 10, 1983.

[117] The term "currency of power" is, I think, more precise than the term "currency of politics" used by L. Namier (*England in the Age of the American Revolution*, London 1930, p. 218) as well as by contemporary White House watchers (cf. *NJ*, Vol. 16, No. 50–51, Dec. 15, 1984, p. 2386). — A subtle analysis of the "political arena" as a "market for power" can be found in: G. E. G. Catlin, *The Science and Method of Politics*, London – New York 1927, pp. 260–279.

are made to determine the amount of currency units involved in the transaction.

The currency of power is a catalyst of politics. It converts most disparate and mainly apolitical elements of human life into a stock of political goods. It enables the participants in politics to pursue their interests in the objective mode of political management: however diverse their interests and, in particular, their resources to look after their interests may be, they can negotiate arrangements of their concerns by the neutral language and medium of exchange which the currency of power provides.

The skilled politician is an expert in political management and negotiation. He dispenses favors, shares out jobs, accepts campaign contributions, provides access to governmental power, considers whose interests will be affected by a policy decision, connects votes with benefits – and yet he will always negotiate, conduct but transactions of politics, use the units of one currency, the currency of politics. And he will not negotiate with anyone who does not understand that in politics favors are not just favors, campaign contributions not just campaign contributions. The currency of power is the safeguard against mercenary politics – against corruption. He who does not protect himself by using it, is deprived of the language and medium of exchange by which he himself and the people he deals with can know the lines between bribe and favor, deal and negotiation, interest and policy, ethical suppleness and political skills. Only fools, dreamers, and inexperienced politicians fail to see the morale that the currency of power represents. They ignore the ethical depth of what they think is the pure game of power.

To associate an "ethic" with the political transactions for which the currency of power is used might seem to be a paradoxical idea, a notion bare of any reality. Yet the apparent contradiction stands: the currency of power is both a medium of exchange and a structure of constraints. For it does smoothe the flow of politics, and it does curb the transactions of politics. What seems to be a paradox actually is a compelling effect that no one intended. As a neutral medium of exchange between various interests, the currency of power not only facilitates but also regulates the interplay of these interests. Whoever uses it does so in complying with an unstated ethic. Through the medium which the currency of power provides various interests are set forth, articulated, and negotiated – and implicitly subjected to the rule not to appear and interact in any direct, unmediated manner.

Mayor White was once offered in his office a stack of dollar bills by someone who had come to ask of him a "favor" – and who was promptly thrown out of the Mayor's Office.[118] There were quite a few reasons for this

---

[118] Source: Interview with senior mayoral aide.

response, of course. The respective person should never have been able to enter the Mayor's Office, in the first place, and had evidently gained the desired access only under false pretences. However, the most compelling reason for the swift dismissal was this person's offence against the implicative ethic that governs the transactions of politics for which units such as "favors" or "campaign contributions" are being used. These transactions are *political* transactions occurring in the modes of negotiation, bargaining, and compromise. They require a political mode of behavior and a political grasp of the situation to be dealt with. The person who sought to "buy" from the Mayor a favor committed the offence of disregarding these conditions by attempting to circumnavigate the mediating sphere of "politics" and to establish instead the direct, private deal between a "buyer" and a "seller." Confronted with the attempt the Mayor could but respond as he did – considering his interest as a politician (as a politician, to be sure, who knew the need for campaign funds), for the attempt struck the core of his political existence. It implied his willingness to forsake politics for a trivial deal. And this was the great offence: the insinuated negation of politics and of the politician's existence. On the part of the politician (as politician) there was but one response indeed: the affirmation of politics and of the rules by which politics is governed, the affirmation of a "political ethic."

A politician cannot use the currency of power and avoid its ethical effect. It orders his behavior precisely because of his being a politician. Using the currency means that one is subject to its ethical effect, whether one intended this consequence or not (the latter is usually the case). Any attempt at dodging the consequence would be an attempt at escaping from politics. The politician would annihilate the reality of his existence.

Therefore, whenever the use of the currency of power is observed, a test of politics is made, for politics must occur when a flow of the currency is found. It is possible to measure the degree of politics in a community by weighing the flow of currency units, according to the question: how many units are in use? What is the frequency of exchange? Which is the scope of their distribution? A simple correlation will disclose a fundamental condition. It will reveal what politics there is in the community: the greater the number of currency units in use, the higher their frequency of exchange, and the larger their scope of distribution, the more will the community be found to be an intensely *political* community.

The currency of power is an excellent quantitative measure of politics because of its quality as a "currency." If a large number of currency units is circulating widely, the currency is readily available to numerous people at various places. Or, inversely put, numerous people at various places can go after currency units and thereby increase their standing in politics. Thus, the currency of power enhances the process of politics. Whoever wishes to participate in this process wants to obtain units of currency, and this desire, to the degree it is felt by many, makes the currency units still more valuable. The general want for currency units will be an incentive to augment their number in circulation, but then the number of people touched by the want will increase, too; and neither the amount of currency units nor their scope of distribution can be enlarged indefinitely.

To the extent that it cannot be satisfied by a quantitative expansion, the general want for currency units makes the process of politics more intense. The distribution of currency units will become a matter of political competition. The competitiveness of each participant in the political process will depend upon the amount of currency units he controls. The currency of power will be used to compete for the currency of power. Or, in political terms, politics will be intensified by politics.

The units of which the currency of power consists − favors, contracts, policy decisions, campaign contributions, etc. − do not therefore circulate "freely." Rather, they are protected, stored away, kept like secret funds. They circulate, but they circulate in the unpredictable and intricate ways of politics. Their "system" of distribution is a moving labyrinth rather than a fixed order, the continuously changing result of decisions made at various places by numerous people who are pursuing different interests in a complex process of negotiation, bargaining, and compromise. All these participants in the process of politics "control" the currency of power and thus nobody really controls it − unless considerable political efforts are made to concentrate upon one political goal a large amount of currency units that circulate in a political community.

In Boston under Mayor White any unit of political exchange was a precious asset. Power had assumed an overbearing and yet elusive presence in the life of the city. Therefore, the means to deal with it were in great demand. It was difficult to ignore it. And it was equally difficult to get in touch with it. There were the transactions of power, however, by which the reality of political power in the city was forged. They made a "market" and in this market the currency of power was used. Anyone who "owned" units of the currency could go to the market and trade them − and thereby enter into the politics of power that nourished the power of politics shaping the city. The elusive yet overbearing presence of this power became accessible to everyone who was capable of trading units of political exchange. Any unit was a precious asset indeed. It could be exchanged for an entry to the political exchange, to the market of power in Boston.

And a market of power existed in Boston − in spite of the Mayor's autocratic regime. Or, rather, the market thrived because of the autocracy. To be what it was, the regime had continuously to soak up from the market as many units of political exchange as possible. The market consequently attracted numerous agents: all the people who found that they had units to offer and all the people who sought units in order to be able to hold their own vis-à-vis the autocracy and the weight of its power.

In the market the regime competed with many other agents. It never did and never could attain at the supreme centripetal strength which it would have needed in order to be capable of draining the market of all the units of political exchange which the latter held. Nor did it always succeed in extracting from the market all the specific units which it tried to obtain at a particular moment for a particular purpose.

Ever so often the Mayor asked his aides to note on a list everyone whom his government had granted a favor or a number of favors and to note, in each case, the nature and the "value" of the favor. Favors were units of political exchange, "hard" currency which the government had not shared out for nothing. It expected its debtors to return the favors and to supply other units of political exchange of which it was in need. To realize the outstanding "debt," a complete list of all the government's favors and their recipients would undoubtedly have been useful. However, such a list was never compiled. It would have been an illogical task, because of reasons which the Mayor, not as head of government but as politician, knew better than anyone else.[119]

Darkness, Shadows, and Light

The market of political finance would not function if every transaction were put on record and spelled out for everyone to know. It is not unusual, for instance, that a transaction is carried out and not one word is spoken as to the transaction itself. The fringe awareness of each participant suffices to understand what the other party to the transaction means and to conduct the exchange while matters of quite a different nature are discussed, matters that hardly give a hint at what they tacitly carry. Any attempt at making the transaction explicit would most likely be tantamount to preclude its completion. The medium for settling it successfully is the obscurity of unspoken words.[120]

---

[119] There were just too many agents in the market who were interested in trading favors for other units of the currency of power — and most of them operated within the government itself. They traded in behalf of the government and they traded in their own behalf.

[120] Cf. P. Grémion, *Le pouvoir périphérique,*op. cit., p. 254: "Les marchandages entre bureaucrates-notables et notables-bureaucrates suivent un rituel immuable. Le vocabulaire est fleuri. Le code est pauvre. [...] Rhétorique plus qu'idéologie, nul n'est dupe du

Darkness is a condition of political finance. So are the shadows of knowledge through which most transactions in the market of political finance are visibly discerned and vainly explored. And so is the light of publicity which beams on the market, such as a beacon meeting the blackness of the sea.

Darkness, shadows, and light – the conditions of political finance of which each is reinforcing the other two conditions. The Mayor's campaigns, as public as they were regarding the courting of votes, blacked out, as much as they could, their financial sources of being. Some contributions, for instance, were tracelessly received and tracelessly converted into campaign expenditures. They were donated in cash and they were used to buy stamps. What tracks there were was lost in the memory of a few campaign workers. Salaries for campaign people were "covered" by business or government. In the preliminary to the mayoral election of 1971, for example, the Mayor's campaign officially employed only one person;[121] however, there were many other persons who worked full-time in the campaign (around 55), and they were paid for their services, too, of course; but they received their wages from a fake employment – they had been put either on private or on city payroll.

All the financing of the campaign could not be concealed; certain records had to be kept, by the government, by the campaign organizations. And these records are public. Not that they afforded full information about the financial transactions of which they tell. They are the outer story of an untold inner story – shadows of knowledge.

In the financial records submitted by the Mayor's campaigns to the appropriate commissions[122] the names of not a few developers, for instance, can be found who are reported to have donated to the campaigns the maximum amount that is legally permitted. A piece of public knowledge, then, one would think. Certain transactions of political finance and their participants being put on record. What more could be told? A considerable part: all the inner story which the outer story of the financial records obscures. Unravelling the full inner story, however, would be a futile attempt. It would not only require an intimate knowledge of Boston politics and much specific research, besides. It would also fail to achieve its goal. The very threads of

---

propos. La rhétorique notabiliaire est un code. L'enjeu d'une négociation se revèle au détour d'une phrase et n'est accessible qu'aux initiés. Les variations insignifiantes permettent à chaque partenaire de savoir 'jusqu'où il peut aller' dans l'assouplissement de la règle. Mais la maîtrise de la rhétorique est sélective et la méconnaissance de son maniement isole immédiatement l'individu 'irresponsable.'"

[121] John Marttila.

[122] The *Boston Finance Commission* and the [Massachusetts] *State Office of Campaign and Political Finance*.

the inner story that were disentangled would make the attempt peter out. It would be a progress of learning unto confusion.

In the financial records of the Mayor's campaigns the names of not a few developers are mentioned, but these names as names are largely unintelligible. They are but words: personal names, or names of nondescript firms. Persistent watchers of politics in Boston will know, at the moment they look at the records, who the persons or the companies are to whom certain names belong; other names will remind them only of something they will recall very vaguely; and quite a number will tell them just nothing. The story, to be further pursued, wants the efforts of scrupulous research. It calls for the discipine of the scholar paired with the talents of the detective.[123] The probe of documents, memories, persons, if undertaken and tenaciously carried on, will bring results. Transactions will be discerned whose financial figures have a political meaning.

Obviously, the story would go on with an inquiry into the politics of these transactions. It would continue being unravelled, if the "truth" of the campaign contributions whose story it is were now uncovered. Yet, at this critical stage, the stock of public records and similar documents dwindles rapidly. The pursuit of the story will acquire the quality of a gamble. There is evidence still to be found, but it eludes the exaction of methodical research. One will not find evidence which one sought but will come across evidence turning up unexpectedly. Such findings will depend upon luck, perseverance, and the whims of participants in the story who are starting to talk or to silently push over their desk a few indiscreet memos. Closing in upon the truth it pursues, the story capriciously begins to meander.

The rills into which it is branching out are so many that a greater number could be staked out only under extraordinary efforts. Under normal conditions, confusion is the whole advice. The sheer number of branches makes the choice as to those one will further explore by necessity an arbitrary decision. And then, all that is successfully explored might still be just dead ends, if luck fails to be the guide to discovery.[124]

Still, discoveries will be made. The political meaning of particular contributions donated by particular developers to the Mayor's campaigns will appear to become transparent. One will learn, for example, that zoning had not been the only issue of a controversy concerning the construction of high rises in

---

[123] Cf. supra, p. 115 and infra, p. 188.

[124] The researcher's predicament can be demonstrated quite easily: a campaign report for *one* of the last years of the Mayor's reign includes the names of at least a hundred (and in some years: two hundred) developers. To pursue the story of each "case" — that is at least a hundred stories — would require extraordinary efforts indeed, not to mention the tremendous task of putting the principal story together again.

the Back Bay, Boston's delicate district of nineteenth-century cosmopolitan architecture.[125] There had been another issue as well: the past and future campaign contributions of the individuals and firms whose interest it was to "develop" the Back Bay. In the past the developers had benefited from the government's liberal zoning policy, and the government, that is the Mayor, had benefited from the developers' liberal financial support. The Mayor was puzzled when he was told that the controversy had been resolved in a way that might well deprive his campaigns of certain contributions in the future, at least in the immediate future.[126]

Or one will hear, to quote another example, that campaign contributions were the reasons why the government gave preference to a developer over the residents in a neighborhood where the developer was planning to build a cluster of high rises which the residents feared would impair the small scale of housing in their community. Aides of the Mayor analyzed the issue and found that the buildings could be lower and would still bring the developer a profit. Since it wanted the flow of contributions from this developer to continue, the government chose to ignore the case of the residents and its own wisdom.

Or one might even be able to acquire written materials such as the memorandum, for example, which illuminates the subtle complicity a refined practitioner of political donations tries to create — clad in a coat of innocence. Written by a close aide of his, the memorandum urges the Mayor to side with a particular developer in the final competition between two proposals for the planned renovation of Boston's Faneuil Hall Marketplace. The case is stated brilliantly, the pros are weighed as dispassionately as the cons, at the close of a perfect argument it appears that choosing the developer in whose behalf the author of the memorandum speaks would only be logical. Perfect indeed, in the sense of the classical definition: nothing should be taken away, nothing should be added.

---

[125] Cf. W. Muir Whitehill, *Boston. A Topographical History,*op. cit.; The Boston Society of Architects, *Architecture Boston,*op. cit.

[126] The controversy took place in 1970. The BRA opposed the proposal for the construction of high rises in the Back Bay. The developers who wanted the plan to be approved worked through the Building Commissioner, Richard Thuma — who happened also to be one of the Mayor's fundraisers. The Mayor continually received briefings about the controversy from one of his aides, Michael Kelly. Eventually, a zoning ordinance was passed — under the active participation of Kelly — which had the effect that a construction of high rises in the Back Bay was possible no longer. This outcome had not been anticipated by the Mayor; he had rather hoped that the controversy would induce some of his financial backers — the owner of the Ritz in particular — to be still more generous with their money.

Nevertheless, a postscript is added, in handwriting. It advises the Mayor of a "late development." The developer whose interest the memo pursues, "has agreed to 'donate' $ 500.000 (free and clear) for the Bicentennial." Free and clear − what an innocence the language of political gifts pretends. But then it does not contaminate the language of logic used in the memo. The two languages are kept distinct, "political gifts" from "political decisions." Of translating nothing is said. But then nothing about translating needs to be said. The developer, the author of the memorandum, the Mayor − they know the two languages and they understand that they understand each other in each language. [127]

The Illusion of Publicity

The truth of political gifts does not have light as a synonym. Even when it emerges "free and clear," it betakes itself to obscurity − an obscurity again of unspoken words. The conditions of political finance, no doubt, they reinforce each other. A darkness of untold transactions casts shadows of knowledge, the shadows of knowledge shape to the light of publicity, the light of publicity spells a darkness of transactions. [128]

The truth of political gifts eludes publicity. It eludes its own reality. Aides in the Mayor's Office could hardly complain of not having enough experience in trading favors for campaign contributions. And yet their vision of the trade's facts were persistently "fuzzy." [129] How many favors were owed to someone, for instance, who had donated two thousand dollars? What was a favor, what was not? And the "value" of both favors and campaign contributions, did it not fluctuate continuously? What were they doing when doing what they did meant to conjecture?

The truth of political gifts shrinks from publicity. It shrinks from its own substance. To be seized, it must be sought empirically. The search for facts through which it bids discovery is a search for figuration − for the figuration of "research" which tells the search its facts. In the mode of empirical research the search is the visualization of the facts it seeks. It converges upon such constellations of persons, actions, events that in themselves appear to be

---

[127] City of Boston and County of Suffolk, Departmental Communication, December 19, 1972, To: Kevin H. White, From: Ira A. Jackson, Subject: Quincy Market-Faneuil Hall.

[128] Cf. the passage on "Die Metaphorik von Öffentlichkeit und Geheimnis," in: L. Hölscher, *Öffentlichkeit und Geheimnis. Eine begriffsgeschichtliche Untersuchung zur Entstehung der Öffentlichkeit in der frühen Neuzeit*, Stuttgart 1979.

[129] The people in the Mayor's government and party were of course used to "fuzzy" appearances of politics. Cf. supra, p. 33 f.

significative. In the parlance of social science these constellations carry the name of "cases."[130] The name suggests phenomena of limited nature; a "case," one is enticed to believe, is a finite number of facts. This is a true notion as long as a "case" is strictly understood to be a mode of understanding. There appear to be "cases" in the reality of people and things, as the figurations of empirical research make for the existence of such "cases." To know a "case" necessarily means to know a *finite* number of facts. A case study of a campaign contribution, for instance, can be conceived of as a terminable search for the truth of political gifts because it *makes* this search a terminable matter.

Yet, the figurations of empirical knowledge do not signify corresponding figurations in the reality of people and things. The finiteness of "cases" is an epistemological, not an empirical phenomenon. A search for more facts relevant to a "case" can well be continued, long after the facts have been found which figured the "case," a constellation of persons, actions, events that in themselves appear to be significative, for any constellation of this kind arises from a circumjacent field of persons, actions, and events whose depth and width, a twigged expanse, potentially are infinite. It resembles a conclusive abstraction and it is actually but a fragment of life. Or, empirically put, from the surrounding field of persons, actions, and events, an endless number of facts could be drawn which all were relevant to the constellation, the particular "case." The finiteness of the case, it seems, could be amended through the infiniteness of the field. What would happen, however, if a search for facts were indeed continued up to the very last fact, the smallest detail, the farthest thread that bore upon the case? Would life then tuck into its fragment or, conversely perhaps, would the fragment attain life?

No. The infiniteness of life would have absorbed the finiteness of the fragment. There were so many facts swamping the case, so many minor and marginal ones, the relevance of each would now be infinitesimal. Since all would equally be valid as "facts," those few were lost which redeemed their infinity through significance. A "case" would virtually have vanished — in that surrounding field of an endless number of persons, actions, and events which a case, to be a "case," needs to be abstracted from as a *finite* number of facts.

The truth of political gifts shrinks from publicity, shrinks from its substance, if it is pursued in the mode of empirical research and if the research is pursued relentlessly. In the controversy concerning the construction of high rises in the Back Bay — to continue the story of a "case" told a few paragraphs earlier — the aesthetic insouciance of the Mayor's principal aide[131] *may* have

---

[130] Cf. supra, p. 172.
[131] Barney Frank.

been of crucial importance. He stood aloof, disclaiming any interest in an "architectural" issue. Of course, the controversy centered on a zoning decision and zoning, the spatial organization of a society, inevitably is intertwined with politics. But the aide chose not to extract from the controversy the potentialities for politics it held. He left it to the market of political finance whose agents, on the "public" as well as on the "private" side, promptly intervened. Why this indifference? That he had no sense of architecture, was this really true? Did he not perhaps grasp the potential gravity of zoning? Or was his insouciance but a ploy in a scheme he could not or did not want to reveal? Or had someone else asked the aide – perhaps compelled him – to put on the mien of indifference and play a silent yet significant role in the other's game?[132]

These questions could of course be turned into problems of empirical research and as such be further pursued. But then the "case" would be thrown open, swarming with "new" facts. And it would by no means be certain that all the additional efforts of research would be indeed a continuation of the original search for facts, for a constellation of persons, actions, events that in themselves appear to be significative. Other cases would very likely be inspired through the host of new facts. The finiteness of the one case would be diluted with the potential infinity of further cases. The story to be told would have begun to meander. In fact, of a story hardly anything could still be told. The thread of a tale would have been lost in a confusion of possible cases that could all be pursued – relentlessly to an ever greater confusion.

The story to be told about the truth of political gifts – or the truth of other political phenomena, for that matter – needs the figuration of empirical research, else it is not a search for truth. As a search for facts, however, it cannot be purely empirical research, or else the infinity of facts absorbs the story.

A publicity of political finance is an illusion not only because the light of publicity spells a darkness of political transactions. It is an illusion also because publicity cannot be the truth it is meant to be.[133]

---

[132] Similar questions could be raised as to the "case" of the memorandum regarding the selection of a developer for the Faneuil Hall Marketplace. What exactly was the position of Ira Jackson, author of the memo? Who induced Rouse to donate $ 500,000? Or had the gift been purely his own idea? What should one make of the fact that Jackson had formerly been employed by Rouse?

[133] In a discussion of Lyndon Johnson's first campaign (for a congressional seat in Texas) Robert Caro relates this experience: having diligently pursued the "truth" of the financing of the campaign he arrived but at conflicting "truths." Cf. Robert A. Caro, *The Years of Lyndon Johnson. The Path to Power,* New York 1982, p. 408.

Political Banking: Phenomenological Approaches

Any reality of politics — as, for example, the reality of political finance, our present concern — can be seized upon in the mode of "facts." This is a possible way of approaching it; it can be grasped as a world of facts — *as* a world of facts. From the possibility of this approach it does not follow, however, that it *is* a world of facts. The "facts" into which it supposedly breaks asunder are facts of knowing, not facts of the reality it is.[134]

For there is the reality of politics preceding, temporally as well as experientally, any political science.[135] It is a reality of patterns, configurations, nodes, of structural phenomena: phenomena that a science can seize. As a reality of structures the reality of politics offers science what science seeks: phenomena of study. Science need not project a mode to seize upon political reality, for it can choose the mode through which political reality appears: the phenomena of politics.

To continue the story of the Mayor's campaigns, then, we shall turn to the phenomena of campaigning through which these campaigns told their reality, the political reality of campaigning. Facts will be part of the story, of course, quite a few facts indeed. But instead of following fact after fact — towards an ever greater confusion —, the story will take up its facts through phenomenological approaches. Not facts, their potential infinity, will be the story's term, but the phenomena that emerge from a sufficient number of facts and that fit the potential infinity of other relevant facts.

The phenomenology which is intended is a phenomenology of political banking. As for its facts, it will draw upon the practices which the Mayor and his party used towards the financing of their electoral campaigns.

Formalities

In Boston, as elsewhere in America, candidates for political office cannot rely on the apparatus and the aid of a political party — as their counterparts in

---

[134] L. Wittgenstein, *Tractatus Logico-Philosophicus:* "The world is all that is the case. (1) — The world is the totality of facts, not of things. (1.1) — The facts in logical space are the world. (1.13) — The world breaks up into facts. (1.2) — The meaning of the world must lie outside the world. In the world everything is as it is and happens just as it happens; *in* the world there is no value, [...]. If there is value that really has value so it must lie outside of all that happens and is the case. For all that happens and is the case is accidental. What makes it all non-accidental cannot lie *in* the world, for if it did, this would again be something accidental. — It must lie outside the world. (6.41)."

[135] Cf. supra, pp. 50 f., 149 f., 160; Chapter 2, notes 6 and 7; supra, notes 92 and 93.

Europe, for instance, can do. They have to build their own campaign organization. And they have to make their own efforts towards raising campaign
funds. They are as much campaigners as they are entrepreneurs – starting
and running their own political business.[136]

The formal conditions of the campaign business are easy to meet. A
"committee" – or a similar body – is founded which serves the candidate
as his or her official organization. The formal body of Kevin White's campaigns was called, quite appropriately, the "Kevin White Committee." The
key position on the committee was held, not surprisingly either, by an
important member of the White family: the committee's treasurer was William
J. Galvin, Kevin White's father-in-law.

On behalf of the candidate secondary bodies are set up and they assist
mainly in the task of fund-raising. Such a body was the "Committee for a
Better Boston," for example. It was formed in 1981, purely for the collection
of contributions to the campaign business of candidate White. Typically, it
originated from the political sanctuary of family members and close friends.
William J. Galvin Jr., brother of Mrs. Kevin White, chaired this committee,
and Theodore V. Anzalone served as its treasurer.

Apart from the necessity of building an organization, there is only one
more formal condition of a campaign business. To comply with the law, the
committees working on behalf of candidate White had to file an annual
report on their financial proceedings. They were required to name each
contributor, to specify the amount of each contribution, to detail their
expenses, and, finally, to disclose their annual balance.[137] The financial
transactions of the Mayor's campaigns thus became a matter of public
records – though not necessarily a matter of knowledge commensurate with
their reality.[138]

Still, in regard of its formal conditions, one might expect a great veracity
of the reporting. In Boston, the critical institution is the "Boston Finance
Commission."[139] Its members are appointed by the Governor of Massachusetts

---

[136] Cf. X. Kayden, *Campaign Organization*, Lexington, Mass. 1978; N. W. Polsby, *Consequences of Party Reform*, Oxford 1983; St. A. and B. G. Salmore, *Candidates, Parties
and Campaigns*, Washington, D. C. 1985; T. Schabert, "Die Freiheit im Labyrinth.
Amerikanische Wahlkämpfe sind chaotisch und schöpferisch zugleich," *Süddeutsche
Zeitung*, No. 255, Nov. 3–4, 1984, p. I; E. C. Banfield, "Party 'Reform' in Retrospect,"
in: idem, *Here the People Rule*, op. cit., pp. 38–52.

[137] At the close of 1982 the Kevin White Committee and the Committee for a Better Boston
had a combined balance of $ 315,350. At the close of 1981 they had a balance of
$ 323,246. At the close of 1980 the balance of the Kevin White Committee was $ 168,208.

[138] Cf. infra, p. 188 f.

[139] The Boston Finance Commission was established in 1909. The legal provisions relevant
to the Commission can be found in: *City of Boston Code*, op. cit., Ch. 9, §§ 300–307.

who, in general, is not inspired by a special affection for the Mayor of Boston — on the contrary. The Boston Finance Commission had no reason, legally or politically, not to look at the campaign business of Mayor White very thoroughly. Yet, it could not probe the Mayor's political finances as exhaustively as it would have wished. For the Mayor had the commission on the purse strings; all its expenses, including the salaries of the chairman and the staff, are paid by the City, and the City's budget is swayed by the Mayor.[140] Through his budgetary powers, Mayor White could — and did — constrain the commission's inquiries into the finances of his campaign business.[141]

The quest for publicity, for knowledge commensurate with the financial reality of the Mayor's campaigns, was thwarted at the outset, when it was still being carried by the law and was dealing only with the formal conditions of campaigning. The Mayor's campaigns patterned themselves upon these formal conditions, but then all they really deferred to were the formalities, hardly the conditions.

The System of Political Insurance

The Mayor came into campaign funds through a system of political insurance which comprised members of his party and his government, and through the tribute which developers, architects, lawyers, businessman paid to his procurators.

The principle by which the system of political insurance worked was simple and effective. The people who belonged to the Kevin White Party mostly wished to play a part in politics, and the party lent a form — quite a promising one at that — to their political passion. But there was no part to play — at least through the party — if one failed to be in the Mayor's good graces. A member of the party was therefore well-advised if he or she responded readily to requests, please to make a contribution to the campaign chest of the Mayor. The contribution did not automatically ensure an employment in the government or whatever it was that one expected from the party, but it ensured an amount of goodwill in the quarters of mayoral power.

A contribution to the Mayor's campaign chest, then, meant two things. On the one hand, it helped the Mayor to finance his campaigns. Thus it

---

[140] Cf. supra, p. 16.

[141] In 1980, for instance, the commission held hearings on certain expenditures of the city government. They displeased the Mayor. In the next fiscal year the appropriation for the commission in the city budget was reduced to the minimum amount ($ 85,000) to which it was entitled by state law.

amounted to a monetary transaction. On the other hand, it helped the person who made it to be insured against mayoral displeasure. And thus it amounted to a precautionary transaction. Both sides wanted a transaction to take place, and both sides knew what each side wished — and what each side had to give. Through the campaign contribution Mayor and contributor entered a tacit contract that served the interests of each. The Mayor (or the procurator representing him) had secured another contributor, and the contributor had paid a premium for his or her insurance policy.

The system of political insurance worked because most members of the Mayor's party and many officials in his government felt that they could hardly afford not to join the system. It drew the large number of these persons into the process of financing the Mayor's campaigns and through this the party — or, more precisely, the Mayor's campaign organization — became, to a large extent, self-supporting. The party ringed the Mayor's clientele and transformed it into financial circles — the Mayor's clients supporting themselves as the Mayor's clientele.[142]

There emerged circles of contributors such as these:

(1) The circle of the *engagés*: prominent or very active members of the party, most of whom also held posts in the government at one time or the other.[143]

---

[142] While the Kevin White Committee encompassed the clientele inside and outside the government, the Committee for a Better Boston collected contributions mostly from city employees and top officials in the government. — Cf. also R. E. Wolfinger, *The Politics of Progress*, op. cit., p. 81: "Control of city or state government, then provides either local party with a formidable array of resources that by law, custom, and public acceptance can be exploited for money and labor. Party leaders reward the faithful and useful by giving them jobs, and then assess these jobholders for sizable contributions to pay the costs of maintaining power."

[143] The following list contains two sets of information: (a) the names of *engagés* and (b) the contribution each of them made to the Mayor's campaign chest in 1978 and 1979: Theodore V. Anzalone 1,350 (1979); Bruce Bolling 200 (1979), 100 (1978); Carolynn G. Connors 1,000 (1979); John E. & Kathleen Drew 200 (1978); Ronald M. Druker 50 (1979), 1,000 (1978); Bertram Druker 1,000 (1979), 1,000 (1978); Ed Dwyer 500 (1979); Harron Ellenson 50 (1979); Arnold & Charlotte Epstein 1,000 (1979); Robert Fichter 175 (1979), 100 (1978); Wendy Grey 1,000 (1978); James Hosker 250 (1979); William & Elisabeth Holland 1,519 (1979), 1,000 (1978); Nancy & Samuel Huntington 200 (1979); Clarence Jones 1,000 (1979), 1,000 (1978); *Katherine* & J. Louis *Kane* 1,550 (1979), 2,000 (1978); Robert Kenney 1,000 (1979), 1,000 (1978); Paul Parks 450 (1979); Jerome Rappaport 1,000 (1978); *Gail Rotegaard* 50 (1979), 100 (1978); Mark J. Weddleton 590 (1979), 100 (1978); John F. & Elisabeth Weis 600 (1979); Robert J. & Jeanne K. Vey 1,100 (1979), 1,000 (1978); Mortimer Zuckerman 1,000 (1979).

(2) The circle of high-ranking government officials: very generous contributors in general, of whom a few had to observe loyalties to the Mayor's government and to the Mayor's party as well.[144]

(3) The circle of mayoral aides: they were all devoted to the party's cause, yet some contributed quite liberally while others did so more modestly; not differences in rank or pay appeared to account for these variations, but rather differences in militancy or the willingness "to please."[145]

(4) The circle of contributors in a governmental agency: they were contributors of whom most paid their premium and not much more. The *Boston Redevelopment Authority* has provided quite an illustrative example.[146]

---

[144] The following list contains: (a) the names of high-ranking officials and (b) the contribution each of them made in 1978 and 1979: Joseph F. & Miriam R. Casazza 500 (1979), 600 (1978); Harold J. Carroll 500 (1979); Newell Cook 100 (1978); Brian Dacey 624,50 (1979); *Francis W. Gens* 1,100 (1979), 1,000 (1978); Andy Olins 375 (1979), 500 (1978); *Joanne Prevost* 1,000 (1979); Lowell Richards 450 (1979); *David Rosenbloom* 1,000 (1979), 1,000 (1978); Robert J. Ryan 1,000 (1979), 1,000 (1978); Marilyn Swartz-Lloyd 100 (1979); Arthur E. Shea 1,000 (1979), 600 (1978); Kane Simonian 1,000 (1979); Edward T. Sullivan 1,000 (1978); Raymond & Carolyn Torto 400 (1979); Robert Walsh 500 (1978); John Vitagliano 1,000 (1979), 500 (1978); James V. Young 350 (1979).

[145] The following list contains: (a) the names of mayoral aides and (b) the contribution each of them made in 1978 and 1979: Chris Bator 100 (1979), 100 (1978); George & B. Bennett 350 (1979); Richard A. & D. Katherine Borten 50 (1979); Susan Clippinger 150 (1979), 200 (1978); Carol Corcoran 400 (1979), 500 (1978); Robert & Roberta Delaney 100 (1979), 100 (1978); Stephen P. Dunleavy 750 (1979): Doby Flowers 600 (1979), 100 (1978); *Herbert P. & Nancy Gleason* 400 (1979), 1,000 (1978); Martha Goldsmith 250 (1979), 100 (1978); Averil Lashley 850 (1979); James Leitner 700 (1979); *Emily Lloyd* 1,000 (1979), 500 (1978); Dennis & Jan Morgan 1,000 (1979); George Nedder 100 (1979), 1,000 (1978); Elaine Noble 1,050 (1979); Mariellen Noris 200 (1979); Lawrence & Mary Quealy 50 (1979); George Regan 834 (1979), 100 (1978); Fred Salvucci 200 (1978); Lisa Savereid 100 (1979); Maureen Schaffner 1,000 (1979); Micho F. Spring 1,000 (1978); Robert & Joanne Toomey 1,100 (1978); Teri Weidner 100 (1979).

[146] The following list contains: (a) the names of contributors from the BRA and (b) the contribution each of them made in 1978 and 1979: Christopher Carlaw 50 (1979); Jeff Chmura 50 (1979); William P. Condo 150 (1979); George N. & Kathleen J. Collatos 1,000 (1979); Matthew A. Coogan 100 (1979); Lucas Di Leo 50 (1979); Alexander & Selma Ganz 425 (1979), 200 (1978); Lawrence & Alexandra Koff 125 (1979); Robert Kroin 125 (1979); Ralph & Sylvia Memolo 200 (1978); Paul L. McCann 150 (1979); Kimberley Robinson 160 (1979); Robert J. Ryan 1,000 (1979), 1,000 (1978); Kane Simonian 1,000 (1979); John Sloan 100 (1978); Rita Smith 125 (1979); David & Rhoda Trietsch 50 (1979), 25 (1978); Philip Zeigler 50 (1979). – For comparative purposes, I give in the following the annual salary of a few contributors (whose names appearing on one of the preceding lists were underlined): Katherine Kane $ 38,500 (1978/79); Gail Rotegaard $ 25,000 (1978/79); Francis W. Gens $ 30,000 (1978/79); Joanne Prevost

Tributes to Power

The Mayor's campaign business prospered with Boston's economic renaissance, especially with the building boom in the central districts.[147] In the 1960's and early 1970's the top officials and civic leaders who pursued the grand project of a "New Boston"[148] were still compelled to court the interest of developers. Invitations to submit proposals for specific development projects usually drew a very small field of entrants, and the task of "selecting" one required not so much jurors as salesmen capable of "selling" to a skeptical developer the future of Boston in general and the project on hand in particular.

In the late 1970's and early 1980's[149] the roles were reversed; proposals for the construction of new hotels or new office buildings were proffered in plenty; the field of bidders could in many cases be reduced to the exceptionally qualified competitors only and a sufficient number of finalists still remained; any developer who succeeded with his proposal in the end had very likely been chosen because he had made the strongly suggested concessions to the political trade and architectural taste of the two principal jurors — the Mayor and the director of the BRA.[150]

Boston had become a hotbed of urban development, and neither the Mayor nor his party missed the chance of cashing in. The developers, architects, lawyers, businessmen, contractors, restaurateurs who were known to have a stake in the city's new economic prosperity were invited to pay a tribute to the party's power. To be sure, the invitation to enter into a tributary relationship with the party's power did not imply the licence to approach the persons in power and to "buy." On the contrary, a tributary relationship had to be established first, and this was a prerogative of the ruler and not of those who owed him a tribute. (The circumstances, after all, were such that the number of potential tributaries quite exceeded the number of tributaries he needed absolutely.) In general, then, the Mayor's procurators observed this rule: they issued their invitations retrospectively, on the basis of lists (compiled by trusty persons in the Court) which told them who the developers, businessmen, contractors were to whom the Mayor, the party, the government had

---

$ 30,000 (1978/79); David Rosenbloom $ 50,000 (1978/79); Herbert Gleason $ 35,000 (1978/79); Emily Lloyd $ 30,000 (1978/79).

[147] Cf. infra, p. 294, note 58.

[148] Cf. infra, p. 278 ff.

[149] In the present context only the *early* 1980's — when Kevin White was still Mayor of Boston — do concern us.

[150] Kevin White, of course, and Robert J. Ryan.

been obliging and from whom the payment of a tribute could therefore be requested.[151]

In 1978 – the next mayoral election was not due before the fall of 1979 – tributes amounting to $ 100.874 were paid by 241 persons representing construction,[152] insurance,[153] real estate companies,[154] banks,[155] law firms,[156] architects,[157] or other enterprises such as the Ritz Carlton, the Old South News Stand, the Boston Center for the Arts, Boston University, the Push Cart Restaurant, the Convention Tourist Bureau, Phillips Candy House, Homer's Jewelry, the Cafe Berkeley. The majority of the tributaries were either the owners or the leading executives of the firms on whose behalf the tributes were paid.

In 1982 – a mayoral election was due again in the fall of 1983 – 194 persons contributed to the Mayor's campaign chest the maximum amount permitted by the law. Much the larger part of them, again, were the Mayor's tributaries in the real estate, urban development, and redevelopment business.

A number of tributaries were particularly attentive to the campaign business of the present and – possibly – future Mayor. They made contributions at very short intervals.[158]

---

[151] Such lists were used also the other way around. Malcolm Dudley, for instance, the Director of Public Facilities in the White administration (and before that in the administration of Mayor Collins) kept in his office a list of architects which had been prepared for him by people in the Court. The understanding was that Dudley looked first at this list before he hired an architect for municipal business. If he found one on the list who was qualified for the job on hand, then this architect got the job.

[152] Some representatives: John J. Appel, General Contractor; Louis N. Cavagnero, Camdele Construction; Mario S. (Jr.) & Natalie Susi, M. Susi & Sons Construction Co.; Edward & Gloria Vozzella, Massachusetts Construction Company.

[153] Some representatives: Maurice Abromson, Maurice Abromson Insurance; Leon M. Cangino Jr., Cangino Insurance Agency; Ambrose J. (Jr.) & Marilyn Redmond, Metropolitan Life Insurance; John P. Riley Insurance.

[154] Some representatives: Francis D. Burke, Maurice Simon Real Estate; Ferdinand Collored-Mansfield, Cabot, Cabot & Forbes; Leo & Emily G. Kahn, Hammond Realty; Edward H. & Joyce Line, Boston Urban Associates; Carole & Brendan White, W. Rr. Realtor.

[155] Some representatives: Russell & Doris Derenzo, Boston Safe Deposit and Trust; Anita R. & Charles F. Murphy, State Street Bank and Trust; Mark C. Wheeler, Merchant's National Bank.

[156] Some representatives: Abraham A. Nicholas, Lawyer; Richard Bisignani, Lawyer; Richard J. Kondel, Lawyer; Barbara A. & Gary A. Pappas, Lawyer.

[157] Some representatives: Graham D. Gund, Graham Gund Architects, Inc.; Robert J. Verrier, Boston Architects; Michael V. & Joan Weinmayr, Architect.

[158] The following list contains: (a) the names of these tributaries and (b) the contribution each of them made in 1982, and/or 1981, and/or 1979, and/or 1978: Paul D. Abbott 1,000 (1982), 800 (1981); Vincent A. Arcieri Jr. 1,000 (1979), 200 (1978); Vincent B. &

And a few formed clusters — echoes of the Kevin White Interest in the city governed by this Interest. They formed "Interests" of relatives and business associates that amassed substantial aggregates of tributes speaking forcefully one single concern.[159]

Nodes of Behavior

Many people were involved in the Mayor's campaign business. And they gave its social reality distinctive contours. They were not just contributors or campaign officials, to be counted merely by their numbers and to be mentioned only by their names. In their association with the campaign they conducted themselves in various manners and according to these they formed at the campaign business into different nodes of behavior.

Some such nodes — circles of contributors, classes of tributaries — have been depicted in the two preceding paragraphs. Presently, four other nodes of behavior will be described. They represent the social essence of the Mayor's campaign business.

(a) *The fundraisers.* A market of political finance is a delicate if not treacherous terrain requiring particular modes of procedures: tacit transactions and unfailing recollections, compelling arguments and gracious manners, a myriad curiosity for the people in the market and a chary

---

Constance Barone 1,000 (1979), 200 (1978); James V. Bennett 1,000 (1982), 1,000 (1978); Gerald S. Berman 1,000 (1982), 500 (1978); Allan S. Bisk 600 (1979), 1,000 (1978); Louis W. Cabot 1,000 (1979), 1,000 (1978); James M. Cashman 1,000 (1979), 200 (1978); John B. Cruz Jr. 1,000 (1982), 100 (1978); Graham D. Gund 150 (1979), 200 (1978); Edward F. Higgins 1,000 (1982), 1,000 (1978); Thomas M. & Florance J. Horan 500 (1979), 1,000 (1978); Frederick M. Lawton 1,000 (1982), 1,000 (1978); George Macomber 1,000 (1982), 1,000 (1978); A. L. Rotman 1,000 (1982), 1,000 (1978); Robert Sage 1,000 (1982), 1,000 (1978); Robert J. Verrier 1,000 (1982), 1,000 (1978); Dennis E. Walsh 1,000 (1982), 1,000 (1978); John E. Drew 1,000 (1982), 100 (1978).

[159] (a) The *Rose Interest*: In 1982 Daniel/Joanna S./Elihu/Susan W./Frederick P./Sandra Priest/David/Rosalie A./Jonathan F. P./David S. ROSE paid a tribute of $ 8,650. – In 1981 Daniel/David/Frederick ROSE paid a tribute of $ 2,400; they were joined by three other tributaries from ROSE ASSOCIATES, Harold & Anne Waxmann and Allan S. Bisk, who made a contribution of $ 600. In 1978 Daniel/David/Elihu/Frederick ROSE paid a tribute of $ 1,000.

(b) The *Athanas Interest*: In 1982 Anthony/Esther/Anthony Jr./Michael/Robert P. ATHANAS paid a tribute of $ 5,000.

(c) The *Fitzgerald Interest*: In 1982 W. Kevin Fitzgerald, President of FITZGERALD INVESTMENT TRUST, his wife Robin, and John Casey, company vice president, paid a tribute of $ 3,000.

tongue, a greed for the currency of power and deference to the reality of political power.

These modes of procedures fit particularly the fundraiser – the quintessential agent in the market of political finance. The fundraiser is the greedy procurator of campaign funds in deference to a politician on the campaign trail – moving hither and thither between shadows and light, between the market and the politician's campaign business, between private interests and political pursuits.

The fundraiser is neither an independent agent in the market nor a fully admitted representative of the politician's campaign business. And yet, it is the fundraiser on whose procedures this business depends. There is the market of political finance. There is the quest of the politician for political power. And there is the fundraiser – the agent who marks the node of behavior where the politician's quest comes into the offerings of the market.

Of all the persons involved in the Mayor's campaign business only a very few were fundraisers, not surprisingly. Nor is it surprising that they worked inconspicuously. Their number appears to be even smaller, however, if it is correlated with all the years of the Mayor's reign. Since they were not active all at the same time, the burden of procuring the Mayor's campaign funds rested sometimes on very few shoulders indeed. The social background of the fundraisers perfectly matched the needs. They were either friends of the Mayor's or government officials and they were closely tied up with the forces in the market of political finance. And they excelled in the one virtue a fundraiser must have: they shielded the Mayor from the financial necessities of his political pursuits.[160]

(b) *The faithful.* A diachronic analysis of the campaign records will detect, among other phenomena, a number of persons whose contributions to the Mayor's campaign business stretched over all or at least a larger part of his mayoral career and added up to considerable and even very considerable amounts.[161] Through their contributions these persons displayed the conduct of the Mayor's faithful – and apparently all the

---

[160] Fundraisers in the Mayor's campaign business were: Theodore V. Anzalone, Richard M. Dray, Mortimer Zuckerman, Robert J. Vey, Barbara Cameron, Richard Thuma, Robert T. Kenney, Phil David Fine, George Nedder.

[161] The following list contains (a) the names of the faithful, (b) the total amount of their contributions (according to the campaign records), and (c) the years in which they made their contributions:

Katherine & J. Louis Kane	7,050	1979	1978	1974	1971	1968
Herbert Gleason	3,650	1979	1978	1974	1971	
Mortimer Zuckerman	3,400	1979	1978			1968

more so as the zeal expressed by this behavior lacked an adequate share in mayoral power.[162]

(c) *The gifts of a few.* Many people were involved in the Mayor's campaign business: as officials and organizers, precinct captains and volunteers, aides in the government and consultants, as party members and friends. At the time when the party was "geared up" to an approaching mayoral election they numbered several thousands.

The people on whom the Mayor built his campaigns also included those who contributed money to his campaign chest. They numbered not many. In relative terms, they were only a few. In comparison with the party primed as a campaign organization for the election, their number appears to be quite small, and it appears to be exceedingly small in comparison with the number of voters in Boston.[163]

In 1982, for instance, the Kevin White Committee received contributions amounting to $ 374,120, and it received all that money from but 660 persons. And the circle of contributors seems to be even more narrow if one considers that over half of the total ($ 194,000) was donated only by 194 persons.

(d) *Separate worlds.* The campaign records, finally, reveal a clear-cut cleavage in the people of Kevin White. As contributors, they marked two separate worlds: the world of the party, on the one side, and the world of business, on the other. With the exception of a very few who belonged to both worlds,[164] they associated themselves with the Mayor's campaigns either through the party and not through business interests or through business interests and not through the party. Business persons paid tributes to the reality of political power, and persons affiliated with the party paid

Robert J. Vey	3,100			1979	1978		1971
Joseph & Susan Berlandi*	2,800	1982	1981	1979			1971
William E. Holland	2,519			1979	1978		1968
Jerome Rappaport	2,500	1982			1978		1968
David Rosenbloom	2,200			1979	1978	1974	
Theodore V. Anzalone	2,000			1979			1971

* (Joseph Berlandi's characteristics: developer, former planning official in the BRA.)

[162] Katherine Kane and Herbert Gleason, in particular, as zealous as they were for the Mayor's cause, held a disproportionate share in mayoral power.

[163]

Years of mayoral election	Number of registered voters
1983	288,986
1975	256,961
1971	294,717
1967	286,798

[164] Mortimer Zuckerman, Jerome Rappaport, Bertram A. Druker, Joseph Berlandi.

premiums for their political insurance. Both tribute and premium were contributions to the campaign fund of one and the same politician, but both symbolized also the divide running through the realm of this politician.[165]

Riddling Oddities

With the records submitted by the Mayor's campaign business something would be amiss if they were wholly transparent and did not also tantalize the curiosity of the researcher. However exhaustively the researcher examines the records, there remain some patterns and single facts which might tell something or might not. Whatever they are, they are certainly odd — appearing in records of a documentary and public nature. And they are riddling, precisely because they appear in such records.

The installments. Quite a few of the contributors in the party and the government gave the contribution which they made in one year by installments. The individual installments were reported individually, on separate records. It takes the deliberate effort of investigating to come across this pattern of installments, and then it is still necessary to expend some time and arithmetic if one wants to determine the full amount given by each of these contributors.

The missing contributors. A number of likely contributors seem to have ignored, evaded, or withstood the drive of the mayoral party towards supporting itself by collecting campaign gifts from its members, associates, and friends. Their names — including some conspicuous ones — do not appear on the lists of contributors that are parts of the records. Perhaps they enjoyed a freedom to withhold their dues, but then this freedom would not have been in line with the encompassing character of the party.[166]

The frugal contributors. On the other hand, one could wonder why some very prominent members of the party were not as generous with their campaign contributions as one might think they should have been.[167]

John Enigma and family. As to the contribution lists submitted after 1981, finally, much of the evidence that is provided is bland. A city ordinance passed in 1981 by the City Council — over the Mayor's veto — had barred

---

[165] Cf. infra, p. 196 f.

[166] Some of the names that do not appear: Lawrence & Barbara Cameron, Jack Murphy, Buford Kaigler, Ira Jackson, Brian Fallon, Reginald Johnson, David Mundel, David Davis.

[167] Micho F. Spring and Lawrence M. Quealy, for example.

employees of the city from contributing to municipal campaigns.[168] Many former contributors appear to have vanished. The traces of their disappearance leave no doubt. For, reading the lists, one will discern some familiar names — the names of government officials. Only the names, the family names, however, as one will realize at a second glance. John Enigma, the well-known official, is not listed as a contributor, for instance. There is only a Robert Enigma, and a George Enigma, and a Mark Enigma, and a William Enigma. And they are, as concerns the government, *personae obscurae*.

The Patrician Moment

In this section on the currency of power the continual quest of Mayor White for political power was analyzed in its elementary, periodically predominant mode as a quest for political money. The Mayor and the people on whom he relied in this quest were observed forming a distinct "agent" in the market of political finance: the campaign business of the mayoral party. For the study of the campaign business was a study of the mayoral party, of the Kevin White Party, emerging in the market of political finance as an "agent" for the renewal of its own life and thus for the Mayor in quest of ultimate power — power deriving from the consent of the governed.[169]

The campaign business was the Mayor's campaign business because the party it represented was the personal party of Mayor White. Moreover, the contemporary conditions and practices of campaigning in America are such that they conduced to the personal character of the campaign business.[170] A person defined the quest for political money. And this person made the quest a circular movement. Kevin White sought money for Kevin White.

To the observer it should not be too astonishing then to discern a patrician moment in the life of Mayor White. With his ever greater success in financing a grand enterprise in politics through the means of his friends and tributaries the Mayor tended to assume in money matters the views and habits of a Roman patrician:

> Is there any news to tell you? Well — yes. The consul Messalla has bought Autronius' house for 13 400 000 Sesterces. What concern is it of mine, you will

---

[168] The "Ordinance Prohibiting Employees from Making Political Contributions" was passed by the City Council on October 14th, 1981. Cf. *CR*, No. 14, April 5, 1982, pp. 381 – 82 (Text of the Ordinance); *CR*, No. 28, July 12, 1982, p. 512, pp. 536 – 37 (the Mayor's veto); *CR*, No. 30, July 26, 1982, p. 553 (report on the motion of the City Council overriding the Mayor's veto).

[169] Cf. supra, p. 122; note 37.

[170] Cf. note 136.

ask. Now it matters much to me, for this purchase proves that my house was a good investment too; and it begins to dawn upon people that it is quite legitimate to use the means of one's friends to buy a house and thus to attain a certain dignity.[171]

Cicero's view was not lost upon the Mayor of Boston. In 1981 and 1982 considerable improvements were made in the town house of the White family on Beacon Hill. The bills amounted to $ 26.724. They were paid by the Kevin White Committee — that is, with the financial help of the Mayor's political friends.[172]

The public life of a patrician family entails responsibilities, and in meeting these responsibilities the members of the family draw on the resources of the patrician household: time, energy, skills, personal and material assets, residences. And money. Money in a dual sense: the money the patrician household has and the money its members "lose" for practicing a patrician life rather than a money-making profession.

Classic patricians own property. They meet their responsibilities because they have them — property. Whatever is theirs is more than wealth. It is, above all, a social institution. Their money is public money. It is natural for a patrician household to support a community's life. Classic patricians do not solicit their friends for money. They pay them.

The family of the Mayor shared in his political pursuits but did not dwell in the comfortable circle described by private property and public responsibilities. The resources of the family were limited and, besides, it was "losing" money — all the money which members of the family could have earned if the time, energy, skills they had spent in serving Boston had been invested in jobs that paid. The Mayor publicly entertained this kind of calculation.[173]

---

[171] Cicero, *Letters to Atticus,* I, 13 (My translation, T. S.). — In Latin the passage reads as follows: "Novi tibi quidnam scribam? quid? etiam! *Messalla* consul Autronianum domum emit HS CXXXIIII. 'quid id ad me?' inquis. tantum, quod ea emptione et nos bene emisse iudicati sumus et homines intellegere coeperunt licere amicorum facultatibus in emendo ad dignitatem aliquam pervenire."

[172] Kevin and Kathryn White bought their townhouse on Beacon Hill in 1963. It is being held in the name of Mrs. White. — In March 1983 Kevin White, upon the advice of the Massachusetts State Office of Campaign and Political Finance, agreed to return to the Kevin White Committee $ 5,000 which the Committee had spent on a new heating system in the townhouse.

[173] Asked about the consultant payments to his wife, White said that she received the fees "for showing up at any event that I don't get to [...]. There is an assumption in American life that you get the wife for nothing. I don't buy that. [...] She's said she's worth $ 50,000, but I can't afford that." (*BG,* Jan. 13, 1982.)

Money was needed to alleviate the financial predicament of Boston's first family. With a sense of conduct becoming to its dignity the mayoral family chose the patrician solution. It accepted funds from its political friends. In 1979, 1980, 1981, and 1982 the Kevin White Committee paid several members of the family substantial "fees" — for their services as "consultants" to the Committee.[174]

13 The Pathology of Politics

A political regime will at no time attain fully to the truth of its form. If attempts are made to realize a polity absolutely, this regime will be pushed to its ruin. A democracy can never wholly be democratic, at least as long as its subjects are men of bodies and passions and not angels of transparency and lucidity.[175] A tyranny can never entirely become tyrannical, it would before have been reduced to the solitude of the tyrant.[176]

---

[174] The following table gives three kinds of information: (a) the names of the family members who received "fees," (b) the amount of each "fee," and (c) the year each "fee" was paid.

	1982	1981	1980	1979
Kathryn G. White (wife of KHW)	26,000	19,000	15,000	
Mark H. White (son of KHW)		2,500	1,500	3,000
Caitlin White (daughter of KHW)		3,500		
Beth White (daughter of KHW)			4,980	
Carolyn G. Connors (sister-in-law of KHW)			1,500	

[175] The insurmountable problem is the problem of the *perichoresis*. Cf. T. Schabert, *Natur und Revolution*, München 1969, pp. 63–74; idem (ed.), *Der Mensch als Schöpfer der Welt*, München 1971, pp. 73–82; idem, "The Roots of Modernity," *The Independent Journal of Philosophy*, Vol. IV, [1983], pp. 27–29.

[176] Cf. Plato, *Politeia* 567 a: "And if, I presume, he [the tyrant] suspects that there are free spirits who will not suffer his domination, his further object is to find pretexts for destroying them by exposing them to the enemy? From all these motives a tyrant is compelled to be always provoking wars? Yes, he is compelled to do so. And by such conduct will he not the more readily incur the hostility of the citizens? Of course. And is it not likely that some of those who helped to establish and now share in his power, voicing their disapproval of the course of events, will speak out frankly to him and to one another — such of them as happen to be the bravest? Yes, it is likely. Then the tyrant must do away with all such if he is to maintain his rule, until he has left no one of any worth, friend or foe." (English translation from: Plato, *The Republic*, II, transl. by P. Shorey, Cambridge–London 1970 = Loeb Classical Library.) — Cf. also R. Oser, "Robespierre/St. Just," in: T. Schabert, ed., *Der Mensch als Schöpfer der Welt*, op. cit., pp. 191–94 and ibid., pp. 12–15.

The perfection of a regime is its death. Or, in sequential terms, it does the more degenerate the closer it is brought to perfection. A truth inheres political regimes that is paradoxical.[177] They produce through themselves the seeds of their decay. A democracy, for example, either is a democracy in the process of becoming what a democracy is thought to be – and hence a democracy that is not yet "sufficiently" democratic; or it is a democracy in the process of absorbing more and more the society whose political form it merely should be – and hence a democracy that is "too much" democratic.

If the former process is discerned, it is natural, for democrats at least, to pursue the promise of democracy further and further, from the process of an emerging democracy to a process of democracy that has no limits other than the democratic extreme: democrats pursuing democracy as a pursuit ("perfection") rather than as a promise. If the latter process is discerned, it is equally natural, for democrats at least, *again* to pursue the promise of democracy and to pursue it inventively – desisting the democratic extreme in a process of democracy that lays down limits ("forms") to the zeal of democrats.[178]

The "true" form of a political regime is a movement, the movement of its actualization between promise and perfection. It "occurs" best somewhere between a "not yet" and a "too much." Its true form is a relative form, namely its best form relative to the two extremes of its realization: its nonexistence as pure promise, on one side, and its dissipation as pure perfection, on the other. The movement of the regime leads to its best form if it leads away from either extreme. But in leading away from the one, it leads to the other. The best form of the regime is the movement of the regime leading to one extreme as much as to the other or, in other words, leading

---

[177] On the *paradoxos logos* of politics, cf. Plato, *Politeia* 472 a – 473 e; the passage on the "aporie fondamentale de l'ordre politique," in: R. Aron, *Dix-huit leçons sur la société industrielle,* Paris 1982, pp. 86 – 88.

[178] Cf. H. Mandt, "Kritik der Formaldemokratie und Entförmlichung der politischen Ausein-andersetzung," *Zeitschrift für Politik,* Jg. 32, NF, H. 2, 1985, pp. 115 – 132; the passage on the "politics of perfection" in: M. Oakeshott, *Rationalism in Politics,* op. cit., pp. 5 ff.; *Federalist* No. 10 (Madison): "[...] a pure democracy, by which I mean a society consisting of a small number of citizens, who assemble and administer the government in person, can admit of no cure for the mischiefs of faction. A common passion or interest will, in almost every case, be felt by a majority of the whole; a communication and concert results from the form of government itself; and there is nothing to check the inducements to sacrifice the weaker party or an obnoxious individual. Hence it is that such democracies have ever been found incompatible with personal security or the rights of property; and have in general been as short in their lives as they have been violent in their deaths." (*The Federalist Papers,* op. cit., p. 81.)

away from one as much as from the other or, in still other words, occurring in between the two extremes of the regime's realization.

The best form of a political regime lies in the balance of its process. It is a fleeting phenomenon, for the process of the regime commonly tends towards one of its extremes – and hence towards a deficiency if not annihilation of the regime. If the best form of the regime occurs, it occurs in between the regime's intrinsic degeneration. The truth of a political regime is largely its pathology.

Once it has been seized, the paradoxical truth of political regimes is a practical matter. It is an inescapable truth. The question only is: how can the process of a political regime be balanced? In the history of political wisdom three answers essentially have been known.

(1) The *form* and the *process* of a regime are supposed to be two separate things (which in reality they are not, of course). All the phenomena of politics held to be deficient, faulty, or pathological are (if they are not ignored or just dimly perceived) associated with the *process* of the regime. With the *form* of the regime all the anticipations and satisfactions are identified which the regime implies: the pure promise. The paradoxical truth of political regimes is resolved by a classic device – hypocrisy.[179] Nothing is wrong with the form of the regime, people would say, it is "true." Whatever it is that may be wrong with the regime is solely due to the insufficiencies of its process. The "theatrical show of society" – to use Bagehot's metaphor for good government – could hardly be improved upon. It is the works of the show that needs correcting.

(2) The proponents of the second answer – Plato being the foremost among them – hold that neither institutional nor purely political agents suffice for alleviating the intrinsic degeneration of a political regime. The para-doxical truth of political regimes stands. It is an antinomy of politics, political wisdom must square. The answer to the degeneration of a regime lies not in the regime but in the virtue of a number of its citizens: persons ("philosophers") who have been actualizing the virtue of wisdom and whom among their fellow citizens is accorded a status that allows them to bring their judgment and counsel – their wisdom – to bear upon the process of the regime. The paradoxical truth of political regimes is resolved by a rare instance of politics – the reign of virtuous men.

---

[179] Cf. R. Aron, *Dix-huit leçons sur la société industrielle,* op. cit., p. 87: "La solution démocratique comporte une permanente hypocrisie, car aucune société n'a jamais pu égaliser ni les tâches, ni les revenus, ni les prestiges des individus. L'ordre de l'égalité est inévitablement un ordre formel que chaque pouvoir établi essaie d'exalter tout en dissimulant les inégalités réelles."

(3) All political regimes exist in time, they are temporal phenomena. If they degenerate − and they do −, the process of degeneration unfolds as a sequence from one point in time to another, from an "earlier" state of a regime to a "later" one, from the regime tending to flourish to the regime tending to decay. While a sequence of this kind starts whenever a regime is founded, it does not have to run its full course, "down" to the ruin of the regime. The sequence can be suspended at any point in time and it can be cut so radically that a "new" sequence begins − the novel instance of politics as it is brought about by a general election or, under extraordinary circumstances, by a revolution.[180] This, in principle, is the third answer. The paradoxical truth of political regimes is resolved through the classic recourse of a new beginning.[181]

Political wisdom, however, has often been superseded by political doctrines,[182] and through the history of these doctrines another two "solutions" have been transmitted as to the "true" form of a political regime. The word "solution" is used here on purpose, for "answer" would be too weak a word to convey the intention which the two solutions carry. Each is thought to be *the* form of a political regime through which the intrinsic degeneration of political regimes can be and, if established rigorously, indeed will be arrested. "Solution" is their proper term as they suggest a final truth: the process of a regime being vanquished through its form, its degeneration being quenched through its fixture.

(4) The formula of the first solution owns the appeal of apparent simplicity: Make a polity transparent and it will not degenerate. If the process of a regime were made a process openly conducted among all citizens, the form of the regime, too, would be defined through this process of transparent politics among all citizens. In the inter-awareness of all citizens as being both the subjects of politics and the participants in the making of politics, the form and the process of a regime would coincide continuously. The intrinsic degeneration of political regimes would be vanquished through an omniscient regime − through the vigil of "all citizens" over "all citizens," a vigilance which would allow

---

[180] Cf. supra, Chapter 2, note 61; Plato, *Politeia* 591 b − 592; E. Voegelin, *Plato and Aristotle*, op. cit., pp. 123 − 29 ("The Sequence of Political Forms"); H. Arendt, *On Revolution*, New York 1963, esp. Ch. V: "Foundation II: Novus Ordo Saeclorum."

[181] There are three answers and there is a "fourth" possibility, of course: some combination of two of the three or of all three answers.

[182] Cf. L. Strauss, *What Is Political Philosophy?*, op. cit., p. 12 ff.

everyone immediately to perceive any transaction(s) "some citizens" might want to except from the full transparency of all things political.[183]

(5) The transparent politics of the first solution would, if practiced perfectly, exclude from a polity every trace of secretiveness. The second solution consists in secretiveness. It is usually thought to be inspired by a sense of "realism." The intrinsic degeneraton of political regimes is considered the natural course of their affairs which to oppose would be futile, if not foolish. There are deficiencis of politics, the "realist" would say, but they tend to be the greater the more people participate in the business of a political regime and the more these people learn about its conduct. Shrouding a regime in secrets would therefore seem to be the obvious solution for its natural tendency to decay. Secrets would sharply restrict access to the process of the regime. An arcane regime would halt the intrinsic degeneration of political regimes. An arcane regime: that is the small circle of guardians who would share the secrets of the regime and who alone then would control its process.

These two latter "solutions" are both products of political fantasy. They substitute states of political imagination for the reality of political life. A polity cannot be made "transparent." All attempts at doing so will only deliver it to masters who excel in hypocrisy and lies, fanaticism and persecution.[184] Nor can secrets be made the foundation of a regime. Their very nature, privy as it is, renders secrets inimical to political affairs which are, by definition, public. A regime resting on secrets causes its guardians and the people alike to harbor sentiments of discord rather than sociability: suspicions and hostility, fear and contempt, a distrust akin to betrayal and strife.

Two seeming "solutions" which are no solutions. They are something else. They are the opposite of what they seem to be: not remedies for the intrinsic degeneration of political regimes, but sources of their decay. Thought – or, rather, imagined – to rescue the process of a regime from its deficiencies, they aggravate the degenerative tendency of the process. Contrary to what

---

[183] This is the classic political dream of a society ruled by *perichoresis*. Cf. supra, note 175. – At present times, it is Jürgen Habermas, the German sociologist and political writer, who communicates the dream, quite exclusively yet evenly quite vociferously. – Occasionally, ordinary politicians, too, articulate the dream. Cf. the following passage from The [British] *Prime Minister's Committee on Local Government Rules of Conduct* (Redcliffe-Maud Report): "The honesty of the individual must be visible if it is to win public confidence. [...] [An] essential safeguard for honesty in local government is therefore that of maximum openness. Things should be seen for what they are [...]" (*The Prime Minister's Committee on Local Government Rules of Conduct*, London, H. M. S. O., Vol. 1, Report of the Committee, 1974, p. 5 f. = Cmnd. 5636).

[184] Cf. supra, notes 175 and 176.

they suggest, they do not reveal a final truth — te process and the form of a regime coinciding continuously. However, they conceal the truth that matters: politics or, to be more precise, the paradoxical truth of political regimes which makes politics their perennial mode of being.

The image of a transparent polity and the image of a regime shrouded in secrets appear to be true forms of a political regime. And yet they vitiate the regimes to which they are applied. A transparency of all things political and a secretiveness in the conduct of political affairs seem to be "ideal" modes of political life. And yet they sow distrust among people. Politics is being made and yet this is not politics. This is a process of rescuing political regimes that destroys these regimes altogether. Poltics occurs and yet something else transpires: the pathology of politics.[185]

The Kevin White Party made politics, and all who were concerned — inside and outside the party — knew politics and knew politics to be the mode of participating in, or of responding to, the politics of the party. Moreover, the party radiated creativity, and this considerably enhanced the pull of its politics. It would have been highly unusual, if the starkly political reality that the party was did not have any pathological traits.

It did have such traits, though, and it had them to a significant degree. The party provided a lesson in political creativity. And it provided a lesson in the pathology of politics.[186]

Being the predominant carrier of politics in Boston, America, on the one hand, and being the coterie of Kevin White, on the other, having democracy as principle of its public life, on the one hand, and having an autocracy as principle of its existence, on the other, the party was forever torn between two images — the image of a transparent polity and the image of a regime shrouded in secrets.

To make up for the coterie and the autocracy, the party sought to impress everyone by its ostensible transparency. To protect in the open process of democracy its private roots, however, the party also sought to set an intricate series of screens between itself and the public. It tantalized everyone's curiosity and it failed to gratify the public's "right" to "know." It projected on everyone's mind an omnipresence of its power and it left everyone in the dark as to where exactly this power lay. It meant to exist for the people of Boston. And it meant to exist for one person: the autocrat, the Mayor, Kevin White.

---

[185] In reading C. J. Friedrich, *The Pathology of Politics. Violence, Betrayal, Corruption, Secrecy, and Propaganda*, New York 1972, one will be disappointed. The promise of the title is not carried out; the book assembles disparate phenomena — which *per se* are by no means pathological — for an inconsequential discussion.

[186] Cf. also supra, p. 158 f.

Its very essence made the party produce the pathological modes from which it suffered. That there were such modes was not accidental. They arose from the party's unceasing struggle with its divided "soul": open to everyone, on the one, withdrawn, on the other. To the extent that it was consumed with this struggle, the party itself formed a phenomenon of political pathology. The large majority of the people, however, who participated in the politics made by the party, were preoccupied most of their time with practical policies rather than the innate state of the party. They experienced it in its pathological modes, but did so superficially: in Boston almost everyone, we should not forget, is in the habit of equating "politics" with "corruption."

Their innocent cynicism aside, the modes of participating in the party included modes of political pathology, and these modes were consciously perceived, casually adopted, or eagerly embraced by a number of different persons in a number of different situations. In the political reality which the party defined, politics occurred: the life of the party. And there was something else occurring, too: pathological politics, the death of the party.

(1) Everyone knew something about the party, no one knew everything. Many persons were involved in the politics of the party. Yet it would be difficult to imagine anyone among them not to have made the experience of a *partial* knowledge as to the life and the affairs of the party. Experience only told what common sense had known already: we know things but partially.

Some persons, nevertheless, exhibited a "knowledge" which they could not have but claimed to have. Everyone who cared was given to understand that they had a fully transparent view of everything: the party ... and the people in the party ... and the government that the party formed ... and the politics that the party pursued. They seemed to watch for opportunities to spill the "truth." They appeared to long for listeners to whom they could "disclose" the "secrets" of a power with which they seemed to be obsessed.[187]

(2) However the tales of these persons were judged, their presence and their behavior alone — not to mention their claim to see through the party, its life, its politics — introduced an element of irreality into the public image of the party. Evidently, one's ordinary sense of politics did not suffice to grasp the political phenomenon for which the informants stood. These were informants, after all, who said, at one moment, that they belonged to a realm of secrets and who said, at the next, that they would of course relate all the secrets.

A plain contradiction, an inconsistency. The informants confused their perception of the party with the party's reality. In fact, they themselves

---

[187] In various degrees.

produced the "mystery" which they purported to "resolve." They were able to tell "everything" about the party, its life, and its politics because the party about which they talked was largely their own invention.

(3) The party formed the city's government and the government, too, was engaged in perceptual twists. By applying the contemporary art of "communication," it constructed − for the benefit of the public, as it were − the artificial reality of a governing process occurring under everyone's very eyes. In the transparency of a "government by press release"[188] everyone knew everything: officials in the government appeared to be as knowledgeable or as ignorant as the citizens who were engrossed in the story written, performed, and produced by the actors in City Hall.

Sometimes, though, some actors performed too well and made the artificial reality more "real" than anyone would have thought. The Mayor, in particular, excelled in the confusion of reality and irreality. To "prove" a point he was making at a press conference, for instance, he just "pulled figures out of his head," drawing upon his fancy to shore up the "reality" he performed. Since his performance had been intended to contribute to the construction of a governmental "reality" in which everyone believed, the Mayor's fanciful figures could not be left simply as they stood. Aides rushed to find "true" statistics which would back up the "real" figures. They succeeded.[189]

(4) The participants in the life and the politics of the party did not resist the general tendency to speak and to write about the party in the conventional language of machine politics. The largely derogatory character of this language aside, its common use inferred an equally common experience of the party's reality.

However, the many persons who partook of this reality experienced it in a large variety of modes − as has been shown in this chapter. The experience of machine politics was but one of these modes and a mode of experience, besides, through which not everyone had to pass. That the public liked to be entertained by a party spoken about in the language of machine politics, and that censuring critics relished portraying the party in this language, about this hardly anyone could have been surprised. Much less usual, however, was the linguistic indifference of the persons who partook of the party's reality. It was not only unusual because one would think that they would have wanted to have their experiences related as they had indeed made them. It was also unusual because

---

[188] Source: Interview.

[189] Source: Interview.

these persons must have felt the peculiar consequence of their linguistic passivism. On the level of their experience they perceived the party in a large variety of modes. On the public level, however, only one mode was left: the party depicted in the language of machine politics. This was a gross distortion and it must have bothered them every day. Yet, they helped this distortion to gain ground. Rather than educating the public through speaking the language of their experience, they acquiesced in a public language of clichés.

(5) Quite a few members of the party, of the government were led, by the linguistic pollution of their experiences, to mistrust these experiences. In their minds the "party" of the public discourse had become the party which they felt they had to disavow. It had become the "party" from which they wanted to dissociate themselves. Since this "party" − a caricature vagabonding in a public, yet cliché-ridden language − did not exist, they could only dissociate themselves from the real party. They became rigid and fought − in some cases with considerable zeal[190] − what, in effect, was the essence of the party: institutional arrangements that were perennially fluid, power that was extremely pervasive, organizations of government that were thoroughly confused, procedures of political finance that were frustratingly finessed, structures of influence that were unassailably personal. In short, they fought the "secrets" of political creativity. Insisting on a rigidity of politics, they were fighting politics. Figures of pathetic distress, they tried to prove that their experiences of political life − true as they were − were wrong.

(6) The party, of course, continually provoked the suspicions which were falling upon it. It held "secrets" of its creativity. Quite a few of them were known − potentially known at least in the form of records, reports, testimonies which everyone, in priciple, was free to consult. Many others, however, were very hard to get at and often guarded so well that simple rumors about them had an air of disclosure.[191]

Both, the party and the government formed by the party, surrounded themselves with a climate of secrecy.[192] In this climate the simple fact, for instance, that an outsider knew the identity and the function of a

---

190 The most notable case in the early 1980's: the attitude of a large part of the historic preservation community in Boston and of the executive director and the staff of the Boston Landmarks Commission, in particular.

191 Cf. the story of the "black book," supra, note 68. The "black book" was never publicly produced, and its existence was acknowledged only under juridictional pressure at an offical hearing. The acknowledgment confirmed what not a few people in City Hall had known all along: the "truth" of rumors.

192 Cf. supra, pp. 14 f., 17, 26, 91, 165, 171 f., 175, 196 f.

mayoral aide provoked indeed splutters of inquisitiveness on the part of the first circle of guardians, that is the secretary who answered the phone: "Mayor's Office. – Whom do you want to speak? – Martha Goldsmith? Who are you? How do you know her name?"[193]

While the bureaucracy in City Hall had not yet overcome the insufficiencies of the "green-shade bookkeeping style of 1901,"[194] the government hardly bothered. The city's administrators could go on producing statistical figures which were largely inaccurate and incomplete, and, due to the chaotic nature of the government, rarely relevant for more than a couple of weeks. Data were viewed by the government as political tools and it looked therefore quite favorably at the patches of opacity into which everyone ran who sought to obtain from City Hall integral sets of financial and economic data. The longer one observed this opaque world of data, the harder it became to dismiss the conclusion that its effect – diffusing the curiosity of outsiders – was precisely its purpose.

The climate of secrecy was quite transparent. The public should "see" the secrets and see that they were secrets. To the people of Boston it should be known that the city's government did not want it to know certain data. When a member of the Court gracefully explained that – "Of course, you cannot get the data you seek, because we keep that information off the computer"[195] –, the frankness was the secrecy.

(7) Perceptual twists, distorted experiences, a confusion of reality with fantasies, a pollution of language, a climate of secrecy, the false frankness of guardians – the party had accumulated a redoubtable mass of pathological traits. And it produced more of it the more it strove to escape from its natural progress unto decay, either through making itself fully transparent or through turning itself into the great secret. The "therapies" intensified the pathology.

Various factors, however, prevented the party from succumbing completely to the seeds of its decay which it brought forth continuously

---

[193] Source: Field note. – The phone conversation took place in May 1981. Martha Goldsmith was a member of Mandarin Spring's "Policy Management Staff." Her areas of responsibility, broadly defined, included "economic policy" and "urban development." It was her main task, though, to keep Robert Ryan, the director of the BRA, and the development policies of the BRA under the Mayor's control. She interfered (or was consulted in time by prudent BRA staffers). "Control" for her meant also to "protect" the Mayor – from any development which the Mayor might eventually want not to be associated with or which he might wish solely to blame on the BRA (or an handy substitute).

[194] Source: Interview.

[195] Source: Interview.

through its very being. Although it was viewed with resentment, suspicion, and awe by a large part of the people who participated in its life and politics, most of these people did not let themselves be overwhelmed by their emotions. They maintained a sense of proportion. They discerned the party also in the light of the creativity which it carried. And they discerned it in the light of their own personal life in which the party did not matter so much, after all.

(8) There were other, external factors which prevented the party from succumbing to the seeds of its decay. They will shortly be noted. Still, some participants in the life and the politics of the party fell prey to its pathology. Their experience of the party grew into a blight that affected their personal integrity, moral constitution, and mental disposition. A few insights into this blight we may gain from the story of an employee in the Boston Redevelopment Authority.[196]

The young man had, by birth, a name quite common in England. He was not a native of Boston, he had come to the city from the South of the United States. He wished to get his PhD at one of the universities in the Boston area. And he wanted a job, preferably in city government. Not much time had passed since he had started to look about and he had become sensitized to the political parameters of governmental work in Boston. He drew and applied the following conclusions: First, I better change my name and adopt an Irish identity. Secondly, I better move to South Boston – the tribal territory of the Boston-Irish. Thirdly, I better join the Mayor's party, volunteer all the time and loyalty it wants, and ask no further questions.

He got a nice job in the BRA. He had, besides, plenty of time to write his dissertation. And he was profoundly disturbed. His false Irish identity proved to be too beneficial. He carried the same name as one of the Mayor's principal aides, many people mistook him for this important person: and he could not resist the temptation to frequently exploit the error. When he succeeded, he reproached himself for being an impostor. When he did not, he reverted to more lies to cope with the awkward situation into which he had maneuvered himself.

His privileges as a political appointee – job security, much license as regards the time he was actually doing his job – were almost more than he could bear. When the BRA was cutting its personnel, he did not have to worry – others were fired. When projects were debated by the staff and different views, different interests clashed, he could be sure to be among the winners – others lost, because they lacked the political connections. "Everything" was "political," everything: his job, his work, his salary, his

---

[196] Sources: Interviews.

prospects for promotion, his relationship with his colleagues, the meetings they held, the opinions they had of each other. The pervasiveness of politics protected him, yes. But it annihilated also his experience of a differentiated social reality: there was politics, politics, politics and – nothing else.

A private life? A social or a mental niche of his own to which he could retreat? No. He had lost his freedom. The party ruled over his mind – as a very capricious master. At one moment it requested loyalty to this person, at the next it requested loyalty to that person, the former's enemy. At one moment it demanded a commitment to this policy, at the next it demanded a commitment to that policy, the former's contrary. Again, everything was political: alliances, loyalties, commitments, promises, plans, words, perceptions, judgments, thoughts. Everything was political, nothing authentically real.

The young man repeatedly used the word "nihilism" to describe his experience of the party. He said he had lost his sense of right and wrong. And he reflected upon his not knowing really who he was – the planning official or the party hack, the shrewd politician or the impostor, the victor or the victim, the initiate or the waif.

Through its pathology the party disclosed the paradoxical truth of political regimes. It degenerated the more, the more it became what it potentially was. It existed through politics and politics corroded its life. Still, the party existed for quite some time. And it did so as an extraordinary carrier of social and political creativity. What, then, sustained the party's existence? How could it "live," if living meant to degenerate?

(1) Participants in the life and the politics of the party maintained, for themselves and thus for the party, their sense of proportion.

(2) "Government" and "Party" were generally conceived of as two separate things (which they were not, of course, as I have repeatedly pointed out).[197] All manifestations of a personal regime – those modes of government which an "unimaginative Protestant ethic"[198] hat not foreseen and of which the public felt that they were the intrusion of "politics" into the city's "public service" – were attributed to the party, and not to the government, their real source and *raison d'être*.The autocracy built by Kevin White did not feature in the eyes of the public as the truly

---

[197] Cf. supra, p. 93 f.

[198] "Behind the gossip lurked an ancient worry that councillors might use their position to enrich themselves. Socialists are often the worst culprits in impugning their colleagues' honesty and they have deep suspicions of new-fangled jobs like public relations. This is not a shabby trade, but its value is not grasped by those who believe in everyone working steadily from nine till five. The unimaginative Protestant ethic dies hard." ("The Rewards of Public Service. The Case of Dan Smith," *New Statesman*, July 16, 1971, pp. 65 – 66.)

astounding phenomenon. Whatever faults the public found in the government of Boston, it associated these faults with the process of government — as to be seen through the party — rather than the form of the government, the Mayor's autocracy.

Succinctly put: Though the autocracy was the cause of public criticism, it was the party on which the main brunt of the criticism fell.

To cope with its role as the autocracy's bad offspring, however, the party was compelled again and again to muster the faculties through which it existed: productiveness, inventiveness, resilience, adaptivity. Thus the distinction between "government" and "party," as artificial as it was, had quite a practical effect upon the life of the party. It could not afford to give in to the natural sluggishness of political bodies. It had to be alive, vibrant, volatile. To counter all the criticism whose subject it was, the party had to counter itself. It was induced to impede through its creativity the process of its decay.

(3) Pathological tendencies of the party were checked, furthermore, by those codes and standards of public conduct which are generally called "mores."[199] Naturally, the mores did not inhibit every wrong desire of every participant in the life and the politics of the party, nor did they inhibit every wrongful impulse of the party itself.[200] But they marked

---

[199] Cf. E. Litt, *The Political Cultures of Massachusetts,* Cambridge, Mass. 1965; E. D. Baltzell, *Puritan Boston and Quaker Philadelphia. Two Protestant Ethics and the Spirit of Class Authority and Leadership,* op. cit.; D. J. Devine, *The Political Culture of the United States,* Boston 1972. – Kevin White commented upon the subject as follows: "I think the public has a very mixed, almost adolescent view of what they expect in terms of morality in their public officials." (*BG,* Febr. 10, 1986.)

[200] Two examples:
(a) The "birthday party" for Kathryn White, the Mayor's wife, which did *not* take place, as planned, in the Boston Museum of Fine Arts on March 27, 1981. As the plans for the "party" developed and became known gradually to the public, it turned out that it would have served as a fund-raiser for the political organization of KHW. Hundreds of invitations were sent out – mostly to members of the Kevin White Party – which solicited contributions "payable to the Birthday Gift Celebration Committee" (reporters quickly discerned the connection between this Committee and William Galvin, the father of Kathryn White and treasurer of the "Kevin White [election] Committee"). Kevin White eventually canceled the "party," on March 26. However, the collecting of money in connection with the "birthday party" became the subject of an investigation by the Massachusetts State Ethics Commission in 1981–82. The Commission found "evidence of possible cash laundering." In the fall of 1982 federal investigators, too, began to probe the circumstances surrounding the "birthday party." As to the whole story and the various outcomes, cf. *BG,* March 16 and 20, 1981; October 29 and December 17, 1982; March 11 and June 6, 1983; Sept. 29, 1984; *Time,* Jan. 2, 1983; G. V. Higgins,

limits – the limits that formed in the public consciousness the divide
between legitimate and illegitimate, rightful and illicit politics.

(4) The party, finally, recurrently had to face the possibility of its end: it had to
face elections. The moment the Mayor lost a bid for reelection, the party
was lost.[201] Elections were the first check on the pathology of the party.[202]
To win elections, it had to be at its best. It had to carry all the creativity
which it carried when it had first appeared in the Boston theater of politics.

14 The Autocrat, the Government, and the Party

Creativity: The Movement unto Creation

On May 26, 1983 Mayor White announced, with the touch of grandiosity he
had come to adopt,[203] that he would not be a candidate in the mayoral
election to be held in the fall of that year.

Style versus Substance. Boston, Kevin White, and the Politics of Illusion, New York
1984, pp. 233 – 235.

(b) Throughout the years 1982 – 85 George N. Collatos lived the story of a "liar whose
testimony was for sale to the highest bidder." Before he was arrested on extortion
charges on October 21, 1981, Collatos had been employed by the BRA as an administrative assistant. After he was convicted of the attempt to extort money from a contractor
who wanted to do business with the City of Boston, Collatos continued to receive
additional sentences as he assembled a record for perjury, in the role of a "prosecution
witness" whose testimony had been supposed to provide evidence for a "corruption" of
the White administration. Instead, Collatos proved to be a pathological liar. As to the
whole story, cf. BG, Jan. 25, Febr. 16, 17, March 13, Sept. 30, Oct. 29, Dec. 17, 1982,
Febr. 9, 1983, Sept. 29, 1984, April 1, 1985; NYT, Jan. 26, 1983.

[201] Cf. infra, p. 207.

[202] My formulation is borrowed, of course, from Walter Bagehot. Cf. The English Constitution, intr. by R. H. S. Crossman, Glasgow 1963, p. 243: "Custom is the first check on
tyranny." – Cf. also: Th. Paine, Common Sense (1776), in: The Writings of Thomas
Paine, ed. M. D. Conway, Vol. I, (1774 – 1779), New York 1967, p. 97: "Let the assemblies
be annual, with a president only." – J. Adams, Thoughts on Government(1776), in:
The Political Writings of John Adams, ed. G. A. Peek, Jr., New York 1954, p. 89: "And
these and all other elections, especially of representatives and counsellors, should be
annual, there not being in the whole circle of the sciences a maxim more infallible than
this, 'where annual elections end, there slavery begins.' "

[203] Cf. BG, May 27, 1983, p. 13: "Late last night, the mayor's pollster, Richard Dresner,
said that an April poll he did for White and subsequent focus group interviews indicated

The public had long been trying to divine the Mayor's decision. His friends and associates had been wondering, too; their accounts of what they thought the Mayor would think — the media storytellers eagerly picked them up, of course — had been inconclusive, confusing. And the Mayor himself had been playing upon conflicting signals.[204] Now everyone knew that the reign of Mayor White would soon be "history."

Without delay, the Mayor had struck in his announcement a tone of "history." It sounded like a conventional historical tale: "When I became Mayor in 1968 [...]." Yet it conveyed "history" of a different mode: "[...] I began [...] to create a process that would guarantee our future [...]."[205] Kevin White reviewed his reign in the language of the creative politician. A process of social creativity had occurred, and he had been the source of creativeness of which this process came.

The Mayor's friends, followers, and aides understood the announcement primarily in view of its immediate consequences. Quite a few might lose their jobs, many would feel compelled to explore possibilities of employment outside city government, and all would go through the painful experience of the final act in the great drama of politics of which they had been the cast. While the Mayor moved on to his fame, they had to face an uncertain future.

The field of political creativity which the Mayor's reign had rested upon did still exist. But it began to disintegrate, under the crisscross of all the particular interests which in the quest of candidate White had converged and which the Mayor's announcement now had released. The zealots behaved as arrogantly as ever and searched for ways to deplete as much as they could the resources the future Mayor would need and to tie him down to a framework of governing which they had put up. Not a few officials in the government displayed a courtesy of which they had not been known before; through all the years of power there had been people, in the public, in the private sector, whose calls they had never returned — now they were choosing these people addressees of one urgent message, of one confidentiality following the other. And among those who had adhered to the Mayor's party many

---

White would have won re-election had he decided to run. Dresner whose results are dramatically ad odds with samples done by most other pollsters, added, 'There's no question the mayor would have been in the runoff election and would have beaten anyone.' Dresner estimated that White spent about $ 110,000 for his polling and the preparation of last night's address." — BG, May 26, 1983, p. 38: "Added David I. Finnegan, who is running for White's job: 'I shouldn't think someone would spend that much money to say goodbye.' " (It was estimated that White, to make known his plans, had spent $ 30,000 to $ 35,000 for radio and TV time.)

204 Cf. BG,Febr. 10, 25, March 18, 21, May 26, June 6, 1983.
205 BG, May 27, 1983; CR, June 27, 1983.

simply withdrew from the depressing reality of its death into the final triumph of their nostalgia.

The Mayor's people parted, drawing no longer the power of creativeness from the discordant particles of political life. The quest for mayoral power for which they had fused turned into memories. They abandoned the future they had lost. The movement of creativity ceased. It acquired the character of a movement in the "past" tending towards the finality which it now revealed. The political creativity that the Mayor's reign had portrayed had been a process of creativeness unto a portrait to be finished. The movement of creativity had been a movement of creativity unto creation.

Creativity: The Movement unto Forms

On December 31, 1983, his last day in office, Mayor White bade farewell to a small circle of aides and department heads – the senior members of the Court. In the speeches which were exchanged the notion of "history" was repeatedly introduced to articulate a sense of continuity: the sense of continuity that arose from the experience in government which all present shared and would still share beyond this final day.

A few friends of the Mayor's, though, carried a special "historical" responsibility. Kevin White had appointed these friends his posterity in government. The Mayor of Boston, as I have noted at the beginning of this study, is vested by the City Charter with the prerogative to fill by appointment a good many posts in the local government of Boston.[206] Kevin White used this right, in the last few months of his tenure, to place a number of friends in such posts and thus to ensure a "continuity" not only in the mode of "history" but also in the mode of governmental influence – in the mode of power.[207, 208]

---

[206] Cf. supra, p. 15 f. – The Boston City Council has virtually no appointment power, except that over the city clerk and the small Council staff.

[207] Most noteworthy is the reappointment of Clarence Jones, Joseph Walsh, James Flaherty, and Robert Farrell to the Board of the Boston Redevelopment Authority. – In 1985 Micho F. Spring still held seats on the Massachusetts Center Convention and the Cable Access Foundation, and Robert J. Ryan a seat on the Massachusetts Center Convention Authority.

[208] Cf. BG, Oct. 7, 21, 1981, Oct. 14, 17, Nov. 12, 18, Dec. 9, 10, 16, 1983, Dec. 9, 1984. – The predecessor of Kevin White, Mayor John F. Collins, also attempted, after he had left office, to exert a continued influence upon the government affairs of Boston, and the Boston Redevelopment Authority and its policies in particular. He had allies on the Board of the BRA, among whom James Colbert proved to be the most pertinacious carrier of the former Mayor's interests. Hale Champion, the director of the BRA, was

Still, these were a very few, compared with the thousands the Kevin White Party had counted. And there remained but these few. The party, as a body politic, did not survive the Mayor's departure. It disappeared. For the party had existed only through and for Kevin White. His political career had been the sole purpose of the body politic the party had formed.[209] The remarkable strength which it rendered him again and again had failed to materialize whenever this strength had been supposed to be lent to others — as, for instance, to those candidates in a City Council election whom the Mayor had promised his support.[210] Even he himself — to whom it aspired, after all — had had little success in using the party as a tool of power separate from his person.[211] The party was

---

unable to restrain Collins' influence on his own. The Board of the BRA "ate Champion for breakfast," Kevin White remarked rather contemptuously. Champion succeeded eventually in blocking the interferences of Collins and his allies — through the support he received from the Mayor, Kevin White. — Towards the end of Mayor White's reign, in the fall of 1983, a group of officials in the BRA tried to put Boston's development community in an organizational configuration favorable to *their* development policies, on the one side, and inimical to the incoming administration, on the other. The configuration was supposed to include: this group of BRA officials, the Boston Chamber of Commerce (its "Boston 2,000 guidelines" group, in particular), and Kevin Lynch, the eminent urbanist. — A most instructive parallel to Mayor White's attempt at ensuring a continuity of influence beyond the loss of power, through placing friends in governmental posts while it's still time, has been provided by François Mitterrand, President of France, in March 1986, that is, shortly before he lost his hitherto autocratic powers. Cf. C. Pégard, "Administration: les copains d'abord," *Le Point,*No. 702, March 3, 1986, pp. 52 – 53; Th. v. Münchhausen, "Die Freunde zuerst," *Frankfurter Allgemeine Zeitung,* March 13, 1986.

[209] Other purposes such as patronage or helping people to start a political career were secondary.

[210] Cf. *BG*, Sept. 12, 19, Oct. 31, 1981. — From time to time, a few Councillors managed to build their own — however small — "organization." In doing so, they relied mostly on a tissue of friends and buddies in their neighborhood (the North End, South Boston) and in the city administration (at the lower echelons). An exemplary case: Frederick C. Langone.

[211] An old and leading member of the party observed: "Whenever we try to turn out the organization for someone else, the troops resent it. Working for the Mayor is o. k., but not for someone else. White has a proprietary interest in this organization. He would love to see this organization intact after he leaves office, but I doubt it will last after White is gone" (Source: Interview). — Cf. also M. Wagner Weinberg, "Boston's Kevin White: A Mayor Who Survives," op. cit., p. 101: "Election to Boston political office [...] has always required a personal organization, something that is difficult to build in the face of a powerful and well-organized incumbent. Historically, political loyalty has not been transferable from one person to another in Boston."

the Mayor's. As he withdrew from politics, he withdrew from the party, as a body politic, the reason for its existence.[212]

The party had already existed, to repeat it once again, at the beginning of the Mayor's reign.[213] The reality of its existence, however, had still been obscure. Neither had any of the far-flung forms yet appeared, through which it would stand out as the Mayor's carrier of power. Nor had yet the process of public curiosity set in, through which it would become the subject of much notoriety. But, in the subsequent process of its differentiation, the party had taken on form after form, and the public, in the parallel process of its increasing awareness, had caught on the party's reality piece after piece.

The reality of the party's existence had been a movement: the movement of the party from its origins as an "interest" of friends to its exposure as a body politic carrying an autocracy. It had been a movement of "revelation." It had been the movement unto the forms which the party in a process of differentiation had shown were the forms of its existence. It had been the movement unto the forms which the public in a process of disenchantment had learned to view as the forms of its growing disillusion.

Creativity: The Movement unto Time

On an unknown day, at an unknown time, an unknown number of its adherents failed to hold the farewell gathering of the party. A farewell party would have been redundant. The party was over.[214]

---

[212] There are no political party positions (Democratic, Republican ...) of any authority in Boston as there are in both Chicago and New York.

[213] Cf. supra, Chapter 2, note 14. – In the fall of 1967 Barney Frank had his first appointment with Kevin White, at White's house. Kevin White never appeared to keep the appointment. While Frank waited in the living room for two hours, he read a book which he had found on the bookshelf: *Ward Eight*, Joseph F. Dinneen's novel about Martin Lomasney, the quintessential political "boss" (the novel first appeared in New York in 1936). The tale about the lesson which Frank, still a political neophyte, had received in his house, engaged very much Kevin White's attention. – In April 1972 Jack Walsh was working for Mayor White on political relations. He handled ward committee contests. – In July 1983 a "longtime City Hall Insider" explained: "Of course, it was always like that [that there existed a political organization of Kevin White]. The difference was that in 1979 it was there for all to see. The one thing Kevin White had going for him before then was that there was never one person – with a handful of exceptions – there to watch the entire sixteen years. His staff people came and went. City Hall reporters came and went. Everyone saw the man in three-year chunks" (*BG*, July 26, 1983).

[214] Cf. supra, note 45.

In a way, the reign of Mayor White had been at an end before it actually came to an end. A few months after he had returned to private life Kevin White confided to the *Harvard Crimson* that he had lost his love of people:

> If you want to go into politics [...] you got to like people. In the end I began not to like people. It was time to get out of politics.[215]

And the Mayor had not been alone in feeling that his enthusiasm for people had waned. Throughout his reign the culture of friendship had largely been exhausted. Old friends had worn their friendships away and of new friends there had gathered too many. The mass of "friends" to whom the Mayor had become the symbol and nucleus of great expectations had stretched to a point at which the word "friendship" had virtually become meaningless. The zealots had turned against people. They were trying to intimidate everyone, to impede the "friends" who swirled about the corridors of mayoral power. The volunteers in the party had come to regard people primarily as a voting population to be treated statistically: as "White supporters," "negative votes," "White probables," as the "Chinese vote," the "black vote," as "pro-White voters," or "positive White voters." And the professionals in the government had discovered the "love" of people which "constituency builders" have. They "loved" people whenever they needed a constituency for a new project or a new policy and when they wanted to work people into a community group supporting their plans.

The soul of the regime had gone. The Mayor no longer liked people. Kevin White had arrived at Cicero's conclusion:

> For these designing and feigned friendships of mine bring some public *éclat*, but private satisfaction they have none. And so, when my house has been crowded with the morning *levée* and I have gone down to the forum amid a throng of friends, I cannot find in the whole bunch a single man with whom I could freely jest or whom I would want to hear my sighs.[216]

It was time to get out of politics. The movement of creativeness which Kevin White as "The Mayor" had catalyzed, had been a movement in the time of relationships between persons. There had been "rhythms," there had been "beginnings," "continuities," "stages." "Time" had occurred. And this

---

[215] Quoted in: *BG*, April 28, 1984. — Cf. also White's further remark: "[...] something just told me it was time. It was time [...] I just knew it was time. You're in this business as long as I am and you just know. You just know. You just know" (*BG*, May 27, 1983).

[216] Cicero, *Letters to Atticus*, I, 18. — The Latin text: "Nam illae ambitiosae nostrae fucosaeque amicitiae sunc in quodam splendore forensi, fructum domesticum non habent. Itaque, cum bene completa domus est tempore matutino, cum ad forum stipati gregibus amicorum descendimus, reperire ex magna turba neminem possumus quocum aut iocari libere aut suspirare familiariter possimus."

time had been defined through the movements of people: movements of people, among people, towards people. The movement of creativeness had been a movement of creativeness in time unto time. It had been a movement in the time of the persons who carried the creativeness unto the time their creativity was exhausted. It had been a movement in the time of persons who moved among themselves towards themselves unto the time their movements staled and each moved away from the other.

Chapter 4
The Government, Movements of Creativity

αὐτὸ μὲν καθ' αὐτὸ μηδὲν εἶναι, ἐν δὲ τῇ πρὸς ἄλληλα
ὁμιλίᾳ πάντα γίγνεσθαι καὶ παντοῖα ἀπὸ τῆς κινήσεως
οὐδὲν εἶναι ἓν αὐτὸ καθ' αὐτό, ἀλλά τινι ἀεὶ γίγνεσθαι,
ἀλλὰ κατὰ φύσιν φθέγγεσθαι γιγνόμενα καὶ ποιούμενα καὶ
ἀπολλύμενα καὶ ἀλλοιούμενα·

... nothing exists in itself, but all things of all sorts arise
out of motion by intercourse with each other ...
... nothing exists as invariably one, itself by itself,
but everything is always becoming in relation to something ...
... in accordance with nature we should speak of things
as "becoming" and "being made" and "being destroyed"
and "changing."

Plato, *Theaetetus*, 157 a – b

1 Philosophical Argument: The Politician's Progress

The "New" and the "Old"

Politics has its beginnings in myths. Incipient politics is mythical politics. And mythical forms sustain politics while it goes on.[1]

The politician enters politics through mythology. Whoever takes upon himself or herself politics, the quest for social creativity, cuts a mythical figure — more or less explicitly.[2]

The distinction between "new" politics and "old" politics is the primary tenet of political mythology.[3] Persons entering politics as politicians always ride on the revolution of time, on the "change" this revolutions appears to bring on. They invoke the "novelty," the "freshness," the "purity" of their project. And they call whatever it is they oppose in politics the "old" ways and views of "outmoded" politicians. They enact the son — the daughter — of the people through whom politics returns to its "origins," to the plain habits and concerns of common folk. And they criticize the "political establish-

---

[1] Cf. Ch. N. Cochraine, *Christianity and Classical Culture. A Study of Thought and Action From Augustus to Augustine*, London 1940; M. Eliade, *Cosmos and History. The Myth of the Eternal Return*, New York 1959 (= Harper Torchbooks); K. Hübner, *Die Wahrheit des Mythos*, München 1985, Chapter 25; E. Voegelin, *Order and History*, Vol. I, *Israel and Revelation*, Baton Rouge 1956, Introduction; Vol. II, *The World of the Polis*, Baton Rouge 1957; Vol. III, *Plato and Aristotle*, op. cit.; Vol. IV, *The Ecumenic Age*, op. cit., Chapter 1; idem, *Anamnesis*, op. cit., pp. 45 – 54 (English version: pp. 23 – 30); idem, "Configurations of History," in: P. G. Kuntz, ed., *The Concept of Order*, Seattle – London 1968, pp. 23 – 42.

[2] The best known examples in contemporary politics: Charles de Gaulle and John F. Kennedy. — It was Machiavelli who demonstrated most clearly that a politician, to be creative, has to cut a mythical figure. Cf. his *Vita di Castruccio Castracani da Lucca* (1520) and E. Voegelin, "Machiavelli's Prince: Background and Formation," *The Review of Politics*, Vol. 13, No. 2, April 1951, pp. 142 – 168. — Cf. also the statement by Rick Smith, an "admirer" of KHW: "Kevin White is a fundamentally more serious man than Curley [former Mayor of Boston], one whose chief competitor is history itself. Like one of the historical figures whom he admires, Charles de Gaulle, he might be described as *a man of the day before yesterday and the day after tomorrow*" (my emphasis, T. S.). (R. Smith, "Remembering Kevin. An Admirer Predicts History's Blessing on Our 'Jackhammer' Mayor. Stylish Visionary in an Era of Mushy Pluralism," *BO*, Vol. 2, No. 10, Dec. 1983, p. 25.)

[3] Cf. M. Eliade, *Cosmos and History*, op. cit., Chapter 2, and the texts of Eric Voegelin quoted at note 1.

ment" for a "decadence" which they assert could be discerned everywhere: in the social, cultural, the political life of the country and, especially, in the government.

Raymond Flynn, successor to Kevin White as Mayor of Boston, entered mayoral politics through mythological perceptions. There was not the politician, the City Councillor and former State Representative, running for another political office. There was a man, of the most humble origins, summoned by a noble yet apparently quixotic call, struggling with it pathetically: "When he stood out in front of the D Street Housing Project in South Boston [...] on an unseasonably hot day to announce his candidacy for mayor, few gave him any chance at all."[4] As if the life of a professional politician of 43 years had not been a life in sharp relief against the anonymity of everyman, the candidate was said to be "just plain Ray Flynn of Southie."[5] "Ray Flynn," a retired shoe factory worker was quoted as having observed, "of course, I know him. Almost everybody in this town knows Ray."[6] Yes, no doubt. For who would not have recognized "the son of a longshoreman and the son of a cleaning woman" – Flynn revealing hiself in the primeval language of mythical politics?[7] There was not the politician, there was "Flynn," the subject of a mythological transfiguration. (Almost) everyone knew "Ray" because (almost) everyone knew the figurations of "Ray" in popular mythology: "hometown boy," "son of a longshoreman and a cleaning woman," "Southie boy," " 'contra' to the incumbent Mayor," the "Lech Walesa figure of Boston politics."[8]

In the process of mayoral politics turned mythical politics the "new" fought the "old" – or else it would not have been "new." There had to be the "old," the "tired," the "corrupt" politician – or else there could not have been a "new" politician. The logic of mythical politics did not give Kevin

---

[4] P. Lucas, "Just Plain Ray: A Political Coup," *BH*, Sept. 30, 1983, p. 35.

[5] loc. cit.

[6] *BG*, Oct. 13, 1983, p. 27. – Cf. also *BPh*, Oct. 4, 1983, pp. 1, 6: "Flynn has put together a campaign that is fueled by ideology and blood ties [...]. These elements of the Flynn campaign rubbed elbows recently at a house party in the heart of St. Margaret's Parish in Dorchester [...]. At the close of one of the candidate's monologues [...] Mike Griffin, a former longshoreman, rose to address the crowd of 50 or so. As he spoke, it was clear that for him, what the candidate had said wasn't nearly as important as who he is. 'I said to your father 15 years ago that you'd be the first boy from Southie to be mayor of Boston,' Griffin proclaimed."

[7] *BG*, Nov. 16, 1983, p. 36: "Flynn, whose win means he will take over in January as the first mayor elected from South Boston, last night described himself as 'the son of a longshoreman and the son of a cleaning woman [...] [and] I'm very proud of that.'"

[8] Cf. the diverse articles on Flynn in: *BG*, Oct. 13, Nov. 16, 1983; *BH*, Sept. 30, 1983.

White a chance to choose his part. He was the sitting, and hence the "old" Mayor, subject of the mythological transfiguration too, was the villain. Several months had passed since Kevin White had removed himself from the mayoral race and the "new" still could not do without the foil of an *ancien régime*. "City government needs a total change from the present and recent past. It has become tired, corrupt and generally ineffective. We need new energy and new ideas in City Hall."[9]

A total change? Nothing was "new" about the "Flynn agenda for change in Boston": That "Downtown" should not be sole site of Boston's renaissance? That Boston's neighborhoods should be given a greater share in the city's political affairs and, especially, in its economic resources?[10] Kevin White, in 1968, had announced precisely this agenda.[11] And − contrary to popular notions − he acted on it, throughout his reign.[12]

"New" politics is "old" politics, is "new" politics that has not yet grown old. Or, conversely put ,"old" politics has been "new" politics, has been "new" politics growing old − old through its process in time unto time, old through its wear in its passage past the eyes of the public. But "new" politics is very new indeed as it repudiates the past it will become in the future: old politics. It is new politics, not because of the "new" things it will bring forth (it will bring forth the old), but because of the new beginning it sets in the process of politics, quest for creativity.

Raymond Flynn could not have been a "new" Mayor − a new focus of political creativeness − if he had been filled with his predecessor's experience, if he had imagined himself reflecting some day upon his time as Mayor of Boston, reaching a conclusion not unsimilar to the one Kevin White eventually reached, after two years of ex-mayoral reflection: in the end, White confessed,

---

[9] *BG* Magazine, Nov. 13, 1983.

[10] *BPh*, Oct. 4, 1983, p. 7: "The Flynn agenda for change in Boston is quite specific. Its explicit goal is to transfer political influence and public resources from real-estate developers working in downtown Boston to low-and middle-income tenants living in the city's many ethnic neighborhoods."

[11] Cf. the first inaugural address of Mayor White delivered at Faneuil Hall on January 1, 1968, reprinted in *CR*, Vol. 60, No. 1, Jan. 6, 1968.

[12] KHW reiterated again and again his promise, first given at his inauguration in January 1968, to "reduce the distance" between Boston's Downtown and its neighborhoods. Cf. for instance, *CR*, Jan. 3, 1977, Jan. 7, 1980. According to a member of Mayor White's transition team (preparing the transition to Mayor Flynn's new administration), $ 680 million were invested in the infrastructure of Boston during Mayor White's tenure. Only a small part, $ 100 million, was invested in Downtown, all the rest in the neighborhoods. (Source: Interview.)

he had become "an embarassment to everybody [...] making errors, getting petulant, tired, impervious, autocratic."[13] Raymond Flynn, of course, entered mayoral politics through mythological perceptions and "Ray" — the mythological transfiguration — superseded all experience of the "old." For "Ray" embodied a new beginning in mythical politics, and in mythical politics every beginning represents the absolute beginning.[14]

Within two years the "new" politics of Mayor Flynn had grown, in several respects, quite similar to the "old" politics of Mayor White.

- He had his aides search the United States for a new police commissioner, in order to find the "best qualified person." And he appointed, in the end, one of his friends from South Boston. With the help of a personal follower the new Mayor apparently sought to make, like the old Mayor had done, an important part of the city government an instrument of his political power.[15]
- He contrived and arranged "quiet shifts at City Hall," making reporters curious — and suspicious — again about the subtle enactments of politics in the theater of governmental institutions.[16]
- He built up a communication office that was discovered to equal the one his predecessor had kept: in size, the number of persons employed, as well as in financial resources, the money spent. A Mayor gone megalomaniac, people had said, in the case of the predecessor.[17]
- He dealt with the City Council high-handedly and did what he could to prevent the Council from exerting the bit of power it had, its power of control in the budgetary process. The device which he used represented old politics in classic form: the budgetary "information" which his office released was simply not adequate, essential tracts of data remained unavailable or were incomplete.[18]
- He seemed to be set on running the city alone; he stubbornly insisted on having the final say in even the slightest matter.[19]
- He did not oppose or obstruct the building boom that had captured Boston's Downtown, but not Boston's neighborhoods. On the contrary, he was found to be actively involved in the process of accelerating the

---

13 *BG*, Febr. 10, 1986, p. 21.
14 Cf. the literature quoted at note 1.
15 Cf. *BG*, Febr. 9, March 15, 1985.
16 Cf. *BG*, March 11, April 9, 1985.
17 Cf. *BG*, March 9, 1985.
18 Cf. *BG*, April 11, 1985.
19 Cf. *BG*, March 2, 1986.

building boom in Downton Boston. "Sometimes," a critic of "Flynn's heedless pursuit of development" wrote, "sometimes you forget where you came from and what promises you made along the way."[20]

The Discovery of the Politician

Floating up from the Prudential Center. When Kevin White first ran for Mayor in 1967, he was made the "hero" of a fictitious anecdote that quickly went the round of Boston. The candidate stood at the edge of the platform on top of the Prudential Center (the only high rise in Boston's Back Bay at the time and the building which symbolized a "New Boston").[21] Someone pushed him over the edge – and the aspirant to the Mayor's weight in the city did not fall, he floated up! The meaning of the anecdote was obvious: There was a political lightweight whom an illusory ambition had seemed to have told he was a politician.

Candidate White evoked sympathy, youth, reform politics, liberal attitudes. But he certainly did not evoke the image of a master in the art of politics. "Bland" was the word people used to convey their impression of the candidate. Nor did the candidate himself discern the politician's fibre he possessed.[22]

I didn't know I had that in me. The existence of the politician is a voyage to the depth of his art through the discovery of himself as a politician. The politician knows his art to the extent that he has learned wherein he is realizing in himself the person of a politician. His is a reflexive nature. Only in considering the potential for politics he has actualized does he comprehend the potential for politics he has been having. Only in grasping what it is that has made of him a politician does he apprehend the character of the politician.

Every politician, in being politician, discovers "the" politician each politician represents. Every politician practicing his art discovers an art which, to be practiced, has to be discovered. The discoveries each politician makes, may not – and indeed usually do not – encompass all of his art, all the characteristics of "the" politician. He is politician in becoming politician, in

---

[20] Webb Nichols, "Flynn's Heedless Pursuit of Development," *BG,* Febr. 14, 1985; cf. also *IHT,* Oct. 14, 1986.

[21] Cf. infra, p. 280 f.

[22] Cf. also the following exchange between Bob Crane, the old friend of KHW, and Kevin White: "Hey, you know something,' Bob Crane said. 'You made the right decision this year [1983]. What did they call you in '67? Bland?' 'Bland,' the mayor agreed with a laugh." (quoted in: *BG,* Nov. 16, 1983.)

becoming politician by his discoveries on the voyage to the depth of his art: the politician's progress.

> Kevin White related in November 1983, when I was running in 1967, I had a guy come in to see me and he handed me a contribution, a big one. I didn't even know him. The next time I saw him was a few weeks after I was sworn in, and he came in the office like he owned me and I resented it. I told him, "Look it, I don't really know you, but I know how much you gave me and I'll tell you what I'm going to do: I'm going to spend the next year looking for ways to screw you and, when I've done it for a year, you come back here and see me and then, may be, we'll be even." I didn't know I had that in me until that day.[23]

Our priorities shift every day. Whatever progress a politician will make on his voyage to the depth of his art, he will never "arrive." There is no solid base upon which he could rest and simply "be" the politician. All is in progress — in his own existence, as he discovers in himself "the" politician and discovers his art, the art of discovering in his practice of politics the art of politics he is practicing. And all is in progress — in the constellation of politics upon which he should act, as he discovers every day another political constellation. "The average business," Kevin White observed, "has the same priority every day." The situation of the politician, however, would radically be different: "Our priorities shift every day."[24]

The politician will never "arrive." He will never simply "be" the politician who is prepared for "everything" — as if his progress was a progress in learning and he had only to digest the definitive companion to political problems, as if his progress was a progress in the administrative routinization of politics and he had only to follow the guide to the political management of wholly pliant societies.

White, in his progress as politician, understood the politician in politics. He understood that the grounds on which the politician in politics moves, are themselves perennially moving. The progress he had to make was not a progress towards routine. It was the progress towards creativity:

> It would be great if they handed you a checklist of problems, and after you were elected you could go down the list bing-bing-bing and take care of all the problems. But that's not what happens. I had no way of knowing that two months after I took office as mayor of Boston, that the biggest problem I would face would be getting fuel oil into the city to keep the people warm. That's not the kind of thing you can anticipate. What you need in office is a man who can cope with situations as they arise, situations that no one even thought of.[25]

---

[23] *BG,* Nov. 16, 1983.
[24] *BG,* Aug. 4, 1974.
[25] Quoted in J. Napolitan, *The Election Game,* New York 1972, p. 129.

If it doesn't turn out right, we can modify it as we go along. In politics, the progress towards creativity is a progress in chaos – in the authoritative chaos of power as it has been described in the first part of this study. "Our priorities shift every day," Kevin White observed, and for this reason, he concluded, the politician in politics should not "formalize a structure."[26] In a firmly structured government having strict lines of responsibility, "rigidity sets in, a form of paralysis"[27] – the suffocation of creativity. However, Kevin White aspired to become a creative politician, and he built a fluid government that followed the fluidity of politics. The creativeness he actualized in his progress as politician became the creativity of the government he formed; nothing was established, all was attuned to the perennial test of politics: "If it doesn't turn out right, we can modify it as we go along."[28]

You never knew what he was going to do next. In his progress the politician moves more and more beyond the common habits of men. It appears that he acquires qualities of uniqueness, outside the sphere of everyday life. The fluidity of his political attitudes and the fluidity of his governmental procedures – the effects of his progress in his being the politician – frustrate the ordinary longing of men for certainty, for categorical promises, for positive security. "Developers want absolute assurances," a senior aide to Mayor White complained;[29] and she continued her lament to deplore their total insensitiveness to politics, an insensitiveness that was all the more startling, she thought, as they did not seem to lack susceptibleness, imagination, and intelligence in the economic conduct of their own interests and affairs. The politician cannot give categorical promises, he cannot provide security, and he cannot afford certainty. Politics knowing but a fleeting reality would simply pass by if he tried to fix it to firm foundations, leaving him stranded in the waste of his art. Kevin White, the Mayor, the politician, recognized the uniqueness of his social position. He had to subdue the general desire for "absolute assurances" – for the sake of politics. And he realized the personal uniqueness that is required of the politician in the uniqueness of his social

---

[26] *BG*, Aug. 4, 1974.

[27] loc. cit.

[28] This formulation is President Franklin D. Roosevelt's. Cf. A. M. Schlesinger, *The Age of Roosevelt*, op. cit., p. 531. – The political action of Chancellor Konrad Adenauer was equally attuned to the perennial test of politics. Cf. A. Poppinga, *Meine Erinnerungen an Adenauer*, op. cit., p. 28 f.; idem, *Konrad Adenauer*, op. cit., p. 26. – In reflecting upon the art of medicine and that of politics, Marguerite Yourcenar arrived at a formulation which is as admirable as pertinent: "Cette science trop proche de nous pour n'être pas incertaine, sujette à l'engouement et à l'erreur, mais rectifiée sans cesse par le contact de l'immédiat et du nu." (*Mémoires d'Hadrien*, Paris 1951, 1974, p. 38.)

[29] Source: Interview.

position. He who was about to master politics, the art, had to be as unpredictable as politics, the capricious thing.[30] "That was," a friendly critic wrote, "the great thing about him: You never knew what he was going to do next. That is a great political art; and Kevin White is the reigning master of it."[31]

To be as big a man as he can. Where does the politician go who has his art about him? Does he espouse burning ideas? Does he embrace the notion of the far-seeing statesman who can lay down plans for ages yet unborn?[32]

The answer appears to be deceptively prosaic. Above all, the politician takes care, much care, over his "office" — over the people and institutions with whom and through whom he pursues his art. Kevin White could not have been outside the sphere of everyday life and yet the focus of politics in his city, unpredictable and yet the skilled politician, unique and yet the head of a government, if he had not used the "liberty" which is the liberty of the politician in office, be it as Mayor, governor, or president: "The President is at liberty, both in law and conscience, to be as big a man as he can [...] His office is anything he has the sagacity and force to make it [...] His capacity will set the limit."[33]

The accomplished politician enjoys the rarest liberty of all. The progress he has made as politician has made him a politician at the peak of the politician's progress. He is the creative politician. And he is: the creative politician who is able to create the conditions of his creativeness. He is political leader. And he is: autocrat. He is Mayor. And he is: Kevin White.

The Revelation of Power

Ultimately, every politician runs a tragic course. To be the politician, the creative politician, he must be powerful. But the more progress he makes in accumulating power, the more progress he appears to make in the display of

---

[30] Machiavelli very much caught the capriciousness of politics through the symbol of *fortuna*. Cf. esp. Chapter 25 of *The Prince*.

[31] D. B. Wilson, "A Grand Finale for Master of Political Art," *BG,* May 31, 1983, p. 17.

[32] I adopt a phrase from W. Bagehot, *The English Constitution,* op. cit., p. 115: "We know, at least, that facts are many; that progress is complicated; that burning ideas (such as young men have) are mostly false and always incomplete. The notion of far-seeing and despotic statesman, who can lay down plans for ages yet unborn, is a fancy generated by the pride of the human intellect to which facts give no support."

[33] W. Wilson, Constitutional Government in the United States, in: *The Papers of Woodrow Wilson,* ed. A. S. Link, Vol. 18 (1908 – 9), Princeton 1974, p. 115, p. 116.
In his *Roosevelt: The Lion and the Fox* (New York 1956, p. 486) James Mc Gregor Burns observed: "The creative leader in the long run seeks to broaden the environmental limits whithin which he operates."

power. The power he owns is useless if it is not known by the people whom it is meant to move. Power, to be power, is necessarily ostentatious. It attracts attention – a pernicious attention. For the collision of power and curiosity engenders awe, fear, hostility. People like to probe the presence of power, glittering politics. But they do not like what they view when power appears bare: the power of power. And they like even less the power of accumulated power: it shows them all the power which they themselves potentially have and now see through the politician who has managed actually to own it. They rebel.[34]

Politicians who are powerful and prudent, besides, make the extent of their power appear smaller than it really is. They calculate its display, dependig upon the circumstances, showing as much of it as they feel they need, confronting people very rarely, if ever, with the power of their power. They play upon the attention that their power attracts, feeding it with a profuse spectacle of political symbols, rituals, figures, roles – with the masks of power.[35] They withdraw their personal presence from the presence of their power and carefully cultivate the perceptual distance at the outer end of which the power they own does not appear in the mode of its reality, as their power, but in the mode of its aura: as the power of the "office." They "disappear" behind the power that is displayed and exert through this display the power of their power – "in order to gain a discreet domination [...] and to rule without being felt, which is the great mystery of policy."[36]

Kevin White made, as has been shown, much progress in the accumulation of power and, inevitably, much progress in the display of his power. He needed both, all the power he accumulated and all the power he displayed, for Boston knowing him to be the Mayor, the politician, who made Boston

---

[34] Cf., for example, the article by J. W. Germond and J. Witcover in: *BG,* Febr. 9, 1983 and the article by K. Scharfenberg in: *BG,* Oct. 22, 1983. – During his last years in office Mayor White was very much "worried" about the public perception that he was "too powerful" (Source: Interview). The Mayor should have made a tour through the offices of his aides and subordinates in City Hall. There were pictures of him all over, on the walls, on the desks. In visiting City Hall one could not avoid forming the impression of an omnipresent Mayor, staring at you from every wall.

[35] "This is my article of faith about your profession and mine," White once explained to an interviewer, "That a story has to have a life. Otherwise it will not fly." (*BG,* Dec. 31, 1982.)

[36] Cf. J. Galt, *The Provost* (1822), ed. I. A. Gordon, Oxford 1982, p. 8: "Having thus reached a seat in the council, I discerned that it behoved me to act with circumspection, in order to gain a discreet dominion over the same, and to rule without being felt, which is the great mystery of policy."

move, as a "City": Boston, urban imbroglio, not so much a city, for itself, as a complicated and confusing patchwork of extremely diverse people, cultures, neighborhoods, institutions, talents, traditions.[37] To be the Mayor of the patchwork, he had to be the autocrat of "his" city. And he exercised indeed a "discreet domination" over Boston during the first half of his regime, ruled the city as an autocrat without really "being felt" as such, was a surprisingly well-set autocrat, as it seems, in view of the later years when he himself and his regime became the subjects of much adverse publicity, local and national.[38]

However, the perceptual distance upon which a "discreet domination" depends, shrinks naturally and shrinks all the time. A politician must be very fortunate, as regards his own disposition and the conditions under which he acts, to be able to remain within the balance of prudence and power, to be able to stay behind the masks of power and yet in the forefront of its display. *Fortuna* tended Kevin White − for a time. Then the autocracy and the public, the Mayor's power and the people's curiosity clashed. The autocrat revealed that he was the autocrat: "I got very possessive about the city in my later years. You lose sight of things."[39] And the public perceived what it felt was

---

[37] Cf. the following section from Kevin White's inaugural address of 1980: "When I first took office in 1968, 70 percent of the wards in Boston were unrepresented on the [City] Council, today, the situation has not improved. [...] That must change, and it *will*. I am not proposing district elections exclusively, and neither am I advocating any change in the electoral system in favor of partisan elections for Mayor. If at all, this proposal can only serve to undermine my own political authority. But the example of political organization in this last campaign, which spanned every precinct and every ward and every ethnic group, only serves to underscore my conviction that politics is the *one* institution in this city above all others which can motivate a diverse people to work in pursuit of common goals, and to feel a part of the larger whole." (*CR*, Jan. 7, 1980, p. 6−7).

[38] Cf. Chapter 1, notes 28 and 32, Chapter 3, note 200 and *BG*, March 15, 1981, Febr. 25, 1983. − White's "admirer" Rick Smith concluded: "[...] the crowd can accuse. It can vacillate, dream, demand, or resist. It can hardly create, nor can it prohesy. It is unattuned to the mystic feelings of a moody Irishman who is happy with a new building and happier still with a new idea. Perhaps an instinctive understanding of the crowd is what made Kevin White such a political loner. He became increasingly reluctant to yield to the gray conformity of modern pluralism [...]" (*Remembering Kevin*, op. cit., p. 28). − And Martha Wagner Weinberg remarked: "Kevin White won his gamble in the 1979 election. He placed his bets on assembling power visibly and on risking the electorate's perception of him as a strong, if at times unscrupulous, leader and, once again, survived" (Boston's Kevin White: A Mayor, Who Survives, op. cit., p. 104).

[39] *BG* Magazine, Nov. 13, 1983, p. 48.

no longer the mayor but "King Kevin", "Emperor White," the "Imperial Mayor," the "Despot of City Hall."[40]

Once a politician is generally derided as the „despot" and the image of a "Napoleonic office"[41] is evoked to describe the place where he rules, it appears that any further progress he will make is a progress in reverse: a progress in the loss rather than the acculumation of power, a progress in the mimicry rather than the mastery of his art, a progress in the management rather than the pursuit of politics. The revelation of power kills the politician's progress.[42] The myth has become the "big lie."[43] The formerly "new" politician has become very "old," everyone sees the man and his power and asks: Why he, just he? And there is not an answer, really. There is but a new beginning, there is but another politician's progress.

2 Persons and Institutions

In politics, a new beginning becomes factual with a new "administration." A politician, in his progress, has risen to a position of executive power in politics. He appoints the members of his government. To be more precise, he places in governmental posts friends from his "home turf," a neighborhood or a town, a county or a state.[44] The "new" are the new faces filling the executive offices of governmental power.

---

[40] Cf. *NYT*, April 28, 1981; *Newsweek*, May 11, 1981; *BG*, May 27, May 30, 1983; *Time*, June 6, 1983. – The revelation of power goes on on its own, whether a politician knows how to withstand it or not. Cf. the unjust verdict of Henry Adams: "[...] not one politician living has the brains or the art to defend his own cause. The ocean of history is foul with the carcasses of such statesmen, dead and forgotten except when some historian fishes one of them up to gibbet it" (*Democracy. An American Novel* [1980], New York 1983, p. 108).

[41] Cf. *BO*, Vol. 2, No. 10, Dec. 1983, p. 1.

[42] Typically, the negative image of the White administration prevalent in the media during its last years, still dominated the mind of a student in "Professor" Kevin White's class at Boston University, one and a half years after he had left office: " 'It will be beneficial to see the other side of the coin,' said Tracy Gordon, 21, a senior from Hartford [...] Gordon added that her earlier perception of White's administration was that it was 'sleazy, if you will' " (*BG*, Sept. 7, 1982).

[43] Cf. the passage on the *gennaion pseudos* (big lie) in Plato's *Politeia*, 414 c ff.

[44] In his book *Working With Truman. A Personal Memoir of the White House Years* Ken Hechler observed: "Luck seems to play a big part in getting assigned to the White House staff. Still, one can make generalizations that apply in any administration. A president surrounds himself with people whom he trusts. They share his goals, or are flexible

This reality of a new beginning in politics has always been well known. The very first act, let us recall, which new rulers and their administrations usually perform is the public ceremony of their accession to the power of government. Everyone should see and behold the renaissance of purpose and creativeness which the new ruler, the new administration embody. All are supposed to "know," to have viewed the new people making up the new regime. They are supposed sensibly to perceive the reality of a new beginning in politics. Or else it would never be a new beginning.

Much less known is the practical paradox of a "new beginning" in politics. The "new" cannot be "new" forever. But the qualities which it carries — the sense of a purpose, the momentum of creativeness — are not meant to be exhausted with the short moment of the "beginning." They are continuously needed to sustain the "new," its continuum: a "new" era, a "new" regime, a "new" administration. A "new beginning" turned into a continuity of the new beginning is a practical paradox. Yet, this is the problem that presents itself to every politician who has acceded to the power of government and who goes about to govern, that is, to create.

In general terms, the problem requires institutions: carriers of continuity. And it requires institutions which produce continuity: continuous creativity. In more specific terms, a certain formula has to be found for the reality of political institutions (not for a prototype of political institutions, to be sure).[45] The formula which creative politicians did find (and do find) makes institutions occur in a continuous flow of cohesive creativeness among a number of persons.

(1) The make-up of an institution is fully attuned to the "institutional" conduct of the persons through whom it appears and "exists." The institution is where these persons are, nowhere else.[46] Its "form" follows

---

enough to embrace and enthusiastically support them. [...] Every president — and Truman was no exception — appoints people from his home state whom he has known a long time. Thus he tries to insure there is mutual trust and loyalty between the president and staff members." (op. cit., p. 35.) — This observation was of course reaffirmed by the appointments policy of subsequent presidents. Presidents Kennedy, Johnson, Nixon, Carter, Reagan surrounded themselves with people whom they trusted. They placed in their governments friends from the (respective) home turf: New England, Texas, Southern California, Georgia, California (Northern and Southern).

45 Any prototype of political institutions would be an empty abstraction, removed from politics by the very act of reification through which alone it would be conceivable. Cf. also supra. p. 28.

46 Cf. Ch. H. Cooley, *Social Organization. A Study of the Larger Mind* (1909) in: *The Two Major Works of Charles H. Cooley*, op. cit., p. 314: "In the individual the institution exists as a habit of mind and action, largely unconscious because largely common to all

their reality, their free movements of association among themselves towards an "institutional" creativeness. There is a first condition of institutional creativity: an absolute primacy of persons over institutions.

(2) Of all possible institutional forms, the least institutional one is constantly preferred. If the purpose of institutions is creativeness, the "best" institution is hardly an institution at all. It is the loosest possible arrangement of people. In the politics of Ancient Rome such an arrangement was called *consilium*.[47] The *consilium* is a second condition of institutional creativity.

(3) The politician masters the institutions through which he is governing. They are but an expression of the politics he pursues. Hence they are "political" institutions in the fullest sense of the word. Politics governs their reality, the reality of institutional government. The politician's politics governs the "institutional" conduct of the persons through whom the institutions of his government appear and "exist." It provides for the medium of inducements within which these persons engage in free movements of association among themselves and yet move towards the "institutional" creativeness through which the politician's politics actually becomes politics: movements of political creativity which, as "government," effect a process of social creativity, politics' essence.

There is a third condition of institutional creativity; institutionalist politics, politics pursued through the institutions of politics.

Under Mayor White the reality of political institutions in Boston mirrored the "institutional" formula just described. The formula has been applied by politicians in the past and is being applied, increasingly as it seems, by politicians in the present.[48] Thus the White Administration, as a subject of study, affords an example of "government," that is, of political creativity. A "new beginning" in politics, Kevin White's accession to the power of government, found a continuum in the White Administration. It was translated into institutional creativeness, into political institutions which continually became what political institutions essentially are: continuous movements of creativity.

---

the group: it is only the differential aspect of ourselves of which we are commonly aware. But it is in men and nowhere else that the institution is to be found. The real existence of the Constitution of the United States, for example, is in the traditional ideas of the people and the activities of judges, legislators and administrators; the written instrument being only a means of communication, an Ark of the Covenant, ensuring the integrity of the tradition."

[47] Cf. J. Crook, *Consilium principis,* Cambridge 1955; J. Bleicken, *Die Verfassung der römischen Republik,* Paderborn 1975, p. 132 ff.

[48] Cf. Chapter 1, notes 9, 34, 35, 40; Chapter 2, notes 38, 39; and S. Cassese, "Is There a Government in Italy?" in: R. Rose, E. N. Suleiman, eds., *Presidents and Prime Ministers,* Washington, D. C. 1980, pp 171−202, esp. pp. 180−81.

3 The Primacy of Persons

This guy, that guy, and that other guy. The White Administration was built on people whom the Mayor had selected. The choosing of his advisers, lieutenants, and assistants was his – and it was theirs. In some way, at some place, at work on some job, each had singled out himself or herself. Each had singled out himself or herself to the extent that he or she had attracted the Mayor's attention and had made him think he or she might just be the person he had been looking for: the right person for a job for which the Mayor had not had found the "ideal" candidate before, or the right person for a policy project which the Mayor would not have thought of, if this particular person, through his or her special experience and skills, had not suggested it.[49]

Any concept of a government is useless, if it is a concept without persons, if *the* persons are not known (and not available) through whom alone it would work. Or, inversely and thus still more pointedly put, persons, through their presence, their skills, their availability, define, in any particular situation, the government that is possible.

The White Administration was a political administration particular persons made. They themselves cast, as has earlier been explained, their governmental roles and took part in the government – in the Court – at places, in positions which had not been part of the government before.[50] The Mayor's government was largely tailored to the persons whom the Mayor wanted to serve in his "government."[51] Persons joined the administration, others left, a different "government" followed: some of its institutions fell apart or disappeared (with the persons who had left), new institutions emerged (with the persons who had joined the administration). Persons within the administration moved from tasks to tasks, from one function to another, a different "government" followed: existent institutional mechanisms dissolved (with the tasks which no longer any persons stood for), new mechanisms were set up (with

---

[49] Senior officials in the White Administration "chose" most of their principal aides in the same way.

[50] Cf. supra, p. 67 f..

[51] Cf. supra, p. 56. – Cf., for comparative purposes, the observation by Herbert Weichmann, Mayor of Hamburg: "Die Mitarbeiter der Staatskanzlei müssen [...] vor allen Dingen auch schöpferischen Instinkt [...] haben. [...] Unter diesen Umständen glaube ich auch nicht, daß sich ein bestimmtes Schema einer Organisationsform festlegen läßt. Die Geschäftsverteilung muß sich in diesem Falle nach den zur Verfügung stehenden Persönlichkeiten und ihren Fähigkeiten richten, also elastisch bleiben." (H. Weichmann, "Vorarbeit für den Staatschef," in: *Die Staatskanzlei: Aufgaben, Organisation und Arbeitsweise auf vergleichender Grundlage,* Berlin 1967, pp. 35.)

the tasks to which persons in the administration had turned).[52] All fluctuated with the persons who, through their being a "government," defined the institutional "form" of this government.[53] That there was a government and that this government worked depended more on the presence, skills, and availability of particular persons than on anything else. "The bodies" counted, not institutions, nor any administrative schemes. "To succeed in government," a mayoral aide explained, "you shouldn't think in terms of issue politics, but of this guy, that guy, and that other guy."[54]

If I want clowns, I should be able to have them. Once the Mayor had convinced himself of the abilities a particular person lent to his government, he was likely to take a very personal interest in that person.[55] He would offer the young aide ("youth" was one of the qualities the Mayor greatly preferred) much opportunity for displaying his or her skills and thus for a rapid rise to the upper echelons of the government. And he would be disposed to a kind of administrative jealousy. The career he wished the young aide to make was meant to be a career in his government, not somewhere else. Realistically, the Mayor did of course expect that not a few of his associates would, sooner or later, consider an employment outside his government. Yet he also expected his aides not to entertain such considerations, not to conceive of the possibility that they could find anywhere else a greater chance of politics and/or professional achievement.[56]

Moreover, he would view his aides possessively. When he had chosen someone to be among the few with whom he governed, the Mayor was unwilling to let the person thus selected act, in his or her personal life, as he or she pleased. In his eyes, an aide of his was not free, for instance, to assist

---

[52] Cf. supra, p. 26 ff.

[53] The former Secretary General of the French Government, Jacques Fournier, described this government in similar terms: "[...] la structure du gouvernement est fluctuante. Elle varie dans le temps puisqu'il y a ce mouvement de longue durée de croissance du nombre des ministères. Elle varie d'un gouvernement à l'autre. Elle tient compte des évolutions à long terme et des nécessités du moment, des personnalités en présence aussi, car souvent un poste ministériel sera taillé à la mesure d'une personne déterminée." (J. Fournier, *La coordination du travail gouvernemental,* Paris, Fondation Nationale des Sciences Politiques, Service de Polycopie, 1985 – 86, p. 8.)

[54] Source: Interview.

[55] Not only the Mayor, but other officials in the government, too, practiced this personal touch; BRA director Robert J. Ryan, for example.

[56] The Mayor's possessiveness fostered, on the part of some aides, a false sense of security. Caught by the Mayor's attention, they neglected to think of themselves and to tend their own interests. They became all the more disappointed, if not bitter, when they realized the truth of their professional advancement: they had advanced very much in the realm of the Mayor and very little "out there" in the world.

a friend in running for a political office, if he found that this particular person did not deserve any assistance to his campaign.[57]

On the other hand, though, the Mayor stood by his aides whenever their employment in his government appeared to be threatened. The financial, that is budgetary conditions of their employment were not completely under the Mayor's control, and the City Council regularly tried, through the budgetary process, to shake his regime by slashing the number of people who were this regime.[58] The Mayor reacted against the attacks so fiercely as he did because they involved, in his view, not only a threat to the stability of his regime but also, and more importantly, a threat to his, that is the politician's, freedom to form a government with whomever he pleased. There was no government if the government there was to be was not a government of persons very personally selected. The politician had to be given the freedom of his choice: "If I want clowns, I should be able to have them."[59]

I don't really see women in [female] terms. The Mayor defended and exerted a freedom of choice by which − it is still necessary to stress the point − women especially benefited. While he governed, "affirmative action" was still a largely unfulfilled promise. His administration, however, could be viewed as a striking exception. It did not hold out to women only the secretarial jobs which conventionally were theirs. It offered them quite more: career opportunities, chances of professional advancement. Since the early 1970's a fair number of women could be found in the White Administration holding positions of responsibility in matters of administration as well as policy.[60] And they could concentrate on being successful executives rather

---

[57] The candidate: Peter Meade, a *former* aide of the Mayor. The aide whom the Mayor did not want to help Peter Meade: Jane Deutsch.

[58] Cf. *CR,* March 23, 1981, p. 700; March 30, p. 719; April 4, p. 754 f.; May 8, p. 45 f.; May 11, 1981, p. 32; August 2, 1982, p. 565, p. 577; *BG,* March 14, 15, 18, 19, 1981; April 1, 2, 1981; Febr. 2, 1982; *BHA,* March 17, 1981.

[59] Kevin White as quoted in: *BG,* May 14, 1981, p. 26.

[60] This is a partial list of women and their positions in the White administration: Susan Allen, chief project coordinator, Director's Office, BRA; Martha Bailey, project coordinator, BRA; Genie Beal, Environmental Affairs, Conservation Commission; Barbara Cameron, Commissioner, Assessing Dept.; Shirley Campbell, manager, Little City Hall, Franklin Field-Mattapan; Susan Child, Director, Revival Programm, Public Facilities Dept.; Alice Christopher, manager, Little City Hall, East Boston, Director, Administrative Services; Nancy Clark, senior mayoral aide; Betty Cook, senior aide, Office of Cultural Affairs; Carol Corcoran, Head, Commission on the Status of Women, Director, Rent Control; Dorothy Curran, Recreation Director, Parks & Recreation Dept.; Pat Dannenberg, Administrative Services; Mary Davidson, assistant for social services, Mayor's Office; Roberta Delaney, manager, Little City Hall, Charlestown, Director Neighborhood Services; Claudia Delmonaco, Director, Office of Public Services, Commissioner, Traffic

than on being successful women. For they had not been appointed on the grounds of gender but solely on the grounds of their talents and skills. As the Mayor upheld the politician's freedom to form a government with whomever he pleased, he made discrimination pointless: "I don't really see women in [female] terms."[61]

They share a vision — sometimes. A government does of course have — as every other social species — its "natural" structure. Its members do differ from each other "in terms" of gender, age, ethnicity, geographic origins, biography. There are men in this government and there are women; there are persons who approach old age and there are persons of tender years; there are people in the government who have been in politics all their life and there are others who are new to this trade.

The makers and members of a government who see their government being built upon a primacy of persons cannot but set this "natural" structure aside, as they must set aside any preexistent structure.[62] They presume the government nothing until it becomes "something" through themselves. They view themselves within a structural void where various persons — they themselves — freely converge upon themselves forming figurations which,

---

and Parking Dept.; Susanne DelVecchio, assistant corporation counsel; Norma Fine, senior aide, Overseas Development; Doby Flowers, Deputy Director, Manpower, Deputy Administrator, Employment and Economic Policy Adm.; Kathy Fraser, Deputy Director, Empl. and Econ. Policy Adm.; Judy Glasser, Public Information, BRA; Martha Goldsmith, economic adviser, Mayor's Office; Wendy Gray, senior aide, Mayor's Office; Elaine Guiney, Commissioner, Affairs of the Elderly, Head, Housing Improvement; Nancy Huntington, Special Projects; Katherine Kane, Deputy Mayor; Vicky Kayser, Public Information Assistant Director, BRA; Christine Knowles, Economic Development Officer, BRA; Averil Lashley, promotions director, special assistant to the Mayor; Ann Lewis, adviser on women in politics, Mayor's Office; Emily Lloyd, transportation adviser, Mayor's Office, Commissioner, Traffic and Parking; Gerry Marcinowski, assistant director, Health and Hospitals; Anne Muenster, manager, Little City Hall, Allston-Brighton; Marcia Myers, executive director, Landmarks Commission; Mary Perot Nichols, Director, Office of Communications; Elaine Noble, senior aide, Mayor's Office; Joanne Prevost, Commissioner, Real Property; Maureen Schaffner, Commissioner, Elderly Affairs; Lucille Sims, zoning officer, BRA; Joan Smith, relocation officer, BRA; Micho Spring, Deputy Mayor; Marilyn Stickler, assistant corporation counsel; Marilyn Swartz-Lloyd, capital project administrator; Teri Weidner, Special Projects; Jane Weisman, Commission on Women; Fran Welton, Office of Program Development; Lisa Zankman, Director, Community Schools, Administrative Assistant, Rent Board.

61 *CSM*, Sept. 19, 1977.

62 They never fully succeed, however. Natural structures such as differences in age or gender cannot really be made irrelevant; they can only be ignored — for some time, that is until they prove to be stronger than the governmental structure that denies them.

after they have visibly emerged, seem to be recognizable as the "structure" of a "government."

The people in the White adminstration looked upon themselves as such a creation. There was nothing except themselves. But among themselves they experienced the great concentration of creativity. They entered into relationships with one another which were very "personal."[63] They gravitated towards the positions that seemed to suit best their own personal inclinations and their notions of how they might best assert institutional influence within and governmental power outside the administration. They did not shun but rather sought political crises, courted politics at the edge of catastrophe, leapt at the events that furnished what they thought were their opportunities for personal recognition, fame.[64] And they realized an "osmosis" of separate yet cohesive creativeness as they pursued their work through each other while each continued to pursue the own, individual work.[65] When one of them was asked what it was that sustained this "osmosis," he replied: "They share a vision — sometimes."[66]

They hate each other. This was a reply, but a reply with reservations, evidently. The great concentration of creativity engendered freedom. It made people free to join each other, to be a government. And it made people free to oppose each other, to be a quarrelling government.[67] The creativeness which they collectively produced was fueled by the personal aggressiveness of each. As each of them made the government as much as the other, none could claim a greater prestige or a greater power than anybody else. Or, inversely put, each enjoyed whatever prestige and power he or she had won in opposition to all others. Each made the government to the extent that he or she aggressively pushed back the others doing exactly the same. They shared a vision, sometimes. For something else was true, as one of them said, talking about all: "They hate each other."[68]

When he left, there was no one who took his place. Feelings symbolized a government. The people in the White adminstration knew that they were a government because they knew that they were personally involved in the

---

[63] Source: Interview.

[64] They tended therefore to prefer politics in dramatized form: as a succession of "visible events" which made the actors shine.

[65] "Osmosis" was the term a number of people in the White administration used to describe the mode of their interaction.

[66] Source: Interview.

[67] That the government of a free people ought to be a "rational" and hence "harmonious" government is one of the great misunderstandings in contemporary politics. Political freedom is the freedom to dissent — to quarrel.

[68] Source: Interview.

existence of "the" government. "They" were the government, but "they" were John X, Judith Y, Robert Z ... individual persons. When John X or Judith Y left, "they," that is the government, became different. And "different" not only meant a difference in the institutional, but also and above all, a difference in the personal sense. Someone who had made the government, together with them, no longer made, with them, "their" government. With this person having left, the government, that is "they," were suffering from a loss which could not really be repaired. Persons made the government and every person leaving the government unmade the government. For those who stayed, it was not only important to note that someone had resigned from his or her post. It was equally, if not more, important to note that a part of the government had disappeared: "When he left, there was no one who took his place."[69]

4 The Consilium

Ubi multa consilia, ibi salus. Politics, as a quest for social creativity, is always a quest for very practical solutions to very specific problems. Should this or that person be appointed Head of the Transportation Department? Should the budget for sanitation services be increased or not? Should the government institute rent control or reject the role of arbiter in the market of rental housing? Should a strike of public workers be broken or should their demands be met? Should the regulatory mechanism of a minimum wage be revoked or maintained? Should the government, confronted with a surge of crime, seek much stiffer penalties?

Each problem or, in the parlance of politicians, each "issue" calls for a government that is prepared to handle this problem or issue. Politics, however, abounds in issues; and these issues tend to arise uncontrollably, in numbers the government could not choose, at moments the government could not decide upon; and they tend to arise unexpectedly, presenting themselves hardly in line with the government's agenda.

The government as *the* government there is cannot achieve for what it appears to exist: to cope with issues, the stuff of politics. Politics is issue

---

[69] Source: Interview. – Cf. also the following remarks as to the demise of the "Boston Plan": "More importantly, the reason why we haven't heard much of the Boston Plan is the fact that a lot of us have gone – and, most importantly, John [Drew]. Certainly John was the glue that held that thing together – [...]" (J. B. O. 'Connell, *The Boston Plan*, (D), op. cit., p. 4). – "Once you lose a guy like John Drew, if you don't find someone like that to take his place, things start to fall apart. [...]" (ibid., p. 5.)

politics and issue politics requires issue government. Hypothetically, it requires *a* government that is prepared to handle each issue. Actually, it demands a host of governments at one moment and another host of governments at the next. *The* government, however, cannot be all kinds of governments – as there are all kinds of issue. And yet, it has to be all kinds of governments, as all the issues – all kinds of issues – arise which *the* government has to handle.

One other paradox of politics.[70] The "solution" has long been known, by politicians in Ancient Rome, in the Middle Ages, and the Renaissance, in our modern centuries.[71] It is a classical solution, a political solution to politics, a very practical solution: The government has to be a government of as many committees as there are issues – currently, of course. *Ubi multa consilia, ibi salus* – Where many councils meet, there is well-being, we are told by a proverb from the wisdom of medieval statecraft. A government is what it is supposed to be, that is a government attuned adequately to the task of coping with each of those thousand things that arise as "issues" in politics, if it actualizes itself predominantly in the mode of *consilia:* task forces, councils, commissions, working groups, meetings, advisory bodies, committees … committees … committees. The *consilium* – a commission, a committee, a task force, or any any other such group – is the most flexible instrument of governing. It can freely, "spontaneously," be set up and it can freely be dismantled – or just fades away – whenever it is needed no longer. Its members are the persons whom one selects, no one else, and one can select persons from within and, without much ado, from outside the government. A *consilium* can be convoked momently, "ad hoc," as contemporary politicians would say, with a brevity of expression quite pertinent to the transitory institutional event which an *ad hoc commission* presents (the politicians in the Italian city states of the Renaissance still used a noun for it: *balia*). It can afford excellence, if the "experts" chosen for the committes – the *savi,* as the ancients said – match perfectly the issue that has been put in their hands. And, finally, a *consilium* can be created for each issue and it is still a *consilium*

---

[70] Cf. infra, p. 242; supra, p. 9 – 12.

[71] Cf. Chapter 3, note 6; U. Pasqui, *Documenti per la Storia della Città di Arezzo,* Florence 1879 – 1920, Vol. II, p. 462 ff.; R. Rose, E. N. Suleiman, eds., *Presidents and Prime Ministers,* op. cit., Th. E. Cronin, S. D. Greenberg, eds., *The Presidendial Advisory System,* New York 1969, esp. the contribution on "ad hoc commissions" by A. L. Dean, pp. 101 – 116; Th. T. Mackie, B. W. Hogwood, eds., *Unlocking the Cabinet. Cabinet Structures in Comparative Perspective,* London 1985; on the French parallel in general, cf. J. Fournier, *La coordination du travail gouvernemental,* op. cit., pp. 151 – 190; on the French practice during the *cohabitation* between President Mitterrand and Prime Minister Chirac, cf. *Le Point,* No. 714, May 26, 1986, pp. 30 – 32; *L'Express,* July 11, 1986, pp. 44 – 45.

of the government there is. The *consilium* is the perennial answer to the perennial problem of politics. There are a thousand issues in politics and there ought to be a thousand governments, for each issue arising a government matching it. However, government cannot occur through a thousand governments. It can only occur through the thousand commissions one government is in coping with politics, a thousand issues.

Adhocracy. It is impossible to enumerate all the *consilia* through which the White adminstration worked as a government. Meetings were held all the time, "lots of meeting," as a senior offical said,[72] every working day (and

---

[72] Source: Interview. — The French government, too, works through "mille réunions interministérielles." Cf. *L'Express*, July 11, 1986, p. 45. Cf. also Table 15.

Table 15: French Government: Interdepartmental Meetings and Commissions, 1961 – 1985

Year	Interdepartmental Meetings	Permanent Interdepartmental Commissions	Interdepartmental Commissions
1961	141	13	105
1962	164	8	72
1963	283	10	72
1964	395	7	111
1965	355	6	112
1966	312	10	135
1967	310	9	108
1968	312	7	89
1969	307	7	88
1970	526	11	134
1971	589	19	127
1972	583	9	83
1973	517	9	65
1974	555	6	76
1975	792	9	84
1976	572	8	44
1977	738	10	53
1978	603	10	72
1979	1002	20	54
1980	1070	20	39
1981	1147	21	57
1982	1855	22	112
1983	1500	26	43
1984	1356	12	39
1985	1307	12	8

Source: The French Prime Minister's Office.

not infrequently on weekends, too), over 16 years; the sheer number one would have to count is staggering. Counting, however, would not be the sole problem. Of the larger part of the *consilia* nothing, in the form of records or documents, summons up their existence, as if the White adminstration had followed the old wisdom of European Chancelleries: What is not on record does, for the world, not exist (*quod non est in actis, non est in mundo*). And the recollections of the former participants in the *consilia* cover, of the innumerable meetings they attended, only those which they can remember. *Consilia* have literally vanished. There is nothing that would give a hint. There are not even memories that would tell a trace.

Once again, the inquiry seizes ignorance where it is seeking knowledge. The story presently to be told is the story of the *consilia* through which the White adminstration worked as a government. Yet, this story cannot be "fully" pursued. An unknown number of unknown kinds of *consilia* composed by an unknown number of persons in unknown ways eludes all efforts of inquiry. The government of *consilia,* which the White adminstration working as a government was, partially remains inaccessible. It is possible to tell its story as a government *of* committees. But it is not possible to tell its story as a government having consisted precisely *in* that many committees of that particular kinds composed by that many persons in that particular ways. We can grasp significance, but we cannot grasp all that signifies.[73]

From the names the *consilia* of the White adminstration were given we can gather the conventional nomenclature of adhocracy: task force, ad hoc mechanism, meeting, team, commission, conference, advisory group, working group, committee. However, these names were used very loosely, and they could therefore tell terminological "facts" – "names" of "governmental units" – to which there was indeed no corresponding reality. The "names" very often did not really correspond to those movements of governmental creativity by which *consilia* occurred. A *consilium* called "task force" could be a task force or something else, a policy review committee perhaps, or a fleeting conference of some officials, or an incipient government agency. Nor did each and every *consilium* carry a designation; some had been given a resounding label ("Boston Commission Against Discrimination," for instance), others were known only as *consilia* "in reference to," in reference to the issue of urban development, for example, or in reference to the interrelations between the City of Boston and the Federal Government in Washington, D. C. (see Tables 4 – 8).

---

[73] This insight is not as new as modern semiotics suggests it to be. It was formulated already around 27 B. C. by the Roman architect Vitruvius, in his *De Architectura Libri Decem:* "Cum in omnibus enim rebus, tum maxime etiam in architectura haec duo insunt: quod significatur et quod significat" (*De Architectura,* I, 1, German-Latin edition, ed. by C. Fensterbusch, Darmstadt 1976, p. 22).

Table 4: Consilia: Boston Government

Boston Plan (1977/78)

A		A'	B		B'		B''
Andy Olins		Charles Atkins	John Drew		Marilyn Swartz-Lloyd		Gordon Brigham
John Drew		("Coordinator")	Robert Walsh		Phil Zeigler		George Bennett
Bob Schwartz	and	+	Charles Atkins		("Coordinators")		Emily Lloyd
Jack Murphy		staff	Michael Westgate		+	and	George Seyboldt
Micho Spring		(appr. 25 persons)	Brian Dacey		Owen Donnelly		Bradley Biggs
			Andy Olins		+		
("Policy Committee")			John Weis		staff		
			("Executive Policy Committee")				

Explanation: On the "Boston Plan" informs note 50, Chapter 1.

Table 5: Consilia: Boston Government

Cable TV (1979/81)

A	B	C
Kathy Kane + staff	Elizabeth G. Cook Robert Ferrante Andrea West Gloria Jean Conway William Morrissey David Thorne Anna De Fronzo Theresa Parks James P. Breedan ("Mayor's Cable Access Advisory Committee")	William J. O'Leary Lian M. Kelly Rev. James K. Allen Rev. Donald C. Luster Stuart H. Rosenberg Daniel J. Finn Charles Cloherty G. Peabody Gardner III Jose Masso	Peggy Charren Bill Owens David Brudnoy Joseph Dimino Michael Lo Presti ("Cable TV Review Commission")

D		D'
Micho Spring Richard Borten Charles Beard Harold Carroll	and	Lowell Richards

Explanation: As to the process leading to the establishment of Cable TV in Boston, cf. the sources quoted at note 19, Chapter 1.

In arranging their movements towards each other and among themselves, the participants in the *consilia* repeatedly fell into a similar structure. They formed three "working" figurations: (a) the members of the *consilium* proper, (b) the supporting staff, and (c) the coordinators "organizing" the proceedings of the *consilium*. However, these figurations were not static forms. They were fluid to the extent that participants in the *consilia* shuttled between two figurations or switched from one figuration to the other or actively shaped a figuration (see Tables 4 – 7).

The members of a *consilium* were not always equally aware of the *consilium* in general and their own status on it, in particular. Some had been chosen member of the committee or the task force and did not know it at first (they later learned of it, of course). Others had shared the considerations

Table 6: Consilia: Boston Government

Review of Rent Control (1977)	Proposition 2 ½ (1980/81)	
Emily Lloyd	A	A'
Micho Spring	David Rosenbloom	David Rosenbloom
Andy Olins	Newell Cook	Harold Carroll
Carol Corcoran	Lowell Richards	William McNeill
	William McNeill	Raymond Torto
	Dennis Morgan	Dennis Morgan
	Ed Sullivan	Lowell Richards
	Raymond Torto	Newell Cook
	Micho Spring	Stuart Marwell
	George Regan	Micho Spring
	Chris Bator (staff person)	Kathy Kane

Boston Commission Against Discrimination (1980/81)	Hispanic Task Force (1980/81)
Ted Anzalone	Jorge Hernandez
Jack Murphy	Carmen Pola
Barbara Cameron	Edwin Blanco
Andy Olins	Alberto Vasallo
Kathy Kane	Awilda Ramos
Bob Vey	Frieda Garcia
Buford Kaigler	Father Wendell Verill
	Bill Meinhofer
	Amelia V. Mederos
	Jovita Fontanez
	Liana Perez-Felix
	Roberta Garcia

Explanation: On "Proposition 2½" informs note 22, Chapter 2.

Table 7: Consilia: Boston Government

Boston Committee (1980/81)		Urban Development (1981)
A	A'	
Rev. Michael Haynes	Lisa Savereid	Micho Spring
Robert A. Corrigan	("Deputy Director")	Martha Goldsmith
Tracy Amalfitano		James V. Young
Ada Focer		Robert Ryan
Jorge Hernandez and		
Richard D. Hill		
William Davis Taylor		
Humberto Cardinal Medeiros		
Kevin White		

Boston/Washington (1981)		Fiscal Task Force (1982)
A	A'	Christopher A. Iannella
David Mundel	David Mundel	Frederick C. Langone
Ira Clippinger	David Rosenbloom	Bruce C. Bolling
Jane Edmonds	Martha Goldsmith	David Rosenbloom
Phil Zeigler	Richard D. Hill	Donald Mausen
Martha Goldsmith	Brian Dacey	
	Robert Ryan	

leading to the committee from the very beginning, but were utterly surprised when they were told that they were sitting on a committee and not, as they had thought, just discussing occasionally with other people what seemed vaguely to be (or rather: to become) an "issue." Often a *consilium* had already done its work for some time, and the names of all participants were still not known to each participant. "Committees" met, "task forces" worked, "advisory groups" deliberated – and the participants in these movements of governmental creativity did not "know" precisely the "form" to which their movements apparently had attained. They could not know, indeed, for as long as they performed these movements, they moved continuously through their movements beyond any form.

Consilia are the loosest institutions of all. They are fragile, fluid, diffuse. They exist to the extent that they are desired. If the persons who make them no longer keep meeting, they disintegrate as snaply as they emerged. They are what is made as *consilia*. They produce what is made through *consilia*. They are the perfect instruments of government, of governing attuned to the agenda of governing. They *are* governing.

Le mouvement qui déplace les lignes. In fact, *consilia* do not really "exist." They have but a floating existence. We call a commission "commission" and thereby suppose a movement of governmental creativity to denote "something" which is not really there. "Something" is a movement and something only in the mode of language, a mode that reifies necessarily (to denote "something"). Strictly told, the movements of *consilia* elude the term *consilium,* or any term, for that matter. For the movement of a *consilium* is a movement that shifts the lines – *le mouvement qui déplace les lignes.*[74] The lines of a *consilium* – names, functions, figurations – depict a flow of shifts (see Tables 4 – 8,10). What is there does not appear to be there – a *consilium.* yet it is there, to be discerned, but not to be told: pure creativity, pure movement.

We can tell the names of persons, however, the names of participants in *consilia.* And in doing so, we are able to recount the movements of these persons within the movements of *consilia.* And something will appear, something indeed. A shape of stability. The movements of these persons, movements of participants "in" *consilia* within the movements "of" *consilia,* tended to be movements towards an ever closer participation. Through all the diffusion of government – through all the *consilia* – "the" government reappears: in the form of familiar names, the names of leading government

Table 8: Consilia: Boston Government

Boston Fair Housing Commission (1982)

A		A'	
Frank N. Jones		Robert W. Upshur	
Jerome L. Rappaport		("Executive Director")	*Transition Team* (1983)
Anna M. Cole	and		Robert J. Ryan
Janet M. Robitaille			David Mundel
Miquel A. Satut			Lisa Savereid
			Micho F. Spring
			Susan Allen
			John Vitagliano
			Paul Grogan
Boston Public Library (1983)			Robert McCloy
Thomas Boylston Adams		Rev. Spencer M. Rice	George Regan
Rev. Michael Haynes		William V. Shannon	Lowell Richards
Doris Kearns-Goodwin		Arthur F. F. Snyder	Arthur Shea
Philip J. McNiff		Robert R. Spillaine	Dennis Morgan
Bettina A. Norton		Micho Spring	
Paul Parks		Sam Bass Warner Jr.	
Ithiel Pool		James V. Young	

---

[74] Cf. Chapter 1, note 48.

Table 9: Consilia: Boston Government

Frequency of Participation in Consilia (Tables 1 – 5)				
Micho Spring	Andy Olins	Lowell Richards	David Rosenbloom	Robert Ryan
8	4	4	4	3
Martha Goldsmith	Kathy Kane	Dennis Morgan	David Mundel	George Regan
3	3	3	3	2
Jack Murphy	Brian Dacey	Phil Zeigler	William McNeill	Raymond Torto
2	2	2	2	2
Newell Cook	Lisa Savereid	James V. Young	Jorge Hernandez*	Richard Hill*
2	2	2	2	2

* Person not holding position in the White administration.

officials (see Table 9). They represent, as they indicate an increasing frequency of participation in *consilia,* a flow of shifts forming a "government." Within the movements of governing, within *le mouvement qui déplace les lignes,* a few persons were drawing lines – the lines of government.

5 Institutionalist Politics

Issue government is the quintessential mode of governing. It is the movement of governing which translates political creativeness into institutional practice and makes the institutional practice follow the process of creativeness all the while. Issue government "institutionalizes" political creativeness – that the creativeness will not be purely intentional. And it upsets the institutionalization – that the institutionalization will not stifle the creativeness.

However, government cannot proceed through this mode alone. It has to exist also in the modes of continuity and stability, being one and the same government – "The Government of Boston" or "The Federal Government," for example – through the passage of time.[75] And it has to cope with issues that do endure much time, if not forever.[76] Neither requirement is met by the transitory institutional events of issue government. What is needed is something else: solid, regular, lasting institutions.

---

[75] Governments borrow money, for instance, due to be paid back only in 10, 20, or 30 years. To do this, they must have a continuing existence beyond the comings and goings of administrations.

[76] Such issues are: the division between the poor and the rich, the threat of war and the fragility of peace, the unequal distribution of political power.

Table 10: Consilia:

BOSTON COMMISSION AGAINST DISCRIMINATION

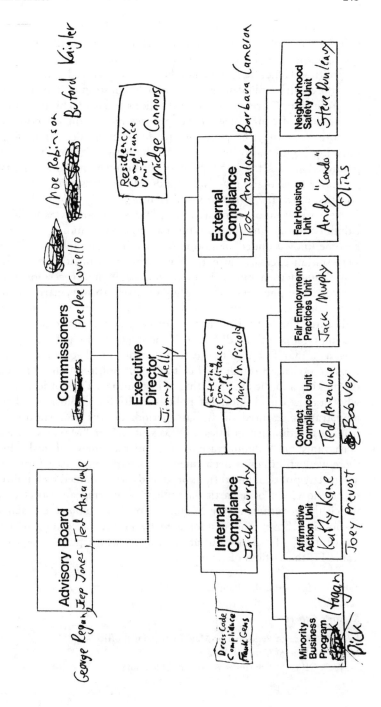

But solid, regular, lasting institutions constrain the creative politician. If in a society politics should reign, that is social creativity, the government through which politics is pursued, ought to be a reflection, not the condition of politics. Hence it should not be institutionalized too firmly. What then does the creative politician do? Submit to the constraints of institutions and betray his profession? Or revolt against institutions and reveal his incompetence?

He does of course neither. He pursues institutionalist politics. Or, to put it more accurately, he continues to do what he does, pursuing politics, in pursuing politics also — and not to the least — through the institutions of politics. He uses the institutions of government not only as *instruments* of politics, but also as *modes* of politics. He governs *with* institutions. And he governs, especially, *through* institutions.

As a result, another paradox of politics appears — as it did in the White Administration. One part of the paradox has, among students of politics, become known under the notion of "overinstitutionalization." As the notion suggests, an excessive growth of governmental institutions is discerned and it is thought to hamper, if not to suffocate, the process of politics. If it is regarded as a phenomenon standing for itself, this hypertrophy of institutions does indeed seem to cumber politics with a governmental structure much too elaborate. The institutionalization of politics appears to have gone awry. But the impression will be different, if the hypertrophy is being grasped as what it is: as a manifestation of creativity. Institutionalist politics is the pursuit of creative politics through the institutions of politics. Politics is being made by the making and the manipulating of institutions. The "office" of the politician who practices institutionalist politics multiplies explosively. The White Administration featured, in its late period, dozens of institutions originating from institutionalist politics: "Offices of ..." or "Mayor's Offices of ..." or "Programs" or "Administrations" or, under a somewhat misleading name (for there were still the line departments) "Departments" (see Table 11). Each was a perfectly political institution: produced and sustained by a political purpose, to be the vessel of a particular policy, projecting an aspect of government which the government (the Mayor) wanted to emphasize. Each was a mode of politics chosen and manipulated by politics according to its modes: an "institution" of politics, but an institution which politics kept changing (see Table 11, the Offices of ... *or* ...).

Table 11: Institutionalist Politics*

Mayor's Offices

Mayor's Office of Personnel or Mayor's personnel office
Mayor's Office of Cultural Affairs
Mayor's Office of Consumer Affairs and Licensing

Offices

Office of Policy Management or Office of Program Management and Evaluation or Mayor's
Office of Management

Office of Program Development or Office of Planning and Development or Office of
Development or Office of Policy Development

Office of Public Service or Office of Public Service and Information

Office of Public Information

Office of Public Safety

Office of Fiscal Affairs

Office of Communications

Office of Neighborhood Services or Mayor's Office for Neighborhood Services or Office
of Neighborhood Services and Programs or Office of Planning and Neighborhood
Services

Office of Public Celebrations

Office of Property Equalization

Office of Governmental Relations or Office of Intergovernmental Relations or Office of
Federal Relations

Office of Consumer Affairs or Consumers Council

Office of Theatre and Art or Office of Theatre District Conservation or Mayor's Theatre
District Committee or Office of Theatre District Coordination

Office of the Bicentennial or Office of Boston Bicentennial

Office of Substance Abuse or Office of Drug Abuse Prevention or Council on Drug Abuse

Office of Housing or Mayor's Office of Fair Housing

Office of Energy Conservation or Energy Office

Office of Human Rights or Boston Commission on Human Rights

Office of Information on Classification

Office of Criminal Justice Staff or Mayor's Office of Criminal Justice Staff or Mayor's
Office of Criminal Justice

Office of Boards and Commissions

One-Stop Business Office

Minority Business Office

Public Safety Office

Equal Employment Opportunity Contract Compliance Office

Programs

Neighborhood Business Program or Neighborhood Business District Program or Neighborhood Business Office

Housing Improvement Program

Administrations

Community Services Administration

Rent Control Administration

Manpower Administration

Employment and Economic Administration or Employment and Economic Policy Administration

Departments

Youth Opportunities Department
Department of Federally Funded Agencies
Public Celebrations Department
Commerce and Manpower Department
Model Cities Department
Department of Neighborhood and Human Services
Community Services Department
Environmental Department

* Table 11 lists institutions which ermerged in the White administration in addition or parallel to the regular city departments. Their existence and their (various) names can be traced through documentary sources (*City Record,* budget lists, newspaper reports, directories, government reports); however, a few offices did not survive the planning stage.

The paradox of institutionalist politics is this: an hypertrophy of institutions obstructs, as it seems, all political creativity; yet, political creativity, pursued institutionally, produces an hypertrophy of institutions. The White Administration was compelled in its late period, to publish "guides" to the government of Boston.[77] The Byzantine growth of offices (and other such structures) threatened to overwhelm everyone, outside and inside the government.[78] The guides — not unsurprisingly — provided only a temporary relief.[79] The practice of institutionalist politics continued and thus did the paradox.

6 Axial Configurations

A government is movement, and none of the patterns it appears to describe does really represent it. Whichever pattern we observe — persons forming a

---

[77] Cf. G. T. Nedder, ed., A Business Community Guide to City Hall, op. cit.; H. Roth, B. Dacey, R. Ryan, Boston Guide to Development, op. cit.
[78] The editor of the *City Record,* the official chronicle of Boston's municipal affairs, is responsible for compiling the *Official Directory,* a selective and indeed frequently obsolescent list of governmental institutions in Boston that appears once or twice a year in the *City Record.* In 1981 the then editor, Arnold J. Epstein, was asked how he would tackle his truly difficult task. "Oh," he said, "I just notice in the newspaper from time to time that there is a new office, so I call them up and ask them: are you the new office of so and so? — And once every year I check whether they are still there." (Source: Interview.)
[79] Only a couple of months had passed since the *Boston Guide to Development* had been published in 1981, and it had already become necessary to release an *Update.*

government, issue government, a government institutionalized hypertrophically — a final form of government we do not find. In following the
movements of government we may, at one point or other, think the movement
could not go any further. Here, here is the "framework" of government, the
"system" through which persons we call "politicians" perform, in handling
purposes we call "policies," a particular genre of actions we call "politics."
Besides the flow and confusing fluidity of our perceptions, we may conclude,
we now have a structure of things, of things political, which absorbs all our
discoveries and problems. Movements of government? Well, there is the
"political system." There are the "uses" to which it is put: planning, bargaining, decision making, policy making. And there are the users: interest groups,
bureaucrats, elected officials, citizens, parties. Movements of government?
What movements other than a system of government being applied to, to what
it is applied?[80]

To questions which we do not ask we do not find answers. If, in the
pursuit of the movements of government, we have stopped pursuing them —
being preoccupied with a "system" instead —, we do not indeed discern any
further movement. We look at politics as if politics suited our categories. And
we "discover" what is obvious: our categories suit politics.[81]

But we must not get trapped in the circle of learnedness that proves but
itself. There is still the original, the classic possibility of observing in the
reality of persons and things patterns which we have not observed before.
We were engrossed in digesting previous perceptions, patterns of creativeness
in the process of creativity we call "government," and the government we
had observed had not ceased to be a government in movement. We had
considered patterns of government, and the movements in which alone we
find government had gone on. Our perceptions were incomplete or rather

---

[80] Cf. the similar reflections supra, pp. 24, 78 f., 94 f., 209 f. — In his study on French local
politics Pierre Grémion wrote: "[...] la science politique, dans le contexte français tout
au moins, n'est pas davantage en mesure de fournir les outils intellectuels adéquats pour
explorer les dimensions du système politico-administratif local. [...] La tradition française
ignore la notion de *local government*. [...] En France, la notion de gouvernement local
ńa pas de sens: on n'y conçoit qu'une *administration locale*. [...] L'étude de la structuration du pouvoir local est inexistante dans la science politique française, tout
se passant comme si l'absence de pouvoir politique local rendait illusoires ou de
peu d'interêt les phénomènes de pouvoir local. Lorsque le politologue s'intéresse aux
problèmes locaux, il analyse plus souvent les facteurs locaux que les acteurs locaux.
C'est-à-dire que pour lui, les phénomènes locaux n'ont guère d'autonomie propre et ne
prennent leur sens qu'en référence à l'ensemble national." (*Le pouvoir périphérique*,
op. cit., p. 158 – 9.)

[81] Cf. supra, p.

incomplete by necessity. A government is movement, but movement, and thus it eludes all attempts at seizing it "completely." All what we really know of a government, is this: it is a movement of creativity and we discern this movement only in pursuing it.

A government institutionalized hypertrophically — the pattern of government we considered last — offers a situation particularly expedient for a further pursuit of government, the movement of creativity. A hypertrophy of institutions does not, of course, bother the political executive who brings it about in governing through institutionalist politics. But what is the situation of all the other persons who, as government officials, have to work within this growth of institutions? Does it not look, to them, like a labyrinth where the ways of political action they can go mostly are dead ends rather than courses of creativity? And is not the political executive, too, but a frustrated mayor or frustrated governor or frustrated president, finding the own government entangled, from all sides, in a maze of hundreds of other governments?

The government officials experience the growth of institutions as a labyrinth. But they apply themselves in the labyrinth to a particular movement: to government along the lines of contacts. The political executive is very often the head of a government struggling with a myriad of other governments. But he applies himself in the maze of other governments to a particular movement: to government along the lines of linkages, conjunctions, joint approaches. The political and hence creative actors in government deploy a pattern of government which I propose to call the construction of "axial configurations."

To construct an axial configuration, it is necessary either to sway, apart from one's own institution, one or more other institutions in the governmental maze, or to know as an ally (or as allies) one or more other persons in the labyrinth at a place (or at places) other than one's own. Normally, one's partners in the construction of an axial configuration tend to their own affairs. They are partners potentially, just contacts one has cultivated carefully, or colleagues to whom one has been obliging, or institutions upon which one has acquired a controlling influence. Within the geography of governments they are located dispersively, here and there, just where one could find and tacitly "recruit" them, and none is associated with all through any formal organization. In the ordinary course of governmental affairs there is no trace of a configuration.

A configuration actually occurs only through a movement of creativity. An actor in government realizes that he or she needs or wishes positively to get "something done." But there is the edifice of government, labyrinthian, inhibitive, restrictive. It thwarts the creativity to which the actor in government aspires. The actor, however, has not been idle. He or she has in the edifice one or more partners whose support and assistance he or she can enlist. The actor aligns himself or herself with his or her partner(s). They form an axis of action that cuts through government: through the red tape, the barriers of bureaucracy, the labyrinth of institutions, the inertia of officialdom. The actor and his or her partner(s) have constructed an axial configuration along which they are now able to move "things" in the government and to move the government to do what they want to have done through the government. A movement of creativity has occurred: government in the form of an axial configuration.

In the sphere of interests which the White Administration pursued axial configurations were often the crucial pattern of government. Configurations were constructed by the Mayor, mayoral aides, agency heads, and middle-level administrators. They involved, exclusively or jointly, partners in the municipal government of Boston, the state government of Massachusetts and/ or the federal government in Washington, D. C

Axial configurations within the Administration. The telling example of the configuration which involved the Mayor, the Court, and the Boston Redevelopment Authority will be discussed in detail in Chapter 5.[82]

Axial configurations aligning Boston and Massachusetts. "Boston" and "Massachusetts" as entities of politics do not relate to each other very favorably. If there is a relationship, it is notoriously antagonistic.[83] To the White Administration (as to any Boston government) the deployment of axial configurations was all the more indispensable, Boston being legally as well as financially under the sway of the Massachusetts Legislature.[84] The antagonism between the city and the state remained, nevertheless, and efforts at constructing an axial configuration at the top level were only exeptionally succesful. The exceptions to be noted were successes which the Mayor had. He built an axis of action through strong personal relationships with two Presidents of the Massachusetts Senate, with Kevin B. Harrington and his successor, William B. Bulger. At the lower levels, however, administrators and political aides, on both sides, managed to establish "lots of liaison," as one of them put it.[85] Pragmatic politics, that is "technical grounds," dictated the need to

---

[82] Cf. infra, p. 301 ff.

[83] Cf. supra, p. 145 f. − Cf. also the editorial "These twelve men," published in the *Boston Globe* on November 5, 1981. The opening sentence of the editorial runs as follows: "Twelve members of the city's delegation to the Massachusetts House of Representatives are endangering the quality of life, if not the lives themselves, of the 563,000 people who live in the city."

[84] Cf. the *City of Boston Code*, op. cit.; and infra, note 105.

[85] Source: Interview. − Mayor White admitted that he never worked too hard to influence the Boston delegation in legislature, although he had done many favors by giving jobs and handling complaints of constituents. (Source: Interview.) − Cf. also the passage on

construct axial configurations that bridged the chasm between Massachusetts and Boston.

Axial configurations aligning Boston and Washington, D. C. In the era of American Politics during which the White Administration existed, cities in the United States became increasingly tied in with the organization and policies of the American Federal Government. There were the laws, programs, and provisions pertaining to a national urban policy;[86] there were the "iron triangle," the "intergovernmental lobby," the "policy community" formed by an intertwinement of political actors from both sides, the local and the federal.[87] And there were axial configurations, our present concern.

Boston did not stand aside. On the contrary, the city made Uncle Sam, to some extent, paymaster of Boston (see Tables 12–14). It exploited the new "fiscal federalism," diligently and adroitly.[88] Boston of course had advantages, as regards its position within the web of local-federal relations. Washington swarmed with graduates from Harvard, MIT, Amherst, Tufts, Boston University, Wellesley, Brandeis, and the other universities in the Boston area. Many preserved fond memories of Boston, and thus were favorably predisposed to

"Levers for effective State action," in: R. Hollister, T. Lee, *Development Politics: Private Development and the Public Interest,* Washington, D. C., The Council of State Planning Agencies, 1979, pp. 53–54.

[86] Cf. Committee on Banking, Finance and Urban Affairs, House of Representatives, 96th Congress, First Session, *Basic Laws and Authorities on Housing and Community Development,* Rev. through Jan. 3, 1979, Washington D. C., U. S. Government Printing Office, 1979, Part II: *Basic Laws and Authorities on Community Development,* esp. Intergovernmental Cooperative Act of 1968, p. 885 ff.; Department of Transportation Act (Excerpts), p. 1033 ff.; Housing Act of 1949 (Title I, as amended, "Urban Renewal"), p. 1103 ff.; Housing and Community Development Act of 1977 (Excerpts), p. 1047 ff.; Demonstration Cities and Metropolitan Development Act of 1966 ("Model Cities Program," Excerpts), p. 1167 ff.; Demonstration Cities ... Act ("Historic Preservation," Excerpts), p. 1183 ff.

[87] Cf. Chapter 3, notes 74–76; and R. L. Lineberry, "Policy Analysis and Urban Government: Understanding the Impact," *Urban Analysis,* Vol. 5, 1978, pp. 143–154. – When the Federal Government started the Model Cities Program, a flow of staff from the BRA to the Model Cities Administration took place. "The HUD proposal," a senior official in the BRA maintained, "was written by BRA people." (Source: Interview.)

[88] The Mayor's Office and a number of other city agencies never failed, for instance, to employ on their staff people of special skills: people experienced in the political-bureaucratic art of "grantsmanship." A series of good appointments in this area helped the city to know about new federal grants before anyone else knew about them or to be very quick in submitting applications, quicker than others. Boston was often successful with its applications in Washington simply because it had submitted the best-prepared application.

Table 12: Public Capital Expenditures in Boston, by Financing Source, 1962 – 1977 (in millions)

Source	Public Schools	Urban Renewal	Water and Sewer	Highways and Streets	Mass Transit	Airport and Port	Municipal Buildings	Health and Hospitals	Misc.	Total
City of Boston	$192	57.6	50.8	61			84.4	80.9	90.4	617.2
Regional and Local Authorities			$30	109	137	395			15.5	686.5
Commonwealth of Massachusetts	$69	11.2	4.2	74						158.4
Federal Government		$270	135.5	97	115	24		7.3	35	683.6
Total	$261	338.8	220.3	341	252	419	84.4	88.2	140.9	2,145.7

Source: Boston Redevelopment Authority, *Boston, Present and Future; Background Information for Infrastructure Planning*, June 1983.

requests, proposals, or calls for assistance submitted to them by former classmates or old friends who worked for the government back in Boston. The city greatly benefitted from numerous axial configurations built on this fertile ground.[89]

Table 13: Federal Grant Funds to Boston: 1968, 1972, 1976, 1978
        (in current dollars, in millions)

	1968	1972	1976	1978
Fiscal Assistance			41	28,85
Manpower	6,65	18,67	27,01	39
Urban Development	25,94	29,80	54,99	61,99
Education	5,81	9,98	13,37	15,10
Human Services	4,78	13,95	14,08	13,59
Public Safety	0,38	2,23	5,42	3,87
Total	43,56	74,63	155,87	162,40

Source: L. Flanagan, *New Directions in Federal Grant Funds to Boston, 1968–78*, BRA, May 1980, p. 6.

Table 14: Total Expenditures by the City of Boston: 1968, 1972, 1976, 1978
        (In current dollars, in millions)

Fiscal Year	Total Expenditures
1968	409
1972	576
1976	855
1978	870

Source: A. Ganz, G. Perkins, *Performance of Boston City Government, 1967–81*, BRA, April 1981, p. 7.

Then the city's government in the federal capital could activate the metastases of the Kevin White Party, axial configurations which I have already described.[90] At the Washington end of these configurations the city continually

---

[89] However, the axial configurations had often to be rebuilt and rebuilt again. "People move all the time," a senior planner in the BRA observed. He therefore kept a special file on his contacts, and recorded each of their movements, a change of position, a change of address, in order never to lose his hold on an extremely versatile network.

[90] Cf. supra, p. 146.

maintained a special office, providing an institutional focus for the Boston lobby in Washington.[91]

Above all, however, Boston — represented by the appropriate person — could again and again proceed along an axis to Tip O'Neill, Speaker of the House, and construct with him (or at least his office) an axial configuration that moved the Federal Government to be concerned with Boston's concern and to render the desired decision or action. The city, furthermore, was able to build, though on a smaller scale, configurations in conjunction with other "Bostonians" in Congress, Senators Edward M. Kennedy, Edward W. Brooke, and Paul E. Tsongas, especially. Finally, we should note, of course, that an axial configuration aligning Washington with Boston often included not only one but several partners. In the case of the "Boston Plan," for example, the White Administration established a configuration of linkages which made *tout Washington* pay attention to Boston.[92]

7 The Appearance of Power

Government is a movement of creativity, the movement of politics unto its form: the existence of a human community. Through government, the movement of creativity, government, the political institution appears. Through government, the political institution, government, the reality of power appears. The movement of creativity has become creation. With the appearance of the power its government is, a human community acquires its ability to exist. It acquires the virtue of life. It comes into being as it becomes an agent of itself, able to pursue intentions ("policies"), to engage in judgments ("politics"), to exercise a will ("decisions"), and to take appropriate measures ("actions"). The appearance of governmental power is, as regards human communities, the ultimate creative act. It turns the communities, products of creativity, into sources of creativity. They themselves continue, as agents of themselves, the movement of creativity from which they originate. Government is a movement of creativity towards creativity. It releases creativity: the appearance of power.

---

[91] Heads of Boston's office in Washington were: Samuel V. Merrick, Stephen P. Cohen, Mark Shields, John Drew, Kevin Kelly. It usually comprised a staff of three persons, as in 1977 and 1981, for instance.

[92] Cf. M. Ferber, E. Beard, "Marketing Urban America: The Selling of the Boston Plan & a New Direction in Federal-Urban Relations," *Polity*, Vol. XII, No. 4, Summer 1980, pp. 539–559; J. B. O. 'Connell, *The Boston Plan*, op. cit.

In the present study this appearance of power has been described. The study, a movement of inquiry into government, followed the movement of government that government is. It discerned the essence of government: a movement of creativity towards creativity, a movement a number of persons (the "few," the "government") perform, towards a movement numbers of persons (the "many," a "city," a "society") pursue. This essence of government has conventionally been called "power." The notion has repeatedly been used in the course of our study, and there is no reason now to discontinue the practice. As the study proceeds, it is a closer analysis of the appearance of power — the reality of power — at which it aims, not a notional discussion.

The preceding paragraph included a statement which is not entirely exact: The study followed the movement of government that government is. It would have been more correct, if it had read: The study followed the movement as well as the movements of government. And it would have been truly accurate, if it had said: The study followed the movement of government as well as the movements within the movement of government. What was studied, indeed, was not just one movement, but a myriad of movements of a myriad of persons, configurations, organisms, institutions. All these movements formed a government, to be sure, and thus could be analyzed as the movements of one government. But the reality of this government, on the other hand, consisted precisely in these movements. Government, the reality of power, appeared. But whose power exactly was it that did appear? The government's power? Not really. The government was a myriad of movements of a myriad of persons, configurations, organisms, institutions. "It," the government, were rather "they": the persons forming the government. Whose power was it then that did appear? The power of all persons forming the government or the power only of one? The power of which some owned the greater part and others just bits and pieces? Who really did it, the government? Who exercised power, the power of government?

Who, indeed? The Mayor, upon retrospection, disclaimed the received opinion:

> The truth is, it looked like I governed with an iron hand, but in fact I delegated an enormous amount of authority and even let the guys get publicity. You knew who Dennis Morgan was. You knew who Kathy Kane was; who Bobby Ryan was; who Ira Jackson was. I did hold power, but I gave it out and let people run with it.[93]

Run they did, so far, so far apart, the power of government appeared to have dissipated. In 1982 a would-be successor to the Mayor observed:

---

[93] *BG*, Feb. 10, 1986.

"A potential developer doesn't know whether to go to [Theodore] Anzalone or [Robert] Ryan or to take a walk with the mayor."[94]

Who, then, exercised power, the power of government? Who indeed?

8 The Limits of Power

An autocrat by being autocrat restrains the autocracy. Mayor White was an autocrat. And he was no autocrat. Extrinsic barriers continually constrained the growth of his autocracy; there existed, in the political world where he staged the autocracy, numerous and, more importantly, insurmountable limits to the Mayor's power.[95] However, the problem of the Mayor's power thus is only half explained. There were still other limits to the autocracy. These limits did not exist before or outside the autocracy. They were intrinsic limits. They were the limits inherent in the autocracy, in the very process of its constitution.

Mayor White built an autocracy. But he built it as a purely political autocracy. The Mayor, no doubt, indulged in Caesarean tastes, and he sought situations of politics where he, the Mayor, was the center of interest and action. Those among his critics, however, who charged Mayor White with having taken Boston on an "ego trip," employed their critical words much too loosely. A glimpse upon modern political history would have sufficed to realize the misconstruction of the charge. If Mayor White had followed the example of the rulers who really drove their people to the abyss of their Ego, he would have striven to make himself the principle of life.[96] He would have tried — by an all-encompassing revolutions, as it were — to transmute not only Boston but all human reality into a pure manifestation of Kevin White.[97] This Mayor White certainly did not do. The Mayor of Boston instigating a

---

[94] James Michael Connolly, former City Councillor and, at the time he sought to succeed Mayor White, Suffolk County Registrar of Probate; *BG,* Nov. 23, 1982.

[95] Such limits were: the classic fragmentation of power in the American republic; the legal and political power held over Boston (and its Mayor) by the Massachusetts Legislature; the persistent financial fragility of Boston, due to a structure of taxation which makes the city chronically dependent upon political and economic actors outside the city; the critical alertness of the people, amplified, channeled and focused by the media, and numerous citizens groups. Cf. also: R. L. Turner, "What Makes a Mayor?" *The Boston Globe Magazine,* Nov. 13, 1983.

[96] As totalitarian rulers in this century tried to do.

[97] On the idea of an all-encompassing revolution by which man would transform all reality into an *imago hominis,* cf. T. Schabert, "Revolutionary Consciousness," *Philosophical Studies* (Dublin), Vol. XVII, 1980, pp. 129 – 142.

revolution of the world? It sounds ridiculous. Mayor White was an autocrat, and a typical one at that. But he was no megalomaniac, no despot.

The Mayor built an autocracy. And this autocracy did not derail into a private obsession of the autocrat.[98] Why? Mayor White acted as a politician and a politician wishes to govern, not to redeem his Self. Government, the pursuit of political creativity, required its condition: it required the power of creativeness. This power, however, was not to be found somewhere. It had to be made, to be produced as the first creative effort of all other efforts of government. With his autocracy Mayor White made — and continued to make — the creative effort from which his power of government derived and upon which it continually depended. Seeking the power of government, the Mayor first of all sought the power of creativeness: a concentration of power (a mode of government) by which power (government) would turn into creativity.

A concentration of power, however, by which power turns into creativity, releases a plurality of power. Mandarin Quealy, in requesting action from commissioners, often invoked the authority of the "Mayor." But whose "authority" was it? The authority of the Mayor, Kevin White, or the authority of the Mandarin acting the Mayor? When Martha Goldsmith, the Mayor's adviser for urban and economic development, was asked to explain what her responsibilities were, she answered: "I give directions." And when she was asked the additional question: "To whom, for example?", she replied: "Ryan." To her, it appeared to be obvious what she did when she talked to BRA director Robert J. Ryan and other members of the agency. "I formulate the Mayor's position." But whose "position" actually did she formulate? The Mayor's position? Or Martha Goldsmith's position?[99]

Under "ordinary" arrangements of government, an answer to questions such as these would easily be found. The lines of responsibility are clearly drawn and one must only follow those lines, if one wanted to come at the person or the body of persons who "is" the "authority" in the given matter — a decision, a request, a directive. However, the Mayor's autocracy was anything but ordinary. The lines of responsibility were confused, like everything else in the fabric of this regime. A chaos of power reigned: the Mayor's power, deliberately confused.[100]

The confusion of power enhanced the presence of the Mayor, the person, to the omnipresence of THE MAYOR — THE MAYOR upon whom, as the "one" power in the general confusion of power, all government converged.

---

[98] On the process of an autocracy derailing into the private obsession of the autocrat (*mónarchos*), cf. Plato, *Politeia* 573 d – 576 b.

[99] Source: Interview.

[100] Cf. supra, p. 33 ff.

The Mayor, Kevin White, wished THE MAYOR very much to "exist." Everyone should know that the Mayor and his government governed. And everyone should know that the Mayor governed his government. Then everyone would also know that only one person really governed: Kevin White, THE MAYOR. No one, however, would be able to check up on THE MAYOR. For THE MAYOR did not exist. The Mayor, Kevin White, the person, he of course was "there" — there in the confusion of power through which he had produced his autocratic presence: THE MAYOR.

The Mayor taught everyone to believe that THE MAYOR decided on everything. And thus he enabled himself indeed to decide upon everything, to the extent that everyone believed in THE MAYOR deciding on everything.

The ingenious contrivance of autocracy. And yet, autocracy on its edges, too. THE MAYOR did not exist. Yet, THE MAYOR did "exist," bringing the autocracy to bear, whenever someone from the government, the Court — not the Mayor, Kevin White — invoked the authority of the "Mayor," formulated the "Mayor's position," or simply said: "The Mayor wants this."

The "ploy," as a senior official called it, worked; very often. A decision was made, or a request, a directive was transmitted. But it was not the Mayor, Kevin White, who spoke. It was THE MAYOR — whoever THE MAYOR, in the given case, was. The autocracy thrived. And the autocrat did not own all of its power. He had to share THE MAYOR with others. Or else there was no MAYOR, and no autocracy.

9 Power in the Twilight

The power of government lies somewhere, but where precisely it lies, this question has always, in every instance, to be settled anew. It is as fluid as the field of persons a government is, to be found here and there, having as only perpetual site the status of its movement. The Mayor, Kevin White, head of Boston's government, marked of course a place where the power of government lay — often, but by no means all the time. Every government is a government in movement, but his government was movement throughout. Being the autocracy that it was, a perpetual pursuit of power defined its essence. The Mayor sought and drew up to THE MAYOR every bit of power his government meant.[101] The power of government was the movement of power: from everywhere a movement of power to THE MAYOR and through THE MAYOR a movement of power everywhere. But — THE MAYOR did not exist.

---

[101] Cf. supra, p. 25 f.

What existed was a field of persons – the government, the Court, other people[102] – and among these persons the movement of power took place. The power of government lay in a multiplicity of movements among numerous persons. It was by all those movements that its reality was made. However, if we should wish to pierce it completely (and retrospectively at that), we would have to search for each movement (not knowing their number and not having traces of all), and we would have to survey each movement (not knowing more than the fact that it had occurred). We would aspire after a "total" knowledge and we would perform but vain attempts, for the same reasons as the ones which I have explained at an earlier instance.[103]

The Mayor, Kevin White, realized the power of government. And everyone else who could and did act THE MAYOR, in some matter, at some moment, realized the power of government, too. But he or she, or they, did not appear. THE MAYOR appeared. Yet, THE MAYOR did not exist. Where, then, did the power of government lie? Always somewhere – in the office of the Mayor or somewhere in the twilight of THE MAYOR.

In the aftermath of "Proposition 2 $^1/_2$"[104] Boston's government had to decide upon various measures of a difficult and complex austerity program.[105] Not a few persons participated in the deliberations concerning the program. Only one person, however, made the decisions by which it took shape. The Mayor, Kevin White.[106]

The Mayor, the Court, the BRA had committed themselves to rejuvenate the NORTH STATION area in central Boston.[107] A group of planners in the

---

102 Cf. supra, p. 49 ff.

103 Cf. supra, pp. 171 – 177. – In his study of the "capitalist process" Joseph Schumpeter observed: "It is not always easy to tell who the entrepreneur is in a given case. This is not, however, due to any lack of precision in our definition of the entrepreneurial function, but simply to the difficulty of finding out what person actually fills it. Nobody ever is an entrepreneur all the time, and nobody can ever be only an entrepreneur. [...] The leading man may, but need not, hold or acquire the position that is officially the leading one. [...] Also, the entrepreneur may, but need not, be the person who furnishes the capital." (J. A. Schumpeter, *Business Cycles. A Theoretical, Historical, and Statistical Analysis of the Capitalist Process,* New York – London 1939, p. 103.)

104 Cf. Chapter 2, note 22; *BG,* Oct. 31, 1980.

105 *CR,* Dec. 15, 1980; Sept. 14, Nov. 11, 1981; April 4, 1982; *BG,* March 12, May 1, 2, 3, 6, 8, 9, 13, 31, 1981; June 1, Sept. 29, Oct. 1, 20, 22, 30, Nov. 4, 6, 18, 19, Dec. 19, 20, 22, 23, 24, 25, 30, 1981; Jan. 1, Feb. 2, 1982.

106 Source: Interview.

107 Cf. BRA, *New Directions for North Station,* [Boston] 1977; BRA/Moshe Safdie and Associates, Inc., *A Development Plan for North Station District,* s. l., s. d.; BRA, *North Station Final Project Report, Urban Renewal Plan,* [Boston] 1980; BRA, *North Station Final Project Report, Supporting Documentation,* [Boston] 1980; BRA, *Commercial Area*

BRA wished to engineer the rejuvenation. They knew where the power of government lay: the Mayor decides upon everything. So they acted THE MAYOR deciding on everything. As their method they chose a gradual set-up of *faits accomplis:* "We hire the consultants. We write the legislation [to be approved by the State Legislature]. We interview the architects. We talk with the Convention and Tourist Bureau. We talk with the Chamber of Commerce."[108] The Mayor would still find himself in the middle of a project having been prepared around him. But the circle of matters to be decided upon had been closed. The Mayor would eventually reach a decision. A decision which THE MAYOR already had made.[109]

In early 1981 the Boston Landmarks Commission approved of protecting the United Shoe Machinery building in Downtown Boston from being destroyed. The Commission designated the building a landmark. Mayor White, however, vetoed the designation. That is, THE MAYOR vetoed the designation. The Landmarks Commission received from the Mayor a letter. It put on the designation a veto that had been exercised by Mandarin Spring.[110]

10 Power and Representation

The reality of politics cannot be politics' reality. We want to know, for instance, "who" holds the power of government. The accurate answer would be: a field of persons. And the answer, if rigorously true to the reality of

---

Revitalization District Plan: North Station, [Boston] 1979; City of Boston, *Boston Enterprise. A Program for Neighborhood Job Creation and Economic Growth,* [Boston] 1981; *CR,* Oct. 20, 1980; *BG,* May 23, Aug. 17, 1980; June 28, July 12, Aug. 6, 1981; June 8, 1983.

[108] Source: Interview.

[109] Cf. infra, p. 258.

[110] Source: Interview. – On the controversy concerning the United Shoe Machinery building, cf. *BG,* June 8, July 20, 1980, March 15, 16, 1981. – Power in the twilight had also its amusing side. A senior assistant to the Mayor once found out that someone had received "meat for the Mayor." A man from the – Market came in to state that he had been having trouble in getting help from some city department. He thought that he deserved consideration because he had been giving meat to the Mayor every week for two years – prime beef. The mayoral aide did a double take. He didn't think the story was true. But White wasn't in his office, so he couldn't ask him outright. Who comes by to pick up the meat, he asked the visitor. When he heard the name, he knew that the Mayor wasn't getting the meat. So he called up the guy and asked him to come into his office. I understand that you have been helping the Mayor with meat pick-ups, he said. The guy replied with a lot of "well-uhs." It stopped. (Source: Interview.)

government, would have a baffling adjective appended to it and then would read: a variable field of persons. A "variable field of persons," however, cannot "govern." Politics' reality is distinct or it is, to us, no reality. In complying with the obligations of citizenship — obeying the laws, paying taxes, being involved with politics — we do not envisage a "variable field of persons." We envision the tangible presence of politics: City Halls, State Houses, State Capitols, Congress, the White House. And we envision the palpable figures of political power: City Councillors, Mayors, State Legislators, Governors, Senators, Presidents. The heads of government, in particular — "The Mayor," "The Governor," "The President" — represent, in our eyes, the power of government. Where they are, there is government: politics' reality.

This is "true" and it is not true. It is "true" in the mode of representation, in the mode of that things and figures which, to us, constitute politics' reality. It is not true in the mode of politics, in the mode of that movements, a myriad of movements, which define the reality of politics. If we want then to know "who" holds the power of government and pursue the question, we arrive but at two answers. The true answer tells us that the power of government is all movement and therefore is only to be found where it just lies but never lies only where it is just found. And the "true" answer tells us that the movement of power comes to a rest through representation: in a city, the City Hall *is* the seat of government and the Mayor *is* the head of government. In knowing the "true" answer we begin to understand that we should know the true answer, and in knowing the true answer we have understood the "true" answer.

11 The Assumption of Power

Bluntly put, the Mayor could not do without THE MAYOR (nor could a Governor or a President do without THE GOVERNOR or THE PRESIDENT). A myriad of movements could not have occurred as the movements of "one" government, if the "One" had not been there, marked by THE MAYOR. The Mayor, however, could not be THE MAYOR all alone. There were others, quite a few, who built up THE MAYOR. They acted THE MAYOR and thereby the "One." They made the movements of government that passed the Mayor's grasp the movement of one, the Mayor's government. The Mayor and THE MAYOR stood in each other's stead.

Mayor and MAYOR, then, could not be allowed to drift too far apart. But what could the means of cohesion be? The simple yet most effective tools of mytho-physical politics: the paraphernalia of power. There was the spatial arrangement of the Mayor's physical presence, for instance. Everyone, whether at home or at work, occupies some space, simply by living. We may adorn our house or we may furnish our office exquisitely, but we will hardly think of mystifying the square feet which we regularly use, the rooms of our house or the space in an office building which is ours. We may wonder at the spatial modality of our existence, trivial yet fundamental as it seems to be, but we will hardly try to disappear from those square feet which define our spatial existence and where we are present mostly: our house and our office.

But "we" are not Mayor and our name is not White. The Mayor who used the office where THE MAYOR dwelled could not be physically present as everyone. The particular architecture of the mayoral floor in City Hall and the row of secretaries assembled there like a palace guard[111] transformed the square feet which Mayor White used as an office into the sanctuary of a remote potentate, into that "Mayor's Office" mystified whereto Kevin White disappeared while he was right there, in his office. THE MAYOR dwelled not too far away from the Mayor. In fact, the veriest place for verifying the Mayor's presence in contrast with THE MAYOR had been used to blur the distinction.

Mytho-physical politics conceals the spatial identity of political power. Its whereabouts become power's own secret, an *arcanum imperii*.[112] In seeing that Mayor and MAYOR did not drift apart in the letters and memos which the "Mayor" wrote, a special assistant to the Mayor[113] administered another *arcanum:* the personal identity of the "Mayor" who signed the Mayor's letters and memos. The assistant controlled the process of the Mayor's communication. He checked "everything" first, letters, memos, notes, and only then did the Mayor sign.[114] Of course, we might think, the Mayor, that is Kevin White, signed merely his, that is the Mayor's, messages. However, he signed THE MAYOR's messages, too. THE MAYOR's signature, as the assistant to the "Mayor" understood it, preceded the Mayor's signature.

Mytho-physical politics makes a riddle of the question, who has signed what. Signatures seem to contain secrets.[115] In capturing all the telephone calls coming in on the mayoral line, the secretaries manning the Mayor's phone guarded yet another *arcanum,* the *arcanum* proper: Kevin White. All

---

[111] Cf. supra, p. 12 ff.

[112] Cf. infra, p. 261 ff.

[113] Christopher Bator, as the Mayor's special assistant in his fourth term.

[114] Source: Interview.

[115] An agency head observed: "I receive letters from the Mayor, signed by him. I do not know whether he has written the letter. And I do not know whether he knows what the letter says." (Source: Interview.)

that the Mayor as MAYOR was, would have been gone, if just Kevin White had answered the phone, saying nonchalantly: "Hello. Glad you call. What can I do for you?"[116] But the telephone guardians fenced Kevin White.[117] They did not bother the "Mayor" or anyone else in the Mayor's Office with calls which they deemed to be insignificant. At the callers they threw empty phrases. THE MAYOR's fence enclosed the Mayor.

Mayor and MAYOR did not drift apart. Indeed. Mayor and MAYOR were not allowed to drift apart. There were the telephonists, the aides, the secretaries — the guardians. They were guardians, because they had assumed a special power: the power of mytho-physical politics. Only the presence of the Mayor as MAYOR sustained this power. But it did not belong to the Mayor. It belonged to THE MAYOR. That is, it belonged to the guardians who watched over the presence of the Mayor as MAYOR. It was their power. The power of mytho-physical politics grew from the power accumulated by Mayor White. Yet, it transcended it: it made Kevin White, the autocrat, the subject of the autocrat's power.

The autocracy produced within itself islands of power which the autocrat could not reach. Mayor White once called a meeting of all department heads. He asked the officials to give him the information about the favors which their departments had done for State Legislators and City Councillors. He wanted to be able to use these favors for political negotiations. The department heads, however, were not very forthcoming. Six months passed, and the Mayor still had not received the required information. In fact, he never received it (although he continued to complain, at least once a year, about this failure to control favors). State Legislators and City Councillors had their own contacts in city departments, mostly employees at the second or third echelon, from whom they could get favors. These lower-level employees felt flattered, of course. Elected officials showed them little attentions. And they minded the use, naturally, which they could possibly make of their political connections. They kept the connections for themselves.

And the Mayor kept wondering at the islands within his realm that he could not reach.

---

[116] Mayor Collins, the predecessor of Kevin White, had in his office a private phone line through which he received calls from a considerable number of people whom he had given the line's number. He personally answered the calls coming in on this line. — Mayor White, on the other hand, accepted unexpected calls, as an associate remarked half seriously, half mockingly, from a very few people only, according to this priority: Ann Landers, Herb Gleason, the U. S. President (if it *was* the President). He did *not* accept calls form the Massachusetts Governor or from Senator Edward Kennedy. (Source: Interview.)

[117] Cf. supra, p. 15.

12 *Arcana Imperii*

Politics, if it is pursued creatively, involves the use of secrets. It cannot occur as a quest for creativity, if it is an absolutely public quest.[118] The creativity to be achieved requires *arcana imperii* − secrets of government.

Mayor White, for instance, never communicated any "plan" of his that would have laid out the future development of Boston. Urban critics reproved him for his failure to convey a comprehensive "vision" of the city. Should Boston, as it passed through the crucial epoch of a "renaissance," be preserved as a city of Old World qualities, or should it fully be developed into a hypermodern American megalopolis? Developers remonstrated with the Mayor and other members of the government about the dangling development decisions with which in Boston they were perpetually compelled to deal. Would the construction of further office towers in the Central Business District be advanced or not? And could not, in an act of rational planning, a blueprint be established that fixed the total number of towers to be built within a certain span of time, the exact construction dates, the sites, as well as the height and design of the buildings?

Neither reproofs nor remonstrations could move the Mayor and the members of his government to issue the desired plan or blueprint. They resisted the pressure to forsake the creative animus of politics. City Hall would not have disclosed just a "plan," if it had released, for instance, a document prescribing in every detail the further development of Boston over a period of 10 years. Real estate prices, for example, would have considerably been affected by the document. In the city areas marked for development the prices for real estate would have risen; in the areas which had been left out they would have fallen. The plan, "rational" as it might have seemed to be, would have played straight into the hands of real estate speculators. All risk of speculation would have been eliminated by a government telling everyone: "This site is scheduled for development in 1986, that site for development in 1991, and that other site for no development at all." Concerning land reserves to be built up or to be set aside for public purposes, the government would have abandoned its "natural" advantage of knowing its intentions prior to anyone else. Once it had published a development plan, the price dynamics ensuing from the publication of the plan would make the assembling of land much more costly, as it would make the preservation of an existing land reserve much more difficult. The government would have lost almost all flexibility for negotiating a concurrence of private and public interests. Land

---

[118] Cf. supra, p. 194 ff.

owners, developers, citizen groups, preservationists, other actors in government would know what it planned and thus be adversaries, in cases of conflict, who could always content that the government stick to its plan and give in to the demands they deduced from that plan.

City Hall would have disclosed a plan. And it would have made itself a prisoner of the plan.

Secrets of government preserve and sustain government. Or, to put it more analytically, secrets of government (*arcana imperii*) preserve and sustain the movement of creativity in which government consists. They are methods (*rationes*) of statecraft, as Arnold Clapmarius explained in his classic study *De Arcanis rerum publicarum* (Bremen 1605), which conduce to the public good (*bonum publicum*) and the conservancy of the commonwealth (*conservatio rei publicae*).[119] In refusing to issue a blueprint of Boston's future development, Mayor White and the members of his government refused to impair

---

[119] A. Clapmarius, *De Arcanis Rerum publicarum*, Bremen 1605, p. 9: "Arcana Rerumpublicarum sic definio; esse intimas & occultas rationes sive consilia eorum qui in Republ. principatum obtinent, tum ipsorum tranquillitatis, tum etiam praesentis, Reipubl. status conservandi, idq; boni publici causa, [...]" − Cf. further: L. Hölscher, *Öffentlichkeit und Geheimnis. Eine begriffsgeschichtliche Untersuchung zur Entstehung der Öffentlichkeit in der frühen Neuzeit*, Stuttgart 1979 (esp. the passage on Clapmarius pp. 131−135); S. P. Huntington, *American Politics: The Promise of Disharmony*, Cambridge, Mass. 1981, p. 75: "Power remains strong when it remains in the dark; exposed to the sunlight it begins to evaporate."; p. 76: "Power revealed is power reduced; power concealed is power enhanced."; p. 78: "Because power is less legitimate in the United States than in other cultures, greater efforts have to be made to obscure it. It becomes necessary to deny the facts of power in order to preserve those facts. [...] the most effective exercise of power is the concealment of power; to cover up power becomes the first imperative of power."; p. 79: "A vicious circle develops: because power is abhorrent, it must be concealed, and because it is concealed, it becomes even more abhorrent. The pervasive threat of publicity to power produces the pervasive need for secrecy and deception about power. Because exposure is more devastating in its consequences in the United States, secrecy becomes more necessary and more difficult to achieve." − Ch. Krauthammer, "When Secrecy Meets Democracy," *Time*, Dec. 8, 1986, p. 46: "Americans abhor secret covenants secretly arrived at because they smack of Old World realpolitik, a way of doing business that the American Republic was to make obsolete. [...] Americans may not like being a superpower, but they have no choice, there being no one else to carry the burden. So they have to face the responsibilities of power. And one of them is the necessity for secrecy." − In contemporary politics *arcana imperii* abound, of course. "[...] the Boston Plan [cf. supra, p. 35] was purposely developed in secret [...]" (M. Ferber, E. Beard, "Marketing Urban America ...", op. cit., p. 552). − Michel Schifres and Michel Sarazin were given the opportunity for gathering extraordinarily detailed information about the French Presidency under François Mitterrand, but they were unable to determine the costs of official travels: "Il nous a été impossible de connaître

their ability to creatively act upon the course of events and the activities of people that were shaping the city. They rejected a "rational" request detriment to the logic of government. As a movement of creativity government occurs only through fluidity, elasticity, flexibility. It must be an open movement, open to as many possibilities of acting and reacting as possible, open to as many and as differing ideas as possible, open to as great a diversity of proposals and projects as possible. A blueprint would have closed the movement of government (in the area of urban development); it would have prevented government still occurring.

The intrinsic openness of government wants an external shield of secrets. In not communicating everything that it possibly could communicate (and that it generally was expected to communicate), the White government maintained itself as a true government. It preserved its options, its ability to negotiate, its readiness to act. It preserved, in short, the freedom of politics.

The City Council, hostile to the power of government from which it was largely excluded,[120] repeatedly tried to interfere with a principal movement of creativity in the government, the Mayor's fluid personnel policy.[121] The Mayor and his aides upheld the movement by keeping it dark.[122]

In the Spring of 1981 the government said that Boston would soon be bankrupt. A severe financial crisis faced the city, no doubt. And Boston depended, once again, upon the goodwill of the Massachusetts Legislature,

---

le coût d'un voyage officiel." (*L'Elysée de Mitterrand,* op. cit., p. 123.) – In their study of governmental committees in the United Kingdom, a "secret garden," B. W. Hogwood and Th. T. Mackie report that Prime Minister Margaret Thatcher, according to estimates, "had established about 25 standing committees and about 110 ad hoc committees in her first five years of office." But: "The British government admits only to the existence of four standing committees of the cabinet (and even the announcement of these and the names of their chairmen was an innovation established by Mrs Thatcher in 1979). However, the revealed information does not divulge the important role played by subcommittees of these standing committees or ad hoc cabinet committees, to say nothing of the small, informal groups of ministers [...]. Unlike recent practice in other Commonwealth countries, the membership and even the existence of most cabinet committees is not made public. [...] the very existence of all other than four standing cabinet committees is kept secret [...]" (The United Kingdom: Decision Sifting in a Secret Garden, op. cit., p. 38, p. 45).

[120] Cf. infra, p. 16.

[121] Cf. supra, p. 37 ff.

[122] The Mayor's policy staff, for instance, was financed for a while from federal funds, that is, from Model Cities funds. Plans were undertaken to keep this secret from the City Council for as long as possible. The financing was done by an internal transfer of funds which was not too visible.

the body politic notoriously inimical to the city.[123] The news that a bankruptcy of Boston was imminent conduced considerably to elicit creative responses to the crisis, on all sides. The fall of Boston was averted and its government could rejoice over the true financial condition of the city which it had not fully revealed.[124]

The tax basis of Boston is rather small.[125] In the late 1970's members of the government became aware of a demographic development through which the tax basis could possibly be enlarged. A greater number of well-to-do persons (later to be called "yuppies") who had previously been expected to prefer suburbia, "returned to the city." The government, housing and tax experts in the White administration thought, could further this development by facilitating the construction of the kind of dwellings which these new urbanites sought, so-called condominiums in particular. Apart from the jobs that would be created by the new housing construction, the city would benefit from the new urbanites in a direct way: through their influx the number of residents in Boston would grow who paid higher property taxes. Within the government a reasoning of this kind took place. But it was conducted secretly. The changes brought by the yuppies formed a very touchy issue, as public

---

[123] Ian Menzies, a leading editorialist of the *Boston Globe* put it bluntly: "It must be remembered that three people, occupying three offices, run Massachusetts – King, Bulger and McGee. They are the people who can reform the nation's most distorted state tax system." ("Don't Blame All on White," *BG*, Febr. 23, 1981.) – On the bankruptcy story, cf. *BG*, March 15, May 5, 1981; *NYT*, April 11, 1981; M. Segal, "Why Boston Should Go Bankrupt," *The Real Paper*, June 4, 1981, pp. 11–12. – Shortly before "Proposition 2 1/2" (cf. supra, p. 60) – principal cause of the financial crisis – passed, the City received a letter from Gerald M. Cohen, Chairman of the Committee on Taxation of the Massachusetts House of Representatives, informing the City about the impact of "Proposition 2 1/2" upon its budget. The letter bears no date and is addressed perfunctorily. Its content could not be more prosaic: "City of Boston Dear Sir; Proposition 2 1/2 will be appearing on the November ballot. If it passes, the amount of revenue that your community would lose is: 1. property tax revenue loss – $ 311,990,200   2. auto excise revenue tax loss – $ 11,264,211   3. total loss – $ 323,254,411. If you have any questions, please do not hesitate to contact me at my office. Sincerely, Gerald M. Cohen, Chairman, Taxation Committee."

[124] Cf. *BG*, May 16, 22, June 12, July 2, 4, 1981.

[125] Cf. City of Boston, Office of the Mayor, *Boston's Tax Strategy. The Fiscal Experience of the City*, May 1974; *BG*, Jan. 11, 1977, Special Report, *Financial Plight of Bay State Cities;* BMRB, Special Report, No. 77, *Tax-Exempt Property: A Boston Burden*, July 14, 1978; T. Sheehan, "Getting and Spending. Living in the Material World. The Mayor and the Budget Crisis," *BPh*, April 1980, pp. 13–14; S. Tompkins, "Proposition 2 1/2 – Massachusetts and the Tax Revolt," *The Journal of the Institute for Socioeconomic Studies*, Vol. VI, No. 1, Spring 1981, pp. 21–32; *BG*, May 11, 1981.

catchwords such as "gentrification" and "displacement" showed.[126] While the government chose, in its public stance, not to relate the ongoing change in the composition of Boston's population to the persistent problem of the city's very limited sources of tax revenue, it silently yet carefully looked at the progress which the yuppies made in improving Boston's tax basis.[127]

13 *Simulacra Imperii*

Governments exist through images. They are images. All government is imagery, figurative product of the human imagination. In the nature of government illusion and reality dwell side by side, the one being an ingredient as essential as the other. There are secrets of government, because government, the creative mode of politics, is a "secret." The reality of government, creativeness, defies the common mode of human perception. It is the great *arcanum* of politics (and, of course, political science).

A "government," we say, conducts the affairs of a city, a state, or a nation. This is not true. And it is true. The government, as we know, is made by persons and these persons, not the government, conduct the affairs of the city, the state, or the nation. The government about which we talk is an image, a figurative product of our imagination. We know, no doubt, that a process of social creativity occurs by which a city, a state, a nation is governed and we know the persons (to some extent) who carry the process. But we do not see the process as process, nor do we grasp the creativity as creativity. We discern only figurations of the process, of the creativity. We recognize our images of what takes place: "government," "politicians," "parliaments," "electorates," "presidents," "governors," "mayors." Government occurs. It is true. And it is not true. A process of social creativity occurs. A process of social creativity of which we know, through its figurations, our images, that it is a process of government. All that occurs, occurs, to us, but in the mode

---

[126] Cf. BRA, *Condominium Development in Boston*, Sept. 1980; Sh. B. Lasks, D. Spain, eds., *Back to the City. Issues in Neighborhood Renovation*, New York 1980; J. R. Dinkelspiel, J. Uschenik, H. L. Selesnick, *Condominiums. Conversion's Effects on a Community*, Boston 1981.

[127] BMRB, *Condominium Conversions in Boston. A Significant Tax Benefit to the City*, Special Report No. 94, April 1, 1980. – That Boston "would benefit as areas of low property-tax productivity were replaced by new structures paying more in taxes," this was an assumption upon which the Boston Planning Board already built its "General Plan for Boston – 1950." Cf. A. Rabinowitz, *Non-Planning and Redevelopment in Boston: An Analytic Study of the Planning Process*, Seattle, Dept. of Urban Planning, University of Washington, Sept. 1972, p. 6.

of imagery. Government is the great *arcanum* of politics. And it is the great tableau of politics. The *simulacra imperii,* the images of government, tell the story told by the *arcana imperii,* the secrets of government.[128]

14 The Government and the City

The White government saved Boston from dissolution, day by day, during the sixteen years that it existed. Every government, in being government, preserves the human community whose government it forms. The alternative to government is not some other condition of social life. The alternative is chaos.

A human community exists through its government or it does not exist.[129] It is a creation, and government is the act of creation. This condition of a human community, be it a village, a town, a tribe, or an empire, involves two aspects of which one in general is not sufficiently appreciated. The act of creation, on the one hand, is the primary act of creation through which a community has come into being. It is the act of foundation that every human community remembers periodically, at the public rituals every year by which it celebrates the historical event of its beginnings. The act of creation is also, on the other hand, the continuing act of creation through which a community, in its existence, is sustained. It is the act of perpetuation that the government of a community incorporates, as the body by which the community has become and is its own agent. The government of a community is the community's life: *creatio continua.*[130]

It is this aspect of the condition under which human communities exist that in general is not sufficiently appreciated. The lack of appreciation is especially noticeable in America, by comparison with Europe, for instance.[131]

---

[128] On the *simulacra imperii,* cf. A. Clapmarius, *De Arcanis Rerum Publicarum,* op. cit., Book VI.

[129] Cf. supra, p. 45.

[130] Cf. E. Voegelin, *Order and History,* Vol. I, *Israel and Revelation,* op. cit., p. 16: "To establish a government is an essay in world creation. When man creates the cosmion of political order, he analogically repeats the divine creation of the cosmos. The analogical repetition is not an act of futile imitation, for in repeating the cosmos man participates, in the measure allowed to his existential limitations, in the creation of cosmic order itself."

[131] The experience that human communities are very fragile, that empires, kingdoms, states, nations rise and fall, emerge gloriously and disappear altogether, this experience is an essential part of the European experience. The American Republic has gone through crises, even a civil war; but it is still the Republic founded two centuries ago. For

And yet, American governments, too, continually create America and the thousands of communities of which America consists. Of course, the immediate praxis of government — elections, policymaking, legislation, administration — tends to overshadow the true process of government, the *creatio continua*. And this effect is particularly compelling in America where the praxis of government is overwhelmingly absorbing. Besides, there is no better manifestation of government, the *creatio continua*, than a very engrossing praxis of government — as the story of the White government attests.

Government, seen as *creatio continua*, poses yet another paradox. It distracts us, to the extent that we are attracted by its manifestations, from pursuing the essence of these manifestations, the true process of government. It appeals to our curiosity and it leads our curiosity astray. The White government drew everyone who watched Boston politics into this paradox, very deep.[132] It produced a spectacle of politics that captivated all one's curiosity. And it diverted one's attention from the pith of the spectacle, by the very excitement which the spectacle conveyed. In the immediate acts of looking at the spectacle flowing on incessantly, the deeper message of what it meant remained largely hidden — not surprisingly, the drama as drama sufficiently filled one's mind. In absorbing one's interest, however, the spectacle stirred an interest in the nature of the absorption. It provoked reflective acts of looking at it not only as a spectacle that amused but also as a spectacle that appeared to tell something. What did it tell that it could be so fascinating?

It told the story of government, the *creatio continua*. The spectacle of politics which the White government produced carried the message of government being a continuing act of creation. As a spectacle, the spectacle concealed this message. As an absorbing spectacle, however, the spectacle suggested the message. The White government was a government: a government that preserved, like any other government, the human community whose government it formed. And it was the White government: the government that manifested through itself the process of creativity by which governments are governments. It performed government: the continuing act of creation through which Boston, in its existence, was sustained. And it performed this act in the most paradigmatic way: as pure creativity.

The White government achieved Boston's *creatio continua*. And it achieved something more: it made Boston a city in creativity.

Americans it is hardly conceivable that America, the American Republic, might some day disappear and be replaced by another form or other forms of political organization.

[132] On the other paradoxes which we encountered, cf. supra, pp. 9–12, 192, 194, 224, 232 f., 242, 250, 267, 307.

Chapter 5
The City, Space of Creativity

κινούμενά τε αὐτοῖς καὶ ἑστῶτα

things in motion are also things at rest

Plato, *Theaetetus*, 181 e

The Spatial Process of Society

1 Philosophical Argument: Politics and Space

All politics happens in the mode of space. All the space wherein human beings exist is this space in the mode of politics. Human beings, through their bodies, are spatial beings. They occupy space, places they fill. Every person is at any moment at a place, at the one place which at the given moment is the particular place of this particular person. This place, then, while it is held, is held exclusively: my place is not your place and your place is not my place.[1] Simply by being bodily beings human beings are indeed social beings, if only in the negative mode that your body cannot be at the same place where my body is and my body cannot be at the same place where your body is. Under the spatial condition of their existence human beings cannot but relate to each other. The space wherein they exist is a space apportioned. To be what they are means to be in a common space where each defines, by being where he is, "his" space and the space of all others. Human existence is a spatial existence and as a spatial existence it is a social existence.

Human beings do not stay continually in the same place, of course. Nor is the partition of the space wherein they exist in any way permanent. They move and they stay; they stay and they move. They congregate and they separate; they separate and they congregate. They mark out spheres of property, influence, or dominance and they engage each other over the extent of these spheres. They mend their quarrels, settle their strifes, and they proceed to seek and to possess property, influence, and dominance.[2]

Human existence is movement and this movement describes space. Or, to put it more painstakingly, the life of human beings is a myriad of movements

---

[1] Cf. Rousseau's classic statement: "Le premier qui ayant enclos un terrain, s'avisa de dire, *ceci est à moi*, et trouva des gens assés simples pour le croire, fut le vrai fondateur de la société civile." (J. J. Rousseau, *Discours sur l'origine et les fondemens de l'inégalité parmi les hommes, Oeuvres Complètes*, III, *Du Contrat Social, Ecrits Politiques*, Paris 1964, p. 164.) – For an English translation, cf. J. J. Rousseau, *The First and Second Discourses, Together with the Replies to Critics and Essay on the Origin of Languages*, ed., transl., and annot. by V. Gourevitch, New York 1986, p. 170: "The first man who, having enclosed a piece of ground, to whom it occurred to say *this is mine* and found people sufficiently simple to believe him, was the true founder of civil society."

[2] Cf. E. Voegelin, *The Ecumenic Age*, op. cit., pp. 115 ff., 212 ff.

and these movements describe the space wherein they exist. Theirs is a spatial existence and there is indeed their space. It is the space wherein they exist: the human space. Yet, their space, the human space, is not a space like any other. It is a fluid space, as fluid perennially as the human movements through which it is described. Human existence is a spatial existence and as a spatial existence it is a social existence. Yet, in being a social existence as a spatial existence it is a social existence of continuous suspense. Its structures are anything but solid and its bounds are anything but firm. The forms it has, they will change eventually. The arrangements it consists of, they will wear out inevitably. It is and it is not, as the space through which it is arises and dissolves, dwindles and materializes with the movements of human beings seeking and leaving, leaving and seeking places of space wherein they exist.

Space, then, produces politics. It is politics. It makes human beings political beings. It makes them pursue their existence as a social existence in continuous suspense. And a social existence in continuous suspense, of course, is a political existence. Human beings exist spatially, and they exist politically: they have to deal with each other perennially, as they relate to each other perennially in the flux and reflux of their spatial movements. Human beings exist spatially, and they exist politically: their spatial existence, as social existence, is all negotiation and agreement, quarrel and conflict. They exist in space. But there were no space wherein they could exist if politics did not create it.

2 Cities

All human space is political space. Wherever the spatial movements of human beings occur, they imply definitions of space produced in the mode of politics. We may think of a vast expanse of land in which but small flocks of nomads roam in search of their subsistence. Politics would follow space, even then and there. The spatial movements of the nomads, as irregular as they might be, reflect in space a character of space that transcends the pure reality of space. They suggest a map of social movements: movements of the nomads towards each other, away from each other, a crisscrossing or a parallelism of their paths, different directions, common itineraries, passages peculiar to each. No one will have drawn the map, of course, and hardly anyone will "know" the map (only a curious anthropologist from outside would be likely to "discover" and thus, inevitably, to destroy it).[3] Yet, the map will be there,

---

[3] The anthropologist who "discovers" a "primitive" people yet "unknown" destroys the cosmos wherein this people existed before he arrived. The questions which he asks makes the "primitive" people wonder at things which they had never thought about

produced by the nomads through their movements that seem only to be movements in space while they are also movements of politics: contacts, diffusion, linkages, detachment, junctions, segregation, rivalries, solidarity, battles, peace.

The lesson of the nomads, it could be reaffirmed by countless other examples. In the course of human history the political character of human space has emerged in very many forms. Politics is everywhere the meaning of human space.

There is only one form of human space, however, in which the meaning of human space — politics — has itself taken on the form of space. This unique form of human space is the city. Cities, as they emerged, have made politics visible. They are the spatial presence of politics; they are politics transposed into space. In a city the meaning of human space is obvious. Spatial movements of human beings occur and the space wherein they occur explains what occurs: the spatial event of human beings living in community.[4]

The emergence of cities has given mankind its memory. Human beings find their fulfillment in the life of their community; the *polis*, common action towards the common good, is the essence of human existence.[5] And yet, this chief thing about human beings does not have a natural vessel as do other human things. Wealth appears in property or money; force figures in bodily strength or weapons; thought shines in words and writings. But where and how is action, the political action of human beings visible?[6] A *polis* convened

---

before — the cosmos becomes shattered from within. The arrival of the anthropologist draws the "primitive" people into the orbit of the modern world — the cosmos becomes shattered from outside. — Kevin Lynch, in the context of architectural planning, put the problem succinctly: "Analysis is not neutral science: any observation changes something." (K. Lynch, *Site Planning*, Cambridge, Mass. 1962, 1971, 2nd ed., p. 96.)

[4] Etymology, of course, captures the point factually: *politics* derives from *polis*, the Greek word for *city*. (Cf. *Pauly's Realencyclopädie*, "Polis," "Politeia." And the founders of political science, Plato and Aristotle, developed their science, of course, in observing the conduct of urban (hence political) affairs in the Greek cities of their time. Cf. further: E. Voegelin, *Plato and Aristotle*, op. cit.; V. Ehrenberg, *Der Staat der Griechen*, Zürich–Stuttgart 1965, 2nd ed.; D. Sternberger, *Drei Wurzeln der Politik*, 2 vols., Frankfurt 1978; Ch. Meier, *Die Entstehung des Politischen bei den Griechen*, Frankfurt 1980.

[5] Cf. Aristotle, *Politics* 1252a24 — 1253a2, 1253a30 ff., 1323b31 ff. — Modern social scientists do attest to the classic insight Aristotle formulated. When Frederick Wirt, author of *Power in the City. Decision Making in San Francisco* (Berkeley 1978), defines, for instance, the city as "a complex set of transactions [...] among its citizens" (p. 5), he says more than he means.

[6] On the special nature of human action, cf. H. Arendt, *The Human Condition*, op. cit., Chapter V ("Action").

vanishes the moment people leave the *agora;* public discourses proceed along the mysterious ways of a people's interior dialogue, between a people talking and the people listening to itself;[7] and decisions have of course the reality of their consequences, but no reality of their own other than the people who made them.[8]

Space is the answer. A people is *polis*. And it is city. It forms itself through common action towards the common good. And it forms itself setting itself down in its spatial existence. It is word and it is space. The words of the *polis* pass as swiftly as they are spoken. The space of the city and the people within that space last; they last as long as their site is remembered. While it does not appear, human action does not disappear. It is preserved through cities, through the space human beings have shaped in common action towards the common good. While its words soon are heard no longer, the *polis* does have a story. It is the story told by the city. The story of politics.

3 Urban Architecture: The Construction of Society

Cities are telling the story of politics, and politicians are caring about cities. The good politician knows that the story cities tell is his own, the politician's story. They constitute the most enduring record of his craft: politics transposed into space.[9] Politicians therefore also like to be architects, city architects

---

[7] Cf. Plato, *Politikos (The Statesman)* 309c – 311c; A. Schütz, *Der sinnhafte Aufbau der sozialen Welt. Eine Einleitung in die verstehende Soziologie,* Wien 1932, Frankfurt 1974, pp. 186 – 193 (section on "Subjektiver und objektiver Sinn. Erzeugnis und Zeugnis"), pp. 282 – 290 (section on "Die mitweltliche soziale Beziehung und die mitweltliche Beobachtung"); M. Polanyi, *Personal Knowledge. Towards a Post-Critical Philosophy,* London 1958, 1973 (Paperback Edition), pp. 204 – 211 (sections on "Communication," "Transmission of Social Lore," and "Pure Conviviality").

[8] Cf. infra, p. 320 f.

[9] Cities represent not only one of the oldest but also one of the most resilient forms of human society. Empires rose and fell, rulers emerged and perished – and Athens or Beijing, Jerusalem or Rome persisted. – It is most interesting to note, furthermore, that the city as political society has again and again emerged and reemerged independently at different places and at different times. Cf. M. Hammond, *The City in the Ancient World,* Cambridge, Mass. 1972, p. 153: "The Greeks do not appear to have been inspired initially either to develop cities or to devise for them a new form of urban government by any direct impulse from the older civilization of the Middle and Near East." – And p. 339: "[...] even for North Italy, pending more evidence, it seems reasonable to regard the rebirth of municipal self-government as a phenomenon unmotivated by Roman antecedents and parallel to the same revival in more northern countries, in fact, as a

especially. They pursue politics as spatial politics and thus through its essence. In constructing the city, they construct the *polis*. In shaping urban space, they shape political space. In being architects of the city, they are the architects of society.

Architecture is social construction. The politician as architect constructs society. And society constructs itself, through the innumerable architectural decisions and acts which its members make and perform every day. People continually participate in the architectural construction of society, simply by doing what they do in everyday life: by renting an apartment or by buying a house; by moving from the old neighborhoods in the inner city to the suburbs or by moving back to the city; by using the automobile or public transport on the daily trips between the dwelling and the workplace; by spending evenings in moviehouses, theaters, concert halls, restaurants or by staying mostly at home with the family, the hifi or the video set; by patronizing the small shops in the neighorhood rather than the department stores in the shopping mall; by filling the streets of the city on weekends with their voices and bustle, or by fleeing every Friday night from the city to the country.[10]

Each of these decisions or acts is a social as well as an architectural decision or act. It affects the unending social process through which the arrangement of society in space is continually composed and recomposed. And, conversely put, it affects the architectural forms through which society has taken on its spatial existence. It bears upon the spatial formation of society. And it bears upon the social formation of space.

A society's architectural construction is the same process as the process of its life. Architecture is the intimate portrayal of society. It reveals its essence. It makes society speak; through houses, streets, monuments, landscapes, vistas and perspectives, styles and ornaments, through colors and shapes. Cities resound with this political language of architecture, it is nowhere better to be heard than here. Through the architectural language of cities our rulers know and express the "secret" of their rule: they rule by representation. Through the architectural language of cities we all know the "mystery" of society: this is the community within which we exist. Society is an abstraction,

---

result of independence from powerful territorial overlords and of the development of wealth from extensive commerce [...]. At present, therefore, it cannot be proved that any municipal institution had a continuous existence in Western Europe from the late Roman Empire through the Germanic invasions and the consequent Dark Ages until towns again came to life in the later Middle Ages."

[10] Cf. M. Castells, *The City and the Grassroots. A Cross-Cultural Theory of Urban Social Movements*, London 1983, p. XVI: "Every day in every context, people acting individually or collectively, produce or reproduce the rules of their society, and translate them into their spatial expression and their institutional management."

it needs exposition, else it is mute. The city, in contrast, speaks, through the language of its architecture:

> In the eye of the Bostonian it [Boston] is something which peculiarly belongs to himself, and no alien person can ever hope to fitly share the proprietorship with him. Strangers coming may get lost in the twisted maze, or almost as bad, may find themselves continually brought back to their startingpoint; and the Bostonian, looking on serenely, feels his love for the city increased by the pleasing comparison of his own familiarity with it. He never gets lost. He was born and brought up to the labyrinth, and it has no unexplained puzzle for him. Even at three years of age he could run away from his nurse and wander around the seven-sided block and safely find his way home again. And in his grown-up passing to and fro, he has discovered little quiet short-cuts, where he meets so few people that in time he comes to look upon those secluded passages as a sort of peculiar revelation to himself alone.[11]

---

[11] L. Kip, "The Building of Our Cities," in: *Hours at Home* 11 (July 1870), reprinted in: L. M. Roth, *America Builds,* op. cit., p. 420.

The Process of Spatial Creativity

4 The Vision

The architectural quality of society greatly appeals of course to social visionaries. How can the vision of a new society or how can the vision of a renewed society be translated into reality? It is architecture that appears to hold the answer. It carries the promise that a new society could emerge from a new formation of human society, or from an exodus to a new place of existence, or from the foundation of a new city.[12] It bears the hope that a society in decline could be regenerated by a rearrangement of its spatial structure, or by a reconstruction of its physical tissue, or by a renovation of its architectural existence.[13] An architectural vision, it appears, is the promise of a social vision. Do know the spatial form wherein the social form you envision could occur, and you know the road to the reality of your vision.[14]

---

[12] Cf. T. Schabert, "*In urbe mundus*. Weltspiegelungen und Weltbemächtigung in der Architektur der Stadt," in: *Eranos Yearbook 1986*, Vol. 55, Frankfurt 1988, pp. 303 – 347.

[13] Cf. S. Giedion, *Architektur und Gemeinschaft*, Hamburg 1956; G. & S. Jellicoe, *The Landscape of Man. Shaping the Environment from Prehistory to the Present Day*, London 1974; W. Braunfels, *Abendländische Stadtbaukunst. Herrschaftsform und Baugestalt*, Köln 1976; R. E. Reed, *Return to the City. How to Restore Old Buildings and Ourselves in America's Historic Urban Neighborhoods*, Garden City, N. Y. 1979; A. D. King (ed.), *Buildings and Society. Essays on the Social Development of the Built Environment*, London 1980; T. Schabert, "The Decentralization and the New Urban Policy in France," *Urban Law and Policy*, Vol. 7, No. 1, March 1985, pp. 57 – 74.

[14] Cf. E. Lissitzky (ed.), *Neues Bauen in der Welt: Rußland*, Wien 1930; M. Holloway, *Heavens on Earth. Utopian Communities in America 1680 – 1880*, New York 1951; H. Rosenau, *The Ideal City in Its Architectural Evolution*, London 1959; R. R. Taylor, *The World in Stone. The Role of Architecture in the National Socialist Ideology*, Berkeley 1974; D. Hayden, *Seven American Utopias. The Architecture of Communitarian Socialism 1790 – 1975*, London 1976; F. Bollerey, *Architekturkonzeptionen der utopischen Sozialisten. Alternative Planung und Architektur für den gesellschaftlichen Prozeß*, München 1977; R. Fishman, *Urban Utopias in the Twentieth Century. Ebenezer Howard, Frank Lloyd Wright, Le Corbusier*, New York 1977; A. Kopp, *L'Architecture de la Période Stalinienne*, Grenoble 1978; H. A. Millon, L. Nochlin (eds.), *Art and Architecture in the Service of Politics*, Cambridge, Mass. 1978; A. Bridgman, "Heavenly Cities on Earth: Urban Planning and Mass Culture in Eighteenth-Century Utopias," in: *Transactions of the Fifth International Congress on the Enlightenment*, The Voltaire Foundation, Oxford 1981; J. A. Leigh, "Space and Revolution: Public Monuments and Urban Planning at the Peak of the Terror," in: *Transactions ...*, op. cit.

For among people as multitude the sluggishness of skepticism usually prevails. Many will discern a crisis: a crisis of government, a crisis of the economy, a crisis of urban life. Yet, for most people the crisis will precisely be the pretext for an indolent anticipation of the imminent catastrophe. Nothing will happen, if the power of a vision does not stall the crisis. Nothing of human importance would ever happen, if the power of a vision did not occasionally encapsule the minds of human beings and enthral them by an irresistible impetus to collective action.

In 1960 the blight of Boston was universally evident and thus for the public mostly a reason to believe that the city was doomed to decay. The party of hope was small, exceedingly small in face of the task to refound a city which seemed to have lost all faith in itself.[15] And the struggle the party

---

[15] Cf. "The Battle for Boston," *The Economist*, March 11, 1961; *Architectural Forum*, Special Issue: Boston, Vol. 120, No. 6, June 1964; W. Mc Quarde, "Boston: What Can A Sick City Do?" *Fortune*, Vol. LXIX, No. 6, June 1964; N. Arnone, *Redevelopment in Boston:* A Study of the Politics and Administration of Social Change, Ph. D. Thesis, The Massachusetts Institute of Technology, 1965; E. C. Banfield, M. Meyerson, *Boston: The Job Ahead*, Cambridge, Mass. 1966; City of Boston − Boston Redevelopment Authority, *Seven Years of Progress. A Final Report by Edward J. Logue, Development Administrator*, Boston 1967; J. W. Rosenblum, *The Boston Redevelopment Authority*, Harvard Business School, 1969; J. Stainton, *Urban Renewal and Planning in Boston*, Boston 1972; A. Rabinowitz, *Non-Planning and Redevelopment in Boston: An Analytic Study of the Planning Process*, Seattle, Dept. of Urban Planning, The University of Washington, 1972; D. Pool, Politics in the New Boston 1960−1970. A Study of Mayoral Policy Making, Ph. D. Thesis, Brandeis University 1974; K. S. Kellerhouse, Redevelopment of the Boston Waterfront, Kennedy School of Government, 1978; R. Memolo, *New Boston: The Politics of Renewal in Boston*, unpublished manuscript; A. Lupo, *Liberty's Chosen Home*, op. cit.; Th. O'Connor, *Bibles, Brahmins and Bosses*, op. cit. − According to the article "The Man With Faith in Boston," published by Victor O. Jones in the *Boston Globe* on July 15, 1966, the party of hope was indeed exceedingly small. It consisted, at the very beginning, but of one man: "There's no particular reason why many people should be aware of this, but this week marks the 10th anniversary of the death of the man who first thought of converting a midtown eyesore railroad yard into what has become our Prudential Center, the keystone to the New Boston. The name, in case you have forgotten it or never heard it, is George F. Oakes, and the date of his death was July 12, 1956. Oh, I know you're going to say that Oakes merely had the idea and that his idea would never have been translated into reality or realty without the work of Mayor Johnny Hynes. Or that without Ed Logue and his genius for extracting money from the Federal government and for handling the City Council there'd be no new Boston. Or that, after all, the actual building of the New Boston took place under the hard-boiled mayoralty of John Collins. Or that without the Chamber of Commerce, or without the Prudential people, or without Boston's business savvy, instead of

of hope waged was two-fold. It had to contend with the party of despair: "Boston has its share of prophets of gloom and doom who think the city is too far gone to be rebuilt."[16] And it had to contend with its own fits of discouragement: "Can Boston really rebuild itself with imagination and beauty?"[17] A third party, meanwhile, stood on the sidelines. Caught between hope and despair, these people wished to be presented with compelling proofs – with the "hard" judgment of statistics – that would relieve them of the doubts which they could themselves not overcome. Was Boston indeed too far gone or did it still hold some promise of recovery? What was the state of the city?

"I suggest that they go and see for themselves," Mayor John Collins, the leader of the party of hope, replied.[18]

Evidence, however, speaks only to those who see the evidence. It is possible infinitely to argue about the blight of a city. It is not possible to argue about the city meant to be in blight. The party of hope discerned in the city of Boston not only symptoms of decay, it discerned also Boston: the idea of Boston as a living city, "rich and populous."[19] It was inspired with a vision and through this vision it saw the evidence. Boston was dying and to death

---

blooming, our city would be withering into graceless decrepitude. And I suppose there'd be a good deal of truth in all this. But the fact still remains that the whole shebang started with Oakes [...]. In the matter of Oakes primacy in the development of the Prudential Center, it's all a matter of record, even though George didn't live to see his dream come true. But back in the early 1950's, Oakes, then a valued operator for R. M. Bradley and Co., tried hard to peddle his idea to Boston developers. He got nowhere. But in May of 1952, he read of the big real estate deal involving the sale of the Empire State Building in New York to a syndicate headed up by Roger L. Stevens. He saw Stevens, sold him on the general idea, and in the next three or four years, worked almost exclusively in furthering the project. A diary of Oakes, which now is in the Bradley archives, shows that from 1953 to 1955, he worked 193 days exclusively on the Back Bay project. There were in that time 161 phone calls with Stevens, 42 conferences with Mayor Hynes, 47 with architects and 110 separate meetings with business leaders. It was he, too, who brought Hynes and Carroll Shanks, president of Prudential, together. [...] How about just a small plaque somewhere in the New Boston for George F. Oakes, A Man Who Believed in Boston?"

[16] City of Boston, *The 90 Million Dollar Development Program for Boston,* reprinted from the City Record, Sept. 24, 1960, s. d.

[17] "The New Boston. City of Ideas 1775 1975", *Boston Sunday Globe,* Febr. 24, 1963, p. 4.

[18] City of Boston, *The 90 Million Dollar Development Programm for Boston,* op. cit.

[19] J. Josselyn, cf. A. Hepburn, *Boston. Biography of a City,* New York 1966, p. 16.

there was no alternative other than the resolution: "Beauty once flourished in Boston. It must again."[20]

And the vision did not seem vain. Other cities had fallen into decline, as Boston had done, and they had put themselves on a course of renaissance. The examples of renewal which they offered helped to sustain the vision of a "New Boston."[21] A vision without paradigms lacks reality; it might be a dreamy conceit. A vision resting upon paradigms to be found in reality does have the quality of truth; it might be possible. The future of Boston had already occurred: in every city that had risen from its decay to its renaissance. And, quite dramatically, the future of Boston was actually occurring, nearby, under the eyes of everyone willing to see. Among the paradigms to be found in reality, New Haven or, more precisely, the story of New Haven's reconstruction formed the one paradigm that strengthened the vision of a "New Boston."[22] There was a city which renewed itself through a renewal of its physical tissue. There was an urban society which revived its sense of a *polis* through a revival of its existence in space: "What is most impressive about New Haven is not its ambitious plans to rebuild and repair itself physically, but the effect that the program is having on people. Because New Haven now has a purpose, it is becoming a community instead of a crowd. This can happen in Boston."[23]

The vision, the vision carried by Boston's party of hope, had indeed the quality of truth. The road to the reality of a New Boston lay open. Architecture led the way. The rebuilding of New Haven formed a paradigm of urban renaissance that would again become true with a rebuilt Boston. And Boston, the reconstructed city, would represent a further paradigm of urban renaissance. The truth of the vision was universal. Boston would renew itself. And it would be, once again, the urban symbol of America: "Once started on its

---

[20] City of Boston, *The 90 Million Dollar Development Program for Boston,* op. cit.

[21] Cf. footnotes 15, 17 and further: J. Q. Wilson (ed.), *Urban Renewal: The Record and the Controversy,* Cambridge, Mass. 1966, esp. pp. 259 – 277 ("Urban Renewal in Boston") and pp. 293 – 335 (on the renewal of Boston's West End); S. B. Warner, *The Urban Wilderness,* New York 1972: St. Thernstrom, *The Other Bostonians. Poverty and Progress in an American Metropolis 1880 – 1970,* Cambridge, Mass. 1973; I. Menzies, "An Upbeat City of Charm, Change," in: *The Dynamic City. Boston at 350.* A Special Supplement, *The Boston Globe,* May 18, 1980, p. 4 ff.

[22] Charleston in South Carolina and Lowell in Massachusetts formed other paradigms. Increasingly, San Francisco became another paradigm for Boston's planners. Cf., for instance, *BG,* June 2, 1983, p. 11: "The model for Boston is San Francisco."

[23] Herbert Gleason in: *BG,* March 31, 1960. – On New Haven's reconstruction cf. R. D. Dahl, *Who Governs?,* op. cit., and R. E. Wolfinger, *The Politics of Progress,* op. cit.

way towards rebuilding, Boston will find all America cheering it on and ready to help. There is, after all, a little bit of Boston in everyone who calls himself an American."[24]

5 Visions and Constraints

It is a universal vision that initiates a process of spatial creativity. The establishment of a society in space equals its foundation. The reconstruction of a society's spatial existence equals its renovation. Both the foundation or the renovation of a society, however, usually involve a large number of individuals. These myriad individuals would not participate in the foundation of a society or in the renovation of their society without a social vision carrying their minds. The community they were supposed to be or to revive had to be a visionary community first, inducing them to make this community eventually. A visionary community is the *causa finalis* of any existing community. A vision of community is the goal "towards" which a community is founded or restored and "from" which therefore its existence or the revival of its existence originates.[25]

In the spatial dimension of a society's existence this principle weighs particularly. A society that will be *built* or *rebuilt*, will be put into a *physical* process which requires, by its very essence, efforts of community. Space as social space will be apportioned, shaped, and structured; and in the space thus produced things will be erected, assembled, and blended into wholes. A process of creativity will occur that will be both physical and social. It could

---

[24] City of Boston, *The 90 Million Dollar Development Program for Boston*, op. cit.

[25] Cf. Aristotle, *Politics* 1252a: "Every state is as we see a sort of partnership, and every partnership is formed with a view to some good (since all the actions of all mankind are done with a view to what they think to be good)"; *Politics* 1253a15: "[...] it is the special property of man in distinction from the other animals that he alone has perception of good and bad and right and wrong and the other moral qualities, and it is partnership in these things that makes a household and a city-state"; *Politics* 1280b30: "It is manifest therefore that a state is not merely the sharing of a common locality for the purpose of preventing mutual injury and exchanging goods. There are necessary pre-conditions of a state's existence, yet nevertheless, even if all these conditions are present, that does not therefore make a state, but a state is a partnership of families and of clans in living well, and its object is a full and independent life." – Cf. further: M. Oakeshott, *On Human Conduct*, op. cit., Chapter 1 "On the Theoretical Understanding of Human Conduct"; H. Arendt, *The Human Condition*, op. cit., Chapter III "The Public and the Private Realm"; E. Voegelin, *Plato and Aristotle*, op. cit., pp. 112–117; idem, *The Ecumenic Age*, op. cit., pp. 244–247.

not occur as a physical process only, nor could it occur only as a social process. The vision of the society to be built necessarily precedes the physical erection of that society; any physical formation of the society would be impossible without a vision of that formation commonly held. The process of spatial creativity is a process of social creativity, for in this process a society builds or rebuilds itself, as its own creation.[26]

While a universal vision initiates a process of spatial creativity, it will not be the sole guide of the process itself, else it will block that very creativeness which it has released. What indeed is spatial creativity, the process of civic architecture, the process of socio-spatial design? Is it a logical process that proceeds from initial assumptions by rational steps to a unique solution? Not quite, for it takes place as an irrational search, conducted over a ground previously prepared by experience, the study of principles, and the analysis of site and purpose.[27] Is it a sequence of events in temporal succession? Not exactly, for the process of spatial creativity appears to occur in quite different temporal modes such as anticipation, synchroneity, and retroaction.[28] Is it a social interaction among certain actors? Not precisely, for the field of actors is diffuse and continually a field of different actors.[29] Is it a projection of physical change in a well-defined area of space? Not really, for the projections vary more often than not and are themselves only parts in a larger process of morphological mutations in the space of a city, of a society.[30]

Processes of spatial creativity occur. Yet they occur — if and when they occur — as unplanned, irregular, fluid, open processes only.[31] Anyone who participates in a process of spatial creativity needs a vision, else he does not "see" what he is creating nor does he "see" why he is creating anything at all. His vision, however, is but one vision among many other visions. He is not alone, he is not the only architectural, hence social "visionary" in a

---

[26] Cf. supra, p. 272 ff. and infra, p. 293 ff.

[27] I adopt an observation from: K. Lynch, *Site Planning*, Cambridge, Mass. 1962, 1971, 2nd ed., p. 249.

[28] In 1968 Hale Champion who was head of the BRA at the time, talked to an interviewer about the planning process and the so-called "infill-program," in particular. He described how "planning" is pursued in different temporal modes (in this case: anticipation and retroaction): "First, the infill program. We're still waiting for Federal approval; yet we've already spent $ 200,000 putting the program together. We had to gamble with time and money if we were ever going to get that program going." (J. W. Rosenblum, *The Boston Redevelopment Authority* (B), op. cit., p. 11. — Cf. also infra, p. 298 ff.)

[29] Cf. infra, p. 284 f.

[30] A splendid example: the continuing morphological mutations of Boston's neighborhoods in the course of the city's history.

[31] Cf. K. Lynch, *Site Planning*, op. cit., p. 246 ff.

society that is continually its own spatial creation. He will never find himself at a starting point from where he might embark upon the actualization of "his" vision. The typical situation is quite different: the participant in the process of spatial creativity will work on a particular project and this work will just be the current contribution to the project in the project's long, often very long history.

Let us consider an example. Let us think of a "planner" who in 1980 has worked on a redevelopment project in Boston, as the *West End Renewal Plan*, for instance, or the revitalization of the *Waterfront*, or the restoration of the *South Station* area, or the *Downtown Crossing Plan*. None of these projects is completed yet. Each is a historical project. The *West End Renewal Plan* has officially been initiated in January 1958, but similar proposals for that area have already been made in the 1940's.[32] The project for the revitalization of the *Waterfront* has been started in August 1964 and the planning for the *South Station* area has begun in the 1950's.[33] The prehistory of *Downtown Crossing* can be traced back to the 1960's when Victor Gruen proposed large pedestrian malls in Downtown Boston. These proposals have not been carried out; but a series of permutations, including a reduction in scale, has resulted in the present *Downtown Crossing Plan*.[34]

What, then, is the situation of our planner or, as he is officially called, our project coordinator? First, his situation is a historical situation; he has not begun the project he is working on, nor is it likely that he will complete it. Secondly, his situation is a participative situation; he may contribute to the project he is working on, but he cannot define it as "his" project. The project is the whole of which the project coordinator is but a part. The planning precedes the planner, and it transcends the planner.

In describing the situation of the planner within the process of spatial creativity I have followed the general practice and have spoken of the "South Station project" or the "Waterfront project" as if it were perfectly clear what is meant by those designations. However, projects in a process of spatial creativity are not only projects of long continuance, they are also the subject matter of frequent permutations. The "South Station project," for instance, was discussed in 1958 in the form of a proposal for a major garage over the

---

[32] Cf. BRA, *Fact Sheets*, 1979, s. l.

[33] Cf. ibid. and footnote 35.

[34] Cf. City of Boston − Boston Redevelopment Authority, *Demonstration Grant Application* [re: Downtown Crossing], May 1980; City of Boston − BRA, *Downtown Crossing*, 1981; City of Boston − BRA, *Background to Planning for Boston's Downtown*, 1973, 1980, 2nd ed.; City of Boston, *Downtown Crossing. An Economic Strategy Plan*, 1983; A. M. Howitt, *Managing Federalism. Studies in Intergovernmental Relations*, Washington, D. C. 1983.

railway tracks; in 1963 it became an "important segment" of a plan for the Central Business District; in 1965 a "South Station Renewal Area" was designated and South Station was included as a "major transportation center" into a *Downtown General Neighborhood Plan;* in 1968 the plan for the Central Business District was abandoned and South Station became a self-contained "mini-project"; other plans that followed put the emphasis on a trade center, commercial facilities, a bus terminal, or a parking garage; in 1972 a larger plan concerning South Station, South Boston, South Bay, Fort Point Channel was considered again;[35] but in 1973 a master plan for South Station as a transportation center was prepared. And in 1980 − our year of reference − South Station is a part of the *Northeast Corridor Improvement Project* which is undertaken by the Federal Railroad Administration; in conjunction with this agency the Massachusetts Bay Transportation Authority and the Boston Redevelopment Authority pursue plans für a *South Station Transportation/Air Rights Development Project.*[36]

Projects in a process of spatial creativity are projects of long continuance and they are the subject matter of frequent permutations. Moreover, they are shifted at some times from one office to another within a governmental agency or from one agency to another in the government or to the office of the head of the government and back to an agency again. In the course of the permutations and shifts, furthermore, a kind of juggling with the different parts of the projects takes place with the effect that quite often an essential component − an "anchor" in the planners' parlance − disappears from one project and reappears in another one.

This plasticity of the projects parallels the fluidity of the social fields which are composed by all those who participate in the process of spatial creativity. As representatives of a city, a state, the federal government, of business firms, of citizens groups deliberate and decide upon a particular project, they constitute a field of configurative action which produces planning acts and planning decisions although its authority is not formalized and although its composition is extremely fluid.[37] Usually, people partake in such a field of configurative action for a much shorter time than the field itself exists. The communication and interaction within the field tends therefore

---

[35] Cf. BRA, *Report on the Proposed Purchase and Development of South Station,* 1964; BRA, *South Station Urban Renewal Project, Environmental Impact Report,* 1976.

[36] Cf. U. S. Department of Transportation, Federal Railroad Administration, *Northeast Corridor Improvement Project, Draft Environmental Impact Statement ... South Station Improvement Project,* Washington, D. C. 1980; [BRA], *Boston South Station, Transportation Center & Air Rights Development Project,* s. d.; City of Boston, *South Station, Transportation Center Air Rights,* s. d.

[37] Cf. infra, p. 315 ff.

to be rather difficult; a collective amnesia concerning earlier deliberations and decisions is not the least problem.

Our planner, then, has to confront the long history of fluid projects as well as the erratic dynamics of the social field evolving around every project. These conditions prevent him from being the master planner; he certainly cannot "plan" planning: the process of spatial creativity. In fact, he has to face not one process but a complex of processes: clusters of events that occur in different temporal modes; social fields of configurative action whose compositions constantly vary; projections of physical change, improvement, or preservation that are undertaken in response to larger morphological processes of mutations in a city. Planning? No. This is not the situation. The problem is creativity: the "planner" responding creatively to the innumerable facets of the creative process.

A process of spatial creativity produces its own constraints. The very creativeness which it does release imposes upon everyone who is involved with it these constraints: You cannot plan, you can only participate. The process of civic architecture is larger than the architect. Socio-spatial design is a history of designs within which each "new" design is but an addition. Any new design requires a vision. Through the vision, however, a process of other visions – "plans," "projects" – opens up, of which each constrains this vision. A building designed can be built only through other designs of the building. A city envisioned can be founded or be revived only through other visions of the city. A process of spatial creativity does not occur as a process "from" a vision "to" its reality. It occurs within a reality of visions and constraints towards the vision to be seen once the creative interplay of visions and constraints has finally released its reality.[38]

---

[38] In a retrospective assessment of the controversy concerning the Waterfront Hotel in Boston (cf. p. 290), a number of architects and planners formulated their general view of the "planning process": "We create the framework but we must leave it open for individual creativity. – The process by its nature has to be subjective. – You don't need to make a competition if the building is already designed [by too tight a set of design criteria]. – Maybe a competition that is orderly and fair is incompatible with creating something new and unanticipated." (K. S. Kellerhouse, *Redevelopment of the Boston Waterfron*, op. cit., Part C, pp. 40–42.) – Cf. further: K. Lynch, *A Theory of Good City Form*, Cambridge, Mass. 1981, p. 289: "No one creates form without precedent." – p. 290: "City design is the art of creating possibilities for the use, management, and form of settlements or their significant parts. [...] True city design never begins with a virgin situation, never foresees a completed work. Properly, it thinks in terms of process, prototype, guidance." – idem, *Site Planning*, op. cit., p. 207 f. – W. Braunfels, *Abendländische Stadtbaukunst*, op. cit., p. 322 ff. (the section on the "Antinomie des Urbanismus"). – F. M. Wirt, *Power in the City*, op. cit., pp. 184–85 (the section on "embattled visions of the city").

6 Constraints and Visions

If we consider the constraints bearing upon the process of spatial creativity, the room for visions appears to be rather small. There are the constraints from within. And there are constraints from outside:

(1) In the sphere of human space no place is neutral; every place is a parcel of space and, more importantly, a social signal. Wherever I go, I am always told, in more or less indicative ways, what import the space carries that I just touch: this is a house and that is a street, this is a sidewalk and that is a park, this is a city and that is farmland, this is a public beach and that is a ranch privately owned, this is an airport and that is an expressway, this is a business district and that is a slum, this is a red light district and that is an upper class neighborhood, this is an artists' colony and that is a quarter being gentrified, this is Irish turf and that is a black neighborhood. As I walk through a city or across open land, I walk through the complex of human society. I move through space and I encounter values, commerce, art, money, power, race, passions, misery, hope, friendship, hate, love, community, strife, life cycles, restlessness, peace. I perceive space and I experience humanity. Every place conveys a message; no place is void of some vision, aspiration, or project, however slight or small it might be. I, the planner, may exert my profession and propose for some space a grand vision of transformation or a global plan of development. Others will have attached to the space their visions or plans long before. The space of human reality for which I have a message is filled with messages:

> Le Corbusier once described his feelings when visiting the statistical bureau of the Paris city government. He was impressed by the labors of the "modest workers of precision" he found there, but he confessed to a deeper horror at their direct contact with the details of the city he wished to transform. They were immersed in a multitude of complicated facts from which no grand pattern could emerge. They would discern the complex web of human relationships that made each street unique. From their perspective, Le Corbusier observed, 'one is afraid to propose even the smallest changes: one can already hear the cracking and the upsets'.[39]

(2) All human space is socially defined; legal provisions regulate the uses to which parcels of space are put; formal rules prescribe the modes by which

---

[39] R. Fishman, *Urban Utopias in the Twentieth Century,* op. cit., p. 210. — Other examples that "illustrate the power of spatially referred values to resist social systems which might violate the symbolic quality of an area" can be found in: W. Firey, *Land Use in Central Boston,* Cambridge, Mass. 1947, pp. 128 – 133. — Cf. also K. Lynch, *Site Planning,* op. cit., p. 226, 358.

structures in space — as buildings, cities, or streets — may be shaped architecturally; governmental policies — as regional, housing, or urban policies — inject social goals into spatial developments.[40] Space is not merely the subject of technical expertise. It is, above all, the legal, governmental, and administrative artefact with which every society has found its spatial existence, each in a more or less systematic way.[41] Any project of spatial creativity, therefore, amounts not only to a spatial undertaking. It amounts also, and more importantly, to a political undertaking. It has to be steered through the social artefact of space. And this means it has to be pursued through a whole web of constraints: laws, ordinances, codes, regulations, rules, policies, bureaucratic procedures, governmental dissension, vested interests, public review, judicial review.

(3) Acts of spatial creativity tend to be costly; they involve labor and materials to a degree that money makes the difference between doing something and doing nothing at all. The financial constraints of spatial creativeness are obvious: the projected creation cannot be more significant than its supply of funds (exceptions notwithstanding). Or, positively put: considerable funds make considerable creations.[42]

(4) The process of spatial creativity is competitive; all places in the sphere of human space cannot equally be places of beauty, of social attraction, of public financial support, places of private investment, of rehabilitation, of protection, of architectural distinction. There is a ceiling to everything — to the amount of public funds, to the private capital ready for investment, to the embellishment of human habitats, to the preservation of historic architecture — and the ceilings cannot be raised at will; at the precise moment a planner applies for public funds, or wants to draw from a developer a concession, or attempts to attract private investment to his city, or desires to enlist an eminent architect for an ambitious development project, the ceilings to his endeavor

---

[40] Zoning, the principal legal instrument regulating land use, is an age-old tool of city design. Cf. W. Braunfels, *Abendländische Stadtbaukunst*, op. cit. L. Benevolo, *Storia della città*, Rome – Bari 1975. It was introduced to the United States quite late, in 1916, when the New York City Board of Estimate adopted the first comprehensive zoning ordinance in the U. S. — The first application of the BRA for an Urban Development Action Grant ran to 30 pages; in 1981 the typical application comprised 500 to 600 pages.

[41] Cf., as an example, my exposition of this artefact in France, in: "The Decentralization and the New Urban Policy in France," op. cit.

[42] Two examples from Boston: (a) Only a large inflow of federal funds made the Government Center possible, as it exists today; (b) Copley Place, on the other hand, has become what it is today because of the importance private money had in its construction.

tend to be absolute.[43] The process of spatial creativity occurs within limits, and within these limits all participants in the process compete with each other: for money, for public support, for media attention, for help from bureaucrats in the federal capital, for this or that developer, for this or that architect, for this or that business firm.[44] Everyone competes with everyone. And all constrain the creativity of each.

---

[43] Efforts to raise the ceilings can be made, of course. But then, time is needed — and the desirable moment of action is gone.

[44] A planner from the BRA, commenting on the policy of the BRA negotiating with developers on behalf of the "public interest," observed: "You can extract from a developer only so much." — And a Boston City Councillor, discussing height limits to office and hotel buildings, stated: "The Dollar will be invested elsewhere if there is no profit." (Sources: Interviews.)

The Politics of Spatial Creativity

7 Statements

Constraints, then, everywhere, within the process of spatial creativity, and outside. A universal vision, it was said, would initiate the process of spatial creativity. Indeed? Do not the impediments that arise with the process itself shatter any grand vision long before it could become true? Pieces of a vision, evocations of a vision, yes. They will emerge from a process of spatial creativity or such a process will not occur. But a great vision, the one vision, no. It will provoke the forces that obstruct it, or a serious attempt at creating something will not have been made. In matters of spatial creativity, progress in the form of a progress in failures is a classic experience. Leonard Kip wrote the following lines a century ago. They have a familiar ring:

> A street is widened here, or a public park laid out there, – and so far it is all very well. But the trouble is, that these efforts are mere disorganized fragments of what should constitute a great, comprehensive design, to be prosecuted with force and energy as a whole; and that, when we accomplish even the smallest results we feel disposed to praise ourselves too highly for our enterprise, to be too leisurely occupied over it, and, at the end, to rest too long before undertaking any additional design. We would fain lay out a new street, for instance; and after years of civic wrangling it is done, or, as likely as not, left undone, because someone may be indirectly going to make something out of it. We decide to put up a public building; – and other years are wasted in first selecting a site and then a plan. While, at each step of the way, we calculate the cost so dolefully, that at last we become horrified at the task we have set ourselves; and the dread of any further expenditure so surely mingles with our complacency over the labor finished, that a long period is certain to elapse before we recover sufficient equanimity and courage to press forward again.[45]

As a process of *spatial* creativity alone every such process will fail in creativity. The critical moment of creativeness is not a spatial, but a political creativity. The constraints which impede the process cannot be passed by "planning" or any other spatially proceeding mode of action. They are constraints that have to be overridden politically. In view of the institutional drags that might thwart the vision of a "New Boston," the city's party of hope formulated in 1960 their resolution for a process of spatial creativity through the politics of autocracy:

---

[45] L. Kip, "The Building of Our Cities," in: L. M. Roth, *America Builds,* op. cit., p. 422.

> No City can renew itself without bold and effective leadership from City Hall. Boston is burdened with a bewildering government structure that encourages devided responsibility. Our program is built on coordinated administration under the Mayor's leadership.[46]

Years later, Mayor White acted in the same vein. A developer and an architect had to be chosen for the construction of a hotel on the Waterfront. The building, because of its site, would have a considerable impact upon the whole architecture of the Waterfront. A significant decision, therefore, had to be made. In steering the selection process, the planners in the BRA refined the architectural criteria for the selection so tightly that the choice to be made had, in effect, been predicated. To affirm the choice, the Mayor chose to be against the foreclosed choice. A city produced itself as its own creation by the logic of politics, not by the logic of schemes. Politics liberates visions, plans constrain them. The Mayor opted for the vision and chose the proposal for the construction of the hotel which he thought was the best: "In my opinion, that's what leading a city is all about [...]. I have chosen a strong statement."[47]

8 Images

Does Marrakesh work? In the process of spatial creativity the good "planner" is a politician. Questions concerning the layout of a city have to be asked and to be resolved, of course. Architectural measures might be applied in the most imaginative and the most perfected way, however, and the city to which they were applied might still lack the quality of a city.[48] In such a case, the architects working on the design of the city will have forgotten to pose themselves a question. It is the simple yet paramount question a planner in the BRA asked when he was shown an aerial photo of Marrakesh, the Arab city in Morocco: "Does Marrakesh work?"[49] It was the first thing he said upon viewing the picture. He did not ask an architectural question. He asked a political question. The social image of a city that "worked" overbore, in his view, all aesthtic perceptions. The general form of a city that Marrakesh represented intrigued the planner. But he would not judge it a good form unless his question was affirmatively answered. For he held a political image

---

[46] "The new Boston. City of Ideas 1775 1975," *Boston Sunday Globe,* Febr. 24, 1963, p. 4.

[47] K. S. Kellerhouse, *Redevelopment of the Boston Waterfront,* op. cit., Part C, p. 24.

[48] Consider Brasilia, Canberra, Chandigarh.

[49] Source: Interview.

of planning. Cities were not just their architects' products. They were there to work.

City Planning is anything and everything. The good politician, being the creative politician that he is, knows the law of his existence: he cannot create, he can only concreate.[50] The good planner – being the good politician that he is – is guided by an analoguos image of planning: "City Planning is anything and everything; it is where opportunity lies; it is where the potential of success exists; it is where *any* type of planning results in something positive happening."[51] Plans can be produced at the thousands. They are all worthless, if the planner producing them does not look about for his chance, for that momentary constellation of persons, events, and things that suggests the actualization of this or that plan. Usually the circumstances are such that a plan is a plan; the circumstances are such that it cannot be realized. The imaginative planner, therefore, proceeds as a political planner. He is less interested in plans than in circumstances. He does not seek the circumstances for a plan, but seeks circumstances upon which he might build a plan. To impose a plan upon reality is a formidable task – not to be tried without a considerable ability to sue illusions or to commit violence. To use reality as a guide to one's plans is a formidable yet promising task – to be tried with the promise the art of politics holds.

"*Guns.*" Politics is the passage to planning. Contrary to conventional wisdom, it is not politics that needs planning, it is planning that needs politics. Planning occurs through politics, else it does not occur. What is a plan? It is an intent, namely the intention to bring forth from nonreality a reality: a thing, an event, a form, an effect. In the process of spatial creativity every plan involves persons and things: many persons and many things. They are all engaged in some pursuit, in all sorts of existential, social, and physical modes, for as numerous as diverse purposes. They normally do not follow the movements which some plan means them to follow. They normally do not stay in the places wherein some plan means them to stay. They naturally withstand any plan to engage them in this or that plan, in this or that project. A plan, to be done, cannot be any other plan than the plan to bring forth from non-reality a reality *within* the reality of persons and things whom it is meant to involve. It has to be a plan that engages the plans that are there: the intentions the people to be involved pursue, the purposes the things to be involved represent. The plan, if it really is what it is meant to be, is a plan not to be executed by a planner. It is a plan to be executed by the players for whom the plan has been made.

---

[50] Cf. supra, p. 149 f.
[51] Source: Interview.

Would then anything at all for the planner in the process of spatial creativity be left to do? Yes, it would, according to a senior planner in the BRA. She would not plan, she said, she would not sue the illusion of overarching planning, no. But she would distribute "guns": the construction of a hotel here and the preservation of an old building there, public housing here and condominiums there. All actors in the field — developers, preservationists, citizens, public organizations, business groups — would have a stake in the development of Boston, but none would control it. Each would have an incentive to stay with the general direction of that development, but none would define it. The field of actors would be the field's own and only guide. And the "guns" — as they were distributed here and there — would shape the field.[52]

A human body, a living thing. Language is an essential tool of planning, as it is an essential tool of politics. The senior planner in the BRA fell into military language to describe her image of her own role in the process of spatial creativity. She articulated the essence of "planning," as she understood it. And she lent to planning, through the language she used, a perspicuous presence. Imponderable purposes became powers to be perceived: "guns."

In the mode of language, planning acquires the reality which it does project. Metaphors, images, symbols obliterate the time and the efforts that still lie between the vision and the creation, the plan and the product, the intention and its execution. They create perceptions of things that have yet to be perceived. But then there are these perceptions and they tend to prescribe future perceptions. In 1964 the "New Boston" still existed mostly in the mode of plans; all the vision a view of Boston appeared to evoke was the vision of a decrepit city. The planners planning the "New Boston," however, had not been idle. They had made plans. And they had produced the "New Boston" in the mode of language. They had been planners, working on their projects. And they had been politicians of language, rendering their projects real in the public perception:

> It seems that investors both within and without the city are beginning to see in the New Boston a metropolis with all the inherited resources to meet the challenge of the new world — a centre of educational thought, culture, research, science and recreation. In simple terms, a stimulating place in which to live.[53]

The process of spatial creativity advances through politics and the politics of spatial creativity advances through language. All the space to be composed is social space and "social space" is the abbreviation for a human society

---

[52] Source: Interview.
[53] Ian Menzies, in: *BG,* Nov. 18, 1964.

building and rebuilding itself as its own creation. The "space" to be composed are people: they form the "city" to be founded, for instance, or the "city" to be revived. Spatial creativity, therefore, would run fatally short, if its carriers did not address their creation to its creature, if the people planning a city did not tell their plans to the people who will make the city, if the persons concerned about a city did not communicate to each other the nature of their concern, if the message a planner in the BRA perceptively phrased did not have as messengers its recipients: that a city is a "human body," a "living thing."[54]

9 The Discourse

A city builds or rebuilds itself discursively. It is founded by discourse and throughout its existence it consists in a running discourse on the human achievement that it represents.[55] It is its own subject, from its beginning bent upon and incessantly concerned with itself.[56] The people who make a city make their city continuously by debating it as a subject of their love, their attachment, their reflection, their criticism, their pleasure, their hate, their irritation, their well-being, their biography, their work, their expectations, their failures, their fulfillment. They form their city as they talk about it. The city is their discourse: their words upon themselves, written in stone.

Every city, therefore, is unique. And the people of every city, therefore, think that their city is unique among all other cities. If we should join in the ongoing discourse on Boston, we should partake of a singular urban experience; the topic invites to the pursuit of an unending story.[57] And among Bostonians themselves there is no greater theme than Boston; they are self-conscious to the degree that they prefer to discuss the discussion that goes on about Boston rather than any simple view on the city.

---

[54] Source: Interview. − In 1964 an assistant planning administrator in the BRA, John R. Rothermel, told Anthony J. Yudis, a reporter from the *Boston Globe* writing on urban affairs: "[...] Boston's resources for economic development lie not in its land, nor in its minerals, nor in its manual labor, but (they) lie in its brains − its tradition for culture, communications and creativeness." (*BG*, Oct. 15, 1964.)

[55] Cf. T. Schabert, "In urbe mundus," op. cit., and the literature quoted there.

[56] Cf. ibid.

[57] There is no lack of books whose principal subject is Boston (cf. Bibliography). *A History of Boston*, however, has not been written yet. Does Boston absorb her historians, perhaps?

As a unique city Boston does not lack epithets of praise. Classical Rome could not have done better, as to the commendations that could be bestowed upon a city and that have been bestowed upon Boston: "Athens of America," "brain of America," "city of the American Revolution," "cradle of liberty," "cradle of the United States," "cradle of art and science," "cradle of the new urbanism," "hub of the universe," "pivot of the solar system."[58] These are universal titles, they introduce a city that appears to be unique indeed: you talk about Boston and − as you may know or as you will soon be told − you talk about THE city, the one city in the world that is the city of the world, the world's urban epitome.

The discourse on Boston runs along ecumenical lines. It has, in recent times, largely been a discourse on a city that nearly died. But then, a city that has been called the "hub to which all roads led,"[59] this city does not die. It cannot be allowed to die. In the political pursuit of Boston's renaissance the theme of Boston's death has been a most effective tool. For the discourse on Boston continued and so did the universal significance the city appeared to carry. Boston did not die. The city that was THE city could not be allowed to die. To the hub to which all roads led, new roads were laid:

---

[58] "Athens of America" cf., for instance, *The Dynamic City,* op. cit., p. 19; "brain of America," cf. *Frankfurter Allgemeine Zeitung* (Germany), Aug. 1, 1987; "city of the American revolution," *The Dynamic City,* p. 4; "cradle of liberty," cf., for instance, *NYT,* June 16, 1985; *BG,* Nov. 17, 1980; "cradle of the United States," cf. *Le Monde* (France), June 24, 1986; "cradle of art and science," cf. Boston Tercentenary Committee, *Fifty Years of Boston. A Memorial Volume,* s. l., 1932, p. 44; "cradle of the new urbanism," NYT, June 16, 1985; "hub of the universe," cf., for instance, A. Hepburn, *Biography of a City. Boston. The Story of a Great American City and Its Contribution to Our National Heritage,* New York 1966, p. 137; "pivot of the solar system," cf. *Neue Zürcher Zeitung* (Switzerland), Oct. 19−20, 1986. − In *Fifty Years of Boston* (see above) we read also: "The first specific reference to a conscious and comprehensive plan for Boston is found in the report of Robert Fleming Gourlay, published in 1844 [...] Gorlay pleaded [...] that [...] Boston should work out its potential destiny as a 'city surpassing all others either in ancient or modern times.'" (pp. 43, 44.)

[59] Boston Tercentenary Committee, *Fifty Years of Boston,* op. cit., p. 53. On the same page we find the sentence: "Boston is itself unique among American cities." − Kevin White, of course, agreed: "This town is unique [...] so unique," quoted in: J. Gogolin, "Kevin's Gospel. The Politics of Property." *Boston Magazine,* July 1980, p. 70. − San Franciscans, too, for instance, maintain that their city is truly unique among American cities. (Cf. F. M. Wirt, *Power in the City,* op. cit., p. 19.) When they speak of San Francisco, they simply say "The City." (Cf. ibid., p. 4.)

Boston persists and prevails. [It has] survived war, revolution, siege, occupation, riots, inflation, panic, depression, fire, flood, the social and educational upheavals of this century, racial and religious strife [...].[60]

[It] is one of America's great urban success stories. Twenty-five years ago it seemed a dying city, its spirit tired. Today it is vibrant, stylish, the downtown bustling day and night. Young people look for work that will take them to Boston.[61]

---

[60] *The Dynamic City,* op. cit., p. 30.

[61] *IHT,* July 19–20, 1986. – Cf. also E. J. Logue, *Memo to Boston Redevelopment Authority,* Dec. 21, 1960: "At a time when federal capital grant funds are becoming scarce, the reservation of almost $ 30 million for Boston is a rare and striking tribute to the Mayor, the Redevelopment Authority, the City Council and to a united community's support for a major rebuilding effort. It is a heartening vote of confidence in an entirely fresh and new approach to the problem of large scale urban blight which confronts most of the nation's older and larger cities. It is also a special recognition of the seriousness of Boston's situation and of its historic importance in the life of our nation."

Movements of "Planning"

10 Off to Utopia

Where Boston is, there is your destiny. "Young people look for work that will take them to Boston." In June 1986, when this point was made, a view of Boston evidently came close to the millenarian dictum: *ubi Jerusalem, ibi salus*.[62] And a visit to the offices in the City where the future of Boston was planned[63] would indeed have given rise to a redemptive view. The planners of Boston, the visitor would have learned, had planned perfectively.

The notions of urban renaissance that had floated around for years, they had been given a focus: Boston.

The issues of urban policy that had been discussed all over the country innumerable times, they had been veered towards a set of guidelines: guidelines on the development of Boston.

Objectives of city planning that had traditionally been thought to be contradictory, they featured in a great urban synthesis: Boston.

The planners of Boston, the visitor would have discovered, had in their offices immersed themselves in an extraordinary movement of planning. Apparently, they had planned Boston to be the place where, like in Utopia, a reality of perfection followed the perfection of plans.

Boston — as it featured in the imagination of Boston's planners — shone by its "Europeanness."[64] It stood out as a city of "historic character" and charmed people with its "physical attractiveness." The architectonic proportions of the city were measured exceedingly well, Boston fulfilled the "human scale." The city excelled in the virtues of urban life: by the "accessibility" of the space and the spaces wherein it consisted, by the "diversity" of the social

---

[62] The biblical image of the "City on the Hill" is, of course, very often associated with American cities and with Boston, in particular. — The tradition of millenarian thought is as evidently present in America as the inscription "Novus ordo saeclorum" on the One Dollar bill.

[63] The Boston Redevelopment Authority and the Massachusetts Port Authority are the principal planning and development agencies in Boston. However, there are quite a few other institutions joining in the process of shaping Boston — municpal institutions (such as the Public Facilities Dept. or the Traffic and Parking Dept.), state/local institutions (such as the Mass. Community Economic Development Assistance Corp. or the Mass. Bay Transportation Authority), federal institutions (such as the Federal Railroad Adm. or the Urban Mass. Transportation Adm.), civic institutions (such as the Back Bay Association or the Beacon Hill Architectural Commission).

[64] In describing the planners' utopian Boston I rely on official planning documents.

and economic uses to which it was put, by the "connectivity" that held all these uses together in one urban vessel.

Boston throbbed with "economic growth," the city's residents found within the city the jobs they sought. A "retail corridor" stretched, like a "spine," throughout the inner city, from the North End to Downtown Crossing, from Downtown Crossing to the Back Bay. "Tall buildings," as they had gone up in the Business District for a while in a row, were now "prohibited"; and for all major new construction "targets" had been set, evenly distributed all over the city, to equilibrate development in the neighborhoods, long neglected, and in Downtown, having boomed too much. "Inclusionary zoning" compelled developers to provide, in conjunction with the hotel or office buildings they constructed, a fair amount of "rental housing"; and a city ordinance prescribed the rate at which old family homes could be converted into condominiums.

The protective measure of "historic preservation" was extended over the great many buildings in Boston that had survived the onslaught of modernism and that the Landmarks Commission had deemed to be worthy of protection (Old Boston had been too poor to destroy itself, in compliance with the Charta of Athens, and when it was ready for being rebuilt, the Charta went out); [65] and other old buildings had been "recycled" instead of being torn down. In Downtown as well as in some neighborhoods numbers of streets had been closed for all automobile traffic and had been transformed into a "pedestrian system"; within the "auto-restricted zone" everyone could move from one place to another either by walking as leisurely as he wished or by using, free of charge, one of the small electric (hence quiet) buses which circulated in the zone on regular schedules.

Boston's historic street pattern was left as ingeniously as it had been mapped out by the cows of the early settlers or as imperially as it had been laid out by neo-classicist architects in the nineteenth century. Everywhere in the city "street furniture," "ceremonial architecture," "greenery" enlivened the "urban landscape"; and a rhythmic sequence of streets, plazas, pathways, alleys, arcades, esplanades, and malls made everyone who crossed the city an explorer of splendid vistas and cozy corners, of irresistible curves and blissful spaces, of lucid views. Boston attracted, no wonder, "lots of inner-city residents"; there occurred in its streets a "continuous activity around the clock"; the city glittered with people, with all the profusion of human life, day and night.

New hotels accomodated the large number of business travelers and tourists streaming to Boston. New office buildings facilitated the resurgence and expansion of Boston's economy. However, tight controls of all further

---

[65] The notable exception was the "modern" demolition of Boston's West End.

office and hotel construction held a balance between supply and demand. A whole web of environmental regulations was spun over Boston: they minimized the pollution of the air circulating in the city; they helped to form clusters of high rises in a way that they did not cause gusts or wirlwinds; they prevented the emergence of "urban canyons," rows of high rises so narrow that the sunshine no longer reached the street below.

No, all shadows were gone: a New Boston shone under the sun.

11 Back to Life

The future as conceived in the present is rarely the future as conceived in the past. When we ponder the future, we usually ponder what we think will be the future of the present. Time goes on and it will go on "from" the present "to" the future. At any moment, the future has already begun: it is arising from the present that it will succeed. Or, conversely put, the future "after" presupposes the present "before." When we contemplate the future, then, we seem to contemplate it on attested grounds. We know of the future because we know the present. There is the future: it is the future the present suggests.

The future whiche we conceive of now might well be the future that other people conceived of before, in the past. Such an assumption would be only natural; why should the future towards which we move be different from the future towards which our fathers and forefathers moved? Is their history not also ours? Not quite, for it is likely that the image of the future which they held will prove, if we research it, to be unlike the one that we have formed. Indeed, in reviewing the future as it was conceived in the past, we shall not find the one image of the future which we might be looking for. We shall find, instead, a plurality of images. The future has at different times been imagined very differently. Seen from the past, the future is but a series of images. It is not, as we superficially suppose, the time that will occur next. It is rather a movement within time beyond time: the movement of the human imagination extracting from the present images of the future. The present, however, changes at every moment and so the images change we hold of the future: we move continually from "future" to "future."

The planners of Boston have, of course, not been exempt from this human rule. They moved from one future of the city to the other; they planned this "Future Boston" and that "Future Boston." The New Boston of 1960 was very different from the New Boston of 1986. And there were other conceptions of a New Boston in between. The planners "planned," this is true — true superficially. To really grasp what they did, "planning" has to be observed — to be reviewed — in the mode by which it actually occurred. It has to be

Table 16: Movements of "Planning," A Prism: The Boston Redevelopment Authority

Mayor	Head of the BRA	Institutional History	"Plans"	Function
John Collins			The Boston Contest 1944/45	
	Edward J. Logue 1960–1967	1957 Foundation of the BRA	The 90 Million Dollar Development Program for Boston 1960	To lead
		1960 Boston Planning Board abolished, BRA becomes the city's planning and development agency a "one-man operation"		
			General Plan for Boston 1965	
Kevin White	Hale Champion 1968–1969	"flipped to neighborhoods"		
Kevin White	John D. Warner 1969–1971	BRA/Little City Halls		To manage
Kevin White	Robert T. Kenney 1971–1976		Growth Program for Downtown 1974	
Kevin White	Robert Walsh 1976–1978			
Kevin White	Robert J. Ryan 1978–1984	"a political body" "primary generator of economic activity in the city"	Boston Downtown Development Guidelines 1981	To market

Table 17: Movements of "Planning", A Prism: The Boston Redevelopment Authority

Orientation	Staff	Type of Projects	Type of Resources
Urban renewal	1957: 17 early 1961: 54 late 1961: 81 1967: 498	Large-scale public (e.g. Government Center, Faneuil Hall)	Large federal funds
Partnership private/public development economic development		Rehabilitation, small-scale public (e.g. Charlestown Navy Yard)	Small federal funds public/private funding annual funding
Economic development, BRA as a "business" Planning for alternative sources of revenue	1981: 225	Large-scale private (e.g. Copley Place)	Scattered federal funds Own resources (ingenuity)

observed in the mode of its movements: movements of planning from this image of a city to that image, from this projection of economic trends to that projection, from this political stimulus to that political stimulus, from this institutional procedure to that procedure, from this figuration of persons to that figuration.

In the following I shall describe a complex of such movements. The Boston Redevelopment Authority will serve as the prism through which particular movements can be detected and pursued. As they are described, the movements may be visualized through the charts on the succeeding pages (Tables 16 – 18). While we pursue the movements, we shall not merely follow movements of "planning." We shall experience more:

Table 18: Movements of "Planning", A Prism: The Boston Redevelopment Authority

BRA – City Government	Mayor – Head of the BRA
A separate body	"Peers"
A part and parcel of city government	Political tutelage/administrative autonomy
A "branch of the Mayor's Office"	The BRA director: "almost a staff person" ("staff" $\cong$ The Mayor's staff)

- We shall see the process of spatial creativity coming into focus.
- We shall discern again, through a major example, the process of institutional creativity analyzed at an earlier instance of this study.
- We shall encounter a further example of politics in the mode of social creativity.
- We shall seize the process of spatial creativity as a process of social creativity, and we shall seize the process of social creativity as a process of political creativity. We shall seize the one process of creativeness by which we live.

Institutional History

The Boston Redevelopment Authority was established in the Fall of 1957. Under the provisions of the National Housing Act of 1949 the Federal Department of Housing and Urban Development had been authorized to enter into contracts with local redevelopment authorities which are duly empowered by state law, to finance slum clearance, urban renewal, open space, urban beautification, and other programs designed to prevent the spread of urban blight through rehabilitation and conservation measures, and to improve the quality of the urban environment.[66] At the request of Mayor John B. Hynes and the Boston City Council the Massachusetts Legislature created the BRA as Boston's local redevelopment authority.[67] It was given sole responsibility for carrying out urban renewal activities in the City of Boston.

When the new Mayor, John Collins, planned in 1960 to appoint Ed Logue — the director of New Haven's renowned redevelopment — head of the BRA, Logue tied his appointment to an institutional condition. He wanted to have both the city's redevelopment *and* its planning function combined into one institution, the BRA. Collins recognized the benefits to be derived from a centralized responsibility for the city's development, for the negotiations with private developers, and for securing the cooperation of individual citizens and civic groups. He prodded the Massachusetts Legislature accordingly, and could deliver to Logue the desired result. Under Chapter 652, Acts of 1960 (Mass. General Laws, Chapter 121A) the City Planning Board, created in 1913,[68] was abolished and all its staff transferred to the BRA which from now on held all the functions, duties, and responsibilities for city planning *and* development.

The BRA had become an institution quite unique in the United States. Logue, now the city's "Development Administrator," had been given "the most massively centralized planning and renewal powers that any large city has ever voted one man."[69] He had been enabled to do both, "to cook and to serve."[70] Logue rose to a position of power that earned him the informal title of Boston's "renewal czar"; he reminded not a few observers of New York's Robert Moses.[71] As he had proved, by making the sweeping empowerment of the BRA the condition for his service to Boston, the Development Administrator possessed an acute sense of power. He ruled the BRA autocratically, practiced power in a way "similar" to the ways that Franklin D. Roosevelt had adopted, and "similar" to the ways Kevin White would adopt. On the one hand, he ran his agency and its activities in the mode of a "one-man show"[72]; and on the other, he kept his staff, by various devices, continually divided. Nevertheless, the BRA under Logue attracted, in its field, "the

---

[66] As to sources, cf. footnote 15.

[67] Cf. ibid.

[68] On the City Planning Board, cf. *Boston Tercentenary Committee, Fifty Years of Boston,* op. cit.

[69] Cf. *Architectural Forum,* op. cit.

[70] W. Mc Quade, "What Can a Sick City Do?" op. cit., p. 136.

[71] On Robert Moses, cf. R. A. Caro, *The Power Broker,* op. cit.

[72] Source: Interview. — Cf. also J. W. Rosenblum, *The Boston Redevelopment Authority,* op. cit., Part A, p. 14: "One employee described the BRA organization in the following

best and the brightest." It was considered to be "the most elite organization in the US."[73] Much of the power to be held in Boston had shifted to the BRA, and its head aspired indeed after the city: "If Collins had permitted it, Logue would have gobbled up a city department or two every so often." But "Logue's Napoleonic complex was checked by Collins."[74] In 1967, though, the Development Administrator tried to attain the position from which, as it seemed, hardly anyone held him back save the outgoing Mayor. Ed Logue wanted to be elected Mayor of Boston – and did not, however, reach his goal. The successor of John Collins was Kevin White.[75]

Logue's unsuccessful quest dispirited the BRA. To seize the Mayor's mantle, the head of the BRA had resigned from his post. Now, with Kevin White being the new Mayor and Ed Logue gone with his electoral defeat, the agency had not only lost its principal, however critical its ensuing predicament was. It had also lost, much more importantly, the creative presence of the person who had formed and who had sustained it. Ed Logue had gone and with him the institutional "soul" of the BRA. The "one-man show" was over; the BRA had ceased to be Logue's "one-man band" and thus the "effective organization" built with and through Logue.[76] There was the BRA, an institution, no doubt. But this institution no longer was what, as an institution, it should have been: an institution of creativity.

The new Mayor, Kevin White, did not seem to discern at first all the creative potential – all the potential for power – to be found in the BRA.

---

manner. Under Logue the BRA really had no organization. There was an organization chart, but if I found it and showed you, it wouldn't mean very much [...]. Although it was pretty close to being a one-man show, I don't think that would be a completely accurate description of the BRA under Logue. Rather, it was a one-clique show. Logue and his pets – his inner circle – really ran the BRA."

[73] Source: Interview.

[74] Source: Interview.

[75] The change from John Collins to Kevin White – including the story of Ed Logue's unsuccessful bid for the mayoralty – is absorbingly told by Alan Lupo in *Liberty's Chosen Home* (op. cit.).

[76] Cf. J. W. Rosenblum, *The Boston Redevelopment Authority* (B), op. cit., p. 8 f.: "Champion [the successor of Ed Logue, T. S.] gave his views on a number of issues concerning the BRA: BRA organization, housing, planning, the community, his first six months as development administrator, and the public record of the BRA in 1968. 'When I took over the BRA, it had been drifting. There had been no central push or drive. Operations just seemed to have slackened off. [...] The organization had been under interim leadership. Few decisions had been made, and where they had, they were not of consequential character. [...] When the BRA had been an effective organization, it was a one-man band. There was only one real decision-maker, very little delegation of authority, and no real organization structure.' "

He assumed a more active role in the agency and its transactions only after Barney Frank, the first in the succession of his alter egos, had departed from his administration. The partial opacity of mayoral power concerning the BRA promptly provoked a senior aide on the Mayor's staff into posing himself as the official overseeing Boston's planning and redevelopment agency.[77] Still, the power over the city's affairs that had once been concentrated in the BRA under Logue had dissipated, and Mayor White gradually and, in a later stage, very determinedly drew the agency within the orbit of his office; he made it finally an extension of his personal political power.

In its history, then, the BRA was largely an institutional subject of creative politics in its autocratic mode. Under Mayor Collins, the BRA was Ed Logue. Under Mayor White, the BRA became Kevin White. Each time, spatial creativity received the practical form of an institution, and the autocratic condition of the institution transposed the creativity into politics, into the political power, resolution, and will through which alone spatial creativity releases its creations: the social creations of a society designing itself in its space.

Kevin White, the new Mayor, wished that all of Boston be included in the process of the city's physical renewal.[78] Upon his recommendation, the Board of the BRA had appointed Hale Champion the new Development Administrator.[79] Champion proceeded to reinstitutionalize the BRA and thus the planning and redevelopment process in Boston. The BRA was "flipped" to the neighborhoods. Within one month, the agency built up a neighborhood staff, hiring 24 new employees for that purpose. In taking steps to reach the people with and through whom the White administration, in the pursuit of the rebirth of Boston, intended to work, the BRA also set up a "District Planning Program" that encompassed the whole city and demarcated 18 planning districts within the city. The agency sent to each district a planner from its staff asking him to work "there" at the periphery, among the people, rather than at the center, in the offices of the BRA in City Hall. In consequence of this institutional policy the BRA increasingly became interwoven with the Little City Halls and thus with the Kevin White Party.[80]

---

[77] The attempt was made by Andy Olins, the Mayor's housing adviser.

[78] "The BRA planning effort until Champion became director," Ralph Memolo reports, "was confined to renewal projects. Indeed, at one point a BRA planner sent Logue a memo in which he outlined the need for planning in non-renewal areas. The memo came back the next day with a short, but direct message scrawled across it: 'That's not on the agenda.' " (R. Memolo, New Boston: The Politics of Renewal in Boston, op. cit., p. 86.)

[79] When he took up his post, Champion did not find an agency fully pliant to his directions. Logue still had allies in the BRA, some of whom he had put in strategic positions shortly before he had left, and he tried very hard to force through them the hand of Champion. Cf. also supra, p. 205.

[80] Cf. supra, p. 135 ff.

From the beginning of his work as Development Administrator, Hale Champion had aimed "to fit the BRA back into the structure of city government."[81] In his view (representing the Mayor's view) the BRA did not only need a thorough reinstitutionalization — however serious he considered this problem to be.[82] The agency needed, above all, a political turnabout. As Champion saw it, "the major factor in the change" to be brought about was "the Mayor's insistence that his administration function cooperatively rather than separately and that the driving central force come from the Mayor's office rather than from individual departments [...]."[83] Writing in July 1968 his first major report to Mayor White and the BRA, the Development Administrator formulated the autocratic approach to government which "his" Mayor was about to pursue. In the case of the BRA the autocracy of Kevin White began with the new head of the agency submitting the agency to the Mayor's ultimate rule.

The tone had been set and it persisted, some variations in the power relation between Mayor and succeeding BRA directors notwithstanding.[84] The movement of planning flowing from Champion's initiatives shaped the BRA more and more along the lines of the Court. It became a major institutional manifestation of mayoral power (and the Mayor's architectural taste). In 1982, Robert J. Ryan, then the director of the BRA, pronounced in a simple sentence the political truth about the institutional form of "planning" in Boston: "We [the BRA] are a political body."[85]

Right — and not quite right. The statement was correct to the extent as it represented the employment of the BRA in mayoral politics. It was not precise, however, representing the actual movement of planning going on through the BRA at the time. The great era of urban renewal and redevelopment had passed, when the agency had been the prime mover of the physical

---

[81] Source: Interview.
[82] Cf. Hale Champion, *Report to Mayor Kevin H. White and the Boston Redevelopment Authority,* July 11, 1968, p. 2: "[...] I must report that I have found this agency in deep administrative and operational trouble. In my judgment, the priorities are out of date, the organization divided and weak, the financing and budgeting undisciplined and sometimes wasteful, the personnel policies an invitation to internal dissension, the relationship to the rest of city government a source of friction and potential impasse, and the ability to deliver on promises of the past eroding rapidly." — Cf. also: [Champion], *Boston Redevelopment Authority Reorganization Plan,* Sept. 12, 1968; J. W. Rosenblum, *The Boston Redevelopment Authority* (B), op. cit., p. 8 f.
[83] H. Champion, *Report to Mayor Kevin H. White ...,* op. cit., p. 4.
[84] Cf. infra, p. 311 f.
[85] *BG,* Febr. 16, 1982, p. 22.

rebirth of Boston.[86] Now, planning meant mainly economic planning; Boston's physical renaissance had made the city more and more attractive economically, the potential for private investment in the city was extraordinary.[87] This economic upswing of the city, however, had to be furthered and managed quite carefully, else it would not yield the desired material as well as social benefits.[88] The secular process of creativity in Boston continued,[89] but it had to be redirected again. The Court chose the BRA — the "political body" employed in mayoral politics — to be the locus and carrier of this reorientation. Through a subtle reorganization of institutional creativity within the BRA, the BRA emerged as the "primary generator of economic activity in the city."[90]

The process of creativity in Boston could continue. It had been given the necessary, "new" institutional form.

"Plans"

Making plans is the most obvious movement of planning. Yet, it is the least understood movement of planning. Plans, to the extent that they become final, arrest planning, the movement. However, the movement of planning alone makes plans useful; if it stops, plans rapidly represent plots of fantasy rather than procedures in reality.[91] Making plans is a paradoxical undertaking and it can therefore easily turn, on the one hand, into a perfection of plans ever more devoid of reality or, on the other, into a compliance with the fluidity of reality frustrating apparently any attempt at "planning." During the stretch of its history considered here, the BRA mostly mastered the paradox of planning. Being an institution of "planning" it pursued the movement of planning in making itself an "institutional" movement towards planning in a continuity of planning. It formed an institutional paradox, in

---

[86] For this predominant role of the BRA there were financial reasons mainly. Cf. infra, p. 308 f.

[87] Cf. BRA, *The Boston Redevelopment Authority. A Special Report on Fiscal Productivity*, June 1981.

[88] Cf. "Outlook for Boston: A Boom. City's $ 1 Building Boom Bucks the National Trend," *BG,* January 11, 1981.

[89] The "last" renaissance of Boston took place a hundred years ago, at the time of the Brahmins in the 19th century.

[90] Source: Interview.

[91] We should not exclude fantasy from planning, of course. In fact, we could not do it, even if we should wish to do so. Fantasy is the mode of mind by which we cognize; but we still have to think — through imagination — about *real* things.

being catalyst and carrier of "plans" that were but plans, yet plans indispensable to the pursuit of planning.

A situation of planning, then, which was hardly conducive to conventional "plans" – to the plans people produce so easily in a free, fancy play of purposes. The paradox of planning – or, concurrently, the movement of planning – is indeed rarely perceived. Usually, only one side of the paradox, isolated from the other, appears to be seen.

There is, on the one hand, the classic complaint, as it was voiced by the Boston Tercentenary Committee in 1932, for example, that the planners of the city thought they could do without a "comprehensive plan" and that they undertook their projects as "separate and isolated problems."[92] The complaint, recurrently repeated,[93] accuses planners of a great neglect: the grand design which they should produce has not yet been produced.

Yet, panoramic plans have been put forward, on the other hand, over and over again – "general plans," "long-range plans," "city-wide plans," "comprehensive plans," plans, and plans, and plans. The list of the grand designs produced in the process of Boston's renaissance is impressive.[94] Each appeared to have been made in disregard of the thwarting effect of finalizing plans: plans that arrest planning, that are not useful, as their proponents like to think, but fatal.[95] Fortunately, there were enough grand designs following each other for the counter effect. Before any of them could be considered for completion, it was superseded by another.[96]

The paradox of planning prevailed. The planners in the BRA pursued what they thought were contradictory activities. They prepared plans and they watched reality. Each of these two activities contradicted the other. If you were consequent in proceeding with the one, you could not proceed with the other. But this was what the planners in the BRA did. They were consequent in being inconsequential. They took the human weakness, being inconsequential, as a professional asset. The movement of planning was given an institution: persons handling through themselves the paradox of planning.

---

[92] Boston Tercentenary Committee, *Fifty Years of Boston,* op. cit., p. 41.

[93] Cf., for instance: *Memorandum,* from Alexander Ganz, to Robert T. Kenney, Subject: Agenda for the BRA; Planning for the City as a Whole, Dec. 20, 1971; BRA, *New Directions for Planning in Boston,* Jan. 1977.

[94] The Boston Contest, 1944/45; The 90 Million Development Program for Boston, 1960; General Plan for the City of Boston and the Regional Core, 1965; General Neighborhood Renewal Plan for Downtown, March 1967; Central Business District Plan, Juni 1967; Growth Program for Downtown, 1974; Boston Downtown Development Guidelines, March 1981.

[95] Cf. supra, p. 285.

[96] The Boston Downtown Development Guidelines, for instance, were continually "developed" throughout the 1980's. Older plans were still valid, although ignored or forgotten, while new plans were elaborated and added to the pile of existing plans.

Shifts of Functions

An institution that pursues a movement of planning pursues a movement beyond itself. It fulfills a function, as a social scientist would say. The movement of the institution in the mode of "planning" does not take place in a void. It occurs within a field of people and institutions of which this institution is a part. The movement of the institution, then, is also a movement within and, to some extent, a movement of that field.[97] The institution pursues a movement of planning and it carries a movement of planning. It pursues the movement of planning that is its own movement. And it carries, through this movement, that movement of planning that is a movement in the larger field. It fulfills, as an institution within the field, a function of the field. For the larger field acquires, through the planning which this particular institution performs, particular qualities of acting: the field can make the movement that the institution pursues.

Within the field of people and institutions wherein its movements of planning took place the BRA fulfilled a series of functions. In the first decade of its existence it assumed and maintained the function of the leading institution in the field of urban development in Boston, thanks to the considerable financial resources of which it could dispose and to the legal powers with which it was vested in the process of urban renewal. In the second decade, dwindling resources and a general reorientation of urban policies towards private investment diminished the status of the BRA at the head of the field; its function shifted to the role of an institution that managed the field, through the art of negotiation and persuasive pressure. In the third decade (during which Mayor White ended off his regime), the BRA shifted its function once again; it took up the task of marketing Boston as the pivot of America's Computer Age.

In its movement of planning the BRA had moved along the movements of the reality that it pursued through its movements of planning. Once a movement of planning that was rightly defined as renewal agency, it hat turned, through a series of institutional moves, into a movement of planning that occurred in the mode of free enterprise: "We have become like bankers."[98]

People

But who was "we"? The remark that the BRA resembled a business was made by Robert J. Ryan who, as its director, run the BRA — in conjunction

---

[97] Cf. also supra, p. 94 f.
[98] Source: Interview.

with the Mayor – indeed in a way conducive to his using the *pluralis majestatis*. In this instance, though, he meant his staff, the persons who formed the BRA in general and those of them who actually pushed its business in particular.[99] The "BRA," of course, did not exist. "We" existed: persons in a field of common movements, the people who knew they were the BRA and who composed, by their continuing movements with and among each other, their institution – a distinctive field of configurative action.[100]

The number of persons forming the BRA varied greatly, between 17 persons in 1957 and 498 persons in 1967. They composed quite different institutions, then, in terms of size, resources, and capacities. The BRA of early 1961 could have hardly encompassed all the engagements with which the BRA of 1967 concerned itself. And the BRA of 1981 could afford but a smaller range of pursuits. The BRA reflected in its own existence, by the changing number of its employees, the fluid character of planning. It made planning as a movement empirically present: as a movement that is a movement from one "institution" to another or, more precisely, as a movement that is a movement from one configuration of persons to another or, still more precisely, as a movement that is a movement from persons to persons.[101]

Shifts in Activity

To the different "BRA's" corresponded different types of activity. The BRA under Ed Logue applied itself exclusively to large-scale public projects. It formed the urban renewal agency as it was nurtured by Washington's urban policy at that time, disposing of large federal funds in the pursuit of large renewal projects. The apparent symmetry between the institution they composed and the type of activity this institution undertook caused the persons in the BRA to view themselves engaged in working towards a common goal: "Everyone knew which way one was going."[102]

The symmetry broke, albeit in the dark, while Logue was still the head of the BRA. When he sought the position of Mayor, the renewal czar rode on the promise that his name implied: the once and future grantsman of Boston's renaissance. Shifts in the federal budget, however, towards the financing of the Vietnam war, were increasingly reducing the funds available for urban renewal. After Champion had acceded the direction of the BRA, Logue told him the truth. He had run for Mayor although he had known

---

[99] Chris Carlaw, Lucas Di Leo, Brian Fallon.
[100] Cf. also supra, p. 142, infra, p. 316 ff.
[101] Cf. also supra, pp. 78 f., 209 f.
[102] Source: Interview.

that there would not be sufficient funds to finish the renewal program he had promised to complete.

Another BRA followed, one that adjusted itself to the shrinking financial supply from the Federal Government and, more critically, to the growing necessity of courting and encouraging private investment that would match the limited public funds. It undertook the corresponding type of activity: rehabilitation of old buildings, small-scale public projects.[103]

With the ascendency of the Reagan Administration — BRA planners derisively called it the "jelly-beans Administration" — the BRA was compelled, once again, to change itself and, congruently, the type of planning and urban development it pursued. The federal support turned into a scatter,[104] and the BRA had to rely more and more upon its ingenuity to find and to develop its own, independent sources of revenue.[105] It took on, as it has already been mentioned, the character of a business. Now the pendulum swung fully around. The planners in the BRA became again involved in large-scale projects. This time, however, these projects were large-scale *private* projects.[106] And the BRA did not form the leading figure in the field of urban planning and development in Boston. It now formed the institutional locus in the field to which the interests that shaped Boston's development were drawn and at which they were submitted to the art of negotiation, arbitration, and, of course, politics.

Political History

Planning, let us remember, is politics, and an institution marking the process of spatial creativity inevitably creates a crossroads of politics.[107] The BRA

---

[103] This shift in activity was caused by a new funding policy of the Federal Government. Funds were no longer granted for a period of several years, but strictly on an annual basis only. By this new rule the BRA lost its financial ability for planning on a large scale, that is undertaking projects whose completion would take several years. It could not run the risk to start with a large-scale project and then, if the Federal Government decided to stop its support in one year, to be left with all the financial burden. The responsible choice was clear: the BRA switched to projects as restricted as the financial planning still possible under the federal rule of annual funding.

[104] Still, a few BRA planners managed to orchestrate, through axial configurations, packages of federal support.

[105] The agency started a new policy concerning the property it owned in the city. It intended no longer to sell property but to lease it in order to secure for itself a steady flow of income.

[106] "You do not do a UDAG project on a small scale." Source: Interview.

[107] Cf. supra, p. 301 f.

confirmed the rule. It did so in changing ways, however. Founded as an autonomous agency, it did not belong to the machinery of the Boston government proper.[108] Yet, the development of Boston was its domain. No mayor of the city could afford not to have a vivid and continuing interest in the agency; none of its heads could ignore the attraction and importance the agency held for the mayor and his government. The agency stood not quite outside nor quite inside the Boston government, rather somewhere in between. But where?

During the administration of Mayor Collins the BRA took up the place of a separate yet concurrent body within the Collins government. Through its head, Ed Logue, the agency retained its own part of power. But it pursued the redevelopment program of Mayor Collins.[109] The Mayor and his Development Administrator knew the power each of them held: "Logue and Collins had a relationship of peers."[110]

Mayor White dabbled in architecture, from the very beginning of his rule.[111] But it took him some time to realize, as an associate phrased it, "that the BRA is a political tool."[112] At first he requested the BRA, like all other units of the Boston government, to recognize his institutional preeminence, a wish which Hale Champion, his first appointee as head of the agency, quite willingly complied with. Inside the regime which the Mayor was erecting, however, the BRA came to a measure of latitude. Under the direction of Robert T. Kenney, in particular, the agency realized some of the autonomy that it legally owned.[113] Still, the reins of the autocracy twined through the

---

[108] Chapter 150 of the Acts of 1957, which created the BRA, provides for the appointment of five *independent* board members, each for a term of five years. Four of the appointees are named by the Mayor of Boston, the fifth by the Governor of Massachusetts. Mayor White put "his" appointees under his influence by keeping them in a holdover status once their original term of appointment had expired. In 1975 the board members were: Paul Burns (appointed by the Governor), James G. Colbert, Robert L. Farrell, James K. Flaherty, Joseph J. Walsh. In 1978 James E. Cofield Jr. replaced Paul Burns, as the Governor's appointee. All four appointees of Mayor White's remained on the board.

[109] Ed Logue routinely professed that he followed Mayor Collins' program. Cf., for instance: E. J. Logue, *Memo to Boston Redevelopment Authority*, op. cit.

[110] Source: Interview.

[111] In 1968 White prevented a motel to be built near City Hall. He wanted to have a tree planted at the very spot on which the motel was supposed to be erected. I. M. Pei, the architect chosen for the construction of the motel, pleaded with White, "on his knees," not to insist on the tree and to give his agreement instead to the construction of the motel. White refused to yield. Later, Pei congratulated White on his "sound architectural" decision. (Source: Interview.)

[112] Source: Interview

[113] A representative story: One day Kenney received from White a memo telling him: "You will stop and desist from [...] and will sign this memo as indication of your agreement

government, reaching ever more into the BRA, too. Already in 1971, the agency had been described by one of its senior officials as "the Mayor's planning and development policy office."[114] Its annexation was preconceived before the Mayor actually consummated the autocratic conquest.

Upon the appointment of Robert Walsh, successor to Robert T. Kenney, the conquest was publicly made complete. The Mayor's institutional preeminence had changed into the Mayor's personal predominance:

> Robert Walsh was asked two questions during the press conference at which he was introduced as director of the Boston Redevelopment Authority. Mayor White answered one of them; Robert Kenney, Walsh's predecessor, answered the other.
>
> Walsh may or may not be articulate. Time will reveal that. What the press conference made clear is that he will not be independent, nor will he have much power. Power, as Mr. Kenney can testify, is access to the mayor and Walsh will not have that. At the same press conference, White himself said so. Deputy Mayor Robert Vey will be the real BRA director. Walsh will be able to communicate with the mayor, through Vey. And Vey, who already has checkoff authority on all BRA contracts, will be the conduit for the mayor's orders to the agency.[115]

Only two years later, White brought Walsh to resign, in consequence of the dispute over the Waterfront hotel.[116] The new BRA director, Robert J. Ryan, member of the Court, friend in the Kevin White Party, fully believed in the personal authority of his boss (as he called him), the Mayor. He ran the agency in the Mayor's name. Kevin White had appointed himself chief architect of Boston and he expected the BRA to enable him to reach the decisions he would make by preparing for his gracious consideration options from which he could choose. Would, for instance, a new office building that had originally been designed to have 40 storeys financially also be feasible if it had 15 storeys only? Some homework would be needed. It would be done by the BRA, now referred to as a "branch of the Mayor's Office," as an "extension of the Mayor's Office."[117] Then the boss and his deputy in his planning office would meet or, in some other way, communicate with each other.[118] And things would move, and plans would be negotiated, and deals would be struck, still in the Mayor's Office, in the Court − not in the institutional void that remained of the Boston Redevelopment Authority.

---

to my decision and you will return the memo to me by 5 o'clock." Kenney threw the memo in his waste basket and asked the people in the BRA who pursued what the Mayor did not want them to pursue "to accelerate their planning activities." (Source: Interview.)

[114] A. Ganz, *Memo to R. J. Kenney,* op. cit., p. 2.

[115] *BG,* Nov. 18, 1976.

[116] Cf. supra, p. 290.

[117] Sources: Interviews.

[118] On the character of the relationship between Ryan and White, cf. supra, p. 129.

The Rise in Creativity

The future is creativity. We do not know the future. Yet we know images of the future held by the past. And they tell us the gait of the future: our creativity.

At different points in the history of the BRA different configurations of planners in different institutional modes of the agency pictured to themselves, under different circumstances, with different policies in mind, very different images of Boston in the future. There were not a few cities of Boston, if each image had indeed become the anticipated future. None, of course, has fully defined the future of Boston. Was the future of Boston — during the historical period considered here — then planned chaotically?

No, it was planned creatively. The planners of Boston would have betrayed Boston, had they forsaken its future for an image of its future. They would have tried to freeze and thus would have lost its future for the sake of an image to which things would less and less correspond. They chose the other way: flexible responses to a fluid reality, new visions under new circumstances, other configurations of people for other goals, plans following politics, policies pursuant to resources, moves designedly contradictory to each other.

In the pursuit of creativity they met Boston's future. Ed Logue could dispose of a great deal of money. In his mode of creativity all of Boston would have become very new. Bob Ryan had much less money to dispose of. In his mode of creativity all of Boston would have become a charming city attracting investors. Logue could buy. Ryan had to negotiate. The early BRA was master in its field. The later BRA had to maintain its status in the field with much ingenuity. Something paradoxical occurred: the greater creativity emerged when the BRA had lost its lead. But then, good plans are made in the hour of need.

12 Within Reality: Boston Regained, Boston Lost

The renaissance of Boston has taken place. Its refound splendor radiates throughout the world.[119] The vision of a new city, "rich and populous" once again, tried for by a few three decades ago in the midst of Boston's decay, this vision has be come an experience of the many. Boston appears to be saved.

Not quite. The struggle for a "new" Boston goes on and it has not been a struggle without costs. Boston has regained, in different ways, a good part

---

[119] Cf. footnote 58 and *IHT*, April 8, 1985; *Süddeutsche Zeitung*, June 2, 1987.

of its former beauty and erstwhile importance. But it has also lost, irredeemably, parts of its Old World character and very special urban charm.[120] There is a mixed lesson to be learned. Movements of planning have to involve utopian hopes, else they do not hold the promise for which people engage in the necessary struggles. Yet they occur, if they occur, within the reality of things – nowhere else. They run into a reality of structures that resist them, of interests that bow them, of people that neglect them, of procedures that split them, of developments that surpass them. The project is a paradox: To seek within reality the utopia of our vision.

"Boston has forgotten about its streetscape," said (in June 1983) Simone Auster, vice president of community development for the Greater Boston Chamber of Commerce. "Big buildings are going up, and I don't see a park bench, I don't see trees."[121]

The movement towards hotel and office complexes had been stronger than the movement towards street furniture.

"If a city told us, 'Put in housing before you build your project,' we'd answer, 'You just changed our mind for us. We're going somewhere else,' " said (in June 1983) R. John Griefen, vice president of Hines Industrial.[122]

Naturally, people investing their money seek a maximum profit. Utopia had to be reconciled with reality. No power, not the most puissant one, could have imposed upon reality a perfect new Boston. In the mode of a city a society is building or rebuilding itself as its own creation. It may seek its spatial perfection. And it will not attain it. For it is not perfect, as a society, and it never will be. As a social quest for its spatial perfection the city must necessarily fail. It is its own and it is therefore an imperfect creation. "Boston," Edward C. Banfield and Martin Meyerson in 1966 predicted,

> will be one of the most beautiful cities in the world a generation hence. It will not, however, be as beautiful as it might be. No city that is built by a free people will ever be a great work of art, for freedom allows the expression of bad taste as well as of good. Let us be reconciled to the prospect that we will make mistakes in civic design in the future as we have in the past. To the extent that a choice must be made between civic freedom and civic beauty, we trust that the former will be preferred. The great challenge for Boston is to pursue the two goals simultaneously.[123]

---

[120] Cf. J. H. Kay, *Lost Boston*, Boston 1980; "Boston Old, Boston New," *The BG Magazine*, Aug. 2, 1981; R. A. Jordan, "The Two Faces of Boston,", *BG*, Aug. 26, 1982; D. Golden, D. Mehegan, "Changing the Heart of the City," *The BG Magazine*, Sept. 18, 1983.

[121] *BG*, June 2, 1983.

[122] ibid.

[123] E. C. Banfield, M. Meyerson, *Boston: The Job Ahead*, op. cit., p. 117.

Politics, Space, and Creativity

13 Gravitational Structures of Creativity

Spatial creativity occurs as creativity in the mode of society: human beings create human space. And it occurs as creativity in the mode of space: human beings as planners plan here and there, in this relationship to each other or in that relationship to each other, in this range of planning or in that, in wide dispersion or in close concentration. Spatial creativity produces things in space: the artefacts of human space within physical space. And it produces a space of things: the space of its production.[124]

While it planned human space, the BRA made its own space of planning. It formed a place or, rather, places at which the planners *in* the agency pursued the planning *of* the agency. The Boston Redevelopment Authority planned. But, in probing this agent of plans one would not have asked the most expedient question in raising the query: Who? The more utile question was: Where? Where, in the BRA, were those movements of creativeness to be found that made up the creativeness of the BRA?

They could be found, in the era of Mayor White, at myriad loci in a moving space of perennial expansion and contraction, formation and restructuring, coalescence and dissolution. They could be found, in the mode of "planning'," where, in the mode of "politics," the same moments of creativeness took place: in the chaos of power.[125]

The Boston Redevelopment Authority mirrored Mayor White's autocracy. The organization of the agency did not involve any delegation of authority.[126] It followed the policies and decisions of the director. If someone else exercised authority inside the agency or outside the agency on its behalf, this authority had only been granted temporarily, by the director. The head of the agency deliberately kept his house divided. He did not work with members of his staff other than individually, in the mode of a one to one relationship. He strongly discouraged, if not prevented, contacts between his staff and the staff of the Mayor.

Employees in the BRA, in general, could not count on job security. Nor had they been given precisely defined positions and areas of responsibility.

---

[124] And a creative government creates the conditions of its creativity. Cf. supra, p. 24.

[125] Cf. supra, p. 40 f.

[126] The following description of the BRA "mirroring Mayor White's autocracy" is based on information obtained through interviews. It relates mostly to the time when Robert J. Ryan was head of the agency.

To the question: "Could you describe your work in the agency?" a senior BRA planner responded typically: "The work I am supposed to do or the work I really do?"[127] All the agency's organization was fluid. The planners formed but transitory teams, each being constituted for a particular project and each being dissolved or just disintegrating once the project had been completed, deferred, or abandoned. One group of planners knew very little of the projects which the other groups of planners worked on; and the projects themselves had but fluid contours. Projects really became projects only under pressure; sooner or later, the planners had to think about the financing of a project and a developer who would undertake it; then, and only then, did they put their projects into a more formal shape.

When members of the BRA spoke about the procedures of the BRA, they stressed the discontinuous character of these procedures. Shifting frequently from one task to another, from one project to another, from one team of planners to another, they hardly achieved a comprehensive view of what they were doing. They rather felt that all what they made were fragmentary and fleeting experiences. In the moving space where they moved all the bearing provided were the movements of things towards each other, away from each other.

Gravitational structures of creativity prevailed. The space produced in the event of spatial creativity spread beyond the BRA into the city. In the planning of Boston more places of planning in Boston emerged. A city of planners arose within the city present. This city of planners was marked mostly by neighborhood associations, community groups, citizen committees — by those countless carriers of social and political concerns that exist in Boston as configurative manifestations of civic authority. It represented an elaborate, labyrinthian, puzzling city, as evanescent as real, as obscure as ostentatious, as small-sized as far-flung, only scarcely populated, but then also teeming with people. The space it spanned appeared the more infinite the more it was explored. In the city of planners the moving space of planning endlessly expands.

In the following, three neighborhood associations are chosen in order to approach the city of planners, the *Downton Crossing Association,* the *Back Bay Association,* and the *Park Plaza Civic Advisory Committee.*[128] All three

---

[127] Source: Interview.

[128] The Downtown Crossing Association, established in 1980, is a private, non profit organization focused on the civic and economic development of the Downtown Crossing area. Its offices are located at 38 Chauncy Street, Boston. It is connected with the Back Bay Association, Washington and Tremont Street Neighborhood Association, Theatre District Neighborhood Association, Bay Village Association, Friends of the Public Garden, Beacon Hill Civic Association, Chinese Consolidated Benevolent Association. –

associations marked, at the time when they were examined for the purpose of this study, a significant space in the city of planners; each did this, however, in a differing way. In setting out at the Boston Redevelopment Authority, and in stopping first at the Downtown Crossing Association, and in moving on to the Back Bay Association, and in coming finally to the Park Plaza Civic Advisory Committee, we shall pass over increasing distances through the space of planning in the expanding city of planners. We shall travel from a "central" place to the periphery. And there will be central places at the "periphery," too.

The Downtown Crossing Association comprised mainly merchants of the old retail sector in Boston near the Boston Common. Its founders intended it to become the local partner in this area for other planning agencies and institutions in the city, in particular for the BRA. And they expected it to emerge as the meeting place of all those who were concerned with "Downtown Crossing," that is, with the plan to reestablish in the middle of Old Boston an economically as well as socially vibrant urban center. Years after its foundation, however, the association remained dependent upon infusions from the BRA, infusions of ideas and initiatives as well as infusions of money. It did have an institutional form: a staff, an office, a newsletter. But this "institution" did not carry the association. If it was heard or noticed in the city of planners, the association had been made vocal by its two active members.[129] The pith of the association lay in the BRA, with the planners who worked on the Downtown Crossing project there. Yet, an essential part of the project was the attempt to set the merchant's association firmly on its

---

The Back Bay Association, established in 1926 as a corporation, is dedicated to commercial and civic improvement in the Back Bay. Its offices are located at 20 Providence Street, Boston. Together with the Neighborhood Association of the Back Bay the BBA has formed the Back Bay Federation for Community Development; it has also helped to create the Back Bay Architectural Commission. – The Park Plaza Civic Advisory Committee, established in 1973 and organized as a corporation under Chapter 180 of the General Laws of the Commonwealth of Massachusetts, is a council of fourteen civic and business organizations to serve as an advisory group to the Boston Redevelopment Authority and to assure citizen participation in the planning of the Park Plaza Urban Renewal Project. Its offices are located at 24 Rutland Square, Boston. The members of the CAC are: the Back Bay Association, Back Bay Federation for Community Development, Bay Village Neighborhood Association, Beacon Hill Civic Association, Boston Conservation Association, Boston Building and Construction Trades Council of the Metropolitan District, Chinese Consolidated Benevolent Association of New England, Friends of the Public Garden, Neighborhood Association of the Back Bay, Greater Boston Real Estate Board, League of Women Voters of Boston, Park Square Improvement Association, Retail Trade Board of Boston, Stuart Street Neighborhood Association.

[129] Dawn Marie Driscoll, Alvin Schmertzler.

feet. The senior planner in the BRA sometimes masqueraded and acted for the party in the project whom he was wanting so much to act on its own. He pushed for an expansion of spatial creativity at the place which the Downtown Crossing Association marked but did not fill.

At the place in the city of planners at which the Back Bay Association could be found, the presence of spatial creativity that it made could hardly be overlooked. Whereas the distance between the Downtown Crossing Associ- ation and the BRA was very short, the Back Bay Association took up in the city of planners a place much farther removed from the BRA (and thus from City Hall). Yet it held the place very visibly and quite exclusively. It appeared to be an independent authority in the area of interests that it defined as its own through the power of its presence.

In the Back Bay — the neighborhood whose civic concerns the Back Bay Association primarily represented — the city government had to share its "central" authority with a "local" power. Carried mainly by businesspeople, the Back Bay Association formed in the neighborhood the principal agency of spatial creativity. It encouraged such commercial activity in the Back Bay that it deemed to be beneficial to the sleek prosperity of the neigborhood and it repelled the establishment of such enterprises (a cheap sandwhich shop or a blue movie theater, for instance) that should taint the Back Bay with urban sleaziness. Issues of zoning or questions concering the design of new houses or restored buildings were, by the parties concerned, first addressed to the Back Bay Association which, in turn, reviewed the matter and, on the basis of its own resolve, discussed the desirable way to proceed with concur- rent agents in the city of planners ... and the city government. The Association undertook its own planning studies — on the circulation of pedestrians in the Back Bay, for instance — by hiring consultants from leading institutions (like MIT) to do the empirical research and to elaborate the findings. It formed indeed a "parallel agency," as BRA director Ryan acknowledged,[130] concentrating in the hands of its members the power of spatial politics in the Back Bay.

Whence did this power come? The Back Bay Association was an old institution, deeply rooted in the local community, well financed by wealthy businesspeople. Its members were friends with many people: neighborhood activists, planners, legislators, leading businessmen, people in the Kevin White Party. The Association made, in many instances, common cause with a host of similar organizations;[131] it had gathered around itself a wide-ranging network of political allies. The executive secretary of the association[132] had

[130] Source: Interview.
[131] Cf. supra, note 128.
[132] Stuart Robbins.

been its principal agent for a long time and thus had acquired an experience and sophistication as to his handling the affairs of the Back Bay that was unequalled by anyone in the city of planners and, for that matter, in his own organization. He held, in fact, the central place in the planning of the Back Bay, quite consciously, in being very much aware both of his "independence" and of the people in whose service he practiced this independence. Through his office the process of spatial creativity in the Back Bay took shape that shaped the spatial character of the Back Bay. Here, center and periphery in the city of planners appeared to have shifted, the nominal center (BRA, City Hall) to the periphery, the periphery to the center.

From the vantage point of the Park Plaza Civic Advisory Committee the space of planning wherein it moved had yet another gravitational structure. BRA and City Hall seemed to have receded from the stage upon which the Committee acted – and appeared to lurk peremptorily, though, in the shadows cast by the Mayor's power. The space into which the Committee chiefly reached lay beyond Boston, in the larger world formed by cosmopolitan development interests, the Massachusetts Legislature, the Federal Government in Washington, and the lovers of Boston – of the Boston Common, to be precise – all over the United States. The Park Plaza Civic Advisory Committee answered to Boston; the place it filled in the city of planners had the marks of the city itself; the periphery fell into the center, the center fell into the periphery.

This status of the Committee could astound. It was but an aggregation of civic association, after all. And the matter for which it existed was just a particular development project – the Park Plaza Project.[133] Yet this project, in its long and controversial history, had proved to be a project of the intractable kind. It touched one of the most sensitive spots in Boston, the point where Beacon Hill, Boston Common, and Back Bay converge. It had lastingly aroused the interest (and suspicions) of a widely dispersed and well connected, hence powerful lobby of Bostonphiles. In the "battle" fought about the project in its original form, the Bostonphiles had won. Now they swayed the course which the project was taking, through the Committee. And the

---

[133] Cf. *Park Plaza. Urban Renewal Project. Final Project Report. Urban Renewal Plan*, s. l., 1971; *Park Plaza. Interim Report of the Park Plaza Civic Advisory Committee*, s. l., s. d.; *Report of the Park Plaza Civic Advisory Committee on Parts IV, V, and VI of the BRA's Draft Environmental Impact Report*, s. l., 1976; *Supplemental Report of the Park Plaza Civic Advisory Committee on the BRA's Environmental Impact Report*, s. l., 1976; BRA, *Park Plaza Urban Renewal Project. Urban Renewal Plan*. Amended, s. l., 1977; [T. Blackett], *Park Plaza: Urban Design in Practice*, s. l. 1977; CAC, *A Progress Report on the Park Plaza Urban Renewal Project*, s. l., 1978; BRA, *Park Plaza Streets Urban Systems Project*, s. l., 1981; cf. also: BG, Nov. 24, 1976; Dec. 20, 1977.

BRA played the role of a spectator rather than that of an actor. Its representative tended to participate in meetings of the Committee as briefly as passively, or did not come to a meeting at all. On the basis of a contract which these two "partners" in the city of planners had concluded, the BRA did, however, finance the organizational life of the Committee: staff, lawyers, consultants, newsletters, office expenditures.[134] It had to. The president of the Committee[135] knew which place she filled in the city of planners. The director of the BRA, she explained, would without delay return her calls. In the process of spatial creativity the power of creativity had gravitated: "They have to listen to us."[136]

14 People and Decisions

Politics is a spatial phenomenon. It produces space. It happens in the space it produces. It is the space through which it happens: movements of people towards each other, away from each other.

Politics, therefore, is best observed through an inquiry into the movements of people who make politics. They make a field of creativity, and the inquiry into politics will be an inquiry into the three dimensions of this field.

(1) It is a field of social creativity: the event of creativeness in a society towards the creation of the society.

(2) It is a field of political creativity: the gathering of creativeness in a society towards a creativeness of the society.

(3) It is a field of spatial creativity: the space of creativeness in the creation of space.

Politics, indeed, is best observed in the mode of the *polis*. The process of creativity human beings can perform through movements with and among themselves in the space they will create by these movements, this process has a paradigmatic form, it is the city. In the city, politics is essential. The process of social creativity coincides with the process of political creativity, and the process of political creativity coincides with the process of spatial creativity. All human space is local space and politics is the mode of its production. All politics is spatial politics. All politics is local.[137]

An inquiry into the movements of people who make politics will fall short of its objective, therefore, if it does but follow the conventional way and

---

[134] In 1981 the CAC received from the BRA the amount of $ 25,000.

[135] Joan Wood.

[136] Source: Interview.

[137] Cf. Thomas "Tip" O'Neill, *Man of the House,* New York 1987, p. 6 and p. 26.

proceeds to seize "decision making" as its subject. It would not recognize the spatial quality of politics. The conventional study of "decision making" assumes, in any given case, a process of politics "from" a point of origination "to" a point of completion on an axis of unilinear time. It presupposes chains of events and presumes that the people who make politics indeed line these chains. It imagines a dramaturgy of decision and considers politics to be indeed the staging of these decisions.

Politics, however, takes place in a multiplicity of time and in an infinity of space. It is creativity and thus its own source of what it is. It creates time and it creates space. It happens in the times it takes and it occurs in the spaces it produces. To be apprehended, it has to be followed, wherever it leads —

— to that man, for example, who, from the distance of a private citizen and acting under a personal sense of time, formed a juncture in the spatial politics of Boston's renaissance; although he pioneered the Prudential Center he has remained almost unknown;[138]

— to that architect in the BRA who, without any specific purpose, took a walk with a colleague one day in the North Station area and came back from the walk with the idea of a great development project, and the skills to enlist a few other people for launching the project; he has not been identified with the origin of the project, the public acclaim for the North Station Project having gone to Mayor White and Moshe Safdie;[139]

— to that consultant who, actualizing both the quick interests of the business politician and the perennial wisdom of the vernacular architect, suggested a way that would give a developer his high rise (the Rose Tower) and the urban designers another chance to preserve Boston as a walking city; he proposed that the ground floor of the tower consist of public passages; it was he who had fused two contradictory pursuits, urban design and free enterprise, yet the developer and the planners celebrated their great art of negotiation.[140]

Things are made through politics. "Decisions" occur. But this is not the question. We would not live, if politics did not make what it makes. The question is the making. Where is the creation that creates itself — politics, pure human creativity? It is to be found only in its own process, in the process of creativity people perform through movements with and among themselves, towards each other, away from each other. The space of these movements, however, is infinite. Politics can be found everywhere. It is creativity. But then, creativity is quite distinguishable. We do know politics — once we have discovered the process of its creativity.

---

138 George F. Oakes. — Cf. supra, note 15.
139 Robert Kroin.
140 Frank Keefe.

Bibliography

I Primary Sources

1. *Interviews*

Series A. Transcripts of 118 interviews which the author obtained in 1980, 1981, 1982, and
1983 from politicians, planners, government officials, neighborhood activists,
businesspeople, and journalists in Boston.

Series B. Transcripts of 43 interviews which Prof. Arnold Howitt (then at Harvard University) had obtained in 1972 and 1979 from politicians, government officials, and
planners in Boston. Prof. Howitt kindly made these transcripts available to the
author.

2. *Field Notes*

36 transcripts of notes taken by the author on the basis of his observations in the field.

3. *Documents, Reports, Memoranda*

A Reprint of the Massachusetts Port Authority ENABLING ACT, Chapter 465 of the Acts
of 1956 as amended through December 1981 (with Appendices), s. l., s. d.

[Blackett, T.] *Park Plaza: Urban Design in Practice,* s. l., 1977.

Boston Municipal Research Bureau, City of Boston Employees – How Many Are There?
Special Report No. 97, Boston 1980.

Boston Municipal Research Bureau, Proposition 2 $^1/_2$: Impact on Boston, Special Report
No. 98, Boston 1980.

Boston Municipal Research Bureau, Down the homestretch on reevaluation and classification, Special Report No. 82 – 8, Boston 1982.

Boston Municipal Research Bureau, Changes in Boston's Personnel Levels, Special Report
No. 83 – 1, Boston 1983.

Boston Municipal Research Bureau, Boston's Personnel Reduction Program, Special Report
No. 82 – 4, Boston 1982.

Boston Municipal Research Bureau, Condominium Conversions in Boston. A Significant
Tax Benefit to the City, Special Report No. 94, Boston 1980.

Boston Municipal Research Bureau, Tax-Exempt Property: A Boston Burden, Special Report
No. 77, Boston 1978.

Boston Redevelopment Authority, Boston, Present and Future; Background Information for
Infrastructure Planning, s. l., June 1983.

Boston Redevelopment Authority, Commercial Area Revitalization District Plan: North
Station, s. l., 1979.

Boston Redevelopment Authority, Condominium Development in Boston, s. l., 1980.

Boston Redevelopment Authority, New Directions for North Station, s. l., 1980.

Boston Redevelopment Authority, North Station Final Project Report. Urban Renewal Plan,
s. l., 1980.

Boston Redevelopment Authority, North Station Final Project Report. Supporting Documentation, s. l., 1980.

Boston Redevelopment Authority, Moshe Safdie and Associates, A Development Plan for
    North Station District, s. l., s. d.
Boston Redevelopment Authority, A Special Report on Fiscal Productivity, s. l., 1981.
Boston Redevelopment Authority, Boston South Station Transportation Center and Air
    Rights Development Project, s. l., s. d.
Boston Redevelopment Authority, New Directions for Planning in Boston, s. l., 1977.
Boston Redevelopment Authority, Report on the Proposed Purchase and Development of
    South Station, s. l., 1964.
Boston Redevelopment Authority, South Station Urban Renewal Project, Environmental
    Impact Report, s. l., 1976.
Boston Redevelopment Authority, Park Plaza Streets Urban Systems Project, s. l., 1981.
Boston Redevelopment Authority, Park Plaza Urban Renewal Project. Urban Renewal Plan.
    Amended, s. l., 1977.
Boston Tercentenary Committee, *Fifty Years of Boston. A Memorial Volume,* s. l., 1932.
Civic Advisory Committee (Park Plaza), Park Plaza. Interim Report of the Park Plaza Civic
    Advisory Committee, s. l., s. d.
Civic Advisory Committee (Park Plaza), Report of the Park Plaza Civic Advisory Committee
    on Parts IV, V, and VI of the BRA's Draft Environmental Impact Report, s. l., 1976.
Civic Advisory Committee (Park Plaza), Supplemental Report of the Park Plaza Civic
    Advisory Committee on the BRA's Environmental Impact Report, s. l., 1976.
Civic Advisory Committee (Park Plaza), A Progress Report on the Park Plaza Urban Renewal
    Project, s. l., 1978.
Champion, H., Report to Mayor Kevin H. White and the Boston Redevelopment Authority,
    July 11, 1968.
Champion, H., Boston Redevelopment Authority Reorganization Plan, Sept. 12, 1968.
City of Boston, Downtown Crossing. An Economic Strategy Plan, s. l., 1983.
City of Boston, South Station, Transportation Center Air Rights, s. l., s. d.
City of Boston, The 90 Million Dollar Development Program for Boston, reprinted from
    the City Record, Sept. 24, 1960, s. l., s. d.
City of Boston, BRA, Background to Planning for Boston's Downtown, s. l., 1973, 1980,
    2nd ed.
City of Boston, Downtown Crossing, s. l., 1981.
City of Boston, BRA, Demonstration Grant Application [re: Downtown Crossing], s. l.,
    1980.
City of Boston, *City of Boston Code* (Statute, Ordinances, Regulations), s. l., 1975.
City of Boston, *Municipal Register for 1978 – 1979,* Boston 1979.
City of Boston, *Boston's Forty-Five Mayors,* Boston 1979, 2nd ed.
City of Boston, *Neighborhood Boston.* A Guide to Human Services, s. l., 1978.
City of Boston, Boston Enterprise. A Program for Neighborhood Job Creation and Economic
    Growth, s. l., 1981.
City of Boston, Boston's Tax Strategy. The Fiscal Experience of the City, s. l., 1974.
Ganz, A., Memorandum to Robert T. Kenney, Subject: Agenda for the BRA, Planning for
    the City as a Whole, Dec. 20, 1971.
Ganz, A., Perkins, G., Performance of Boston City Government, 1967 – 1981, s. l., 1981.
Logue, E. J., Memo to Boston Redevelopment Authority, Dec. 21, 1960.
Logue, E. J., Seven Years of Progress. A Final Report by Edward J. Logue, Development
    Administrator, Boston 1967.

Nedder, G. T., ed., A Business Community Guide to City Hall, s. l., s. d.
Park Plaza. Urban Renewal Project. Final Project Report. Urban Renewal Plan, s. l., 1971.
Roth, H., Dacey, B., Ryan, R., Boston Guide to Development, Boston 1981.
U. S. Dept. of Transportation, Federal Railroad Admin., Northeast Corridor Improvement Project, Draft Environmental Impact Statement South Station Improvement Project, Washington, D. C. 1980.
Vocations for Social Change, The Boston People's Yellow Pages, 1980 – 81 edition.

4. Newspapers, Periodicals

City Record, City of Boston: Boston Globe; Boston Herald; Boston Herald American; Boston Magazine; Boston Observer; Boston Phoenix; The Christian Science Monitor; International Herald Tribune; The New York Times.

II. Secondary Sources

1. Boston

Adams, R. B., Jr., The Boston Money Tree. How the Proper Men of Boston Made, Invested and Preserved Their Wealth from Colonial Days to the Space Age, New York 1977.
Ainley, L., Boston Mahatma: Martin Lomasney, Boston 1949.
Amory, C., The Proper Bostonians, New York 1947.
Arnone, N., Redevelopment in Boston: A Study of the Politics and Administration of Social Change, unpubl. Ph. D. Thesis, The Massachusetts Institute of Technology, 1965.
Banfield, E. C., Derthick, M., A Report on the Politics of Boston, Cambridge, Mass. 1960.
Banfield, E. C., Meyerson, M., Boston: The Job Ahead, Cambridge, Mass. 1966.
Baltzell, E. D., Puritan Boston and Quaker Philadelphia. Two Protestant Ethics and the Spirit of Class Authority and Leadership, New York 1979.
Burns, C. K., "The Irony of Progressive Reform: Boston 1898 – 1910," in: R. P. Formisano, C. K. Burns, eds., Boston 1700 – 1980. The Evolution of Urban Politics, Westport – London 1984, pp. 133 – 164.
Butterfield, F., "Troubles of Boston's Mayor Are Tied to Political Machine," NYT, Dec. 26, 1982.
Clendinen, D., "Profile in Politics: Boston Mayor's Reformist Style Faded With His Fortunes," NYT, Dec. 30, 1982.
Conzen, M. P., Lewis, G. K., "Boston: A Geographical Portrait," in: Contemporary Metropolitan America, Vol. I, Cities of the Nation's Historic Metropolitan Core, ed. J. S. Adams, Cambridge, Mass. 1976.
Esch, M. D., Killory, J. E., Boston Charter Reform (A), (B), (C), Kennedy School of Government, Cambridge; Mass. 1978.
Ferber, M., Beard, E., "Marketing Urban America: The Selling of the Boston Plan & a New Direction in Federal-Urban Relations," Polity, Vol. XII, No. 4, Summer 1980, pp. 539 – 559.
Ferman, B., "Beating the Odds: Mayoral Leadership and the Acquisition of Power," Policy Studies Review, Vol. 3, No. 1, Aug. 1983, pp. 29 – 40.

Ferman, B., *Governing the Ungovernable City. Political Skill, Leadership and the Modern Mayor,* Philadelphia 1985.

Firey, W., *Land Use in Central Boston,* Cambridge, Mass. 1947.

Formisano, R. P., Burns, C. K., eds., *Boston 1700 – 1980. The Evolution of Urban Politics,* Westport – London 1984.

Frank, B., Transcript of a lecture presented to a class (Government 246, Prof. E. C. Banfield) at Harvard University on March 3, 1977.

Gogolin, J., "Kevin's Gospel. The Politics of Property," *BM,* July 1980.

Golden, D., Mehegan, D., "Changing the Heart of the City," *BG Magazine,* Sept. 18, 1983.

Green, M., *The Problem of Boston. Some Readings in Cultural History,* New York 1966.

Handlin, O., *Boston's Immigrants 1790 – 1880. A Study in Acculturation,* Cambridge, Mass. 1941, rev. ed. 1959.

Harmonay, M., First, D., "Mayor White, Media Mogul: The Politics of Cable TV," *BG Magazine,* Sept. 1980.

Heymann, Ph., Weinberg, M. W., "The Paradox of Power: Mayoral Leadership on Charter Reform in Boston," in: W. Dean Burnham, M. Wagner Weinberg, eds. *American Politics and Public Policy,* Cambridge, Mass. 1978, pp. 280 – 306.

Hepburn, A., *Biography of a City, Boston. The Story of a Great American City and Its Contribution to Our National Heritage,* New York 1966.

Higgins, G. V., *Style Versus Substance. Boston, Kevin White, and the Politics of Illusion,* New York 1984.

Hollister, R., Lee, T., *Development Politics. Private Development and Public Interest,* Washington, D. C. 1979.

Jennings, J., King, M., eds., *From Access to Power. Black Politics in Boston,* Cambridge, Mass. 1986.

Joher, F. C., *The Urban Establishments. Upper Strata in Boston, New York, Charleston, Chicago, and Los Angeles,* Urbana, Ill. 1982.

Joher, F. C., "The Politics of the Boston Brahmins: 1800 – 1860," in: R. P. Formisano, C. K. Burns, eds., *Boston 1700 – 1980,* Westport – London 1984, pp. 59 – 86.

Jones, V. O., "The Man With Faith in Boston," *Boston Globe,* July 15, 1966.

Jordan, R. A., "The Two Faces of Boston," *BG,* Aug. 26, 1982.

Kay, J. H., *Lost Boston,* Boston 1980.

Keller, M., *Historical Sources of Urban Personality: Boston, New York, Philadelphia,* Oxford 1982.

Kellerhouse, K. S., *Redevelopment of the Boston Waterfront,* Kennedy School of Government, Cambridge, Mass. 1978.

Killory, E., *Boston Charter Reform (A), (B),* Kennedy School of Government, Cambridge, Mass. 1978.

Larkin, A., "Cable TV Comes to Boston ... and It's Kevin White's Show," *BG Magazine,* Sept. 7, 1980.

Lorrain, D., La gestion municipale à Boston, unpubl. research report, Fondation des villes, Paris 1976.

Lucas, P., "Just Plain Ray: A Political Coup," *BH,* Sept. 30, 1983.

Lukas, J. A., *Common Ground. A Turbulent Decade in the Lives of Three American Families,* New York 1986.

Lupo, A., *Liberty's Chosen Home. The Politics of Violence in Boston,* Boston 1977.

Marquand, J. P., *The Late George Aply*, New York 1936.

Mason, Th. R., Reform Politics in Boston. A Study of Ideology and Social Change in Municipal Government, Unpubl. Ph. D. Thesis, Harvard University, 1963.

Matthews, N., *The City Government of Boston*, Boston 1895.

Mc Quarde, W., "Boston: What Can a Sick City Do?" *Fortune*, Vol. LXIX, No. 6, June 1964, p. 132 ff.

Memolo, R., New Boston. The Politics of Renewal in Boston, unpubl. ms.

Menzies, I., "An Upbeat City of Charm, Change," in: *The Dynamic City. Boston at 350. A Special Supplement*, BG, May 18, 1980.

Menzies, I., "Don't Blame All on White," BG, Febr. 23, 1981.

Morison, S. E., *One Boy's Boston 1887 – 1901*, Boston 1962.

Murphy, J. V., "Southie Cheers Victory of Their 'Hometown Boy,' " BG, Oct. 13, 1983.

Nichols, W., "Flynn's Heedless Pursuit of Development," BG, Febr. 14, 1985.

O'Connell, J. B., *The Boston Plan*, Kennedy School of Government, Cambridge, Mass. 1979.

O'Connor, E., *The Last Hurrah*, Boston 1956.

O'Connor, Th. H., *Bibles, Brahmins and Bosses. A Short History of Boston*, Boston 1976.

Pool, D., Politics in the New Boston 1960 – 1970. A Study of Mayoral Policy Making, unpubl. Ph. D. Thesis, Brandeis University 1974.

Rabinowitz, A., *Non-Planning and Redevelopment in Boston: An Analytic Study of the Planning Process*, University of Washington 1972.

Rezendes, M., "Left, Right, and Flynn. Profile of a Blue-Collar Crusade," BPh, Oct. 4, 1983.

Rosenblum, J. W., *The Boston Redevelopment Authority*, Business School, Harvard University, 1969.

Segal, M., "Why Boston Should Go Bankrupt," *The Real Paper*, June 4, 1981.

Shand-Tucci, D., *Built in Boston. City and Suburb 1800 – 1950*, Amherst 1988.

Sheehan, T., "Getting and Spending. Living in the Material World. The Mayor and the Budget Crisis," BPh, April 1980.

Smith, R., "Remembering Kevin. An Admirer Predicts History's Blessing on Our 'Jackhammer' Mayor. Stylish Visionary in an Era of Mushy Pluralism," BO, Vol. 2, No. 10, Dec. 1983.

Stainton, J., *Urban Renewal and Planning in Boston*, Boston 1972.

Story, R., *The Forging of an Aristocracy. Harvard and the Boston Upper Class*, Middletown 1980.

Thernstrom, S., *The Other Bostonians. Poverty and Progress in an American Metropolis 1880 – 1970*, Cambridge, Mass. 1973.

Todisco, P. J., *Boston's First Neighborhood: The North End*, Boston 1976.

Travis, T.-M. C., "Boston: The Unfinished Agenda," PS, Vol. XIX, N. 3, Summer 1986, pp. 610 – 617.

Trout, Ch. H., "Curley of Boston: The Search for Irish Identity," in: R. P. Formisano, C. K. Burns, eds., *Boston 1700 – 1980. The Evolution of Urban Politics*, Westport – London 1984, pp. 165 – 195.

Turner, R. L., "Connolly Builds an Organization," BG, Nov. 23, 1982.

Turner, R. L., "What Makes a Mayor?" *The BG Magazine*, Nov. 13, 1983.

Warner, S. B., *The Urban Wilderness*, New York 1972.

Weinberg, M. W., "Boston's Kevin White: A Mayor Who Survives," *Political Science Quarterly*, Vol. 96, No. 1, Spring 1981, pp. 87 – 106.

Weismantel, W., The Collision of Urban Renewal with Zoning. The Boston Experience 1950 – 1967, unpubl. Ph. D. Thesis, Harvard University 1968.

Weston, G. F., Jr., *Boston Ways. High, By and Folk,* Boston 1957, 1974, 3rd ed.

Whitehill, W. M., *Boston. A Topographical History,* Cambridge, Mass. 1959, 1968, 2nd ed.

Wilson, D. B., "A Grand Finale for Master of Policital Art," *BG,* May 31, 1983.

The Boston Society of Architects, *Architecture Boston,* Barre, Mass. 1976.

Financial Plight of Bay State Cities. Special Report, *BG,* Jan. 11, 1977.

Boston. Special Issue, *Architectural Forum,* Vol. 120, No. 6, June 1964.

"The Battle for Boston," *The Economist,* March 11, 1961.

"Boston Old, Boston New," *The BG Magazine,* Aug. 2, 1981.

"The New Boston. City of Ideas 1775 – 1975," *BG,* Febr. 24, 1963.

"Outlook for Boston: A Boom. City's $ 1 B Building Boom Bucks the National Trend," *BG,* Jan. 11, 1981.

"City of Boston", *Fortune,* Vol. VII, No. 2, Febr. 1933, p. 26 ff.

2. General

Achterberg, N., Krawietz, W., eds., *Legitimation des modernen Staates,* Beiheft No. 15, *Archiv für Rechts- und Sozialphilosophie,* Wiesbaden 1981.

Adams, H., *Democracy. An American Novel* (1880), New York 1983.

Adams, J., *Thoughts on Government* (1776), in: *The Political Writings of John Adams,* ed. G. A. Peek, Jr., New York 1954.

Adler, M. J., *The Difference of Man and the Difference It Makes,* New York 1967.

Adrian, Ch. A., *State and Local Government,* New York 1976, *4th ed.*

Albertini, R. v., *"Parteiorganisation und Parteibegriff in Frankreich 1789 – 1940,"* *Historische Zeitschrift,* 1961, pp. 529 – 600.

Alexander, H. E., ed., *Campaign Money. Reform and Reality in the United States,* New York 1976.

Alexander, H. E., *Financing Politics. Money, Elections, and Political Reform,* Washington, D. C. 1976.

Alexander, H. E., *Political Finance,* Beverly Hills 1979.

Allum, P. A., *Politics and Society in Post-War Naples,* Cambridge 1973.

Arendt, H., *The Human Condition,* Chicago 1958.

Arendt, H., *On Revolution,* New York 1963.

Aristotle, *Nicomachean Ethics,* transl. H. Rackham, Cambridge, Mass. – London 1968 = Loeb Classical Library.

Aristotle, *Metaphysics,* transl. H. Tredennick, Cambridge, Mass. – London 1968 = Loeb Classical Library.

Aristotle, *Politics,* transl. H. Rackham, Cambridge, Mass. – London 1959 = Loeb Classical Library.

Aristotle, *Posterior Analytics. Topica,* transl. H. Tredennick, E. S. Forster, Cambridge, Mass. – London 1966 = Loeb Classical Library.

Arnim, H. H. v., *Ämterpatronage durch politische Parteien,* Wiesbaden 1980.

Aron, R., *L'opium des intellectuels,* Paris 1955.

Aron, R., *Dix-huit leçons sur la société industrielle,* Paris 1982.

Bagehot, W., *The English Constitution,* intr. R. H. S. Crossman, Glasgow 1963, 1978, 14th ed.

Banfield, E. C., ed., *Urban Government. A Reader in Administration and Politics*, New York 1961.

Banfield, E. C., *Political Influence. A New Theory of Urban Politics*, New York 1961.

Banfield, E. C., "Party 'Reform' in Retrospect," in: idem, *Here the People Rule, Selected Essays*, New York 1985, pp. 38–52.

Banfield, E. C., *Here the People Rule. Selected Essays*, New York 1985.

Banfield, E. C., Wilson, J. Q., *City Politics*, Cambridge, Mass. 1963.

Baring, A., *Im Anfang war Adenauer. Die Entstehung der Kanzlerdemokratie*, München 1982, 2nd ed.

Barzun, J., *Clio and the Doctors*, Chicago 1974.

Bastid, P. et al., *L'idée de légitimité*, No. 7, *Annales de philosophie politique*, Paris 1967.

Bean, W., *Boss Ruef's San Francisco: The Story of Union Labor Party, Big Business and the Craft Prosecution*, Berkeley 1972.

Becquart-Leclercq, J., *Paradoxes du pouvoir local*, Paris 1976.

Becquart-Leclercq, J., "Légitimité et pouvoir local," *Revue Française de Science Politique*, Vol. 27, No. 2, 1977, pp. 228–258.

Beer, S. H., "Federalism, Nationalism, and Democracy in America," The American Political Science Review, Vol. 72, No. 1, March 1978, pp. 9–21.

Beer, S. H., "In Search of a New Public Philosophy," *in:* A. King, ed., *The New American Political System*, Washington, D. C. 1978, pp. 5–44.

Bellush, J., Hausknecht, M., *Urban Renewal*, New York 1967.

Benevolo, L., *Storia della città*, Rome–Bari 1975.

Berlin, I., *Four Essays on Liberty*, Oxford 1969.

Berti, E., *Il de re publica di Cicerone e il pensiero politico classico*, Padua 1963.

Birnbaum, P., *Les sommets de l'etat. Essai sur l'élite du pouvoir en France*, Paris 1977.

Blau, P. M., "Theories of Organization," in: D. L. Sills, ed., *International Encyclopedia of the Social Sciences*, Vol. II, s. l., 1968, pp. 297–305.

Bleicken, J., *Die Verfassung der römischen Republik*, Paderborn 1975.

Blumenthal, S., *The Permanent Campaign. Inside the World of Elite Political Operatives*, Boston 1980.

Böckenförde, E.-W., "Organ, Organismus, Organisation, politischer Körper," in: O. Brunner, W. Conze, R. Kosseleck, eds., *Geschichtliche Grundbegriffe. Historisches Lexikon zur politisch-sozialen Sprache in Deutschland*, Vol. 4, Stuttgart 1978, pp. 519–622.

Boissier, G., *Cicero and His Friends. A Study of Roman Society in the Time of Caesar*, New York 1970.

Bollerey, F., *Architekturkonzeptionen der utopischen Sozialisten. Alternative Planung und Architektur für den gesellschaftlichen Prozeß*, München 1977.

Bonafede, D., "Costly Campaigns: Consultants Cash in as Candidates Spend What They Must," *NJ*, June 16, 1983, pp. 789–792.

Bookwalter, J. W., *Rural Versus Urban. Their Conflict and Its Causes: A Study of the Conditions Affecting Their Natural and Artificial Relation*, New York 1911.

Bouzerand, J., "La constellation Mitterrand," *Le Point*, No. 660, May 13, 1985, pp. 46–47.

Braunfels, W., *Abendländische Stadtbaukunst. Herrschaftsform und Baugestalt*, Köln 1976.

Breitling, R., "Berufsbeiträge aus Ämterpatronage. Eine vergessene Quelle politischer Finanzierungen," in: M. Kaase, ed., *Politische Wissenschaft und politische Ordnung*, Festschrift R. Wildenmann, Opladen 1986, pp. 291–301.

Bridges, A., *A City in the Republic. Antebellum New York and the Origins of Machine Politics*, New York 1984.

Bridgman, A., "Heavenly Cities on Earth: Urban Planning and Mass Culture in Eighteenth-Century Utopias," in: *Transactions of the Fifth International Congress on the Enlightenment*, Oxford 1981.

Bryce, J., *The American Commonwealth*, abr. ed., New York – London 1920.

Buchheim, H., "Die Ethik der Macht," in: Institut der deutschen Wirtschaft, ed., *Wirtschaftliche Entwicklungslinien und gesellschaftlicher Wandel*, Festschrift Burghard Freudenfeld, Köln 1983.

Cambell, A. K., ed., *The States and the Urban Crisis*, Englewood Cliffs 1970.

Caro, R. A., *The Power Broker. Robert Moses and the Fall of New York*, New York 1974.

Caro, R. A., *The Years of Lyndon Johnson. The Path to Power*, New York 1982.

Cassese, S., "Is There a Government in Italy?" in: R. Rose, E. N. Suleiman, eds., *Presidents and Prime Ministers*, Washington, D. C. 1980, pp. 171 – 202.

Castells, M., *The City and the Grassroots. A Cross-Cultural Theory of Urban Social Movements*, London 1983.

Catlin, G. E. G., *The Science and Method of Politics*, London – New York 1927.

Cattaneo, M. A., *Il partito politico nel pensiero dell 'illuminismo e della rivoluzione francese*, Milano 1964.

Chamberlain, A., *Beacon Hill*, Boston 1925.

Cicero, *De Amicitia*, Lat.-Germ. ed., München 1959, = Tusculum.

Cicero, *Letters to Atticus*, Lat.-Germ. ed., München 1961, = Tusculum.

Clapmarius, A., *De Arcanis Rerum publicarum*, Bremen 1605.

Clifford, Th. P., *The Political Machine. An American Institution*, New York 1975.

Cochraine, Ch. N., *Christianity and Classical Culture. A study of thought and action from Augustus to Augustine*, London 1940.

Cohen, R. E., "Costly Campaigns: Candidates Learn That Reaching the Votes Is Expensive," *NJ*, June 16, 1983, pp. 782 – 788.

Cohen, S., *Les conseillers du Président*, Paris 1980.

Cohen, S., "Les hommes de l'Elysée," *Pouvoirs*, No. 20, 1981, pp. 94 – 98.

Cooley, Ch. H., *Human Nature and the Social Order* (1902), in: *The Two Major Works of Charles H. Cooley*, intr. R. Cooley Angell, Glencoe 1956.

Cooley, Ch. H., *Social Organization. A Study of the Larger Mind* (1909), in: The Two Major Works of Charles H. Cooley, intr. R. Cooley Angell, Glencoe 1956.

Cotta, S., "La nascità dell'idea di partito nel secolo XVIII," *Atti Facoltà di Giurisprudenza Università Perugia*, LXI, 1960.

Cronin, Th. E., *State and Local Politics. Government by the People*, Englewood Cliffs 1976, 2nd ed.

Cronin, Th. E., Greenberg, S., eds., *The Presidential Advisory System*, New York 1969.

Crook, J., *Consilium principis*, Cambridge 1955.

Crozier, M., *The Bureaucratic Phenomenon*, Chicago 1964.

Cumming, R. D., *Human Nature and History. A Study of the Development of Liberal Political Thought*, Chicago 1969.

Dahl, R. D., *Who Governs? Democracy and Power in an American City*, New Haven 1961.

Dentler, R. A., Scott, M. B., *Schools on Trial. An Inside Account of the Boston Desegregation Case*, Cambridge, Mass. 1981.

Desmond, S., "America's City Civilization: The Natural Divisions of the United States," *Century*, Vol. LVIII, Aug. 1924, pp. 548 – 555.

Devine, D. J., *The Political Culture of the United States*, Boston 1972.

Dinkelspiel, J. R., et al., *Condominium Conversion's Effects on a Community*, Boston 1981.

Donovan, H., "The Enigmatic President," *Time*, May 6, 1985, pp. 18 – 24.

Drew, E., *Politics and Money. The New Road to Corruption*, New York 1983.

Dulong, C., *La vie quotidienne à l'Elysée au temps de Charles de Gaulle*, Paris 1974.

Easton, D., "Categories for the Systems Analysis of Politics," in: idem, ed., *Varieties of Political Theory*, Englewood Cliffs 1966.

Easton, D., *Varieties of Political Theory*, Englewood Cliffs 1966.

Ehrenberg, V., *Der Staat der Griechen*, Zürich – Stuttgart, 1965, 2nd ed.

Elazar, D. J., ed., *American Federalism. A View from the States*, New York 1966.

Eliade, M., *Cosmos and History. The Myth of the Eternal Return*, New York 1959.

Ellwein, Th., Zoll, R., *Wertheim. Politik und Machtstruktur in einer deutschen Stadt*, München 1982.

Eschenburg, Th., *Ämterpatronage*, Stuttgart 1961.

Eulau, H., *Micro-Macro Political Analysis. Accents of Inquiry*, Chicago 1969.

Eulau, H., Prewitt, K., *Labyrinths of Democracy. Adaptation, Linkages, Representation and Policies in Urban Politics*, New York 1973.

Evers, H. G., *Tod, Macht und Raum als Bereiche der Architektur*, München 1970 (Reprint).

Faul, E., "Verfemung, Duldung und Anerkennung des Parteiwesens in der Geschichte des politischen Denkens," *Politische Vierteljahresschrift*, Jg. 5, H. 1, March 1964, pp. 60 – 80.

Fénelon, *Télémaque (XVII)*, in: *Oeuvres*, ed. A. Martin, Vol. III, Paris 1837, Reprint 1882.

Fishman, R., *Urban Utopias in the Twentieth Century. Ebenezer Howard, Frank Lloyd Wright, Le Corbusier*, New York 1977.

Flanagan, L., *New Directions in Federal Grant Funds to Boston, 1968 – 78, BRA*, May 1980.

Fournier, J., *La coordination du travail gouvernemental*. Paris, Fondation Nationale des Sciences Politiques, 1985 – 86.

Freeman, J. M., Krantz, D. L., "The Unfulfilled Promises of Life Histories," *Biography*, No. 3, 1980, pp. 1 – 13.

Fried, C., "Comparative Urban Policy and Performance," in: F. J. Greenstein, N. W. Polsby, eds., *Handbook of Political Science*, Vol. VI, Politics and Policymaking, Reading 1975, pp. 305 – 379.

Friedrich, C. J., *The Pathology of Politics. Violence, Betrayal, Corruption, Secrecy, and Propaganda*, New York 1972.

Galt, J., *The Provost* (1822), ed. I. A. Gordon, Oxford 1982.

Gans, H., *The Urban Villagers*, New York 1965.

Gelzer, M., *Vom römischen Staat. Zur Politik und Gesellschaftsgeschichte der römischen Republik*, Vol. II, Leipzig 1943.

Gelzer, M., *The Roman Nobility*, Oxford 1969.

Giedion, S., *Architektur und Gemeinschaft*, Hamburg 1956.

Gierke, O. von, *Natural Law and the Theory of Society 1500 – 1800*, Cambridge 1934.

Gosnell, H. F., *Machine Politics: Chicago Model*, Chicago 1937.

Gosnell, H. F., Merriam, Ch. E., *Chicago. A More Intimate View of Urban Politics*, New York 1929.

Gourevitch, J.-M., M.-Th. Guichard, "La marée des 'têtes d'oeuf,'" *Le Point*, No. 622, Aug. 20, 1984.

Greenstein, F. J., *The Hidden-Hand Presidency. Eisenhower as Leader*, New York 1982.

Grémion, P., *Le pouvoir périphérique. Bureaucrates et notables dans le système politique français*, Paris 1976.

Haider, D. H., *When Governments Come to Washington. Governors, Mayors and Intergovernmental Lobbying*, New York 1974.

Haig, A., "CAVEAT. Realism, Reagan and Foreign Policy," *Time*, April 2, 1984, pp. 28 – 36.

Hammond, M., *The City in the Ancient World*, Cambridge, Mass. 1972.

Hart, J., *The Presidential Branch*, New York 1987.

Havard, W. C., Beth, L. P., *The Politics of Mis-representation. Rural-Urban Conflict in the Florida Legislature*, Baton Rouge 1962.

Hayden, D., *Seven American Utopias. The Architecture of Communitarian Socialism 1790 – 1975*, London 1976.

Heale, M. J., *The Presidential Quest. Candidates and Images in American Political Culture 1787 – 1852*, London – New York 1982.

Hechler, K., *Working With Truman. A Personal Memoir of the White House Years*, New York 1982, 2nd ed.

Heclo, H., *A Government of Strangers*, Washington, D. C. 1977.

Heclo, H., "Issue Networks and the Executive Establishment," in: A. King, ed., *The New American Political System*, Washington, D. C. 1978, pp. 87 – 124.

Heers, J., "Partis politiques et clans familiaux dans l'Italie de la Renaissance," *Revue de la Méditerrané*, Vol. XX, 1960, pp. 259 – 279.

Heers, J., *Le clan familial au moyen-âge. Etude sur les structures politiques et sociales des milieux urbain*, Paris 1974.

Heinze, R., *Vom Geist des Römertums*, Leipzig – Berlin, 1938.

Hennis, W., *Richtlinienkompetenz und Regierungstechnik*, Tübingen 1964.

Hesse, J.-J., ed., *Politikverflechtung im föderativen Staat*, Baden-Baden 1978.

Hobbes, Th., *Leviathan*, ed. C. B. Mac Pherson, Harmondsworth 1972.

Holloway, M., *Heavens on Earth. Utopian Communities in America 1680 – 1880*, New York 1951.

Hölscher, L., *Öffentlichkeit und Geheimnis. Eine begriffsgeschichtliche Untersuchung zur Entstehung der Öffentlichkeit in der frühen Neuzeit*, Stuttgart 1979.

Howitt, A. M., *Managing Federalism. Studies in Intergovernmental Relations*, Washington, D. C. 1983.

Hübner, K., *Die Wahrheit des Mythos*, München 1985.

Humphrey, H. H., *The Education of a Public Man*, Garden City 1976.

Huntington, S. P., *American Politics: The Promise of Disharmony*, Cambridge, Mass. 1981.

Jellicoe, G. & S., *The Landscape of Man. Shaping the Environment from Prehistory to the Present Day*, London 1974.

Joachim, H. H., *The Nicomachean Ethics. A Commentary*, Oxford 1966, 4th ed.

Jones, C., ed., *Party and Management in Parliament 1660 – 1784*, Leicester 1984.

Kayden, X., *Campaign Organization*, Lexington, Mass. 1978.

Kent, F. R., *The Great Game of Politics: An Effort to Present the Elementary Human Facts About Politics, Politicians, and Political Machines, Candidates and Their Ways, for the Benefit of the Average Citizen*, Garden City 1923, Reprint New York 1974.

Kesselman, M., "Research Perspectives in Comparative Local Politics: Pitfalls, Prospects, and Notes on the French Case," in: T. N. Clark, ed., *Comparative Community Politics*, New York 1974, pp. 353 – 381.

Key, V. O., Jr., *Politics, Parties, and Pressure Groups*, New York 1942, 1964, 5th ed.

King, A., "Building Coalitions in the Sand," in: idem, ed., *The New American Political System*, Washington, D. C., 1978, pp. 388 – 395.

King, A. D., ed., *Buildings and Society. Essays on the Social Development of the Built Environment*, London 1980.

Kip, L., "The Building of Our Cities," in: *Hours at Home*, 11, July 1870, reprinted in: L. M. Roth, *America Builds. Source Documents in American Architecture and Planning*, New York 1983, pp. 417 – 425.

Kirschten, D., "Decision Making in the White House: How Well Does It Serve the President?" *NJ*, Vol. 14, No. 14, April 3, 1982, pp. 584 – 589.

Kirschten, D., "Inner Circle Speaks With Many Voices, But Maybe That's How Reagan Wants It," *NJ*, Vol. 15, No. 22, May 28, 1983, pp. 1100 – 1103.

Kirschten, D., "Under Reagan, Power Resides With Those Who Station Themselves at His Door," *NJ*, Vol. 16, No. 8, Feb. 25, 1984, pp. 361 – 364.

Kopp, A., *L'architecture de la Période Stalinienne*, Grenoble 1978.

Krauthammer, Ch., "When Secrecy Meets Democracy," *Time*, Dec. 8, 1986.

Lagroye, J., "A la recherche du pouvoir local," *Sociologia Internationalis*, Vol. 15, 1977, pp. 77 – 90.

Lasks, Sh. B., Spain, D., eds., *Back to the City. Issues in Neighborhood Renovation*, New York 1980.

Laurent, M., *A l'écoute des villes en France*, Paris 1976.

Leigh, J. A., "Space and Revolution: Public Monuments and Urban Planning at the Peak of the Terror," in: *Transactions of the Fifth International Congress on the Enlightenment*, The Voltaire Foundation, Oxford 1981.

Liebich, A., *Le libéralisme classique*, Sillery (Quebec) 1985.

Lineberry, R. L., "Policy Analysis and Urban Government: Understanding the Impact," *Urban Analysis*, Vol. 5, 1978, pp. 143 – 154.

Lissitzky, E., ed., *Neues Bauen in der Welt: Rußland*, Wien 1930.

Litt, E., *The Political Cultures of Massachusetts*, Cambridge, Mass. 1965.

Lockard, D., *New England State Politics*, Princeton 1959.

Long, N. E., "Federalism and Perverse Incentives," *Publius*, No. 2, 1978, pp. 77 – 97.

Lowi, T. J., *At the Pleasure of the Mayor. Patronage and Power in New York City 1898 – 1958*, New York 1964.

Luntz, F. J., *Candidates, Consultants, and Campaigns. The Style and Substance of American Electioneering*, New York 1988.

Lyman, St. M., Scott, M. B., "Territoriality: A Neglected Sociological Dimension," in: R. Gutman, *People and Buildings*, New York 1972, pp. 65 – 82.

Lynch, K., *Site Planning*, Cambridge, Mass. 1962, 1971, 2nd ed.

Lynch, K., *A Theory of Good City Form*, Cambridge, Mass. 1981.

Machiavelli, N., *Il Principe e Discorsi sopra la prima deca di Tito Livio*, ed. S. Bertelli, Milano 1960.

Machiavelli, N., *The Prince and the Discourses*, intr. M. Lerner, New York 1950.

Mackie, Th. T., Hogwood, B. W., eds., *Unlocking the Cabinet. Cabinet Structures in Comparative Perspective*, London 1985.

Macy, J. W., et al., *America's Unelected Government. Appointing the President's Team*, Cambridge, Mass. 1983.

Malbin, M. J., *Unelected Representatives. Congressional Staff and the Future of Representative Government*, New York 1980.

Mandelbaum, S., *Boss Tweed's New York*, New York 1965.

Mandt, H., "Kritik der Formaldemokratie und Entförmlichung der politischen Auseinandersetzung," *Zeitschrift für Politik*, Jg. 32, NF, H. 2, 1985, pp. 115–132.

Manent, P., *Les libéraux*, 2 vols., Paris 1986.

Manent, P., *Histoire intellectuelle du libéralisme*, Paris 1987.

Mansfield, H. C., Jr., *Statesmanship and Party Government. A Study of Burke and Bolingbroke*, Chicago 1965.

Mansfield, H. C., Jr., "The Absent Executive in Aristotle's Politics," in P. Schramm, T. Silver, eds., *Natural Right and Political Right*, Durham 1984.

Mansfield, H. C., Jr., "Gouvernement représentatif et pouvoir exécutif," *Commentaire*, No. 36, 1986, pp. 664–672.

Martines, L., *Power and Imagination. City-States in Renaissance Italy*, New York 1979.

McGregor Burns, J., *Roosevelt. The Lion and the Fox*, New York 1956.

McKean, D. D., *The Boss: The Hague Machine in Action*, Boston 1940.

Médard, J.-F., "Le rapport de clientèle, du phénomène social à l'analyse politique," *Revue Française de Science politique*, Vol. XXVI, No. 1, Febr. 1976, pp. 103–131.

Meek, Ch., *Lucca 1369–1400. Politics and Society in an Early Renaissance City-State*, Oxford 1978.

Meier, Ch., *Res Publica Amissa. Eine Studie zu Verfassung und Geschichte der späten römischen Republik*, Wiesbaden 1966.

Meier, Ch., *Die Entstehung des Politischen bei den Griechen*, Frankfurt 1980.

Merton, R. K., "The Latent Functions of the Machine," in: E. C. Banfield, ed., *Urban Government. A Reader in Administration and Politics*, New York 1961.

Meyerson, M., Banfield, E. C., *Politics, Planning and the Public Interest. The Case of Public Housing in Chicago*, Glencoe 1955.

Millon, H. A., Nochlin, L., eds., *Art and Architecture in the Service of Politics*, Cambridge, Mass. 1978.

Mitterrand, F., Interview, *Libération*, nouv. ser., no. 923, May 10, 1984, p. 6–7.

Moley, R., "The Issue Is Administration," *Newsweek*, Vol. 32, Aug. 30, 1948 and Sept. 6, 1948.

Molho, D., "Elysée an III: Les choses de la vie," *Le Point*, No. 607, May 7, 1984.

Molho, D., "Les stratèges du Président," *Le Point*, No. 644, Jan. 21, 1985.

Mollenkopf. J. H., *The Contested City*, Princeton 1983.

Moreau, P. F., *Les racines du libéralisme*, Paris 1978.

Moscow, W., *The Last of the Big-Time Bosses. The Life and Times of Carmine De Sapio and the Rise and Fall of Tammany Hall*, New York 1971.

Moulakis, A., *Homonoia. Eintracht und die Entwicklung eines politischen Bewußtseins*, München 1973.

v. Münchhausen, Th., "Die Freunde zuerst," *Frankfurter Allgemeine Zeitung*, March 13, 1986.

Myers, G., *The History of Tammany Hall*, New York 1917.

Namier, L., *England in the Age of the American Revolution*, London 1930.

Namier, L., *Monarchy and Party System*, Oxford 1952.

Namier, L., *The Structure of British Politics at the Accession of George III*, London 1957, 2nd ed.

Namier, L., *Crossroads of Power. Essays on Eighteenth-Century England*, London 1962.

Napolitan, J., *The Election Game*, New York 1972.

Neustadt, E., *Presidential Power. The Politics of Leadership with Reflections on Johnson and Nixon*, New York – Toronto, 1960, 1976.

Nolen, J., *City Making*, (1909), in: L. M. Roth, ed., *American Builds. Source Documents in American Architecture and Planning*, New York 1983.

Noonan, J. T., Jr., *Bribes*, New York 1984.

Norberg-Schulz, Ch., *Genius Loci. Towards a Phenomenology of Architecture*, New York 1980.

Oakeshott, M., *Rationalism in Politics*, London 1962.

Oakeshott, M., *On Human Conduct*, Oxford 1975.

O'Neill, Th., *Man of the House*, New York 1987.

Oser, R., "Robespierre/St. Just," in: T. Schabert, ed., *Der Mensch als Schöpfer der Welt*, München 1971, pp. 169 – 206.

Paine, Th., *Common Sense* (1776), in: *The Writings of Thomas Paine*, ed. M. D. Conway, Vol. I, (1774 – 1779), New York 1967.

Park, R. E., "The City: Suggestions for the Investigation of Human Behavior in the Urban Environment," in: R. E. Park, E. W. Burgess, R. D. McKenzie, *The City*, Chicago 1925, 1967, 4th ed, pp. 1 – 46.

Passerin d'Entrèves, A., *The Medieval Contribution to Political Thought – Thomas Aquinas, Marsilius of Padua, Richard Hooker*, Oxford 1939.

Passerin d'Entrèves, A., "Legality and Legitimacy," *The Review of Metaphysics*, Vol. XVI, No. 4, June 1963, pp. 687 – 702.

Pasqui, U., *Documenti per la Storia della Città di Arezzo*, Florence 1879 – 1920.

Patterson, Jr., B. H., *The Ring of Power. The White House Staff and Its Expanding Role in Government*, New York 1988.

Pégard, C., "Administration: Les copains d'abord," *Le Point*, No. 702, March 3, 1986, pp. 52 – 53.

Perkins, F., *The Roosevelt I Knew*, New York 1946.

Peterson, L., *Day of the Mugwamp*, New York 1961.

Picotti, G. B., "Qualche osservazioni sui caratteri delle signorie italiane," *Rivista Storica Italiana*, Nuova Seria IV, Vol. XLIII, Jan. 1926, Fasc. I, pp. 7 – 30.

Pious, R. M., *The American Presidency*, New York 1979.

Plato, *Cratylus, Parmenides, Greater Hippias, Lesser Hippias*, transl. H. N. Fowler, Cambridge, Mass. 1970 = Loeb Classical Library.

Plato, *The Statesman, Philebus*, transl. W. R. M. Lamb, Cambridge, Mass. 1962 = Loeb Classical Library.

Plato, *Lysis, Symposium, Gorgias*, transl. W. R. M. Lamb, Cambridge, Mass. 1967 = Loeb Classical Library.

Plato, *Laws*, transl. R. G. Bury, vol. I, Cambridge, Mass. 1967, vol. II, Cambridge, Mass. 1968 = Loeb Classical Library.

Plato, *The Republic*, transl. P. Shorey, vol. II, Cambridge, Mass. 1970 = Loeb Classical Library.

Pohlenz, M., *Griechische Freiheit*. Wesen und Werden eines Lebensideals, Heidelberg 1955.

Polanyi, M., *Personal Knowledge. Towards a Post-Critical Philosophy*, London 1958.

Polsby, N. W., *Consequences of Party Reform*, Oxford 1983.

Poppinga, A., *Meine Erinnerungen an Adenauer*, München 1972.

Poppinga, A., *Konrad Adenauer. Geschichtsverständnis, Weltanschauung und politische Praxis*, Stuttgart 1975.

Premerstein, A. v., *Vom Werden und Wesen des Prinzipats*, München 1937.

Publius (Hamilton, A., Jay, J., Madison, J.), *The Federalist Papers*, ed. C. Rossiter, New York 1961.

Ragon, M., *L'Architecte, le prince et la démocratie*, Paris 1977.

Rakove, M. L., *Don't Make No Waves, Don't Back No Losers. An Insider's Analysis of the Daley Machine*, Bloomington 1975.

Rakove, M. L., *We Don't Want Nobody Nobody Sent. An Oral History of the Daley Years*, Bloomington 1979.

Rapoport, A., *Human Aspects of Urban Form. Towards a Man-Environment Approach to Urban Form and Design*, Oxford 1977.

Redman, Ch. L., *The Rise of Civilization. From Early Farmers to Urban Societies in the Ancient Near East*, San Francisco 1978.

Reed, R. E., *Return to the City. How to Restore Old Buildings and Ourselves in America's Historic Urban Neighborhoods*, Garden City, N. Y. 1979.

Reinle, A., *Zeichensprache der Architektur. Symbol, Darstellung und Brauch in der Baukunst des Mittelalters und der Neuzeit*, Zürich – München 1976.

Reydellet, M., "Le cumul des mandats," *Revue du droit public et de la science politique en France et à l'étranger*, No. 3, May – June 1979, pp. 693 – 768.

Reynolds, G. M., *Machine Politics in New Orleans*, New York 1936.

Rials, S., *La Présidence de la République*, Paris 1981.

Riordon, W. L., *Plunkitt of Tammany Hall*, New York 1905.

Roberts, St. V., "Carter Discord with Congress: President Is Apparently Seeking to Ease Stains," *NYT*, June 5, 1979.

Rose, R., Suleiman, E. N., eds., *Presidents and Prime Ministers*, Washington, D. C. 1980.

Rosenau, H., *The Ideal City in Its Architectural Evolution*, London 1959.

Rosenman, S. J., *Working With Roosevelt*, New York 1952.

Rousseau, J. J., *Discours sur l'origine et les fondemens de l'inégalité parmi les hommes, Oeuvres Complètes*, III, *Du Contrat Social, Ecrits Politiques*, Paris 1964.

Rousseau, J. J., *The First and Second Discourses, Together with the Replies to Critics and Essay on the Origin of Languages*, ed., transl., and annot. by V. Gourevitch, New York 1986.

Rubinstein, N., *The Government of Florence Under the Medici: 1434 to 1494*, Oxford 1966.

Sabato, L. J., *The Rise of Political Consultants. New Ways of Winning Elections*, New York 1981.

Sabato, L. J., *PAC Power. Inside the World of Political Action Committees*, New York 1984.

Sabato, L. J., *Campaigns and Elections. A Reader in Modern American Politics*, Glenview 1988.

Salmore, St. A., and B. G. *Candidates, Parties and Campaigns*, Washington, D. C. 1985.

Salomon, B. M., *Ancestors and Immigrants. A Changing New England Tradition*, Cambridge, Mass. 1956.

Salter, J. T., *Boss Rule. Portraits in City Politics*, New York 1935.

Sayre, W. S., Kaufman, H., *Governing New York City*, New York 1960.

Schabert, T., *Natur und Revolution*, München 1969.

Schabert, T., ed., *Der Mensch als Schöpfer der Welt*, München 1971.

Schabert, T., "Moderne Architektur – und die Hütten der Epigonen. Menschliches Bauen als politische Kunst der Vergangenheit," *Der Monat*, Jg. 30, H. 2, Dec. 1978, pp. 127 – 133.

Schabert, T., "Ansätze zu einer Phänomenologie der politischen Parteien in Frankreich," *Zeitschrift für Politik*, Jg. 25, H. 4, Dec. 1978, pp. 357 – 376.

Schabert, T., "The Roots of Modernity," *The Independent Journal of Philosophy*, Vol. IV, 1983, pp. 27 – 29.

Schabert, T., "Modernity and History," *Diogenes*, No. 123, Fall 1983, pp. 110 – 124.

Schabert, T., "Die Freiheit im Labyrinth. Amerikanische Wahlkämpfe sind chaotisch und schöpferisch zugleich," *Süddeutsche Zeitung*, No. 255, Nov. 3 – 4, 1984, p. I.

Schabert, T., "Power, Legitimacy and Truth: Reflections Upon the Impossibility to Legitimize Legitimations of Political Order," in: *Legitimacy/Légitimité*, ed. A. Moulakis, Berlin 1985, pp. 96 – 104.

Schabert, T., "Das Paradox der Macht. Anmerkungen zur Regierungspraxis in Washington, Paris und Bonn," *Süddeutsche Zeitung*, No. 188, Aug. 17 – 18, 1985.

Schabert, T., "Revolutionary Consciousness," *Philosophical Studies* (Dublin), Vol. XXVII, 1980, pp. 120 – 142.

Schabert, T., "*The Decentralization and the New Urban Policy in France*," *Urban Law and Policy*, Vol. 7, No. 1, March 1985, pp. 57 – 74.

Schabert, T., "In urbe mundus. Weltspiegelungen und Weltbemächtigung in der Architektur der Stadt," in: *Eranos-Yearbook 55*, Frankfurt 1988, pp. 303 – 347.

Scharpf, F. W., Reissert, B., Schnabel, F., *Politikverflechtung*, Kronberg 1976.

Schendelen, M. P. C. M. v., "Das Geheimnis des Europäischen Parlaments: Einfluß auch ohne Kompetenzen," *Zeitschrift für Parlamentsfragen*, Jg. 15, H. 3, Sept. 1984, pp. 415 – 426.

Schieder, Th., "Die Theorie der Partei im älteren deutschen Liberalismus," in: idem, *Staat und Gesellschaft im Wandel unserer Zeit*, München 1958, pp. 110 – 132.

Schifres, M., Sarazin, M., *L'Elysée de Mitterrand. Secrets de la maison de France*, Paris 1985.

Schlesinger, A. M., Jr., *The Age of Roosevelt*, Vol. I, *The Coming of the New Deal*, Boston 1958.

Schneider, R., "Les 30 hommes du Président," *L'Express*, July 5, 1980, pp. 29 – 35.

Schumpeter, J. A., *Business Cycles. A Theoretical, Historical, and Statistical Analysis of the Capitalist Process*, New York – London 1939.

Schütz, A., *Der sinnhafte Aufbau der sozialen Welt. Eine Einleitung in die verstehende Soziologie*, Wien 1932, Reprint Frankfurt 1974.

Shannon, W. V., *The American Irish*, New York 1966.

Siegfried, A., *Tableau politique de la France de l'Ouest sous la Troisième République*, Paris 1964, 2nd ed.

Simeoni, L., *Le signorie*, 2 vols., Milano 1950.

Simon, H. A., et al., *Public Administration*, New York 1950.

Smith, J. R., *North America: Its People and Resources, Development, and the Prospects of the Continent as an Agricultural, Industrial, and Commercial Area*, New York 1925.

Stave, B., *The New Deal and the Last Hurrah*, Pittsburgh 1970.

Steffens, L., *The Shame of the Cities*, New York 1957.

Sternberger, D., "Die Erfindung der 'Repräsentativen Demokratie,'" in: ed. K. v. Beyme, *Theory and Politics – Theorie und Politik*, Festschrift C. J. Friedrich, Den Haag 1971, pp. 96–126.

Sternberger, D., *Drei Wurzeln der Politik*, 2 vols, Frankfurt 1978.

Stinchcombe, A. L., "Formal Organization," in: N. J. Smelser, ed., *Sociology. An Introduction*, New York 1973, 2nd ed., pp. 23–65.

Straetz, R. A., *P. R. Politics in Cincinnati*, New York 1958.

Strauss, A. L., "Strategies for Discovering Urban Theory," in: L. F. Schnore, H. Fagen, eds., *Urban Research and Policy Planning*, Beverly Hills 1967.

Strauss, L., *What Is Political Philosophy?* New York 1968.

Suerbaum, W., *Vom antiken zum frühmittelalterlichen Staatsbegriff – Über Verwendung und Bedeutung von respublica, regnum, imperium und status von Cicero bis Jordanis*, Münster 1961.

Taft, Ch. P., *City Management: The Cincinnati Experiment*, New York 1933.

Taylor, L. R., *Party Politics in the Age of Caesar*, Berkeley 1949.

Taylor, L. R., "Nobles, Clients, and Personal Armies," in: L. Guasti, et al., *Friends, Followers and Factions. A Reader in Political Clientelism*, London 1977, pp. 179–192.

Taylor, R. R., *The World in Stone. The Role of Architecture in the National Socialist Ideology*, Berkeley 1974.

Tharp, L. H., *The Appletons of Beacon Hill*, Boston 1973.

Tompkins, S., "Proposition 2 ¹/₂ – Massachusetts and the Tax Revolt," *The Journal of the Institute for Socioeconomic Studies*, Vol. VI, No. 1, Spring 1981, pp. 21–32.

Trexler, R. C., *Public Life in Renaissance Florence*, New York 1980.

Trilling, J., "Paris – Architecture as Politics," *The Atlantic*, Oct. 1983, pp. 26–35.

Turner, V., *Drama, Fields and Metaphors. Symbolic Action in Human Society*, Ithaca 1974.

Verrier, P., *Les services de la présidence de la république*, Paris 1971.

Viansson-Ponté, P., *Histoire de la République Gaulliene*, 2 vols., Paris 1970–71.

Vico, G., *Scienza Nuova*, Neapel 1725.

Vidich, A. J., Bensman, J., *Small Town in Mass Society. Class, Power and Religion in a Rural Community*, Princeton 1958, 1968, 2nd ed.

Vitruv, *De Architectura libri Decem*, German-Latin edition, ed. C. Fensterbusch, Darmstadt 1976.

Voegelin, E., *Order and History*, 5 vols., Baton Rouge 1956–87.

Voegelin, E., "Der Mensch in Gesellschaft und Geschichte," *Österreichische Zeitschrift für Öffentliches Recht*, Vol. XIV, No 1–2, 1964, pp. 1–13.

Voegelin, E., *Anamnesis. Zur Theorie der Geschichte und Politik*, München 1966; engl. *Anamnesis*, ed. and transl. G. Niemeyer, Notre Dame 1978

Voegelin, E., "Configurations of History," in: P. G. Kuntz, ed., *The Concept of Order*, Seattle 1968, pp. 23–42.

Voegelin, E., "Machiavelli's Prince: Background and Formation," *The Review of Politics*, Vol. 13, No. 2, April 1951, pp. 142–168.

Voegelin, E., ed., *Zwischen Revolution und Restauration. Politisches Denken in England im 17. Jahrhundert*, München 1968.

Walcott, R., Jr., *English Politics in the Early Eighteenth Century*, Cambridge, Mass. 1956.

Waley, D., *The Italian City-Republics*, New York 1969.

Wann, A. J., *The President as Chief Administrator. A Study of Franklin D. Roosevelt*, Washington, D. C. 1968.

Warnke, M., *Politische Architektur in Europa. Vom Mittelalter bis heute — Repräsentation und Gemeinschaft*, Köln 1984.

Watkins, F., *The Political Tradition of the West: A Study in the Development of Modern Liberalism*, Cambridge, Mass. 1948.

Weichmann, H., "Vorarbeit für den Staatschef," in: *Die Staatskanzlei: Aufgaben, Organisation und Arbeitsweise auf vergleichender Grundlage*, Berlin 1967, pp. 33 – 36.

White, Th. H., *The Making of the President 1960*, London 1961.

White, Th. H., *The Making of the President 1964*, New York 1965.

Wiese, L. v., "Organisation," in: E. v. Beckerath et al., eds., *Handwörterbuch der Sozialwissenschaften*, Vol. 8, Stuttgart 1964, pp. 108 – 111.

Wilson, J. Q., *Urban Renewal: The Record and the Controversy*, Cambridge, Mass. 1966.

Wilson, W., "Constitutional Government in the United States," in: *The Papers of Woodrow Wilson*, ed. A. S. Link, Vol. 18 (1908 – 1909), Princeton 1974, pp. 69 – 216.

Wirt, F., *Power in the City. Decision Making in San Francisco*, Berkeley 1978.

Wittgenstein, L., *Tractatus Logico-Philosophicus*, in: *Schriften 1*, Frankfurt 1969.

Wolfinger, R. E., *The Politics of Progress*, Englewood Cliffs 1974.

Woll, P., *Constitutional Democracy. Policies and Politics*, Boston 1982.

Würtenberger, Th., Jr., *Die Legitimität staatlicher Herrschaft. Eine staatsrechtlich-politische Begriffsgeschichte*, Berlin 1973.

Yourcenar, M., *Mémoires d'Hadrien*, Paris 1951, 1974.

Zink, H., *City Bosses in the United States: A Study of Twenty Municipal Bosses*, Durham 1930.

Zorbough, H., *The Gold Coast and the Slum*, Chicago 1929.

Zuckerman, A., "Clientelist Politics in Italy," in: E. Gellner, J. Waterbury, eds., *Patrons and Clients in Mediterranean Societies*, London 1977, pp. 63 – 79.

Zundel, R., "Die Souffleure der Kanzler," *Die Zeit*, No. 28, July 8, 1983.

"Kanzleramt", *Der Spiegel*, No. 24, June 6, 1966, pp. 32 – 40.

Index of Subjects*

act of creation 128
act of foundation 266
act of social creation 128
action 72, 273, 278
adhocracy 233 f.
Administrative Services Department
  (Boston) 81
alliance of interest 112
alter ego 61, 68 f., 81, 304
America 9, 49, 73, 106, 111, 119, 166, 178,
  196, 266, 281
American cities 296
American city politics 100
American Federal Government 248
American politics 23, 73, 111
American Presidency 54
American Presidents 53 f.
American public life 111
American republic 18, 23, 253, 262, 266 f.
American society 86
Ancient Rome 54, 101, 112, 119, 225, 232
arcana imperii 261 f., 266
arcane regime 195
arcanum imperii 17, 26, 259
arcanum of politics 100, 265 f.
architects of society 275
architecture 3, 12 – 14, 275, 277, 280
architecture
  ceremonial 297
  political language of 275
  process of civic 282, 285
architectural autocrat 18
architectural construction of society
  275
architectural language of cities 275
architectural planning 273
architectural quality of society 277
architectural vision 277
Athens 49

authority 23, 33 – 35, 315
  absolute 17
  circles of 33 f.
  confusion of 33, 35
  legal 16, 20
  lines of 33 f., 41
  manifestation of 33
  personal 35
  purely formal 20
  sense of 35
  structures of 33
autocracy 12, 18 f., , 22 – 25, 38, 40 f., 64,
  75, 148, 170, 196, 202 f., 208, 222,
  253 – 255, 260, 311
  of Kevin White 305
  Mayor White's 100, 315
  principle of the 25
  strategy of the 22
  White's 22
autocrat 18, 20, 22, 26 f., 29, 31 – 34,
  36 – 41, 46, 59, 61, 63, 220, 222, 253 f., 260
  autocrat's government 33, 35, 87
  autocrat's power 260
  autocrat's strategy of governing 31, 40
  power of the 25
autocratic conquest 312
autocratic executive power 18
autocratic power 23, 27
autocratic regime 20
axis of configurative action 146 f.
axial configuration(s) 246 – 248, 250 f., 310
axis of action 247
axis of time 99

Back Bay (Boston) 174, 176, 217, 297,
  317 – 319
  Association 296, 316 – 318
Beacon Hill (Boston) 47 f., 72, 117 f., 319
  Architectural Commission 146, 296, 317

---

* The following lists (Index of Subjects, Index of Names, The Cast) were prepared by
  Claudia Leitzmann, Siegfried König, and Klaus Rudolph.

Index of Names

The Cast

This list presents the set of actors in our story.

The Author

TILO SCHABERT, Dr. phil., is Professor of Politics at the Friedrich-Alexander-University Erlangen-Nuremberg. Previously he taught at the Universities of Munich, Bochum, Trier and at Stanford University. In 1989 he has taught at the Université de Haute Bretagne in Rennes (France). He has been Research Fellow at Stanford University, the Australian National University in Canberra and German Kennedy Fellow at Harvard University. He has held visiting appointments at the European University Institute in Florence, the Joint Center for Urban Studies, and the Center for European Studies at Harvard University, the Institut d'Etudes Politiques in Paris, and the University of Maryland, College Park; and he has been guest lecturer at universities in Germany, Switzerland, England, Ireland, Italy, Australia, Canada and the United States. He was awarded a Heisenberg Professorial Fellowship by the German Research Council. He has also been scriptwriter and filmmaker in the Cultural Programme of the Bavarian TV Network.

His publications include: *Natur und Revolution*, Munich 1969; *Der Mensch als Schöpfer der Welt* (ed. and co-author), Munich 1971; *Aufbruch zur Moderne* (ed. and co-author), Munich 1974; *Gewalt und Humanität*. Über philosophische und politische Manifestationen von Modernität, Munich-Freiburg 1978; articles in the areas of French intellectual history and political thought, political theory, comparative politics, architecture and urban planning, published in German, American, Irish, English, French and Israeli journals. Some of these articles have appeared in Spanish, French, Portuguese, Arabic and Chinese. He has also contributed essays on politics and culture to the *Süddeutsche Zeitung*, the *Frankfurter Allgemeine Zeitung*, and the *Neue Zürcher Zeitung*. A recent study on the cosmology of city architecture ('In urbe mundus') appeared in the *Eranos-Yearbook-55*, 1986. He is married to Dr. Ina Schabert, Professor of English Literature at the University of Munich.

de Gruyter Studies on North America

Politics, Government, Society, Economy, and History

Series Editors

Willi Paul Adams, Helga Haftendorn, Carl-Ludwig Holtfrerich, Hans-Dieter Klingemann, and *Knud Krakau* (Freie Universität Berlin)

Advisory Board

David P. Calleo (School of Advanced International Studies of the Johns Hopkins University, Washington, D. C.), *Robert Dallek* (University of California, Los Angeles), *Robert J. Jackson* (Carleton University, Ottawa), *Roger Morgan* (London School of Economics and Political Science), *Richard Sylla* (North Carolina State University, Raleigh), *Martin P. Wattenberg* (University of California, Irvine)

Vol. 1

The Reagan Administration:
A Reconstruction of American Strength?

Edited by *Helga Haftendorn* and *Jakob Schissler*

1988. 15.5 x 23 cm. XII, 306 pages. With 1 table. Cloth.
ISBN 3 11 011372 4; 0-89925-409-8 (U. S.)

Vol. 2

Values in the Marketplace
The American Stock Market Under Federal Securities Law

By *James Burk*

1988. 15.5 x 23 cm. X, 207 pages. With 15 tables. Cloth.
ISBN 3 11 011714 2; 0-89925-487-X (U. S.)

Vol. 3

Economic and Strategic Issues in U. S. Foreign Policy

Edited by *Carl-Ludwig Holtfrerich*

1989. 15.5 x 23 cm. XVI, 297 pages. With 23 tables. Cloth.
ISBN 3 11 011793 2; 0-89925-535-3 (U. S.)

Walter de Gruyter · Berlin · New York

Metin Heper and Ahmed Evin (editors)

State, Democracy and the Military

Turkey in the 1980s

1988. 15.5 x 23 cm. XII, 265 pages.
Cloth. ISBN 3 11 011344 9; 0-89925-454-3 (U.S.)

Peter Juviler and Hiroshi Kimura (editors)

Gorbachev's Reforms

U.S. and Japanese Assessments

1988. 15.5 x 23.5 cm. XXII, 178 pages.
Cloth. ISBN 3 11 011748 7; 0-202-24168-8 (U.S.)
Paper. ISBN 3 11 011749 5; 0-202-24169-6 (U.S.)
(Aldine de Gruyter)

Robbin F. Laird and Erik P. Hoffmann (editors)

Soviet Foreign Policy in a Changing World

1986. 15.5 x 23.5 cm. XXIV, 969 pages. Tables.
Cloth. ISBN 3 11 010817 8; 0-202-24166-1 (U.S.)
Paper. ISBN 3 11 010997 2; 0-202-24167-X (U.S.)
(Aldine de Gruyter)

Erik P. Hoffmann and Robbin F. Laird (editors)

The Soviet Polity in the Modern Era

1984. 15.5 x 23.5 cm. XVI, 942 pages. Tables. Figures.
Cloth. ISBN 3 11 010295 1; 0-202-24164-5 (U.S.)
Paper. ISBN 3 11 010294 3; 0-202-24165-3 (U.S.)
(Aldine de Gruyter)

Erik P. Hoffmann and Frederic J. Fleron Jr. (editors)

The Conduct of Soviet Foreign Policy

Second Edition 1980. 15.5 x 23.5 cm. X, 761 pages.
Cloth. ISBN 0-202-24155-6 (U.S.)
Paper. ISBN 0-202-24156-4 (U.S.)
(Aldine de Gruyter)

Ilan Greilsammer and Joseph H. H. Weiler (editors)

Europe and Israel

Troubled Neighbours

1988. Oktav. X, 354 pages.
Cloth. ISBN 3 11 009713 3; 0-89925-369-5 (U.S.)

 # Walter de Gruyter · Berlin · New York

Genthiner Strasse 13, D-1000 Berlin 30, Phone (0 30) 2 60 05-0, Telex 1 83 027
200 Saw Mill River Road, Hawthorne, N.Y. 10532, Phone (914) 747-0110, Telex 646677